MANSIONS OF MISERY

A Biography of the Marshalsea Debtors' Prison

Also by Jerry White

Rothschild Buildings
Campbell Bunk
London in the Eighteenth Century
London in the Nineteenth Century
London in the Twentieth Century
Zeppelin Nights

MANSIONS OF MISERY

A Biography of the Marshalsea
Debtors' Prison

JERRY WHITE

THE BODLEY HEAD
LONDON

1 3 5 7 9 10 8 6 4 2

The Bodley Head, an imprint of Vintage,
20 Vauxhall Bridge Road,
London SW1V 2SA

The Bodley Head is part of the Penguin Random House group of companies
whose addresses can be found at global.penguinrandomhouse.com

Copyright © Jerry White 2016

Jerry White has asserted his right to be identified as the
author of this Work in accordance with the Copyright,
Designs and Patents Act 1988

First published by The Bodley Head in 2016

www.vintage-books.co.uk

A CIP catalogue record for this book
is available from the British Library

ISBN 9781847923028

Typeset in India by Thomson Digital Pvt Ltd, Noida, Delhi
Printed and bound by Clays Ltd, St Ives plc

Penguin Random House is committed to a sustainable future for our
business, our readers and our planet. This book is made from Forest
Stewardship Council® certified paper.

For debtors everywhere

Hard-up, Floored, Broke

Hard-cut, hard-run, hard-pushed; at low water mark; cracked up; down on one's luck; fast; in the last pea of time; in the last run of shad; low down; low in the lay; oofless; out of favour with the oof-bird; seedy; short; sold-up; strapped; stuck; stumped; suffering from an attack of the week's (or month's) end; tight; on one's uppers; under a cloud. Dead-beat; basketed; bitched; bitched-up; buggered-up; busted; caved in; choked-off; cornered; cooked; done brown; done for; done on toast; doubled-up; flattened out; fluffed; flummoxed; frummagemmed; gapped; gone under; gravelled; gruelled; hoofed out; jacked-up; looed; mucked out; pocketed; potted; queered in his pitch; rantanned; sat upon; sewn up; snashed; snuffed out; spread-eagled; struck of a heap; tied up; timbered; treed; trumped; up a tree. Dead-broke, clear-broke, clean-broke, stone-broke, stony-broke, braky-broke; wound up; settled; coopered; smashed up; under a cloud; cleaned out; cracked up; done up; on one's back; on one's beam ends; gone to pot; broken-backed; all U.P.; in the wrong box; stumped; feathered; squeezed; dry; gutted; burnt one's fingers; dished; in a bad way; gone up; gone by the board; made mince meat of; broziered; willowed; not to have a feather to fly with; burst; fleeced; stony; pebble-beached; in Queer Street; stripped; rooked; hard up; hopped-up; strapped; gruelled.

John S. Farmer and W. E. Henley, *Slang and Its Analogues, Past and Present*, 7 vols., London, 1890–1904

CONTENTS

LIST OF ILLUSTRATIONS

PREFACE

In the Borough High Street, near Saint George's Church, and
on the same side of the way, stands, as most people know,
the smallest of our debtors' prisons, the Marshalsea.

THESE words from *The Posthumous Papers of the Pickwick
Club* must have been my first encounter with the Marshalsea,
as a schoolboy, a decade or so before my infatuation with
London's greatest chronicler took a hold. It was only in later
years that the inseparable strands linking Dickens's life and
work gave me some sort of understanding of the place of
the prison in both. The Marshalsea haunted him. The
prison's ghosts lived with him more than thirty years after
he had known it as a boy during his father's imprisonment
there in 1824. And his precocious razor-sharp memory
remains our best window on how that new Marshalsea
looked and was run. By a quirk of history, the new gaol
was just twelve years old and so was Charles Dickens when
he knew it.

The Marshalsea lives in the culture, of course, because of
Dickens and other than that I wouldn't have given the place
much further thought. But then, in researching *London in
the Eighteenth Century*, I came across the second report of
the 'Gaols Committee' enquiring into the London debtors'

prisons and published in 1729. There were many horrors in eighteenth-century London but I remember being staggered by what I read. The Gaols Committee led me to John Baptist Grano's journal in the Bodleian – he was a debtor prisoner there in the Marshalsea in 1728–9 – and revived my interest in whatever had lodged in my mind from *Pickwick*, from *The Personal History of David Copperfield* and *Little Dorrit*. I was then asked to give the Raphael Samuel Memorial Lecture in 2008; it was a great honour to me, because Raphael had been my mentor for many years. So I decided to write up the eighteenth-century Marshalsea and say something about Grano's gaol. The lecture was published a year later and I thought this would be the end of my Marshalsea explorations.

At that point I was in the middle of a trilogy of histories of modern London, going back in time century by century from the twentieth to the eighteenth. These metropolis-wide overviews of London and the Londoner, huge canvases as they seemed to me, were not the way I'd begun as a historian in the 1970s and early 1980s. Then my focus was already London, but my first two books were 'microhistories' of small distinctive communities through which I tried to explore small building blocks of the capital, unlocking some of London's secrets and throwing new light on the bigger picture. By the 1990s I'd become frustrated with that approach. How many grains of sand would I have to study before I could hope for an understanding of a city of so many people, of such diversity? So I embarked on that fifteen-year struggle, if I can put it that way, to clarify and sharpen the bigger picture itself. That large venture came to an end in 2012. My subsequent study, *Zeppelin Nights: London in the First World War*, brought the big picture into sharper focus by looking at the whole of London but in a tighter period, that almost unendurable crucible of the four and a quarter years of total war.

This more intimate study of the city gave me a renewed taste for the microhistory approach. But what to choose?

An event, a life story, a neighbourhood, a building? All had their appeal. And I began to wonder whether the Marshalsea might offer me such an opportunity. The question in my mind was whether it could make a book. I had a beginning or something like it in the Gaols Committee's Marshalsea and an ending or something like it in Dickens's prison a hundred years later. But I wasn't sure there would be enough in between.

The puzzle began to unravel, in a good way, when I talked things over with Jörg Hensgen of the Bodley Head. He said it would work best if I focused on the lives of the prisoners who'd gone through the Marshalsea gates, and the more I thought about it the more I agreed. Of course, the debtor would have been given a voice, as far as I could; but this approach brought those voices centre stage. This would not be a book about bricks and mortar but about the people who went through the gaol – or perhaps entered and never came out again, like so many prisoners in the deadly years of 1727–30.

And what people some of them were. A few were stranger than fiction: even Dickens never gave us a debtor like James Stamp Sutton Cooke. All displayed the ups and downs and comings and goings of ordinary Londoners, especially of the shabby-genteel lower middle classes of this city made from trade. Through their lives, brought together by the laws of debtor and creditor which connected the Marshalsea prison to every street and court and alley in London, it seemed to me that fresh insights would be given us into just what it meant to be a Londoner between 1700 and 1842. 'Biographies' of places, even nations, are fashionable subtitles in the historian's trade, but here I felt I might justly lay claim to a biography of the Marshalsea prison.

Ask any other historian – or biographer – and they will tell you that there inevitably grows some sympathy (or perhaps some hatred) for the subject under scrutiny. How

did I feel about the London debtor? I was conscious
throughout that behind almost every one were struggling
creditors leaving yet more debtors in their wake. For everyone
in London in these years was in debt for a while at least,
though most paid their way, often against the odds. But the
thought never left me how easy it is for most modern debtors
to keep our heads afloat and that there but for the grace of
mortgage and credit card would go I. It was, in the end, not
too difficult to imagine myself in the tap with the other
'collegians', as the prisoners called themselves, and being
'made a doctor of the Marshalsea College' in my place.

Acknowledgements

My debts are indeed legion. I would like to thank the archiv-
ists and staff of the National Archives, the British Library,
the Bodleian Library, London Metropolitan Archive,
Southwark Local History Library and Archive Collection,
the Surrey History Centre, the Caird Library at the National
Maritime Museum and Sheffield City Archives. My thanks
go too to my agent Maggie Hanbury, to Jörg Hensgen at
the Bodley Head and to Stuart Williams, my commissioning
editor, for having faith in the project; to Lesley Levene, who
has copy-edited five of my books with consummate skill
and an indefatigable eye for detail; to Sarah Barlow for her
excellent proofreading; to Daniel Binney, who gave invaluable help with my technological difficulties; and to my
colleague Dr Brodie Waddell at Birkbeck, to Michael Allen,
to Jon Levin and to Sally Alexander for reading the book
in whole or part before publication – they have saved me
from many embarrassments. Two collegians whom I've not
met have thrown special light on to Marshalsea obscurities:
John Ginger, who edited part of the Grano journal for
publication, and Professor Angus Easson, whose doctoral
thesis at Oxford in 1967 explored the Marshalsea of *Little*

Dorrit; I am in debt to them both. I owe very special thanks to Ann Stephenson, who undertook research into the life stories of many of the debtors who have made it into these pages: when I am able to say that so and so was born, married or died on specific dates, or had so many children, or was living at these various addresses, more often than not the evidence comes as a result of Ann's gleanings. Her contribution is such that *Mansions of Misery* would have been almost impossible to write without her help; I am deeply grateful. Finally, as always, my thanks go to Rosie Cooper, who has not just borne with the Marshalsea as my own personal obsession for quite a few years but also resigned herself (nearly) to the very real debts incurred in building an unwieldy library of London books at home.

Jerry White
Birkbeck, University of London,
October 2015

A NOTE ON MONEY

In eighteenth- and nineteenth-century sterling

£1 = 20 shillings (20s) = 240 pence (240d).

There is no satisfactory mechanism for calculating the modern value of old money. However, for much of the eighteenth century, 15s a week (75p) was a reasonable wage for a journeyman; comparing that to the 2016 London Living Wage of £329 gives a multiplier of around 440, so £1 of debt in the eighteenth century might be approximately £440 in today's money. From around 1790, inflation brought average wages for the period 1790–1842 closer to £1, though still below it, so £1 might be approximately £350 in today's money.

I

THE DEBTOR'S WORLD

I enter in this little book the names of the streets I can't go down while the shops are open. This dinner today closes Long Acre. I bought a pair of boots in Great Queen Street last week, and made that no thoroughfare too. There's only one avenue to the Strand left open now, and I shall have to stop that up to-night with a pair of gloves. The roads are closing so fast in every direction, that in about a month's time, unless my aunt sends me a remittance, I shall have to go three or four miles out of town to get over the way.[1]

So Dick Swiveller, one of Charles Dickens's more amiable debtors, made shift to exist on an empty pocket in his single room dwelling, somewhere 'in the neighbourhood of Drury Lane' around 1840. As a debtor he was in good company. Everyone was a debtor in eighteenth- and nineteenth-century London, as had been the case for long before. Almost everyone remains a debtor two centuries on too, though with one big difference. In Dick Swiveller's day and before there was no generally applicable credit mechanism available from a bank or building society or credit provider that enabled a debtor to spend freely in many places to an agreed limit. Debt then was personal, between a purchaser needing credit for one or a few items and a seller prepared to provide it. It was a face-to-face arrangement between individuals who would know each other again. So debt, because personal, had spatial consequences, curtailing movement to avoid embarrassing local encounters, as for Dick. It could also involve restrictions of a more drastic kind, as we shall see.

If everyone was a debtor for a time it was not necessarily through inability or unwillingness to pay, for deferred payment on credit was the way business was generally organised. Great merchants or bankers traded not in ready money but by means of bills of exchange, a promise to pay at some point in the future, allowing time for goods to be sold or other debts gathered in. If disaster struck and merchants proved unable to honour outstanding bills they could take advantage of the bankruptcy laws and sell up in gentlemanly sessions with the Commissioners in Bankruptcy, without any of the humiliations of arrest or imprisonment that less wealthy people suffered.

For ordinary folk too, debts were an unavoidable part of everyday life. During much of the eighteenth century, specie – ready coin of the realm – was in such short supply, especially in small denominations, that it suited buyer and seller to allow an account to accumulate till it could be paid in silver or gold or, more rarely, by a banknote or draft. Paying with ready money was reserved generally for transactions between strangers – travellers at an inn, say, or buyers from a street seller or pedlar. An account or tally would be run up with the grocer, baker, butcher or milkman, all on the credit of an address given, confirmed by the tradesman's delivery. Something ought to and might be occasionally paid on account, but otherwise the bill was rendered after a time thought reasonable by both sides: on the four quarter days, for instance, or even, for smart tailors or upholders (furnishers and interior designers) serving the quality, once a year at Christmas, when interest would be openly added to the bill. Indeed, delays in presenting a bill were considered polite. Delivering a bill or account too early was thought greedy or impertinent and could lose a customer for life. Tradesmen built into their pricing an element for bad debts, because it was anticipated that not all money owed could be gathered in.[2]

The poor needed credit too, perhaps none more so, when the absence of ready money might mean a family going hungry. For them special mechanisms had been constructed, like pawnbrokers who would lend money on possessions at high interest, or informal pawning arrangements at public houses or with their grocers. By the beginning of the eighteenth century a new facility had come into fashion: tallymen or 'Manchester' or 'Scotch' drapers selling 'Cloaths and such Things' on credit, but requiring weekly repayments from poor customers at high interest. All these transactions could go wrong and tallymen were seen as 'a sort of Usurers', according to a pamphlet of 1716, 'where some of these Oppressors are said to have above a Hundred of these poor Wretches in the several Jayls in and near *London* at a time'.[3]

Although the tallymen may have been notoriously quick off the mark, the truth is that when people got into debt they usually owed money everywhere. When John Rummells, 'Marriner' of Greenwich, totted up his creditors while in the Marshalsea in 1725 he listed six different 'victuallers', probably publicans, a City tallyman and a 'Salesman', a butcher, baker, candle seller (tallow chandler), 'Fisherman' and 'Fisherwoman', a carpenter, an 'officer' (probably a Marshalsea bailiff), two 'Marriners', 'Elizabeth Baker, alias Read' (no occupation given) and three doctors (a 'Surgion' and two 'Barbers'), twenty-one in all and scattered around the four naval towns of Greenwich, Deptford – or Debtford, as he once appropriately rendered it – Gosport and Portsmouth. It was the butcher who got his claim in first and made the arrest that put Rummells in the Marshalsea for £30.[4]

Many tradesmen devised mechanisms to avoid the losses consequent on untrustworthy credit and an unpaid bill. Landlords, those unofficial and unwilling bankers to the poor, frequently demanded prior references and a week's or month's rent in advance. Many shopkeepers had their own rules for refusing credit: 'Upon my word, Sir, you must excuse me. It is a thing we never do to a stranger,' a sword-maker in the Strand told James Boswell, who had asked to take away a silver-hilted weapon on a promise to pay later, though he relented under his customer's haughty gaze.[5] Others sought security by requiring a debtor to obtain a counter-signature or 'acceptance' to an IOU or promissory note, ideally a known householder or one from a good address; anyone signing, often family members or close friends, could find themselves liable for the whole sum if the debtor defaulted, and this gave creditors a further opportunity to get their money back.

Tradesmen who gave long credit were also, of course, debtors themselves. Tailors would owe drapers, cabinet-makers would owe gilders or timber merchants, shopkeepers would notoriously owe suppliers, employers would owe their journeymen wages, journeymen would owe publicans, publicans would owe brewers and so on and so forth. And any or all might owe the moneylenders if no other resource was open to them, none more experienced in the fine arts of recovering a debt through adroit manipulation of the law.

True it was, then, that all sorts and conditions of men and women were in debt. When the *Morning Post* analysed the occupations of 941 debtors going through the insolvency court in August 1801, it listed 252 distinct walks of life, from labourers (nineteen) to Doctors of Divinity (one). Retailers of one kind or another were prominent among them, with thirty-one 'shopkeepers', many others specifically described, and seventy-five 'victuallers', victims of countless real-life Dick Swivellers. In general, contemporary authorities agreed that debtors ending up in gaol were 'About Two-thirds Manufacturers and Labourers – the remainder Seamen, Dealers and Chapmen [or pedlars] and various Professions'. Those who had most difficulties were additionally burdened beyond the daily vicissitudes of industrial life, tending to be 'married; and many of them have very large Families; some Five, others Six, and others Ten Children'. Added to these, with children or without, was a small but significant proportion of women debtors, including many widows and women abandoned by men.[6]

When a creditor's patience was exhausted the law provided the means to bully or frighten a debtor into paying up at last. The weapons at a creditor's disposal meant that, for countless numbers of debtors, debt could become a galling blight on their lives, never shaken off. Many of those cultured and sophisticated men and women who made the eighteenth century a particular age of genius did so with the shadow of the debtors' prison wall dark upon them. Artists like Gawen Hamilton, George Morland and Thomas Bonner, writers like Daniel Defoe, Sir Richard Steele, Henry Fielding, Laetitia Pilkington, Samuel Johnson, Oliver Goldsmith and John Cleland, actresses like Mary Robinson and Charlotte Charke, all saw the inside of a bailiff's lock-up or spunging (or sponging) house, if not worse. In England, it was said in 1716, there 'are more unhappy People to be found, suffering under extream Misery, by the severity of their Creditors, than in any other Nation in *Europe*'.[7]

Not all of them were innocent victims. Debtors might have subterfuge, dishonesty, even fraud among the weapons with which they waged war on the innocent creditor. Hiding might be the first instinct, as it was for Dick Swiveller, perhaps 'in an obscure lodging, somewhere in the neighbourhood of Kilburn, in order to avoid the *traps*', or bailiffs, it was said in 1821. Because arrests couldn't be made at night or on Sundays, such a discreet debtor was called 'a *once-a-week*

man, or, in other words, a *Sunday promenader* . . .'[8] Obscure
and ancient jurisdictions gave certain places in London immu-
nity from arrest for debt, the longest-lived of these being the
'verge of the court', land belonging to the royal household
around the King's Mews north of Charing Cross and
extending to the royal parks. Sought-after lodgings could be
rented in the verge: 'I knew an artful fellow once', recalled
the Reverend John Trusler in 1786, 'that eluded all his creditors, by residing there; if he wanted to go out of it, he took
water at Whitehall-stairs, which place is privileged, and as
no writ can be served on the water, without a water-bailiff's
warrant, which cannot be immediately procured, he would
land safely in the city, or on the Surry side', where some
Middlesex or City writs had no force.[9]

Experienced debtors would know their way around such
rabbit warrens: that proceedings in the Marshalsea or Palace
court could not be brought if a debt was incurred in the
City or more than twelve miles from Whitehall, nor arrests
made in the City on a Marshalsea warrant alone, for instance,
despite that court offering creditors the cheapest and quickest
grip on those owing debts above the smallest. Even prison
could be an effective hiding place, some debtors intriguing
with family or friends – a man could be arrested at his wife's
suit – to work up sham actions and so stop other creditors
battening on them:

> The idea, that imprisonment can be a punishment to a man
> under these circumstances, must instantly vanish: he prepares
> for his catastrophe with the vizard of distress, and by that craft
> sets every danger at defiance; his property is conveyed by
> previous assignments, apparent gifts, spurious loans, and with
> the semblance of poverty, he possesses a genial fortune, fabri-
> cated on the ruin of the credulous, honest, and unsuspecting
> dealer . . . To the *collusive* Debtor therefore Imprisonment can
> be no punishment, – for he feels it not as such.[10]

Others still might procure two householders to bail them out of custody and then abscond abroad, leaving the creditor to recover debt and costs from the bails, a difficult and expensive process, especially if there was collusion between them all. And many debtors managed to squirrel resources away from their creditors and leave them to legatees, as the few surviving Marshalsea wills tell us: for example, Mary Young, who died in April 1750, probably in prison, left money for gold mourning rings and funeral expenses, amid other bequests; and Joseph Railton left 'all my ffreehold Copyhold and Leasehold Estate or estates' to John Darkin of Goodman's Yard, Minories, in 1776.[11]

In the general sum of things, though, the whip hand lay with creditors. Most no doubt were honest in their intentions to recover money properly owed, aggravated beyond the limits of patience by what looked like their debtors' refusal to pay, even after repeated and exhausting efforts to cajole or harass or shame them into doing so. Many will have been driven on by their own creditors snapping at their heels. Once they reached the end of their tether, however, the law put a terrible weapon in their hands.

A creditor's suit was begun by swearing an affidavit quantifying the sum said to be owed. This was put before a judge by the creditor's attorney and, with only the creditor's word for it and without hearing from the debtor, permission would be granted to begin due process: the affidavit could be rejected only if it was defective in form, though not all defects were spotted until it was too late. If the debt sworn to was over 40s (£2; increasing to over £10 from 1779), then an arrest could be made at that point, still without the existence of the debt being proved in court, under what was known as 'mesne process' – pronounced 'mean' and denoting 'middle'. There were many advantages to the creditor in doing so and this was the way most imprisonments were brought about. At this stage the costs of the action nominally had all to be reimbursed by the debtor. He could escape imprisonment by securing bail from two householders who in effect pledged themselves to pay any proven debt should the debtor default. If bail was not forthcoming (as in most cases), or if it was offered but not accepted by the creditor or his agent because of the inadequate standing of the debtor's bail, then the debtor could be imprisoned – still without the debt being proved.[12]

There were two ways in which a debt came to trial (the 'final' process). A creditor could move straight to this point by way of a writ of execution and without passing through mesne process. He had to do this where debts were below the minimum of £2 (later £10); but even if debts were above these sums, at trial the original debt and costs could be loaded with damages consequent upon the debtor's original failure to pay – debt, costs and damages had, though, all to be proved at the trial. Once proved, should debtors still remain unable to pay, they were imprisoned. The disadvantage to the creditor, however, was that from this point debtors could claim maintenance while in prison, the creditor having to pay 4d (a groat) a day (2s 4d a week) to the debtor; this obligation was introduced in 1759 by 'the Lords Act' and groats were increased from 1797 to 6d a day (3s 6d a week).[13]

Arrest and imprisonment under mesne process, attractively swift and draconian as it appeared, also involved creditors in more costs should they wish to keep a debtor in prison. Creditors had to serve a declaration on the imprisoned debtor, stating the amount of debt and costs and requiring a plea so that the matter could come to trial; this involved further attorney's fees, which creditors would have to pay, at first at least. Declarations had to contain the names of two sureties to ensure creditors' attendance in court to prove a case; but the law provided fictional sureties for him, named 'John Doe and Richard Roe', 'Those charming creations of the poet', as Dickens put it. But 'the Plaintiff generally proceeds in the slowest manner' and in any event could wait till the end of the next law term before making a declaration. There were four of these a year, some with long vacations between them, so that a debtor arrested before Christmas, say – a popular time to do so – could wait over six months before a declaration became due.[14] If no declaration was served, then the debtor was 'superseded' and could be discharged; this was also the case where groats and sixpences were not paid punctually each week. But a discharge could take place only once papers had been lodged and prison fees paid.[15]

Did imprisonment or the threat of it work for the creditor? '[T]ho' it be a common saying amongst us, *That a Prison pays no Debts*', in many cases it did. In 1791, of 12,000 bailable writs issued against debtors only some 1,200 led to imprisonment, the rest paying up in some form, absconding, or proving such hopeless cases that creditors despaired of getting their money and let the matter drop. Arrest was also more straightforward than executing against the debtor's goods, complex and rule-bound as that was. In any event, the goods might not have amounted to anything, while imprisonment could serve to rally friends and family to help discharge the debt. So arrest and imprisonment were widely resorted to.[16]

They were, though, not always fairly resorted to. Most creditors were genuine enough and dunned for their bills, repeatedly requesting then demanding they be paid – like the milkmaid with her tally or score in William Hogarth's *The Distressed Poet* of around 1740. But some failed even to take these steps. 'A man may be arrested from mere malice or caprice, without being applied to for the debt, and without any account being rendered to him of the claim: this has frequently happened . . .' And some used trickery to inflate a debt, perhaps by getting 'an illiterate person' such as Francis Brasberry, a Marshalsea prisoner of 1735, to sign a note he

could not read admitting to a debt far in excess of the value
of the quack medicines he had received. They had been
necessary to cure 'a Rash or Scurvy humour upon him, and
his wife had the Ague or ffeaver', and were sold to him by
Francis Butler, 'who professed a Doctor' but who 'called up
and down the Country with Baggs upon his Shoulders to
Sell Medicines'.[17]

There were cases of a debtor spending 'many months
in prison where the court subsequently decided he owed
nothing', the House of Lords was told in 1814. And in
the dog-eat-dog world of eighteenth-century London it
was always possible to find someone prepared to swear
away another's liberty on a lie. Sarah Dodd or Todd, an
oyster seller, was suborned by a 'Mr. Mitchel' to swear a
debt against one Dancer which landed him for some time
in the Marshalsea; she knew nothing of the man, had
never in fact seen him, but was paid three guineas for her
pains.[18]

The power of imprisonment was a godsend to the vindictive: it got a debtor quickly out of the way and it might
well lead to financial ruin. So we read around 1830 of a
greengrocer ruined by a competitor who loaned him stock
worth 35s and then made a demand for 55s. The greengrocer
offered 35s but this was refused and a Marshalsea writ
issued which he could not afford to defend. The debt was
'proved' and he was imprisoned. His landlord, hearing of
his plight, distrained against his goods for the rent and 'sold
even the bed from under his wife!' And a false or contrived
debt could be used for other reasons, perhaps to remove a
rival in love. The vociferous Ann Cantwell, wife of Walter,
was in the Marshalsea in 1696–7 with her child, 'in a most
miserable Condition Lying on the bare boards'. Sarah Wright,
Walter's lover's mother, had 'surreptitiously obtained an
execution for 5:2:10' against her. When Ann sought relief
from the Middlesex Justices, who issued a warrant against

Sarah to appear and answer the complaint, Sarah was said to have 'told yᵉ Constable she car'd not a ffart for all yᵒʳ Warrants calling them butt Petty Justice . . .'[19]

Similarly, debt was a powerful way of raising the stakes in a family dispute. George Hovey, with his wife and child, languished in the Marshalsea for at least two and a half years from 1702 to 1705 at the suit of his allegedly prosperous mother and his brother-in-law for an affront that has not come down to us. And in 1718 'One Oades, a Quaker, and an eminent Potter, in Gravel-lane in Southwark', was imprisoned by his four sons on an action for the enormous sum of £10,000 arising out of a business difference; they also evicted their mother from the home and barricaded themselves inside with their friends. They were wise to do so, because 'a very great Tumult gather'd about the House, so that it was in a manner Besieg'd, throwing Stones, Dirt, &c. and exclaiming against them . . .' When someone inside opened fire with a musket, killing a woman in the crowd, the Riot Act had to be read and the house was not cleared until a 'File or two of Musqueteers' arrived across the river from Whitehall. Oades's youngest son and his friend were duly convicted of murder – though through influence all escaped punishment.[20]

Family disputes aside, some creditors tightened the screw by seizing debtors at their most vulnerable. In June 1733 it was reported that a boy of four had been arrested and confined in the Marshalsea at the suit of a Quaker surgeon – hypocrisy among the saints a popular target of the eighteenth-century press. The creditor had treated the child's sore finger but it had mortified so he had cut it off. He then sued the child and his guardians for his bill of £15, arresting the boy rather than others involved in the suit. And in 1750 an execution against the heavily pregnant Ann Cox brought her into the Marshalsea, where she was delivered 'of two Boys and a Girl'.[21]

All these abuses, and others, discredited the laws of arrest for debt among many commentators from the seventeenth century onwards. But some abuses were built into the system. They did not require any extraordinary viciousness or turpitude on the part of the creditor, but flowed naturally from the moment a suit was first brought. For there were others besides creditors who sought their lawful penny from the debtor, and they did so by way of costs.

Costs were an oppression frequently far worse than the original debt itself. Debtors proceeded against for very small debts below 40s, where proceedings took place in the courts of conscience or requests, could be imprisoned by a judge on the debt being proved but not paid. The costs of proceedings, borne by the plaintiff but payable by the debtor, were often wildly disproportionate to the original debt:

> A person committed to the Gatehouse for 1s. 6d. was a poor lame industrious creature who had not to pay; this miserable debtor was charged in Execution, and the expences of the prosecution increased the debt to *one pound five shillings and six-pence!* If the man could not pay *one and six-pence*, when at liberty, how was he to discharge this accumulated debt under confinement.[22]

Here the costs amounted to seventeen times the original debt and other egregious cases were frequently cited: in another from 1783, 'A short time since, a poor destitute girl under 20 years of age and believed to be virtuous, was committed in execution for EIGHT Pence, which together with the costs of suit and fees amounted to 18s. and 4d.' And so on. Fifty years later, 'A.B.', in fact John Ewer Poole, tells us that he was sued in the Marshalsea court for a debt of £5. He didn't defend it, 'as the demand was just'; but he then found himself arrested for £13 to include the costs of the action, could not pay and was imprisoned. Had he been arrested under mesne process for a debt over £10 his costs would have been higher; a bill of costs, involving as it might do nearly a score of items, could 'within ten days in London, amount to nearly 12*l.*'[23]

All these costs arose because the law of debt had created a great array of henchmen who leeched on debtors and creditors and made rich spoil from one or the other – for lawyers would have their costs either way.

First among them was the pettifogger, the back-street or 'hedge' attorney with a one-room office and working alone or with a clerk. In 'the eyes of all humane men', pettifoggers were 'a species of *Anthropophagi* that ought not to be endured'. Lord Mansfield, the great Lord Chief Justice, had reportedly 'said publicly in Court – "That he was astonished the populace did not stone the pettifogging tribe of Attornies, as they went to Westminster Hall"'. It was a breed best described by Charles Dickens, who had much experience to draw on, including spells as a lawyer's clerk in two attorneys' offices when he was fifteen and sixteen years old. They crop up throughout his fiction, but none are more memorable than Sampson Brass of Bevis Marks and his fearsome sister Sally, his assiduous clerk. They were both bred to pettifogging by their attorney father, known as 'Old Foxey'. Sally

> had passed her life in a kind of legal childhood. She had been remarkable, when a tender prattler, for an uncommon talent in counterfeiting the walk and manner of a bailiff: in which character she had learned to tap her little playfellows on the shoulder, and to carry them up to imaginary sponging-houses, with a correctness of imitation which was the surprise and delight of all who witnessed her performances, and which was only to be exceeded by her exquisite manner of putting an execution into her doll's house, and taking an exact inventory of the chairs and tables.[24]

Her favourite occupation was 'drawing out a little bill', 'scratching on with a noisy pen, scoring down the figures with evident delight, and working like a steam-engine.' A bill with imaginary and fraudulent costs, perhaps, for serving 'a writ that would be thrown in at the Door': 'Letter for payment of debt (though no letter sent)', 3s 6d; 'Attending Officer for return' of a warrant of arrest when no attendance was necessary, 3s 4d; paid for a messenger when none used, 3s 6d; and so on. Of a pettifogger's bill for £4 9s 6d to get to an arrest under mesne process relayed to the *Oracle and Public Advertiser* in 1799 some £2 7s 6d (so more than half) was said to have been made up in fictional fees.[25]

There were many other opportunities for greedy gleanings. All pettifogging attorneys were commissioned by clients to recover unpaid debts. Many debts were, as we have seen, incurred on the basis of a note of hand or bill of exchange that was countersigned, backed by 'acceptances', persons who undertook to pay on the debtor's default. A bill might have many acceptances, each one potentially acted against. So we hear in 1831 of John Minter Hart, a St Pancras attorney, who presented on behalf of his client an unpaid bill to an acceptor whom he knew to be insolvent and unable to pay. Pretending to sympathise with the man's plight, he asked the acceptor for a list of his debts. He then 'hurried off to the principal creditor', advising him to arrest the acceptor as he had plenty of money. The creditor duly instructed Hart to arrange the arrest and eventual imprisonment. Hart thus represented his original client, the acceptor and the arresting creditor, reaping fees from all sides. He used the name of another attorney without his knowledge when representing the final creditor, so that the acceptor wouldn't realise he was being advised and sued by the same man. The six Marshalsea attorneys at Clifford's Inn, Fleet Street, were said to have acted in not dissimilar ways. 'These men have innumerable retainers, who frequent public-houses, &c., where the lower orders of tradesmen resort, and become absolutely *barrators*, or fomenters of discord' for the resulting fees. As Dickens once remarked, 'The one great principle of the English law is, to make business for itself.'[26]

Fomenting discord, engaging in false representation and fraudulently inflating bills, the pettifogging culture could easily turn into blatant theft. In 1768 a Marshalsea prisoner, John French Esq., anxious to remove himself by writ of habeas corpus to the comforts of the King's Bench, paid Arthur John Plunkett seven guineas to arrange the matter, but Plunkett was a pretend attorney and neither he nor the money was seen again. At the discharge of numerous prisoners from the Marshalsea and King's Bench prisons in September 1797 an attorney who had received money from his client to settle prison fees and costs but not paid it over was remanded in custody. And poor Thomas Jury looked like enduring further time in gaol because of the defalcations of his pettifogger – a small attorney indeed:

Whereas an Attorney at Law, who some time since did Business for Mr. Atwood, an Attorney in Castle-yard Holbourn, had of Mr. Thomas Jury, a Prisoner in the Marshalsea, on Saturday the 5th Instant, a Sum of Money, a Watch, a Note of Hand to pay to the Hon. Commissioners of Excise for the said Thomas Jury's Use, as a Fine of Twenty Pounds for selling of Spirituous Liquors in the Marshalsea, but has not paid the Money, nor since been heard of, but suppos'd to be gone in the West Country towards Exeter or Devonshire; he had on an old dark-brown Coat, a blue double-breasted Waistcoat with yellow Tinsey Buttons, Button-holes the same, a Pair of old Leather greasy Breeches, and a light-brown Wig; he is a very thin spare Man, about four Feet and a half high, of a fair Complexion, very full dark Eyes, and about 36 Years of Age. If he will return or send to Thomas Jury, now a Prisoner in the Marshalsea, in six Days, with the Watch and Note; and if any Part of the Money is imbezzled it will be forgiven; if not, whoever secures him in any Part of England, shall receive two Guineas Reward and reasonable Charges; to be paid at the Bar of the Marshalsea Prison.

May 17, 1739   THO. JURY[27]

The pettifoggers had a casual fringe of clerks and messengers – 'little boys . . . on legal errands', as Dickens called them – and of watchers and besetters and a host of the impoverished who might be relied on to divulge a debtor's whereabouts for twopenn'orth of gin. Other sorts of mackerel scavenged off the debtor too, such as the men who hung around spunging houses in pairs offering to hire themselves as bail, should the necessary ready money and sureties be available: pejoratively, they were often called 'Jew bail', the profession associated in the popular mind with the Jewish community on the eastern borders of the City. But chief among the pettifogger's agents was the bailiff.

Despite their lowlife reputation, bailiffs were substantial men of sorts. Most were appointed and accredited by the county or City sheriffs and so were sheriffs' officers, responsible for serving warrants and summonses or distraining goods. But the tricky business of arrests was generally handled by 'special bailiffs' 'employed by the sheriffs on account of their adroitness and dexterity in hunting and seizing their prey', as Gifford's *Complete English Lawyer; or Every Man his own Lawyer* cheerily put it around 1817.[28]

Among these special bailiffs were the Bearers of the Verges, better known as Marshalsea or Palace court officers. These were men of the middling sort, of substance sufficient to obtain letters of recommendation from the clergyman, churchwardens and other householders of the parish where they lived, to survive scrutiny of their applications by way

of public notice, and to obtain sureties of £500 – ten years'
wages for a skilled worker – before they could be sworn in
by the Marshalsea and Palace court judges. Their business
was lively enough for them to take on, at will, one or more
assistants or 'followers', so there was a casual fringe of
bailiffs' hangers-on, like the attorneys' own: just such men,
perhaps, as shown by Hogarth nabbing the hero of *The
Rake's Progress* (Plate IV, 1735). The Marshalsea officers
themselves seem to have numbered at any one time some
thirty to fifty – in 1805, for instance, there were forty-five,
five of them keeping places of safe custody, or spunging
houses.[29]

It was hardly to be expected that bailiffs as a breed would
attract men of advanced sensibility for the human condition.
They were 'body-snatchers' in the vulgar tongue, and certain
it was that they had a very bad press. 'Bailliffs in General
are a sort of Desolute Wretches made up of the Dregs and
Refuge of Mankind', 'a kind of Beasts of Prey' 'that for their
lude and vitious behaviour are Banish'd from the sober
Conversation of their fellow Creatures . . .' Notable among
them were 'another sort of Vermine, *i.e.* the Bailiffs that
belong to the *Marshals Court*'. These were a 'Barbarous
Gang of Miscreants', *'the very Sink and Outcast of Bailiffs
themselves, a sort of Creature so Ravenous, Wild and
Despicable, that some of the better sort of the Masters of
this Order are ashamed to herd with 'em'*. That's how it
seemed, at least, to an anonymous pamphleteer of 1699 who
thought the ranks of bailiffs of all complexions had swollen
to 'a strange number', 'some say Fifteen hundred, some a
great many more; in truth, I believe there may be a thousand
of them that are *Commission Officers*, besides *Subalterns*
and *Cadees* viz. *Followers* and *Setters*', in all (he said) perhaps
3,000 men *'able to draw Swords upon Occasion'*. Complaints
like these held good for generations, so that, for instance,
an advertisement in 1776 asked for instances of 'The

atrocious robberies daily committed by Marshalsea Court Bailiffs, Sheriffs Officers, Sheriffs Brokers, and other infamous Appendages of the Law' so that offenders could be brought to book.[30]

Abuses there were and the occasional case of perjury was brought before the courts, one Marshalsea officer suffering the tribulations of the pillory at the corner of Chancery Lane and Fleet Street in May 1735, for instance. Indeed, whenever a suit was brought against the Marshalsea officers and other bailiffs for some allegations of oppressive behaviour or of a technical breach of the tight legal restrictions on arrests or distraint, juries generally sided against them. Certainly some oppressions were justly infamous: when bailiffs who had missed their chance to execute a warrant arrested the body of a debtor on the way to his funeral in Hoxton in 1811 – they 'forcibly removed the body into a shell, and conveyed it away', leaving it for a time with the plaintiff! – the arrest of a corpse was declared unlawful by Lord Chief Justice Ellenborough.[31]

Even so, instances of generosity and kindness from bailiffs were far from unknown. George Parker, a popular writer on London life, claimed in 1781 that 'there are many of them who have hearts which would honour a more exalted situation'; 'rarely, if at all, [do] they oppress those who are in their custody' and they frequently 'endeavour to compromise for the Debtor' with the arresting creditor. Certainly this was true for Charlotte Charke, that eccentric cross-dressing actress, petty entrepreneur and Grub Street aspirant, arrested around 1741 for £7 at the suit of 'a wicked drunken Woman' – maybe an exasperated landlady. She found herself held at a Marshalsea officer's spunging house in Jackson's Alley, a place too small for any map. Perhaps it was near Covent Garden, for 'I had not been there Half an Hour, before I was surrounded with all the Ladies who kept Coffee-Houses in and about the *Garden*, each offering Money for my Ransom.' But even though some fourteen ladies gathered, they were unable to raise between them the sum needed to assuage the debt and the costs of suit, arrest and an overnight stay in Jackson's Alley. The officer tried to mediate with the creditor, but she held out for the whole sum due. After another night in the spunging house Charlotte dispatched her eight-year old daughter, who had been left at home, with 'eight and thirty Letters' begging aid from her friends to avoid being shipped to the Marshalsea. It worked and she was released. On the way out the kindly officer suggested she change her flamboyant laced cavalier's hat with his 'smoaky' headgear, 'cocked up in the Coachman's Stile' and draped with crape to keep out 'the Winter's Cold', so that she wouldn't be recognised and nabbed by her other creditors. That worked too. Charlotte took new lodgings out of the way, only appearing after dark and on Sundays, until another arrest and a second sojourn in Jackson's Alley about a year later. Similarly, Charlotte Lennox the novelist, who knew something of this sort of thing, had Mrs Belville, arrested at her landlord's suit, treated with courtesy at a spunging house: 'the officer's wife, moved to some respect by my dress, conducted us to a genteel enough chamber . . .'[32]

The vivacious Mrs Charke did not record whether the officer, while pressing the creditor to take less than her due, had made a similar gesture in respect of his own costs at the spunging house, but it seems unlikely. No debtor could be forced to pay for food and drink, or so the law said. But debtors had to remain twenty-four hours there before being committed to prison – longer if arrested on a Saturday – and who could resist seeking sustenance, even solace, in circumstances like these? If their friends couldn't help they had to order victuals and if they ordered they had to pay – through the nose. Extortionate sums were charged for wine, the right to smoke, for pen and ink and paper, and so on. Samuel Johnson, who knew one or two from the inside, defined a spunging house as a prison for debtors where 'the bailiffs sponge upon them or riot at their cost'. Others found the same. In an unusual reversal of a common case, Sylas Neville found his landlord 'arrested for one of his debts by an infamous plaintiff and more infamous bailiff'. He was confined in a spunging house, 'the Pyed Bull, Grays Inn Lane', where 'the insolence and brutality of a bailiff and his myrmidons are equal to any description I have read of them'.[33]

This combination of public house and private lock-up was common but not universal. Simon Place, bred to a baker but better acquainted with 'Drinking, Whoring, Gaming, Fishing and Fighting', according to his son Francis, was a Marshalsea court officer from around 1768 to 1781. He used his house at Vinegar Yard opposite Drury Lane Theatre Royal as a '"lock-up house", or a "spunging house"', its windows barred with iron to prevent escapes. Around 1772 he took premises of the same kind that fell empty in Ship and Anchor Court off the north side of the Strand, 'a good house but not a large house'. There were no windows at the back but just on the wall fronting the court, all apart from the garrets secured by 'strong Iron bars'; 'on the stair-case leading from the street door to the first floor was a strong door. – This door as well as the street door was secured by a large lock and a peculiar sort of massive key as security against the escape of prisoners. The house was particularly neat and clean.' Francis, who lived there till he was nine, thought it 'was one of the best if not indeed the very best of the sort'. It was 'seldom without an inmate or two of the most respectable or wealthier class of prisoners'. Business declined greatly after arrest on mesne process for debts under £10 was abolished in 1779 and Place sold up two years later, but until then he fared well. On his combination of fees and costs for victuals, messengers and so on, the first no doubt provided by the Ship and Anchor public house next door, 'my father notwithstanding he was an extravagant man accumulated money', keeping a horse and chaise and a mistress 'at a distance from London'.[34]

Yet there were risks, and not all iron bars and stout doors proved effective:

> *September* 23, 1772
>
> WHEREAS John Lloyd, of New-Street, near Carnaby-Market, was this Evening taken into Custody by us the under-mentioned (being at his Bail) at the House of George Ormerod, Officer of the Sheriff of Middlesex, in Chancery-Lane, in order to be surrendered to the Marshalsea Prison on Friday next, and escaped by the Assistance of a Person in the said Ormerod's House: And as the Bail are liable to be fixed on Friday next for the Debt and Costs, we hereby offer a Reward of One Guinea to any Person that will give Information where the said John Lloyd is, provided he is taken by us in Time to surrender him.
>
> GEORGE POWELL,
> Broad-Street, Upholder.
>
> JOHN FOSTER, Hopkin-Street,
> near Broad-Street, Carpenter.[35]

Despite instances of fair conduct, however, bailiffs were generally loathed. This was especially true for those many debtors whose poverty was obvious and whose capacity to sweeten a stay in a spunging house was self-evidently non-existent. The many attacks on bailiffs by pamphleteers and in the press could amount to incitement to violent resistance, occasionally to worse. One Captain Alexander Smith, noting in 1723 the many murders 'committed by cowardly and most rascally Bailiffs', exulted that 'some of them have paid in their own Coyn' and that 'several others of that detestable Tribe have deservedly suffer'd the same Fate'. Among many instances he highlighted Henry or Harry Boyte, a bailiff of the Marshalsea court, who 'only made it his Business to set poor People to arrest one another for meer Trifles'. On Saturday 4 August 1722, 'going along *Shoe-Lane* in *Holbourn*' with '2 others of his odious Society', Boyte struck a dog that had attacked them. An argument followed with the dog's owner, a blacksmith called Butler, and the bailiffs then reportedly set about the smith in his cellar. Butler snatched a red-hot iron from his fire 'and ran it into the Breast of that very honest, honest, honest Fellow *Harry Boyte*', who 'died about 6 or 7 Hours' later, 'to the great Joy of all that knew him'. Butler, committed to Newgate, died of gaol fever before his trial.[36]

This hatred for bailiffs could be personal and vengeful. Patrick McCarty or Carty had kept the King's Head at the corner of Prince's Street, Drury Lane, till the spring of 1760. He had been in and out of debt to various parties and eventually lost possession of the public house. In the process he suffered what he considered harsh treatment at the hands of the Marshalsea court officers, becoming furious with them. McCarty, it was said, was known to be a 'dangerous man, and had often threatened to kill the officers'. On 11 October 1760 just such an officer, William Talbot – whom McCarty said he knew from his schooldays – arrived at the King's Head to arrest him on a writ of execution for a debt of £4 plus costs. Talbot had assistants with him and when McCarty proved unable to pay up they laid hold of him, but he produced 'a naked knife' and stabbed Talbot in his chest, under the arm: 'he clapp'd his hand upon his side, and desired' the publican 'to send for a surgeon; I believe he had receiv'd his death; he said, *I believe I am done for*, or something to that effect'. McCarty walked away, knife in hand. He was followed by Talbot's assistants, who 'call'd out murder'. In Vere Street he was stopped by a soldier who after some difficulty drew his sword but would not cut him:

'the prisoner went two or three doors farther, and a man came out with a poker; I said, break his arm that has the knife in it; the man threatened to strike him with the poker; and another came and took the knife out of his hand, and held it up'. McCarty was hanged from gallows erected at the end of Bow Street and his body 'hang'd in chains on Finchley common'.[37]

There were many reasons why people were desperate and reckless in eighteenth-century London, but there is no doubt that the severe oppressions of arrest and imprisonment for debt bulked large among them. For the first two decades of the century this desperation drove some men and women debtors into collective resistance against the law and its agents. The most extraordinary instance of this was in a district of Southwark west of Borough High Street, five minutes' walk from the Marshalsea court and prison. This was the Mint.

The notion of a place of sanctuary from arrest had long English traditions stretching back before the Norman Conquest. It was carried forward by the ecclesiastical authorities in medieval London, with churches providing temporary protection and two places offering 'the permanent protection of special sanctuary', at the precinct of St Martin-le-Grand in the City of London and at the abbey in Westminster. Sanctuary in church was usually a prelude to forfeiture of all possessions and banishment from the kingdom. But by the end of the fourteenth century the privileges of the special sanctuaries in the City and Westminster had developed into customs and cultures of a more rebellious kind as debtors, thieves and even murderers clustered there to put themselves out of the reach of the law and, through strength in numbers, of their oppressors. It was no accident that this development coincided with a dramatic enlargement of the powers of creditors to imprison for debt in 1352. Of these two places the position of

St Martin-le-Grand proved a fruitful template: its sanctuary
was founded not on the church but on the precinct's accidental exclusion from City rule, a tiny self-governing district
insulated from the writ of Mayor, aldermen and sheriffs,
who had no jurisdiction there.[38]

Ecclesiastical sanctuary was swept away by the Reformation
and felons could no longer claim sanctuary anywhere, but
the idea of self-governing places, immune from outside inter-
ference though land-locked in the giant city, took root. St
Martin-le-Grand was joined in the sixteenth century by
Whitefriars, on the City's riverside, known by many as
Alsatia. Others sprang up and some fell away. By 1697,
when all these 'pretended privileged places' were nominally
suppressed by an act of Parliament, there were a dozen: four
places near Fleet Street, including Whitefriars and Mitre
Court; Fuller's (later Fullwood's) Rents and Baldwin's
Gardens in Holborn; the Savoy in the Strand; in the East
End at the Minories; and four in Southwark – Montagu
Close, Deadman's Place and the Clink Liberty, all in Bankside
along the river west of London Bridge, and the Mint. This
last was largest of all by far. Its suppression would in fact
take another twenty-five years to effect. But the district and
much of its character remained into the nineteenth century.[39]

The Mint took its name from a Tudor mansion, Suffolk
Place, used for a time under licence from Henry VIII as a
genuine manufactory for the coinage. Suffolk Place had
extensive grounds, which were dotted with tenements by
the 1680s. Part of the grounds lay within the 'rules' of the
King's Bench prison, a verge where prisoners could buy the
privilege of lodging outside the gaol in certain designated
streets. Until around 1720 the rules were never defined in
law but had general force nonetheless. Those prisoners living
in the rules were immune from arrest for debt. It was a
popular benefit. By the end of the seventeenth century this
was a privilege claimed by everyone in the Mint, whether

they were boarded-out prisoners or at liberty and whether within the King's Bench rules or not. Within four years of the 'suppression' of 1697, the Mint received a major boost when a builder called Thomas Lant won parliamentary approval to develop the remaining empty land at Suffolk Place began to run up a warren of cheap streets, courts and alleys. It was a happy coincidence for some: numbers of those disturbed from the other London Alsatias were said to have crossed the river and found congenial lodgings in the Mint.⁴⁰

The Mint's notoriety was proclaimed in its very street names, including Dirty Lane, Harrow Dunghill, Robin Hood's Court and Rebel Row, and loudly and luridly in publications such as *A True description of the Mint* by an anonymous resident (1710) or M. Smith's *Memoirs of the Mint and Queen's-Bench* (1713). The population at that time was some thousands strong – ten years later there were said to be 6,200 people there. They were divided, according to the *True Description*, into 'Benchers' or Queen's Bench (as it was in the time of Anne) prisoners and their families in the rules; 'Shelterers' or *'Tag-rag* and *Bob-tail*, all sorts of Trades, Professions, and Religions, from the Circumcised Jew, down to the Pharisaical Christian', living in fear of arrest by the bailiffs; and the 'Minters', former prisoners and unencumbered householders who picked on the Mint as a ripe place to turn a penny from the other residents – landlords, keepers of coffee houses and public houses, bawds, butchers, bakers and all kinds of shopkeeper. Debtor clergymen conducted cheap Mint marriages without licence or banns. Here everything cost more – rents were said to be twice what they were outside – and 'No credit was anywhere obtainable', though that seems doubtful, given what we will see of the Marshalsea itself. All had an interest in sustaining the Mint as a veritable fortress against sheriffs' officers and Marshalsea men of all descriptions.⁴¹

The treatment meted out to bailiffs and process-servers of all kinds was established by traditions particular and peculiar. They were described by their victims in testimony to a committee of the House of Commons in early 1723; rarely in a long history can the House of Commons have taken evidence like this. Richard Poole, 'one of the Badge Porters of *Lincoln's Inn*', had attempted to serve subpoenas on a man and two women at a house in the Mint. They locked Poole in and called for their friends 'to get the Club together with all possible Speed'. When all was ready Poole was allowed to leave. He testified that in the street he

was surrounded by a Mob, who laid violent Hands on him, and carried him to an Alehouse . . . where were divers Persons, unknown to the Examinant, one of which they called Judge: That they searched the Examinant's Pockets, and took an Order from thence; and then cut a Piece of Parchment into small Pieces, and put the same into a Glass of water and Salt, and forced the Examinant to eat the said Pieces of Parchment, and to drink the Water and Salt: That then there came into the Room several other Persons, in Disguise, whom they call the Spirits, who, by Violence, took the Examinant to 7 or 8 Pumps, and pumped him at each Pump a considerable Time: That, afterwards, they forced the examinant (beating and punching him with short Sticks and Truncheons) into a Ditch, into which the Common-sewers, and Filth of the Necessary-houses, runs; and one of them forced the Examinant's Head Three Times under the Surface thereof: That, as soon as the Examinant came out of the Ditch, they led him to a Place, at some Distance, which, as the Examinant has been informed, was the extent of their Bounds; and there they produced a Brickbat, having on it human Excrements; and obliged the examinant to kiss the same, and to express himself in the following Words; *viz.*

I am a Rogue, and a Rogue in Grain;

And damn me, if ever I come into the *Mint* again:[42]

The under sheriff of Middlesex told the committee that he could not 'execute Process' in the Mint without 'the Posse Comitatus', ordering out on pain of punishment suitably active men over the age of fifteen in sufficient numbers to overcome resistance; even then he often waited till the Assizes were sitting, 'when he can have the Javelin Men to assist him'.[43]

The indignation of the House of Commons spurred drastic action. An act to suppress the Mint made it easier for the authorities to call out the posse comitatus; any person resisting the service of an execution committed an offence and anyone resisting arrest or execution for a debt of over £50 could be transported for fourteen years; and, crucially, debts totalling less than £50 could be written off for persons living in the Mint by application to the quarter sessions at Guildford, twenty-five miles or so to the south-west. In the summer of 1723, debtors and their families totalling some 6,000 people shipped out to be heard by the Surrey justices. They 'look'd like one of the Jewish Tribes going out of Egypt, the Cavalcade consisted of Caravans, Carts, and Waggons, besides Numbers on Horses, Asses, and on Foot'. The keeper of the Two Fighting Cocks, a Mint alehouse, sent 'an Ass loaden with Geneva [gin], to support the Spirits of the Ladies upon the Journey'. From this time the most outrageous traditions of the Mint were expunged. But it never lost its hole-and-corner character, its usefulness as a hiding place, its reputation for violence and, most of all, its place as a reservoir for some of the deepest poverty in London.[44]

Even in the Mint's heyday, and especially from 1723, debtors who did not pay up could not easily avoid prison if their creditors proved adamant. There were plenty of prisons to choose from. Every part of London could boast a prison, some more than one. Daniel Defoe thought there were more prisons in London 'than any City in Europe' in the 1720s. He listed twenty-two 'public gaols', added 'Five

Night Prisons, called *Round Houses*' and ended his list '&c'. Around these often ancient institutions clustered a dense penumbra of private prisons where those under arrest were held awaiting bail or commitment to prison proper. For political prisoners and prisoners of conscience there were the King's Messengers' houses, the Serjeant at Arms officers' houses and the Black Rod officers' houses. For seamen there were the Admiralty officers' houses and the Admiralty prison at the Marshalsea. Most numerous of all were the 119 'Spunging Houses' that Defoe calculated were then run by licensed bailiffs for debtors. It amounted to an archipelago of incarceration that stretched across London in every direction.[45]

In the City of London and under the jurisdiction of the Corporation were four prisons: Newgate, Ludgate, and two compters or 'counters', one gaol for each of the sheriffs of London, at Wood Street and Poultry. All held debtors as well as miscreants, with the debtors generally in the majority. Even at Newgate debtors were held in considerable numbers. The debtors in the compters were frequently very poor people taken in execution, the debts having been proved in court, for sums of less than £2, and conditions there were notoriously miserable and promiscuous. Debtors and felons at Wood Street, for instance, mixed together in the prison 'tap' (or alehouse), a cellar under the chapel so dark it needed candles from midday; the prisoners paid for the candles.[46]

Besides the Corporation's gaols and a handful in Westminster and the suburbs, London contained three ancient prisons for debt. North of the Thames, inside the City at its western edge, lay the Fleet prison, there since medieval times, on the banks of the River Fleet. From the early eighteenth century this part of the Fleet had been bricked over for Farringdon Street and the prison lay on its eastern side, north of Seacoal Lane. In the early nineteenth century it would be known to familiars as the Farringdon Hotel.

Like the King's Bench, it had its rules or extensive verge of neighbouring streets and alleys where prisoners, at a price, could lodge out of the gaol without fear of further arrests. Its rules were notorious for Fleet marriages; they were a boon to runaways and abductors, a peril to persons excited by drink, and were finally outlawed from 1774. Prisoners here were of all kinds, the poorest on the common side while the better-off, with resources hidden from their creditors, could take advantage of rooms on the master's side.[47]

South of the Thames, Southwark was a veritable township of gaols. It was no surprise that so many sanctuaries clustered here offering refuge from the prison gates. Walking north from St George the Martyr in 1750, on the right-hand side of the way, one passed the White Lyon or Surrey gaol and its adjoining House of Correction for vagrants and street walkers; then, a few steps further, the King's Bench; and then, within yards, the Marshalsea, all inside a quarter of a mile. The Clink Liberty had its own old prison on Bankside and the City Corporation, with a complex and uneasy jurisdiction in Southwark, had a compter there, at first at St Margaret's Hill on Borough High Street, later moving to Tooley Street, east of London Bridge. The King's Bench and the Marshalsea were the other two great debtors' prisons of London.

Most prestigious of all was the King's Bench. In Southwark from around 1368 at the latest, by the mid-eighteenth century it was worn out and too small for the task, so around 1758 it was moved from the High Street to a new gaol on open land in the west of St George's Fields. Its rules we have met, generally also on the Fields' side of Borough High Street but crossing it to include the Marshalsea prison, where the tap was occasionally kept by a King's Bench prisoner ('Bencher') living out of the gaol and taking advantage of this profitable accession to the rules. It was the largest of the debtors' prisons, frequently accommodating around 500, sometimes many more, distributed between the common and master's sides and, as always, often taking in families too.[48]

Just how many debtors were accommodated here and in the other prisons at any one time is unknown, figures being unreliable and frequently unavailable. The great drivers were periods of economic distress that sent many to the wall, but numbers fluctuated as Parliament from time to time sought to relieve misery by easing the process for debtors to free themselves from prison, as we shall see. After 1750, peak years for the King's Bench, which has to stand as a barometer because of the relative completeness of its records, were 1780–81 and 1793; but there was a general tendency for the numbers of imprisoned debtors to rise during the 1790s and especially from 1807, with between 1,000 and 2,000 committed there each year; in 1817, when 1,647 were brought into the King's Bench for a time at least, the numbers of debtors committed to prison in England and Wales was 9,030. The numbers of family members incarcerated with them are unknown.[49]

The King's Bench prison fell under the supervision of the court of that name, its judges frequently sending to it prisoners convicted of crimes against the state, or of libels on prominent individuals. So politicians, publishers and newspaper editors – occasionally visited in prison by some of the greatest in the land – gave added cachet to the Benchers. In the eighteenth and early nineteenth centuries, for instance, John Wilkes, Tobias Smollett, Sir Marc Isambard Brunel, George Colman the playwright, Daniel Defoe, Benjamin Haydon the history painter, and a host of others were imprisoned here. The gaol was notorious for high living on the master's side. It all contributed to an atmosphere of genteel abandon, nicely summed up by Henry 'Orator' Hunt's first stay there, imprisoned for a political crime, around 1800. On arrival

I had made the necessary inquiry for an apartment, but the prison was represented to be very full; and I was shewn one or two rooms, where the parties occupying them had no objection to turn out, to accommodate me, for a certain stipulated sum. Amongst the number I was shewn up into a very good room, which was occupied by a lady, who, it was said, would give up her room for ten pounds. When we entered the room she was singing very divinely, she being no less a personage than Mrs. Wells, the celebrated public singer. With great freedom she inquired which was the gentleman, me or my attorney, who accompanied me; and upon being informed that I was the prisoner, she eyed me over from head to toe, and then, with that art of which she was so much a mistress, she simpering said, that 'she was loath to part with her room at any price, but that, as I appeared a nice wholesome country gentleman, I should be welcome to half of it without paying any thing.' As I was not prepared to enter into a contract of that sort, I hastily retired, and left my attorney to settle the quantum of pecuniary remuneration with her.[50]

If the King's Bench was the most prestigious of the debtors' prisons of London – indeed of the nation – its near neighbour was considered to be one of the lowest and, outside the City, the smallest. This was the Marshalsea, the third great ancient debtors' prison in London. And it had a long and turbulent history.

2

'THE WORST PRISON
IN THE NATION'

THE beginnings of the Marshalsea are lost in time. No date can be attached to its establishment and no date can be given to the institution whose creature it was. This was the Marshalsea Court of the King's Household, its jurisdiction 'of the highest antiquity', said to be 'coeval with the common law'. The court was established to hear causes arising from disputes both criminal and civil between members of the king's household. There was no appeal from its decisions until 1332, when errors in law could be challenged in the superior court of King's Bench. Over time, the Marshalsea court's functions became extended to hear cases of debt and other breaches of covenant arising within the verge of the king's household, an arbitrary and imaginary realm measured by a twelve-mile radius from the king's dining hall at his palace in Westminster, later Whitehall. The City of London, however, was excluded from its jurisdiction. This extension of the court's original and much tighter purpose was maintained by yet another legal fiction: that one of the parties to an action was nominally a member of the royal household, even when neither was.[1]

All this survived for centuries until it was challenged in the early seventeenth century and held to be unlawful, virtually stifling the Marshalsea court's business overnight. But by charters of James I and Charles I a new Palace court, a subsidiary of the old Marshalsea court, was established to take responsibility for causes arising from debts within the verge. From this time the two courts shared the same judges and were in effect made one, the formula of 'the Marshalsea and Palace court' commonly adopted to describe it. Old forms were respected on court days, when the Marshalsea court was opened and adjourned while the Palace court remained sitting for business.[2]

Even from the earliest days it seems that actions for debt had formed a significant component of the court's business. So too, especially when imprisonment for debt was widened after 1283, debtors would have made up a substantial proportion of the population of the Marshalsea prison. The first traces of a prison of the Marshalsea court date from the 1330s, though it seems likely that the court would have had its own gaol from the outset. Just where that prison lay is unclear, like so much at this time. The first reference to the Marshalsea in Southwark is to be found in 1373, when the 'good men' of the Borough were given permission to build a new courthouse for the Marshalsea court with a prison attached, but it is quite possible that there had been a Marshalsea prison in Southwark long before that. By this time a King's Bench prison had already been established in Southwark, as we have seen.[3]

Just why these prisons should have been situated in Southwark remains a matter of speculation. There was much of the outcast about this ancient transpontine locality of London, juxtaposed to the wealth and pomp of the cities of London and Westminster to the north and west. It was a district of complex and uncertain jurisdictions, the City of London having some rights and powers there from 1327, strengthened in the fifteenth century and after, but never extending over the whole Borough. Even in its Southwark domain, the City acted alongside the jurisdictions of the king's courts of Marshalsea and King's Bench and the Surrey justices, with the powers of each contested and challenged by the others even into the eighteenth century. In and around this administrative anarchy, 'Southwark for the most part pursued its accustomed way, unruly and unruled.' It was long notorious as a hiding place of criminals and a settling place for refugee aliens from across the Channel. It was a convenient location for noisome and stinking industries unevenly regulated by the City guilds, home to slaughterhouses and close to what would become by Tudor times the nation's largest leather-making district. The 'stews' of Bankside, brothels banished by the City, alongside countless taverns and alehouses, made the Southwark riverside west of London Bridge notoriously turbulent in the thirteenth and fourteenth centuries. The many coaching inns and drinking houses that lined Borough High Street, profiting from the trade of travellers and drovers to and from London, made something of an everyday fairground even before Southwark Fair, first permitted in 1444, transported the City's Bartholomew Fair across the river for three days in September each year. Bull- and bear-baiting and dogfighting, bowling, archery and other lively pastimes were all sixteenth-century favourites at the Paris Garden, in the west of the Borough along the riverside. It was here that Southwark's long connection with players and playgoers in the High Street's galleried inns climaxed in the construction of a clutch of theatres beyond the reach of City puritans – the Swan, the Hope, the Rose and, most famously, the Globe, from the 1590s and after, most of them short-lived and all of them unrespectable.[4]

This place of banishment and misrule made a suitable location for the king's courts to plant their two great civil gaols, almost in sight of Westminster but conveniently separated from it by the great tidal river. The very unruliness of Southwark's population rendered prisons a necessary buttress of authority – as we have seen, there were five there for much of the Marshalsea's long existence. Unsurprisingly, however, the prisons proved uncongenial bedfellows for the people of Southwark. Nominally bulwarks of order, they could easily become sites of riot and revolt. John Stow, the great chronicler of London, related how, in 1377, a gentleman (perhaps of the king's household) slew a sailor at a time when the navy had assembled in the Thames. The man's shipmates charged the offender in the Marshalsea court but found the judges partial and discovered that the king's pardon would be granted to the offender while he lay in the new-built Marshalsea prison. The sailors broke open the gates

and brought forth the prisoner with his Giues [gyves, or fetters] on his legges, they thrust a knife to his heart, and sticked him, as if hee had beene a Hogge, after this they tyed a roape to his Giues, and drewe him to the gallowes, where when they had hanged him, as though they had done a great act, they caused the trumpets to be sounded before them to theyr ships . . .[5]

Indeed, the prisons would prove vulnerable to any outbreak of public unrest. Four years later the Marshalsea was again stormed, this time by Wat Tyler's men of Kent in the Peasants' Revolt of June 1381. They freed the prisoners and 'brake downe the houses of the Marshalsey, and Kinges Bench in Southwarke . . .', loathsome symbols of the machinery of law, and ransacked a brothel in Bankside occupied by Flemish women, symbol of the hated foreigners who a day or two later would be massacred in considerable numbers on the north bank of the river. Another Kentish rebellion, Jack Cade's of 1450, once more broke open both prisons on the rebels' road to London Bridge.[6]

There were many reasons for rebels and even ordinary citizens to detest the Marshalsea. Besides debtors and offenders against the king's household, the prison housed religious prisoners and political dissidents from the fifteenth century if not before. It seems likely, too, that around 1430 the Marshalsea took on a function that stayed with it almost to the end, as the Admiralty's prison in London for offenders in the navy and on the high seas, including piracy; the Admiralty prison constituted a separate enclosure or building within the Marshalsea. Whatever the offence, treatment of prisoners could be harsh. The 'houses' of the prison were incapable of securing prisoners from escape without cruel fetters, as in the case of the gyves worn by that unfortunate gentleman in 1377. An inventory of the prison taken in 1483 recorded 'Fedirs called Shakylls', 'Sherys' ('shears', leg irons pinioning the ankles while holding the legs apart with a long rod), 'Devyllis in the neke', 'manacles for menys handis', 'Doble Colers of Iron' with and without 'a Chayne', several pairs of 'Stokkis' and so on. It is from these years and even before that the plight of the prisoners prompted the charitably minded to endow the prison with gifts for the use of its poorer inmates. Sir William Horne, a Lord Mayor of London who died in 1496, left an annual donation of 10 shillings for victuals at Christmas and at Easter for prisoners in the Marshalsea and three other prisons: but a century later Stow recorded that the 'legacies are not performed'.[7]

The prison's oppressions caused resentment inside the walls as well as without. Only a few incidents have come down to us. In 1504, Stow tells us, a mass break-out of prisoners resulted in many being captured and executed, 'especially such as had beene committed for felony or treason'. And in 1592 a crowd of apprentice felt-makers gathered outside the prison to protest at the unjust treatment afforded one of their number then in the gaol. Anticipating an attempt to break open the prison, the Marshalsea officers charged out of the gates in force, 'laying about them with daggers and cudgels' so vigorously that several in and around the crowd were killed. The resulting row over apportioning blame involved the Lord Mayor and City sheriffs, the Surrey justices and the Privy Council, testimony to Southwark's and the Marshalsea's uncertain accountability.[8]

During the Reformation the function of the Marshalsea as a receptacle for religious prisoners, especially recusants (those refusing to bow to authority or give up the old religion) grew in importance. Priests and politicians were imprisoned here in their hundreds during the turbulent sixteenth century, frequently to be interrogated, sometimes tortured and occasionally taken from the Marshalsea to the Tower of London on their way to a grisly death at Tyburn or on Tower Hill.

Imprisonment in the Marshalsea traced every twist and turn of the Reformation and the Counter-Reformation. Under Henry VIII, for instance, George Bucker, otherwise Adam Damplip, a Protestant dissident hanged at Calais in 1543, is said to have asked the prison's keeper before being returned to France, 'Do you think I have been God's prisoner so long in the Marshalsea and have not yet learned to die?' Under Mary, Thomas Mountain was imprisoned there for nearly two years, undergoing interrogation by the Lord Chancellor, but he survived and eventually became vicar of St Pancras, Soper Lane, in the City. Most of all, under Elizabeth the Marshalsea became one of the most important gaols in the land: the former Deans of Exeter and of Worcester died there in 1559 and 1561 respectively; recusant priests were tortured there, such as John Cornelius, who refused to betray his benefactors and was taken in irons to Dorchester, where he was executed in 1594; and some clandestine priests were uncovered there, such as James Fenn, brought in 1581 to the Marshalsea, where he administered solace, especially to the pirates, but was undone when one of his penitents converted to Catholicism. Even the queen's own torturers could end up there, such as Richard Topcliffe, who complained to her majesty of the 'disgrace' of a spell in the Marshalsea for a slight he had perpetrated on the Privy Council in 1595.[9]

Of all the Marshalsea's religio-political prisoners during these troubled times the most renowned was Edmund Bonner, Bishop of London, at first a loyal supporter of Henry VIII against papal rule, rewarded with this great bishopric in 1540. But Bonner's convictions were conservative and he found himself out of step with those Protestant reformers who received a sympathetic reception under Edward VI. Bonner's first spell in the Marshalsea was for preaching at St Paul's doctrine that was opposed to the king's direct instruction; he was imprisoned in September 1549 and deprived of his bishopric in October. For refusal to pay the gaol fees his bed was removed and he lay on straw, kept on the prison's poor – or common – side, with no allowance of food or clothing other than what could be obtained from charity or his fellow prisoners. In 1553, within a month of Edward's death, Bonner was pardoned by Queen Mary and effectively reinstated as Bishop of London on the day of his release, Saturday 5 August; met with popular acclaim in the City, his formal restoration followed less than three weeks later. There followed six years of royal favour, under which Bonner's reputation as a dogged pursuer of anti-Catholic heresy earned him the name of 'Bloody Bonner', responsible for 120 or so burnings in the see of London. His malevolence was not forgotten when Elizabeth succeeded to the throne and restored Protestantism. Refusing to take the Oath of Supremacy in 1559, he was once more deprived of his bishopric and in April 1560 was duly imprisoned in the Marshalsea. Though treated less harshly than during his first imprisonment, Bonner would stay in the Marshalsea until his death in September 1569; he was buried at midnight in St George the Martyr's churchyard close by, the authorities fearing that his interment would provoke trouble among the truculent populace of Southwark.[10]

Alongside these prominent prisoners, the Marshalsea had continued its use as a gaol for debtors and to a lesser extent for seamen. As the times became less troubled under James I, the proportion of debtors almost certainly rose, though no figures survive to prove the point. The decision in the court of King's Bench that the Marshalsea court could no longer hear cases unless one of the parties really did belong to the king's household must have dented the business of the gaol as much as of the court. But this weakening of the strictures enforcing the circulation of capital alarmed tradesmen and merchants everywhere and moves were made to re-establish the effectiveness of the Marshalsea jurisdiction, first under James I in 1611 and then with the foundation of a new Palace court under Charles I in 1631. Even before the new troubles of the 1640s, the future of the court was again put in doubt by challenges to its legality, though it seems to have continued hearing cases until its abolition by the Commonwealth on 1 August 1651. With the Restoration, and in response to petitions from tradesmen and no doubt representations from legal interests, the court began to sit again in 1660. New letters patent were issued by Charles II in 1664 which finally put to rest lawyers' doubts over jurisdiction that had rumbled on for half a century or more, though some pamphleteers continued to argue the point for another 150 years and more. Sometime later, in May 1676, both court and prison would narrowly escape destruction in the Great Fire of Southwark. It began to the north of the Marshalsea in Borough High Street, razing many historic inns, such as the George and the Talbot (Tabard), and required the blowing up of Southwark compter and courthouse at St Margaret's Hill as a fire break.[11]

It seems likely that the Marshalsea prison kept open for business during the Interregnum despite the absence of the court to which it belonged. Prisons were always needed in London, whoever tried to govern it, and in any event the

The Marshalsea on William Morgan's map of 1682, Borough High
Street at this point known as St Margaret's Hill.

Admiralty duties continued. It is likely, too, that debtors were committed there from the inferior courts in both Middlesex and Surrey, and possibly felons, housed there for convenience as the old county gaol at the White Lion fell steadily into decay. From 1681 or perhaps later, the Surrey magistrates arranged with the Marshalsea authorities that some felons, eventually many, were kept there rather than the White Lion pending its rebuilding. The doubling of the Marshalsea as a Surrey county gaol continued to some degree until 1724. So we read, for instance, of the pursuit of 'eight Highway-Men' from Kent Street in 1717 where one was seized there and another in the Mint, both then taken to the Marshalsea; or of 'several Pickpockets . . . apprehended practising on People in Southwark Fair, and committed to the Marshalsea' in 1721. This intimate connection with the affairs of Southwark, the prison tied by old-established attachments to the Mint with its debtors and outcasts, to the White Lion with its felons, and to the excitements of the fair, whose stallholders made collections for the Marshalsea prisoners each year and where theatre booths were cheek by jowl with the prison – plays were advertised as performed at 'Mrs. MYNNS's Great Booth, in the *Queens-Arms* Yard near the *Marshalsea* Gate' in 1715, for instance – was a great feature in the life of the gaol, at least in this early period. And the local connections persisted, for it seems that the Marshalsea helped lodge debtors from the City's rebuilt Southwark compter when it moved from St Margaret's Hill on Borough High Street to Tooley Street around 1787.[12]

Despite this local immersion, though, the prison retained some of the national importance it had possessed in the time of Elizabeth. The Marshalsea continued to imprison those convicted of offences against God (including blasphemy and recusancy) and the king (including 'treasons, conspiracies, riots and tumults'). These old functions were kept alive through the period of Marlborough's wars. The prison thus proved useful in helping deal with prisoners captured during the Jacobite Rebellion of 1715, when sixty or so of the 200 prisoners brought to London from Preston were committed to the Marshalsea in December 1715. Some proved more troublesome than others, the Jacobite gentleman-poet William Tunstall using the occasion to publish two pamphlets of Marshalsea verses in 1716, while at least one other made his escape.[13]

Once in the gaol, these and all other prisoners held there over the previous 300 years or so were nominally the responsibility of the Knight Marshal of the King's Household, who was also one of the two (from the time of Charles II, three) judges of the Marshalsea and Palace courts. Knights Marshal were appointed by the Lord Chamberlain and retained their office for life 'on good behaviour'. Over the generations they had been able to distance themselves from responsibility for both court and prison, while continuing to reap profit from the fees attaching to both. Thus, by the seventeenth century if not before, the Knight Marshal came generally to be represented on the Marshalsea bench by a deputy judge or 'steward'. Similarly a deputy marshal was appointed by the Knight Marshal to be keeper of the Marshalsea and to live in the prison and govern the prisoners on his behalf.[14]

In every case, profit was made from these appointments too. And all profits made from official positions were intim-ately intertwined with politics. 'Places' were granted to the 'friends' of the party in power: emoluments and stipends were bought and sold for substantial capital sums and in expecta-tion of subsequent political favours of one kind or another. That was no doubt true of any preceding age, but we might see how profit and politics came together during the early eighteenth century. The Knight Marshal from 1700 was Sir Philip Meadows, who managed successfully to be acceptable to both Tory and Whig regimes either side of the Hanoverian succession. He had long spells out of the country as ambassador to Holland and then Vienna from 1704 to 1709, while sitting as MP for Cornish pocket boroughs. Meadows was said to have paid the Lord Chamberlain £5,000 for his place as Knight Marshal. He accorded to custom by sending his steward to the Marshalsea and Palace courts, and from 1706 he appointed as new deputy marshal and keeper of the Marshalsea prison John Darby, a printer of Bartholomew Close, Smithfield, where William Hogarth was a close neighbour. Darby died around September 1720 and in November Meadows came to a similar arrangement with Darby's son, also John and also a printer. John Darby the Younger was a dissenter – 'a finished Christian', as an admirer put it – and accordingly a Whig. He was a prominent publisher and printer of tracts in favour of the Hanoverian succession and, as far as can be surmised, was four-square in the emerging camp of Sir Robert Walpole. We do not know how much Darby paid Meadows for the privilege of being his deputy in 1720, but it would have been a lot. This is clear because in March 1727 Darby was able to 'farm' the Marshalsea prison to its former turnkey, William Acton, a Southwark butcher by trade, on a seven-year lease; Acton became deputy keeper of the Marshalsea and undertook to pay Darby a total of £400 per year, with Acton paying all taxes on the prison. We shall meet him again.[15]

There was profit to be made from the business of the Marshalsea in other ways too. The lawyers in the Marshalsea court – restricted in number to two counsel (barristers) and six attorneys – bought their positions from the Lord Steward of the court, the senior judge sitting with the Knight Marshal or his deputy. Occasionally this practice was frowned upon and disowned by a conscientious Lord Steward, but in general in the eighteenth century counsel paid £1,000 for their positions, and attorneys, who managed most of the business, £1,500; the purchases were for life and could be sold on and the purchase money was shared between the Lord Steward and Knight Marshal. The Marshalsea attorneys had their chambers at Clifford's Inn, at the side of St Dunstan's in the West, Fleet Street. These arrangements continued for the life of the court and prison; the six attorneys' initials can still be seen against the names of prisoners brought into the Marshalsea in the surviving 'Day Books' of commitments and discharges. By 1831 it was said that the closed shop of Marshalsea lawyers had become even more expensive to enter: 'The barristers give from three to four thousand pounds for their appointments, and the attorneys from fifteen hundred to two thousand.' Their monopoly position enabled them to fix high fees before appearing on behalf of clients in the Marshalsea or Palace court, attorneys demanding '21s. to 25s.', it was said in 1833, 'and the money must be *paid down*', for rather understandable reasons. Presumably similar fees and demands had been normal long before. But some could be found to defend the Clifford's Inn 'Six': their secure position was said to mean that 'no *harsh* measures are pursued to drive a human being to despair'; to 'deprive them, therefore, of their monopoly [would mean] an end of all happiness in the Marshalsea prison'.[16]

When Sir Philip Meadows made his bargain with John Darby the younger in 1720 the Marshalsea prison was already an antique institution whose buildings showed their great age. On the east side of Borough High Street, bordered by Mermaid Alley (now Court) to the south and Ax and Bottle Yard, later King Street, to the north (now Newcomen Street), it was squeezed between the backs of buildings on the north and south sides of these places and behind those fronting the High Street. The gaol was entered by a gateway and narrow passage to the right-hand side looking from the Borough. There is no reason to suppose that this arrangement had changed since permission had been granted to build the prison in the 1370s, for William Morgan's map of

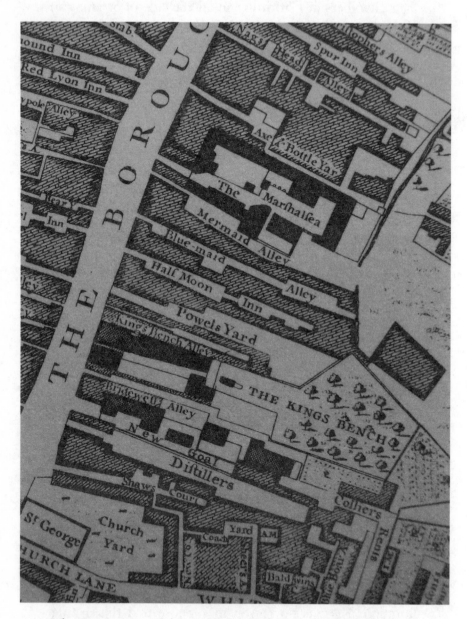

John Rocque's map of 1746 shows the Marshalsea extended to the
south into Mermaid Alley.

1682 shows terraces of gabled and other houses, some of apparently late-medieval design, on all four sides of a central long quadrangle of open space, with some of it encroached upon on the north side. Part of the quadrangle appears to be walled off, enclosing buildings on some of the north side and the west – this the common side of the gaol. The wall is indicated more clearly in John Rocque's survey of London in the 1740s. By that time the prison site had been extended to the south, largely taking in the north side of Mermaid Alley. The land for this extension of the prison was leased originally from 'the Gosling family'. Exactly when is unclear, but it was done 'when the prison was considered "too straight"', or too small, for its purpose, probably sometime between 1730 and 1745. It no doubt required the enlargement or redevelopment of the buildings on the south side of the gaol. This became a complication when plans were contemplated to rebuild the prison in the 1780s, by which time the lease had been acquired by or otherwise assigned to W. Marston, the prison's then deputy marshal, and subsequently his widow.[17]

Apart from this extension to the south, what evidence we have indicates that the buildings in the gaol throughout the eighteenth century were already very old. Although John Strype, the antiquary, called the gaol in 1720 'a large and strong Building', it was more properly described as a collection of buildings of various ages and styles. Fifty years on it was described thus:

As you quit the main street, a dirty court presents itself to your view, which is terminated by large gates, closed with a massy bar of iron, fastened with an enormous padlock. The top of the high wall over it is guarded by a *chevaux de frize*, to prevent the unhappy prisoners making their escape. By a narrow door, which you go up three steps to, on your right hand, and which is secured with a weighty chain and a large

lock, you enter through a dirty room, which is the station of
the turnkey. The horrid clanking of the chain, or the dreadful
sound of the lock, is sufficient to terrify you; but when you
descend into the prison, it is wretched almost beyond description. Houses, in which are apartments for the prisoners, with
scarce a window, except in those whose inhabitants can afford
to pay for them. Walls tottering to their fall . . .[18]

A view of the terrace on the north side of the prison taken
in 1773 shows five three-storey houses of old-fashioned form,
perhaps dating from the sixteenth or even fifteenth century.
An annotation to one of these buildings, double-fronted and
next to a blank wall, describes it as 'the Original Prison,
now called the Common Side'. By this time the common
side was not separated from the rest of the buildings by any
wall, and nor is one shown on Horwood's map of 1792–9,
though the remains of a wall that might have stretched some
way across the Park (as the open central quadrangle was
known by the prisoners, in ironic reference to Hyde Park
and its continuations into Westminster) are shown in an
engraving from around 1803. Next to this terrace of houses
and also on the north side was the courtroom, in which the
Marshalsea and Palace courts were held every Friday except
on religious holidays; on court days prisoners would be
locked in their rooms until the judges, lawyers and suitors
had assembled to minimise the risk of escapes in the confusion. The court building appears on Morgan's map of 1682
and its encroachment into the Park is plainly shown. It was
probably newly built at that time, because a later authority
gives its builder as John Lowman, who erected it on land
he leased within the prison, the lease dating from 1688.
Apart from this and the Goslings' lease, the prison and its
site belonged to the crown.[19]
Later sketches made of the prison and engraved in 1803
show these old buildings to be still standing, though some

were now extensively propped up by timber raking shores. They show too, on the west side of the gaol, next to a blank wall against which prisoners played fives, clapboard-covered buildings dating probably from the seventeenth century, possibly earlier. Watercolours and engravings from 1801–5 also show buildings on the south side of the gaol, galleried and partly timber-faced, probably from the seventeenth and early eighteenth centuries.

The accommodation provided in these and other buildings was detailed in a schedule in the report of a parliamentary inquiry into conditions in the Marshalsea published in 1729. The '*Master-side*' comprised five houses or buildings named the Horsepond (then partly empty), the 'Oake' or Oak (part of which was for women prisoners), the Nursery, the Park and the Long Gallery, the last 'in a very Ruinous Condition', its 'Walls being very weak' and unsuitable for keeping prisoners who might be tempted to escape. The master's side contained in all twenty-four rooms occupied by eighty prisoners, of whom six were women; nine rooms were empty; one other was let to prisoners as a workroom, one was a coffee room and one a chandler's shop. The 'Tap-house' or alehouse was in a separate building within the prison. On the common side at that time were sixteen rooms or wards in what appear to be three houses or buildings, including one sickroom each for men and women. They were occupied by 281 prisoners, or some eighteen persons per room, of whom sixty-eight were women. There was thus a total of 361 prisoners when the parliamentary committee visited in 1729, although the schedule does not tally with the text, which claimed 'upwards of 330 Prisoners' on the common side alone.[20]

We shall see that the 1729 inquiry uncovered many abuses, some of them utterly horrifying. But as the 1483 inventory and the sufferings of religious prisoners in the Marshalsea tell us, abuses there were no new phenomenon. The loose

oversight of the Knight Marshal and the tradition of delega-
tion to a contractor who paid a high price for the privilege
and then still had to extract a profit from the prisoners
tended towards exploitation and oppression in the closed
world of the Marshalsea. The injustice was not always taken
lying down. In 1639 the prisoners mutinied against the keeper
or his deputy, attacking the officers 'with stones, brickbats,
and firebrands'. One of their complaints concerned twenty-
three women kept in one room too small for them to lie
down.[21]

Evidence for the state of things in the first three decades
of the eighteenth century abounds, foreshadowing the findings of the parliamentary committee of 1729. A pamphleteer
of 1699 discovered there '*a Woman almost naked and
perish'd*' after seventeen months in prison, for in the
Marshalsea 'ther's no Allowance at all for Debtors that are
brought in by the Marshals Writs, so that unless they have
Money to subsist themselves, they must inevitably be starv'd
to death'.[22]

Over and above the travails of destitution there was the
capacity of the gaolers to make any prisoner's trials worse.
Peter Drake, perhaps held as a traitor during Marlborough's
wars, had 'Irons put upon him, which he had once bought
off but has them now put on againe, in hopes as is most
probable of extorting more Money from him. I must
acquaint you,' the Secretary of State wrote to the keeper
of the Marshalsea, 'that he was sent to you, to keep him
in Safe Custody, not to punish him by putting him in Irons,
and you are to take his Irons off, and let him have Better
usage for the future.' A year or so later, a Jacobite officer
in the French army, Lieutenant Charles Aslaby or Aislaby
complained of being 'Severely loaded wth Irons not
Consistent to Prisoners of Warr', and now 'being Threatned
for want of Money, to be put into the Dungeon . . .' Another
Jacobite, Alexander Dallzell, complained to the Secretary

of State for the Home Department (Henry St John, Viscount
Bolingbroke) in December 1711 that in the Marshalsea he
had been 'heavy loaden with Irons these eight Months past,
in which in the Summer occasioned two severe fits of sickness that had almost taken me off . . . I am perswaded if
these irons are not Removed they and ye pinching Cold
weather, together wth Lying upon ye bare boards will
Inevitably cutt me off in a short time.' He asked that the
irons be removed but they were not; a further letter in
February 1712 begging the same relief seems also to have
gone unanswered.[23]

The Marshalsea, day to day, was the keeper's fiefdom,
and the irons and worse would remain part of the armoury
of oppression there for a generation to come. For the mass
of prisoners – the debtors – misery was indiscriminate, at
least for the poorest sort. A petition to Parliament in April
1714 'of above 600 poor insolvent Debtors in the *Marshalsea*
Prison' claimed they 'were now perishing in Gaol for want
of Necessaries, some of them dying daily', or so they
affirmed. Parliament duly resolved to bring in one of its
periodic bills for the relief of insolvent debtors. A pamphlet
that same year pleading the cause of debtors asserted there
were some 700 or 800 prisoners in the Marshalsea of whom
two or three died each day. No poor prisoner was immune,
even those of high rank: it alleged that one Captain Derew,
a debtor, 'was found roasting a Rat for his Subsistence';
and Sir George Seaton, Bart, 'was forced to pick up those
smaller Sprats from a Dunghill, which had been thrown
there by another prisoner, who thought them too small to
eat'.[24]

Similarly, an anonymous verse effusion by a prisoner,
with copious explanatory notes about conditions in the
prison, was published in 1718. *Hell in Epitome: or, A
Description of the M—SH—SEA* spelled out the various
abuses of the gaol:

Stands an old Pile, most dreadful to the View,
Dismal as Wormwood, or repenting Rue.
Thither the Graduates in Sin resort,
And take Degrees becoming *Satan*'s Court;
There are instructed in the Paths of Vice,
There sell good Linen, there they purchase Lice.

It complained of insolent and oppressive gaolers – the keeper or deputy marshal was 'the Monarch'; of the lack of provision for the poor prisoner, 'at Liberty to chew upon the very Iron Bars that confine him; for no one helps him under the pinching Streights of Hunger'; of the frequent deaths – 'dead Bodies lie here sometimes a Week together unburied'; of the 'Dungeons' where prisoners who cannot pay their fees are kept 'ne'er to see the Day.'

But what provokes my Spleen, and makes me write,
Is the strong Room, begirt with endless Night;
A Prison in a Prison, where Men live,
And Corm'rant-like, on Wreck or Rapine thrive[.][25]

This Marshalsea prisoner proved far from a lone voice. In 1719 Sir William Lowther reported to the House of Commons that 'a Hundred Persons have died in less than Three Months' in the Marshalsea. In 1722 a petition of 'between Three and Four Hundred insolvent Debtors' in the Marshalsea complained of 'the Burthen of all the Misery that can attend them, in the worst Prison in the Nation; where there is no Allowance but Water; by which Hardship many poor Souls die, as many of the Petitioners can witness'. And in 1724 the prisoners bolstered their case by stressing that 'they are so numerous, and so closely confined, that they may occasion an epidemical Distemper to the whole Nation, in case of a hot Summer', perhaps seeking to play on fears of the plague that had arrived in Marseilles and caused a panic in London a year or two before; it would be an argument their successors would exploit on and off for more than a hundred years to come.[26]

The 'worst prison in the nation' was an extravagant claim. But within the hierarchy of London's debtors' prisons the Marshalsea was assuredly at the bottom, certainly compared to the King's Bench and the Fleet. The author of *Memoirs of the Mint* of 1713 had been arrested by a bailiff, taken to a spunging house and from there 'to an Inchanted Castle, called (as I have since learn'd) the *Marshalsea*':

> The various Spectacles in this Place were amazing, in one Place you hear a Fiddle, in another a Groan; here a Piper, there a Penitent; in another place a fat Baud, and after her a Skelleton, at the Head of fifty walking Diseases, tho I rarely met a fighting Face, yet there's scarce a Man, that is not a thousand strong, and what is strange, he feeds all these, while he starves himself. Within you hear the Chinking of Irons, and Vollies of Oaths, while they are fetter'd from throwing ought else, at one another's Heads. The most wretched here, Fare the best, and eat out of the Basket, while those on the other side, are ready to eat them up.

By a writ of habeas corpus he quickly removed himself at some expense to the Queen's Bench prison, as it then was. Many others able to do so would take the same route over the years. It was just a few yards to the south, but really another country: '*Pimps, Bullies, Bauds, Punks*, &c. are never Naturaliz'd here, but stay at the *Marshalsea* . . . not being able to defray the Charge of their *Pass-port* hither: Perhaps some may shelter in the *Mint*, but that (tho' on our Borders) is a separate *Common-wealth* . . .' And if those who could afford it fled to other prisons, the privilege could operate in reverse. Prisoners in the King's Bench too clamorous of their rights would be threatened with removal to the Marshalsea and the refractory would be sent there for punishment, loaded with irons 'and lock'd down in the Strong-Room', 'a Dungeon, or dark Hole, with a Ring in the middle of the Room, to fasten down Prisoners to the Floor'. In 1724 a mutiny in the King's Bench prison required the assistance of gaolers 'from Newgate, the Marshalsea, and elsewhere' to suppress it, not without a long struggle. Finally, 'the Ringleaders were put into Irons, and some of them sent to the Marshalsea'.[27]

Most debtors able to do so, then, would avoid the Marshalsea if they could. But those without money to spare on legal process and a more expensive gaol had no option, and they comprised all sorts and conditions of men and women, whether polite or plebeian, educated or ignorant, wily or innocent. And just a few years after the King's Bench mutiny, it was into this fearful prison that John Baptist Grano, a gentle musician of Italian stock, was committed from Johnson's spunging house on Thursday 30 May 1728. He would remain in the Marshalsea for almost the next sixteen months; and he kept a journal for every day he spent there.

3

'HARDLY ANY ONE BUT VILAINS': GRANO'S MARSHALSEA, 1728–9

JOHN Baptist Grano

was brought to this Hell between 7 & 8 at Night when I was introduc'd, by those Masters of Cerimony call'd Bailies into the Lobby or what is call'd Here yᵉ Lodge I spy'd a Man whom I knew who happening to be yᵉ Master Turnkey, told me I should be us'd <with> all yᵉ good Manners in the World; made me set down & offer'd to treat me with some thing to drink. after asking a few Questions about Mʳˢ Cuningham (, for he was turnkey to yᵉ golden Lyon Sponging=House when Mʳ Cuningham was in trouble, for so I got acquainted with him) he ask'd me if I was for yᵉ Master's Side and if so wither I was provided with five Shillings advance for a fortnights Beding, a Shilling for Sheets, and six pence for the Bed Maker, I told him I was not provided, but yᵉ next Day I should. So he told me he would treat me as a Friend and he would answer for my paying the next Day, so he left me in the Lodge and went to find me a Room habited of the best People: in about an Hour he came to me and told me he had provided me a Room with good Company a clean Bed=fellow and clean Sheets. about the Hour of ten the unhappy Prisoners began to cry one another to their diferent Wards as they term it, but in my life I never heard any thing so hidious the sight of the Dead and Wounded the groans of the latter the Moans of each relation the Day after a Battle is harmony to y^e Crys of these Miserable wretches; when the gentlemen \<were call'd\> of y^e Quarter was alloted me my friend the turnkey who now I'll remember by y^e Name of Wills came and call'd me to follow him; accordingly I did, and was introduc'd \<by Him to my\> bedfellow & Companions when I came in, they Saluted me with S^r we are sorry for y^r Misfortune as soon as which I was lock'd in with them; after some Minutes Silence examining one another's looks, one of y^e Gentlemen told me he was y^e Youngest prisoner or him of the latest Date therefore was oblig'd to speak for his Brethren & in behalf of him Self, I ask'd him what he had to say he told me that at ye Entrance of a new Prisoner 'twas a Custom to treat ye Company with a tall Boy of Drink, in answer to which I reply'd I was not provided being brought away unawares, however that if they'd call for it Mr Wills would answer the paying of it which accordingly they did and we drank it, sate up till about 11 and so went to bed to my new Bedfellow.[1]

At the time of his arrest John Grano was a musician of some celebrity in London. Though the outlines of his career can be gleaned from the newspapers from 1714 on, much else about his life is obscure. His father, Johon Baptist Grano, was probably Sicilian and likely to have been a regimental musician in one of the Dutch armies of William of Orange, arriving in England as part of the invasion of 1688 or soon after. His wife, Jane, née Villeneuve, was French and generally gave her married name as Granom. Taking full advantage of this endowment, John Baptist Grano spoke French and Dutch and almost certainly Italian – he wrote his name on the vellum cover of 'A Journal of My Life Inside the Marshalsea' as Giovanni Battista Grano. He was the eldest son, a first-born, baptised John Baptist, having been buried in the church-yard of St James's, Piccadilly, in 1691. We do not know when the Marshalsea's John Baptist was born but it is likely to have been around 1693. Three other children lived to adult-hood: a younger son, Lewis, also a musician, and two daugh-ters, Jane and Mary (Molly). The whole family was staunchly Roman Catholic, John performing his 'Religious Exercise' almost every morning in prison, his parents and siblings attending mass at the Venetian and Sardinian ambassadors' chapels, and taking religious counsel from a Jesuit who would pay frequent visits to Grano in the Marshalsea, for the good of his soul and the benefit of his pocket, passing family donations to the prodigal son. Catholicism was at this time still a proscribed religion, practised with circumspection, almost secrecy; and its adherents were aligned politically with Jacobites, supporters of the Stuart line to the throne. But all this did not prevent the family from making their way in the world. The Granos rented a small house and haberdashery shop on the south side of Pall Mall, on the site of today's Reform Club, Jane and Molly running the family business at the sign of the Golden Ball.[2]

John Grano was short of stature, black-haired and attrac-tive to women. He married Mary Thurman at St James's in 1713, when he was about twenty and she only fifteen. Before an amicable separation four years later they had a son, Peregrine or Perry Grano, who would later leave for sea as a midshipman, but not before time spent usefully running errands for his imprisoned father. Grano played a noteworthy part in London's musical life from his teenage years. He was an orchestral musician at the Opera House in the Haymarket even before Handel arrived in London in 1709. Possessing an outstandingly fine ear, from 1714 Grano was a prominent solo performer on the German (transverse) flute and the trumpet, often exploiting both in the same 'consort'.

Newspaper cuttings show him playing concertos by Corelli, Vivaldi and others at all London's leading music venues of the time: at Stationer's Hall in the City, at Hickford's Room then at James Street, Haymarket, at the Haymarket 'Tennis-Court', at Lincoln's Inn Theatre and the Theatre Royal, Drury Lane, at the 'Great Room' in York Buildings, Villiers Street, and so on. He performed in the same programme with the capital's leading instrumentalists such as Jean Kytch, the Dutch oboist, and the violin prodigy Matthew Dubourg, and singers such as Mrs Fitzgerald, Mrs Barbier, Mrs Fletcher among others. These were frequently prestigious occasions, Grano performing at benefits for his fellow musicians and for the architect, playwright and impresario John Vanbrugh, for instance, and sometimes announced as performing 'At the desire of several Persons of Quality'.[3]

Grano was also well known as a composer of some repute for a range of instruments, his pieces published on their own merits even when he was a prisoner in the Marshalsea, and in collections with other composers: his 'trumpet march was long used by the guards', it was recorded later in the century. And he was a well-known teacher, his most famous pupil the black trumpeter 'Mr. William Douglas, commonly called the Black Prince, a Scholar of Mr Grano', as the papers put it. His career seems quickly to have recovered from one unseemly interlude: accepted into a troop of the Horse Guards as 'servant and trumpeter' to its commanding officer, the Marquis of Winchester, he absconded to The Hague in 1719, taking his master's expensive livery with him – perhaps to escape his creditors or caught up in some complication involving his marriage – but he was back on the London stage within a year. From 1720 he played in the Opera House under Handel, though how frequent a performer he was there we do not know. The Opera itself went through many difficult times until a temporary closure just after Grano entered the Marshalsea.[4]

A musician's life in early-eighteenth-century London was full of uncertainties and vicissitudes, even for such a skilled and comprehensive talent as Grano's. At the top, in the salaries obtainable by the greatest Italian singers, the London music market was the richest in Europe. But there was no mass audience that could sustain the careers of all the musicians who flocked in emulation to the capital. To make the best of things music was a career that needed steadiness and application to pursue. Grano could draw on those qualities – they helped him survive in the Marshalsea, as we shall see. But he also had flaws that both undermined his industry and robbed him of its fruits. He was greedily sociable but could not separate cheerfulness from drinking to excess. He deliberately sought associations where he could indulge these propensities, like the Horse Guards, notorious for high living, and the Freemasons, more restrained but dedicated to fellowship in this city of strangers. More fatally, though, Grano had aspirations to gentility. He adored people of 'rank' and 'quality' and clamoured to be thought one; and he embraced the other side of the coin, displaying haughtiness verging on disgust for those he considered beneath him. Charles Burney, writing fifty years later from memory or hearsay, called Grano 'a kind of mungrel *dilettante*, who during many years condescended to make concerts and give lessons, *en professeur*, always insinuating that it was merely for the pleasure of amusing the public and instructing individuals'.[5]

Perhaps Grano saw the taint of trade spilling out of the Pall Mall haberdashery and tarnishing the necessity of earning money by his talents. Irksome it might have been, but necessity it was. For gentility came at a high price. Unfortunately for Grano, he had slipped into the habit of purchasing gentility with money he had not yet earned, perhaps never could. That was the immediate cause of his downfall this spring of 1728. He was nabbed by a bailiff at the suit of 'Andrew Turner et al' in the sum of £99 – better than two years' wages for a journeyman. But he was in debt everywhere. He woke in the spunging house on the day of his committal to the news that Mrs Thomson, landlady of his lodgings at Chelton's Court, Bedfordbury, behind St Martin's Lane, 'had clap'd another Action upon me'.[6]

When the fog cleared from Grano's mind after that first night in the Marshalsea, he began to ease his way into prison life. He discovered his 'chum' or bedfellow to be 'Mr Blunt', properly David Blount, a 'Cloathier', perhaps in the haberdashery business like the Granos. Two other 'Gentlem[n]' lodged in the same master's-side room, 'M[r] Sandford a young Fellow, the son of a Rich Man but under the displeasure of his Father, and a M[r] Blundel an unfortunate Jeweler'. These two almost certainly shared a bed at the same rate charged Grano and Blount, 2s 6d each a week: bed-sharing was customary for working men in lodgings and for travellers in inns, so this was no uncommon arrangement, though certainly a blow to gentility.[7]

From his chum and room-mates Grano quickly learned the language of the Marshalsea. The prison was 'the Castle', sometimes 'this inchanted Castle', occasionally 'our College', its prisoners 'Collegians'. Outside the high walls 'the Living World' was contrasted to 'this Dead World'. The open ground within the prison was 'the Park'. Grass, however, was in short supply: walking with a fellow prisoner 'under the Admiralty', they were 'almost killed with Dust <the Wind being at that Time very High as its call'd>'. The Park, with all its faults, could be enjoyed in the lengthy hours of free movement granted to the prisoners, 'for we are lock'd up every Night between Nine & ten and let loose a little after 5' on every day except Fridays, court days, when doors were kept locked until later in the day. Grano took his exercise walking in the Park and, though not an especially active man, occasionally played with battledores and shuttlecocks there with other prisoners. He also, as presumably others did, used to piss there.[8]

Within days of his committal the crowded room had become to him a 'Hell whole of a Place', made more crowded still by his chum's propensity to entertain the occasional 'Damsel of the Town'. Grano had been impressed early on by another prisoner who had visited his room-mates, one Adam Elder, 'a pretty well behav'd Man, of very good Education and fine Parts'. Elder had a room to himself, so Grano asked William Acton, the prison 'Governour', to let him chum with Elder and within three weeks or so the move had been made. There was still just one bed in the room but the new arrangements must have eased living conditions considerably for him. Pretty much everything had to be done, especially after locking up, in a room unlikely to have been larger than ten feet square. Grano recorded early on, for instance, after a drinking bout in the room, that Elder 'went to Bed while I sat up sounded a dozen airs on the Trumpet Wash'd my Manhood Legs and Feet read a little and went to Bed between 12 & 1', and something similar was likely on most nights.[9]

In this close-closeted existence Elder's surface gentility would soon wear thin and there would eventually be a fractious falling-out, to be recounted in its place. Grano thus pressed Acton once more to permit him to move, this time to an empty but ruinous room next to Elder's which Grano undertook to fit up at his own expense. With labour from inside and outside the gaol, the building work proceeded slowly and piecemeal. He had to have casement windows fitted, 'a new Door, new Chimley Piece, Window Seat, Feet [skirting?] Board and Cornish [cornice]', a new tiled fireplace and stove with a stone hearth and brass 'Ornimentals', and a 'double cas'd' brass lock to keep his possessions safe. At first he used his room for privacy during the day but then moved in a bed and bedding, and 'I lay in my own Room for the first time' on 3 December, some six months after entering the prison. Domestic necessaries like a kettle and a

'Dresser' for his clothes would be accumulated in the coming weeks. But peace, so much desired, was unobtainable in the Marshalsea. The ramshackle state of the old gaol meant that noise from the rooms above and below and all around could never be kept out. He could hear conversations from prisoners under him because his floorboards were loose and 'the ceiling Plastering [was] broke' below; rows or drunken merriment in his building and even beyond could enliven the days but shatter the nights. Sometimes the prison sounds were pleasing: 'the Nymphs of this Place Sang till about one in ye Morning, which with the Silence of the Night and formation of the Place had a very agreeable Effect'; but surprisingly pleasant or otherwise, they could never be ignored.[10]

Those singers may well have been common-side nymphs, but in general the two sides of the gaol were for Grano entirely separate worlds. He knew the common side was there, had heard it locked up on his very first night, but he avoided the thought and sight of it as much as he could. When a gentleman acquainted with Grano visited him and invited him to drink in 'the Bar', he suggested instead a bowl of punch in his own room, for the tap was 'a Vilainous Place being in Sight of all ye Lower degree of People'. Keeping the common side out of sight was essential to the preservation of gentility. That September Acton permitted a dance and entertainment arranged by Grano and other master's-side prisoners at their own expense: 'assoon as ye Common Side people were lock'd up we walk'd two's & two's up to the Court Room'.[11]

Yet the common side could make itself felt. On 1 March 1729, the queen's birthday, 'a parcel of Fellows from the Common Side came and Hollow'd in our Park enough to rend ye Skys'. The Catholic Grano deplored the Hanoverian succession and made no demonstration of the loyalty customary in such situations, but soon 'being Advis'd there was a Plott 'gainst my Windows (for so I may call them since I paid for ye Same) onless I set up Candles accordingly I did'.

Only once did he venture into the buildings occupied by his poorer fellow sufferers, accompanying Mr Le Lart, his Jesuit adviser, and an apothecary who had come 'to administer som releif to a Poor Prisoner on the Common Side, where attending them I thought it would have kill'd me'.[12]

The bar or tap, run at this time by Mrs Acton, the deputy keeper's wife, herself reputedly the daughter of a Marshalsea prisoner who had perhaps caught the eye of Acton when he was chief turnkey, was plainly accessible to both sides of the gaol. Drink could be consumed there but the tap would also send out beer to prisoners' rooms in pewter tankards; Grano refused to use them because 'the Major Part of yᵉ Inhabitants of this Hell (if not all) do piss in these same Potts'. The Park was divided by walls into master's and common sides, although some sharing clearly went on from time to time. And the common side had a cook, renting a room for 4s a week and selling food to those who could buy. But the gaol's other amenities seem to have been in and of the master's side alone, if only because it required money (or the reasonable expectation of money) to take advantage of their wares. On the ground floor of the Nursery, with four rooms on two floors above occupied by a total of sixteen men, was a chandler's shop, run by a prisoner, George Cary, and his wife, rented at 6s a week. From this the prisoners would buy candles, coals and other domestic necessities. There was then a 'Coffee House' on the ground floor of the Oak, the building used for women prisoners. It was run by Sarah Bradshaw, a prisoner since 1721, who rented it for 2s 6d a week. Coffee could be sent out to prisoners' rooms or drunk at Bradshaw's, so it was large enough for a few tables and chairs at least. Coffee and bread and butter made up Grano's customary breakfast.[13]

Mrs Bradshaw also cooked meals, but the chief cook shop or chop house of the prison was on the first floor of the Oak, known variously by Grano as 'Titty-Doll's', after the celebrated gingerbread vendor of the day, or 'MacDonnell's', after its keeper, Robert McDonnell, a prisoner since 1726, who ran it with his wife. McDonnell cooked dinner – the main meal in the prison, eaten around 2 or 3 p.m. – and supper, sending out a boy or girl to the master's-side rooms to let prisoners know what was cooking and to take orders. Meals could be eaten there or in prisoners' own rooms. Drink at mealtimes could be had from the bar, Mrs Acton keeping spirits and wines under lock and key, or brought in from the numerous public houses around. Food too could be brought in from outside. Street vendors visited the gaol, selling door to door and in the Park, Grano buying 'half a dozen Whiting . . . and half a Dozen Places' from 'a Woman that call'd at our Door by Chance', for instance. Food brought in could be cooked and dressed at Bradshaw's or McDonnell's; the cooking of large quantities could be organised by one of the Borough inns. Alternatively, unlikely as it sounds, some prisoners employed prisoner-cooks of their own, men and women dependent on these in-house earnings for a livelihood, cooking dishes on the grate or stove in their own rooms or more likely their clients'.[14]

The relationships between prisoner and trader could prove problematic. This was the more so because, astonishing as it seems in a debtors' prison, both Bradshaw and McDonnell gave credit to oil the wheels of business. Grano, his fame, manners and air of politeness all inducing confidence, inevitably ran up debts all over the Marshalsea. The debts most troubling to him were with these two purveyors, because to a large extent his comfort and peace of mind depended on them and because his inability to pay first exposed and then undermined the genteel appearance he presented to the world. In July 1728, after a night spent drinking very heavily with Acton and others and unable to settle to work, he was playing 'Wist' in the lodge, where prisoners were kept for some time so that the turnkeys could study their faces and figures to prevent escapes. There he 'was interrupted by Mrs Bradshaw', probably asking him to settle his bill, 'which I have taken so very ill that I am resolv'd neither to lay out a Farthing my Self with Her and I shall do what I can to influence my Acquaintance not to do it'. Mrs Bradshaw now became 'Mother Ragdab' in the journal for some time to come. But the gaol's resources were so thinly spread, and his reliance on her for his breakfast comforts so complete, that within a month or so he was patronising her 'Hovel' again. Two months on, complications over money turned another screw in their relationship, for in the Marshalsea a shilling was equivalent to a guinea or more in the living world. At the end of November he was drinking two dishes of coffee at Bradshaw's only to find he

> was Dun'd heartily for 2 shillings altho I have Spent there above a Crown a Week for these 2 Months past and never fail'd in my payements according to promise and receiv'd for Answer a kind Offer of lending her a Crown to buy in Provision for the Court Day; but Ah! S^r pay me what you owe me already; which piece of Ingratitude shock'd me to that Degree that I never felt such an imotion of Contempt and Revenge since I have liv'd on Earth; for not only that Proffer I have assisted the old Cocotrice several times when she has not known which way to turn her Self[.]^15

From this point he took his coffee at McDonnell's, but by early February 1729 Mrs Ragdab and he had made things up, possibly because his relations with McDonnell were heading for a fall in their turn.

Besides these various shops and refreshment houses in the gaol there was one further public amenity which Grano frequently paid to use. This was 'the Parlour', a name with an old Marshalsea pedigree, for such a place was mentioned in the 1483 inventory. From the furniture recorded there, 'a pair of Trestillis', 'a Table, 'a fourme', 'ij Chayres' and so on, it seems to have served as a place to welcome visitors and host the occasional entertainments. By Grano's day the parlour had migrated to the newest buildings in the prison, either underneath the court building or on the first floor of the Oak adjoining, perhaps 'the drinking Room' indicated on the view of 1773. It could be used for an after-dinner conversation or hired out as a place to meet important visitors when a prisoner's cramped room would not serve. So, for instance, in August 1728 Grano had some unexpected company who came to his room, where 'we drank one another's health in Bumpers, drank two 3 shilling Bowls [of brandy punch], then proposing to give them a Tune on the Germain Flute we adjourn'd into the Parlor'; 'about 10 a clock Mr Acton came to us and push'd the Glass about briskly and what between one thing and another, I got very Drunkish . . .'[16]

The common side's reputation for starvation cast no dark shadow over John Grano's time in the Marshalsea. Certainly his appetite was unaffected. The journal meticulously records almost every meal he had there. He never stinted and never went hungry. The daily odours of cooking must have been a maddening goad to those in hunger just a score or so yards away, but that impaired Grano's belly not one jot. So, to pluck a few instances from hundreds, these from a single week in October 1728: 'some <Beaf> Stakes were sent for, and we got to Dinner about one a Clock. I ate very Heartily which was owing to abstaining from Eating in ye Morning'; 'sent to the Cooks for to know what they had, near ready: they brought us Word they had part of a Loyn of Pork which proving Acceptable we sent for the same which with the remains of ye Nuckle of Veal hash'd made us a very good Dinner'; 'we went to dinner on ye Cod was sent to Mr Pott [a fellow prisoner] which Mac-Donel drest for us'; 'met Mrs Smith going up to Mac-donel's where I was going my Self when we came there we Ate each of us a Mess of good Pease Soop', followed by 'a Leg of Pork' at dinner; 'we ate the Pigeons <for Dinner> were brought to Mr Pott ye Night before, (NB. nothing that ever was sent him we have hither to nor will accept of, but with allowing Him their Price; and the Reason I judge his Friends chuse rather to send him Victuals than Money, is that He Seems to have no government over him Self)'.[17]

Perhaps he was not the only one, for two weeks or so later Grano was sent by the steward of the Jacobite Lord Leeds 'a Leg of very fine Mutton and excellent Turnips; a handsome Young Pig, and a Couple of pretty Fowls'. Such a feast would have stretched the Marshalsea's resources, so Grano sent them out to be cooked and dressed at the Royal Oak inn, next to St George the Martyr. That afternoon he gave a dinner in the parlour for a number of friends who were visiting from outside the gaol: 'it was approv'd of by the whole Company not only for the quality of the provision but the Dressing also, which gave me a great deal of Pleasure, being I had sent it out for that purpose'.[18]

But if Grano always fed well, he fed best at the table of his gaoler, William Acton. Grano was a frequent visitor in Mr and Mrs Acton's rooms above the lodge, where he would be invited to sing songs of his own composing or play the flute or trumpet to amuse the Actons' friends. Acton, we might recall, had been a butcher in Southwark and roasts were a main feature of his family dinners: on a Thursday, 'an exceeding fine Leg of Mutton and Turnips as also a pretty piece of Roast veal'; on a Sunday, 'a Noble Buttock of Beef and Turnips and the fine quarter of Lamb and Sallad we bought the Night before' on Borough High Street; on another Sunday, 'a fine Chine of Pork and a glorious piece of Roast Beef', and 'after a handsome Apple Pudding'; on another Thursday, 'an Extraordinary fine boned Leg of Veal with Greens and a Roast Stufft Fillit', with 'a quart of y^e

Rack to be made into Punch which my Governor did himself and prov'd very good', and so on. Grano shared the Actons' Christmas dinner and was invited to some other family events, most notably the celebration of their five-year-old son's birthday on Friday 22 November 1728:

> we went to Dinner about 2. and had for the same a Charming Leg of Mutton and Turnips, a Glorious Chine of Pork, a rare Pudding and special Chiscakes with good Bread Butter & Cheese. after Dinner we Smoak'd a Pipe and a Very Handsome Bowl of Punch was set on the Table and when that was empty'd 'twas so large and discreetly Drank that 'twas time to go to Supper, as accordingly we did; and after Supper we had a Bowl of the same Magnitude. and was so extream Merry Singing and Telling of Stories that I never was happier in my Life . . .[19]

There can be little doubt that Grano was excellent company, with many stories to tell of his amours, of his quality acquaintances on stage and off, of his travels to The Hague, to Ireland and elsewhere. He was a fine musician and must have had a large repertoire of tunes at his finger-tips. He exuded politeness, adopted fine airs, dressed as well as he could, even keeping his sword in his room at the prison and carrying it with him when he went out. And he was frequently drunk, contributing to the general mirth of the company in that way too: 'there was wagers offer'd, I should and should not get Drunk', he was told when joining a dinner party held in the courtroom for 'several Masters of Prisons'.[20] But he was of value to Acton in other ways too: for instance, by telling his friends, some of whom were not only wealthy but powerful, of Acton's kindnesses to him. Most of all, Acton could farm Grano as he farmed the Marshalsea: for lucre. Everyone in the gaol needed money to survive and those on the master's side needed a significant income to stay there. Failure to pay rent would consign them to the common side, which Grano knew 'would have kill'd me'; and failure to pay Bradshaw or McDonnell would mean hunger or worse. So a debtor had somehow to put money in his purse. In the Marshalsea there were many ways of doing so.

It was a godsend to the poorest that what walls there were between common side and master's side proved porous. From the common side were recruited the ragged reserve army of labour that made the beds, swept the rooms and did the washing for their more comfortably placed neighbours across the Park. Take Hannah Shant, a prisoner since 1726, committed for a debt of just £4 19s, who was servant to Elder and Grano in their shared room. She was there every day and was paid as much in kind as in cash, sharing the food and drink the men consumed in the room. Hannah washed two shirts a week for Grano, for which he paid her, though we don't know how much; this too was money he owed and poor Hannah had to pawn what clothes she had to get money to live. When she asked Grano to buy her a pair of shoes he refused, the two men wrangling over which of them owed her what. Even so, despite the difficulties of the arrangement, Hannah was without doubt better off than many on the common side in the two bleak years of 1728 and 1729.[21]

Besides these domestic services, common-side prisoners were the gaol's internal messengers, taking orders back and forth to the cook shops, hanging around the lodge in case a prisoner was needed or a visitor had to be shown to a room – 'one of ye poor Slaves of this place came to let me know Mr Gardiner wanted to see me, I went and met him at the Lodge'. Former prisoners almost certainly swelled the ranks of messengers from outside the gaol who waited each morning for unlocking, ready to run errands to and from the living world; some prisoners were trusted to do the same,

like 'old Hand', 'the Ranger of this Park', an elderly prisoner
given free run of the gate. He was sent out on weighty
matters of trust, Grano giving him an order for vellum, for
instance, so that subscription sheets for a concert he was
planning might be handsomely presented. Hand brought
back 'a Skin of the Same and told me he paid three and
sixpence for it therefore return'd him his Money with
Thanks'. When in his own room, Grano had his coals carried
and his fire made up by 'Baily a fellow prisoner who waits
of me'; he used a girl to run errands for him – 'my Female
Mercury', he called her, probably a prisoner's or turnkey's
daughter, because she sped freely in and out of the gaol; and
'my Maid Molly', who was his Hannah and who occasionally bedded down in his room at night. Other prisoners
earned pennies by taking on peacekeeping duties on the
common side as constables for each ward, or as watchmen
throughout the prison and even, under Acton at least, turnkeys. All these positions were well placed for tips from
visitors and other prisoners.[22]

Indeed, money could be earned from other prisoners on
both sides of the gaol. All benefited from garnish money
charged of new prisoners that went to their room-mates. If
garnish on the common side was not forthcoming prisoners
could be stripped of their best clothes, which were then sold
or pawned, a procedure known as '*Letting the black Dog
walk*'; and on the master's side Grano dined 'on the Garnish
of yᵉ poor Countriman came in last Thursday' in his first
apartment, for instance. Many, men and women alike,
gambled with cards and dice for low stakes, hazard, piquet,
'Wist', 'Cribbidge' and backgammon apparently the most
popular. Others could exploit the skills they came in with.
So, on the master's side, 'Trim' the barber shaved and cut
hair in his own room, which he shared with a chum, or in
the rooms of his customers; Sam Street 'yᵉ Joyner' made
Grano a writing desk and helped fit out his room; Joshua

Poole, a gentleman prisoner with a copperplate hand, copied Grano's subscription 'Proposals' for a concert at Greenwich on to vellum and did the same for Lewis Grano at half a guinea per commission; John Horn, 'a fellow prisoner who is an upholsterer, (and will make my Bed and Hang my Room)', helped finish Grano's new abode; and Benjamin Brown, a prisoner-attorney, provided him with legal advice during the last months of his stay. The prisoners also freely bartered among themselves, 'a Pott of Drink' legal tender in the Marshalsea, for sealing wax, for instance, or to borrow a razor. Grano gave the upholsterer some spare timber left over from fitting out the room, probably for something in return, and helped others write letters and compose petitions, and translated 'some Letters are writ in French and Dutch', all for fellow prisoners.[23]

But overwhelmingly Grano's earnings came from outside the gaol. If his case is anything to go by, hundreds of pounds flowed each year into the Marshalsea – far more, one imagines, than ever flowed back to frustrated creditors. The Marshalsea was not only a microcosm of London life; it was a crucible of the metropolitan cash nexus, attended by all the uncertainties of the age. Grano's sources of income were many and varied but none was steady, few could be relied upon and most proved less profitable than he expected, so that despite his extraordinary efforts his 480 days in the Marshalsea were characterised by little more than a hand-to-mouth existence.

First was the money he had from his family, mainly his doting mother and his less susceptible father. Grano sometimes called this his 'Pension', 'a Gentlemanlike and Christian like Allowance ever since I have been here'. When it came it was in gold, half a guinea or a guinea at a time, but it was frustratingly irregular, Grano complaining at one point of not receiving a farthing in this way for some weeks. At Christmas 1728, in response to one of Grano's many begging letters addressed to home and elsewhere, his father sent him a guinea and a half with the explanation that 'Trade was very dull or he would have sent me more'. We should not underestimate the drain on the funds of this superficially prosperous family. that their delinquent son, now thirty-five or so years old, represented to them. Besides these gifts from his family, Grano also received 'Presents' in cash or kind from one benefactor or another, any contribution, however modest, of value to him.[24]

In general, though, Grano had to rely on work to get him through. A steady source of income for much of his time in the Marshalsea was from teaching. Early on, Grano obtained permission from Acton to use an empty garret above the courtroom as a 'School', and his celebrity as a performer – and now the likelihood that his fees would be cheapened by his Marshalsea stay – ensured that he had no shortage of pupils. He was sought after especially to teach the trumpet and he had a selection of pupils: a few were young soldiers who aspired to become regimental trumpeters, like two black youths, one of whom, John Anthony, Grano called his 'Tawny-Moor'; others learned probably more for pleasure, like the son of Thomas Yeates, the showman and theatrical booth impresario, who took the opportunity of proposing his son to Grano while showing 'Postures, Monsters &c.' at Southwark Fair; or a 'Young Fellow' who was a member of a Southwark Freemasons' lodge which held a musical club, and so on. Grano seems rarely to have been without a pupil and frequently had two, giving lessons most weeks. But agreeing his fees and getting his money were always prob-lems. He asked the Southwark youth, for instance, for a guinea entrance and a guinea a month, but debtors could not be choosers and he had to settle for half a guinea and two guineas for three months thereafter.[25]

A second source of earning for him was composing, to commissions mainly from his brother Lewis, who was an occasional concert soloist in London, Bath and elsewhere. John was extremely versatile, composing concertos for flute, hautboy (oboe), bassoon, trumpet, violin and harpsichord, as well as orchestral pieces. He worked at great speed, writing 'a grand Concerto for the Trumpet' in less than a week and a bassoon concerto in 'five Moods' or movements in around ten days.[26]

But most of his energies went into performing and for this he had to have William Acton's permission to move in and out of the living world. Ten years earlier, the author of *Hell in Epitome* had warned gentlemen prisoners in the Marshalsea that whatever urgent business they had outside the walls, 'the Favour of setting Foot over the Threshold of the Prison (tho' they would pay a Keeper to go with them) would be denied. They may walk where they please round the Prison, but not a Step farther.' If that was true in 1718, then all had changed under Acton. His high annual burden to John Darby meant that the farmer of the gaol had to take dangerous chances in search of profits. The risks of escape were real. It was easy enough to give a turnkey the slip in the crowded streets of London, especially if he'd been liberally plied with drink in advance. Once gone, and if not recaptured, then Acton became liable for the prisoner's debts plus costs, in Grano's case a tidy sum. On the other hand Grano was well known about town, his whereabouts could be readily tracked unless he fled abroad, and his spirit was not of the kind to tarnish honour and dent decorum by an undignified flight. Thus Acton must have reasoned when deciding that this particular milch-cow might be permitted to graze the fat pastures of the West End and City in search of charity or work. And of course Grano had to pay Acton or his minder handsomely for the privilege of bringing money into the deputy keeper's pockets. In this way Grano was able to pursue some small part of his previous musical career and maintain limited acquaintance at least among 'Persons of Quality'.[27]

It was Grano who first proposed the notion of a benefit concert, suggesting it within a month of his arrival in the gaol. Acton embraced the idea with enthusiasm. The more flush Grano was with money the more secure were Acton's fees and rents and the profits of the tap. Either Grano or Acton lit upon 'the Borrough Hall' as the best venue, this in Southwark town hall just a few steps to the north on St Margaret's Hill, as that part of Borough High Street was known. Acton had been bred to trade in Southwark and must have known everyone of worth and influence in this crowded commercial township. He engaged 'the Gentlemen of the Borough' in favour of the benefit, many of whom might also profit from the affair by printing advertisements and tickets, or supplying food, drink and candles on the night; some of these latter costs came to £3 6s and Grano also had to pay £2 for room hire, the Borough Hall in fact a great room in the King's Arms tavern that formed part of the town hall. Grano also had to pay some of his musicians, a couple of whom at least were Southwark men living in or near the Mint – not a reassuring sign; those who refused to play without money in their hands first he called 'those coin thirsty Villains'. Because Grano was short of ready money himself he had to give tickets away in lieu of the debts he incurred in getting the evening together and, in the nature of things, he proved unable to sell all the remaining tickets at his disposal. The concert came off on 5 September 1728. How much, if anything, he made from it is questionable, for just three weeks later he complained he would have starved without a friend's 'Present', having received not 'one Six pence for the Tickets my Friends have dispos'd of (as they were pleas'd to term it) for my Advantage'.[28]

In making all these arrangements Grano was permitted by Acton to roam about the Borough accompanied by Acton himself, a frequent event, or with one or other turnkey. He tipped the gaolers and paid for their drink, taverns the most frequent meeting places for his contacts. It was no doubt on one such occasion that he undertook to be godfather on behalf of a loose-living turnkey, Thom Nichols, a duty he shamefacedly performed probably at St George the Martyr, a few doors away from the Marshalsea: the child was a boy, christened John Baptist after his illustrious benefactor. But the godfather was disgusted at having to stand with 'the poor People'. 'About 7 a Clock Mr Acton sent for me and I can say this, that not withstanding I am in Prison I was more oblig'd to Mr Acton for sending me back than ever I was for his giving me leave to go out'.[29]

Making a friend among the turnkeys, even lowly Thom Nichols, was no doubt better than making an enemy, but despite its disappointing financial outcome the Southwark benefit did make other friends for John Grano. He was admired and sought out by many a local worthy from this point on. He was befriended by the son of Justice Maltys Ryall, a City coal merchant and Southwark magistrate, who gave him a chaldron of coals to see him through the winter. He was made at home by a number of tradesmen and in several of the Borough inns. He was a member or honorary member of the Freemasons' lodge meeting at Thurtle's coffee house near Bankside. Some of these connections offered him more opportunities to perform for money. There was another benefit, this time at the Crown tavern in November, and although Southwark's music lovers proved thin on the ground he was philosophical about the outcome: 'I am about 30 Shillings in Pocket by the whole: but however as the thing was kindly intended, I am and think myself as much oblig'd to the Gentlemen of the Borrough as if I had put 20£ in my Pocket'. And there would be a longer relationship with a 'Musical Club' meeting on Thursdays at Thurtle's, where Acton seems to have been a member of the lodge and accompanied him most weeks. The club was honoured by Grano's presence and he was told it would be recognised by 5s paid him each week 'under ye Rose', or secretly. It was all a comedown compared with his life before the Marshalsea, 'for I have had 2 3 4 &5 Pounds or Guineas a Night for as much as I have done for a Crown to oblige the Gentlemen of ye Musical Club at Thurtle's'. His crown also proved annoyingly hard to get.[30]

Grano's capacity to roam abroad was far from constrained by the borders of Southwark. He frequently took a boat for the north shore of the Thames and St James's, where he had been brought up: seeing his parents, having breakfast or dinner with them at Pall Mall, very occasionally worshipping with them on Sundays, seeing friends in coffee houses – all for the purpose of supplicating alms, calling in favours, pursuing benefactors. Of these last the most potentially fruitful was Alderman Humphrey Parsons, the great brewer of St Katharine's by the Tower. Parsons was one of the two Members of Parliament for the City of London, a Tory and a Jacobite committed to the Stuart line, a favourite of Louis XV of France and a sympathiser if not closet follower of the old religion adhered to by Grano. He was one of the richest commoners of his day, with one of the nation's best stables at his country house in Reigate.[31]

Grano's relationship with Parsons seems to have begun through serendipity and was not of long standing. In 1728 Parsons was the Master of the Grocers' Company, ranked second in the City's livery company hierarchy. Each year at the end of October, the company's barge was prominent in the regatta that accompanied the Lord Mayor elect from the City to be sworn in by the king at St James's Palace, Westminster. Each barge carried its water music, an orchestra frequently playing compositions newly written for the occasion. But this year Parsons and the Grocers were incommoded by the illness of their master musician. Someone recommended Grano to step into the breach, to select and order the programme of music and to direct the musicians on the barge. A Drury Lane musician of Grano's acquaintance brought him the news and Parsons paid Grano the notable compliment of coming by carriage from the City to Southwark – not to the Marshalsea but to the Three Tuns inn nearby. Acton, inevitably, conducted Grano to meet him and shared in the conversation and the refreshments. On 29 October Acton and Grano took a coach together to the Fleece at the Royal Exchange, where Parsons and the company assembled to join their barge: 'assoon as they stept into yᵉ Barge I struck up one of my newest Marches with Hautboys Bassoons French Horns, which was yᵉ tune we mostly perform'd yᵉ whole Neptunian Entertainment; I must own 'twas a Glorious Sight, a true emblem of yᵉ Riches of our Charming City and the Gallant Minds of the People'. Acton was waiting for Grano and the alderman when the company returned to the Fleece for a celebration supper that same night. Parsons took to Grano, 'Johnny' as he called him, though the alderman's looked-for intervention to liberate the musician from his travails seems never to have taken place.[32]

Amid all these efforts to bring money into the Marshalsea and so keep himself afloat on the master's side of the gaol, Grano had to labour against his own constitutional flaw of drunkenness. Frequent evenings of unrestrained excess, in the parlour of the Marshalsea, in Acton's apartment or in the Borough taverns would render him half paralysed by lassitude, occasionally disordering his head and his bowels for a couple of days at a time. But there were other difficulties in the way to which drink, perhaps, was an antidote. For the cramped living conditions of the gaol, the noise and unrest and absence of privacy, and, worst of all, the dog-eat-dog tensions between prisoners that were an inescapable fact of life there, at times became intolerable. His peace of mind and capacity for work were constantly shaken by his room-mates and neighbours. And the superior airs he no

doubt adopted rendered him from time to time an exasper-
ating provocation to his fellows. In these circumstances,
enemies were easily made in the Marshalsea.

Adam Elder, Grano's second chum, proved an enemy
eventually, falling out with Grano over responsibility for
shared expenses and other matters, frequently centring on
his treatment of Hannah Shant. Hannah shared Elder's bed
as well as making it, frequently while Grano was lying in it
too: 'I would faign know who in such a Place would bear
being three in a Bed or suffering his Chum to have . . . a
Wench at Bed and Board with Him'. Elder mistreated her
too, 'Beating and Pinching a Poor Wench who Bears it on
no other Account than that She is a Prisoner and has no
Support but which we give Her'. Rancour over how much
Grano should pay towards Hannah's keep and other house-
keeping expenses remained even after the room-sharing
ended, and we might remember the trouble over a pair of
shoes for her. In pursuing his dispute with Grano over money
owed, Elder would look for allies around him.[33]

In the room beneath the new lodging that Grano had
fitted up lay Captain Benjamin Tudman, a veteran of
Oudenarde but a man of more bluster than courage in the
Marshalsea. He had been a prisoner since 1725 and would
die there at the end of 1730. Around 3 one morning Grano
was woken by a row between Tudman and his chum, the
latter accusing the gallant captain of stealing Grano's coals
from his locked storeroom, having 'a Turnkey and Picklock'
to open the padlock on the door. The coals were indeed
depleted and Grano made no secret among other prisoners
of who had stolen them. Theft was a crime that the prisoners
took seriously, organising trials among themselves and
carrying out summary punishments (usually a drenching
under the pump) without involving the gaolers, and Tudman
challenged Grano with spreading false rumour. But Grano
stood his ground and said how he'd come by the knowledge:

'Mr Tudman spluter'd and spoke more like a Porter than ye fine Gentleman He pretends to be for he did nothing but Swear Curse and you Lye like a Rascall &c.'[34]

An alliance was now forged between Tudman and Elder with violent consequences. Grano took an interest in an attractive woman, Mrs Elizabeth Smith, and was frequently in her company. One morning Elizabeth was returning to his room from Mrs Bradshaw's when Hannah 'came behind Her pull'd Her down and beat Her most inhumanly saying she was a Bitch for reporting that she saw Mr Elder at ye Window'. Elder had reportedly been bedridden, too ill to endure the noise of Grano's trumpet practice next door, but Elizabeth had 'certingly' spied him at the window, or said she did. Mrs Smith was badly beaten and lay ill and feverish for days. Grano sought justice through Acton, who was reluctant to fall out with Elder and would not interfere, and spoke noisily of involving the local justices. It was around this time that Grano told Justice Ryall that 'I had ye Misfortune to be in a Place where there was hardly any one but Vilains'.[35]

That was in February 1729. In April, Elder now restored to health it seems, a sustained campaign began to make Grano's life a misery. Elder joined with Tudman and half a dozen others, including Joshua Poole, who had written subscription notices for Lewis but had never been paid. Late one night, Grano was disturbed by these and other men who had gathered in the room 'over my Head Singing and Dancing when they got into ye Park and broke my Windows'. The disturbance continued the next night and at intervals thereafter, leaving Grano unable to sleep, practise or find much peace for composing – he was working on a concerto for Lewis. Finally 'the Hell-Fir'd Crew' made such a row screaming and shouting that 'ye whole Park' was disturbed and with support from other prisoners Grano wrote letters of complaint to Elder and Acton. It merely provoked

impudence from Elder and his friends, whom Grano had
unwisely described in the letter as a 'Mob'; he was brazenly
warned, 'There was no Law in a Jayl'. Things stayed tense
for a time, but in May Acton managed to smooth things
out between Grano, Elder, Poole and others over a bottle or
two.[36]

These flare-ups were distressing, even frightening, perhaps
especially to a man like Grano, who was not 'Fram'd by
Nature or Education to Box'. Yet they did not displace the
overall impression one has from his journal that even more
dominant were the many consolations of life in the
Marshalsea to be derived from prisoner fellowship. Grano
was not a benevolent man but even he took occasional
pleasure in giving – perhaps, more properly, patronising –
sufficient to note it in his journal: 'gave a Pott of Drink to
old Drunken Sedgwick or Fudge', or 'drank two pints of
Wine I bought of a fellow Prisoner out of Charity'. There
was, too, the opportunity to have quiet conversation with
like-minded persons discovered in gaol: 'about eleven a Clock
I took a Turn in yᵉ Castle with Mʳ La Roche a very devout
Roman Catholick', rumoured to be a priest, who became a
support for Grano in his troubles.[37]

Sociability was indeed a large part of Marshalsea life, like
any contemporary coffee-house club or Freemasons' lodge.
It took place everywhere in the prison. In the coffee room
and chop house, of course, but also in the Park, in the lodge
as prisoners came and went, perhaps even on the communal
wooden seats of the earth closets which Grano is too polite
to mention but which remained a noisome feature of the
gaol for more than a century to come. And it took place
most of all in prisoners' rooms among chums and room-
mates and among friends and acquaintances invited in for
an evening pint of wine or bowl of brandy punch, or for
morning coffee or afternoon tea. Cards were a frequent aid
to conviviality, and so was fortune-telling from the tea leaves

and coffee grounds, especially in the ladies' rooms of the Oak – luck, good or ill, a large part of the debtor's world-view. Grano received gratifying news early in his confinement that 'I should have some Part or other in the Government <e're long>' and, more modestly, 'I certainly should receive Eight Sums of Money successfully but they would be small, thô enough to support me in this Place very well and that while I staid here, I should want for Nothing', a pretty safe bet on the fortune-teller's part.[38]

Most memorable perhaps were the spontaneous eruptions of sociability. On the master's side they seem to have been sparked off somewhere almost daily. They were no doubt especially likely on Saturday evenings and on Sundays, favourite visiting days in the Marshalsea and other gaols, but for Grano any day might be a holiday. One Wednesday in November 1728, for instance, a gregarious afternoon and evening were had by Mr Blount, his first chum, and a friend of Grano's from outside who brought with him two young women, one of whom Grano had known sometime before. He recognised her even though, 'say'd she I was so much leaner when you knew me first . . . which indeed was very true'. Dinner, a forequarter of lamb, was brought in from the Royal Oak: 'we was very innocently Merry'; 'we Sung round and now and then I perform'd on my Flute or Trump" – 'I can't say I have past many Evenings with more Mirth'.[39]

Similar superlatives, reminiscent of that happy evening at the young Acton's birthday party, had been elicited some six weeks earlier when 'Charly' Potts, the Southwark apothecary, had settled his debts and was released from the Marshalsea. It was an evening of extremes. After dinner Grano and Elder, then still his chum,

play'd a few Games at Cribbidge and about Candle light seating our selves by the Fire intending to smoak a Pipe and drink a little Malt Liquor Mr Fargueson paid us a Visit and Smoak a Pipe with us. (Mr Fargueson is a Live Guard Man and a Prisoner at the Suit of an Old Bawd also a Prisoner by Name Clayton) between 6 and 7 a Clock Charly came Home who had his discharge in his Pocket and beg to give us a Bowl at Parting; he inform'd us 'twas by his Mamma's Indulgence, who at a Word speaking gave him what he ask'd that he had been ill us'd by his Brothers &c a Six Shilling Bowl of Punch was Order'd and a Fire in the Parlor Mr Fargueson came down with us and Charly M^r E—r and my self sent our Services to Mr Acton and inform'd <Him> that Charly was a taking a leave of us and would be glad he would give him an opportunity of performing the same to him in answer to which Mr Acton was so kind as to send us Word he would come immediatly. just as we had drank two or three Glass<es> each, my dear Governor came, which rejoyced us all exceding: we had hardly drank above half the Bowl before Charly fell as drunk as David's Sow, and made such a Work to be gone that he did not let us rest till Mr Acton sent him about his Business; at his departure he exprest a great deal of Grief that he could not take us with him, but particularly me whom he kiss'd from the Parlor door to the Lodge and embrac'd me there an hundred times; gave a Tall Boy of Drink to the Servants &c. when I return'd to the Company we were exceeding happy in a Moral Manner entring upon devinity which was introduced by talking of the Church Musick I had Compos'd Mr Thorton was in Company who sung us an Hymn and who had not sung before these 20 Years at least; we whipp'd our Shillings a Piece more for another Bowl, which being four shillings we had a three shilling Bowl and half a Pint of Rasbury Brandy more Flung into it: – I can't say that I was ever better pleas'd with company nor Liquor since I have known what Company was not withstanding I have gone throw all ye Granduer possible.[40]

It is some testimony to the conviviality of the Marshalsea master's side that many prisoners revisited it after their discharge. Sometimes no doubt that was for charity's sake, regaling their friends with food and drink brought in from outside or bought in the prison. But the firm impression left from the journal is that on the master's side at least it was mainly for pleasure – for the sake of reminiscence and to hear news of former prisoners' fortunes, within the gaol or out. Surprising numbers of former prisoners turned up like bad groats in this way. A Mr Williams, a friend of Elder's 'and a fellow Prisoner in this Castle', had dinner with Elder and Grano one Thursday, then 'went in to the Park smaok'd a Pipe & drank a Mug of Drink play'd at half Penny hazzard most of ye after Noon'; a month later he returned for a similarly leisurely day. Next month Grano 'met with Mr Gardner a late Prisoner chatter'd a little with him', and the month after that 'Mr Wigstead, a late prisoner came to pay us a Visit'. For a few weeks after Charles Potts was discharged he seemed hardly able to keep away, missing its companionship so much. Once he brought with him a gaggle of friends: 'Phil Pott [his brother]; Mr Nicholls, a Lawyer; Mr Hogs Flesh, a Fat Personage; and <a> fourth was a Lean Watch-Maker; all as Drunk as Dutch Sailors, just landed from the Indies'.[41]

The liveliest time of year for the Marshalsea was September, before during and after the days of Southwark Fair. This was the great festival of the Borough and the Marshalsea was at the heart of it. Though the fair was nominally restricted to the three days of 7 to 9 September it was customarily extended, with much bustle involved in setting up and taking down. It was a tradition for the stallholders and showmen to collect money for the Marshalsea's common-side prisoners and give it in at the gate when they left the fair. It was a boon much anticipated in the prison. When it failed to happen in 1743, the Southwark justices 'crying down' the fair after just its lawful three days, to the great cost of the booth-keepers' profits and the Marshalsea alms, the prisoners 'got together a large Quantity of Stones and flung over the Prison-wall upon the *Bowling-Green* [an open space on lower ground behind the gaol, entered by steps from Mermaid Alley and used for shows during the fair], whereby a Child was kill'd in a Woman's Arms, and several People wounded and bruised'.[42]

Even during normal times the prisoners could not escape the racket and excitement of the fair. When Grano sent out a flute to the mender's it was returned to him during fair time: 'try'd ye German Flute but could pass no Judgment on the same, there being such a Noise with ye Fair which began last Saturday Sen'net that I could not possibly hear ye tone of ye Flute'. Something of the fair might also be seen from the prison. Acton permitted Grano and some other prisoners to climb to 'the Turrit', possibly one of the garrets of the courthouse, where they saw 'a fellow got up a Rope which was fasten'd at ye Head of a Pole about Six Yards high thrô ye Top of a Booth in ye Fair from whence he Slid down to the Bottom, which is call'd flying'. This was a French acrobat, one of a multinational troupe of rope dancers and tumblers at the 'Great Booth in Bird-Cage Alley' that year.[43]

Indeed, Acton seemed at his busiest during fair time, entertaining at his table friends and visitors who wished to see the prison. Once he invited Grano to dine and drink with them, Grano his celebrity prisoner of the moment: 'when we had supp'd ye Ladies went to see the Beggar's Opera', then playing at Fielding's Booth in the fair. John Gay's musical play was the theatrical sensation of the early eighteenth century, opening at the Lincoln's Inn Fields theatre on 29 January 1728 and soon performed by travelling companies up and down the land. It had been performed at the George Inn, Smithfield, during Bartholomew Fair by 'the Company of Comedians from the New [Little] Theatre in

the Hay-market' and was now at Tim Fielding's booth 'at
the lower End of Blue-Maid Alley, adjoining to the Bowling-
Green'. Everyone was speaking of it and Acton took Grano
to see it that same night. They spoke to Fielding, who told
them the show began at 10, so 'we took a Tour about yᵉ
Mint, where we pick'd up some Company took a Bottle
between six' and managed to catch the last act, and then
'about Half yᵉ Quaker's Opera' at Lee, Harper and Spiller's
Booth at the Queen's Arms tavern yard, next to the
Marshalsea Gate.⁴⁴

For the eponymous James Spiller, Southwark Fair was a
real coming home. He was one of the originals of Macheath
the Highwayman's crew in the Lincoln's Inn *Beggar's Opera*.
He played Mat o' the Mint, a thief and debtor who finally
snitches on Macheath and puts him in Newgate. This was
clever casting, for Spiller was well known as a feckless debt-
ridden actor in and out of prison for his extravagancies. He
did indeed know the Mint well, and the Marshalsea. A
pamphlet *Life* of Spiller, published in 1730, claimed that in
the Marshalsea 'his jocose Conversation so won upon the
Good Nature of the Person who was then *Deputy-keeper*
of the Goal, that he found a very sincere, generous and
serviceable Friend in him ever after . . .' This was not Acton
but a predecessor, said in 1730 to be a publican in Clare
Market, Holborn.⁴⁵

Spiller found difficulty in staying out of the Marshalsea,
even voluntarily. For in September 1728, just as the fair was
setting up and after a late afternoon unlocking at the end
of a court day, 'Mʳ Spiller the Player or Comedian came to
see me so I got out and came into the Parlor, where we
call'd for some Punch'. Spiller only knew Grano by reputation, but he knew Blount, who was invited to join them;
'soon after which, my Governor joyn'd us', Acton probably
knowing Spiller from his time as turnkey but in any event
loving a celebrity. A year or so later the genial Spiller was

dead, collapsing with an apoplexy or stroke on stage at Lincoln's Inn in January 1730 and dying a few days later. Among his friends was William Hogarth, who designed a famous benefit ticket for Spiller, showing him nabbed by bailiffs outside a spunging house.[46]

Among the former prisoners who kept up their acquaintance in gaol were women, and both women and men would sometimes be visiting old flames. Not just friendships but love affairs were sealed in the Marshalsea crucible. Sex played a large part in debtors' prison life and continued to do so throughout the Marshalsea's long history. London's lively trade in sex for sale could not be kept out by gates or spiked walls. We might remember Blount's damsels of the town coming to the room he shared with three other men, and the bed he shared with one; this was no isolated incident, Grano being summoned to view some women brought to the same room about one of whom he had heard a particular story. There was no shortage of supply, for the Park on summer evenings would be visited by numbers of 'yᵉ Nymphs'. Elder, Grano's second chum, had Hannah living with him who Grano thought 'as been Common on the Town these many Years &c.' Perhaps this was right, for Hannah claimed to know both the women who had delighted him on that evening of mirth with dinner from the Royal Oak, 'saying that one had been a Whore about the Town these 12 Years and the other a Bunter as long; what is meant by the last Phraze I do not understand' – it generally denoted the cheapest kind of young prostitute.[47]

But it was the potential for genteel sexual partnerships among the middling sort, physical and psychic compensation for the deprivations of prison, that played such a part in Marshalsea life. When Grano conducted two lady visitors to the chamber he shared with Elder, he explained that 'one of them would be deem'd my Wife or Cloe [mistress] for that yᵉ most Miserable wretch in this direful restriction had

one of ye two if not both to attend them'. Grano himself
had flirtations and friendships with women prisoners, the
details of which he leaves unsaid. He was smitten to something just short of delirium by Mrs Myngs, whom he christened Indiana: she, her sister (Emerentiana to Grano) and
their mother, a Southwark hat dyer, were all prisoners for a
time. Grano entered into this consuming infatuation within
weeks of arriving at the gaol, but the confined space and
crowded quarters rendered intimacy difficult and sexual
jealousy rife. One of the sisters' room-mates, 'One M^{rs}
Migean', 'was so highly incens'd at Indiana's Whispering
when she came in . . . that had we not all of us made our
escape out of the Room I do not know what might have
follow'd'. There were other scenes of envy and discord until
the sisters obtained their release; they revisited the gaol to
see their mother and friends, including Grano, for a while.[48]

Grano's admiration for Indiana seems not on this occasion
to have blossomed into sexual romance, but others quickly
established bonds that were openly acknowledged in the
prison. Charles Potts, the local apothecary, had his 'Cloe',
that same Mrs Elizabeth Smith later befriended by Grano.
One Tuesday Charles was out of the gaol with Acton, trying
to arrange his discharge. While out he was visited by his
brother Phil and a friend. Phil asked Grano to invite Charles's
Chloe to share a bowl of punch. They were all 'exceedingly
Merry' in Charles's room, which he shared with a chum,
when Mrs Potts came to visit her husband. When 'her Charles
came Home 'twas Matter of Surprise to Charles to find his
Wife and Cloe setting near each other and also a greater
uneasiness to Cloe thô to do her justice She sate with the
same infeasible Countenance as usual'. Mrs Potts perhaps
knew how things lay; certainly she partook of her husband's
easy manner. Grano noted she left the room frequently to
attend to something in his and Elder's room, 'I suppos'd
upon some Natural Occasion our Hannah might be assisting

to her', but when Grano went to check he found Phil 'making love to his Sister', Charles's wife.[49]

When Potts was discharged Grano and Mrs Smith struck up a friendship and probably became lovers: Acton certainly thought so, for he twitted Grano as a 'man that always Pleaded so much Chastity & would not have any Person to think he was in any need of a Bedfellow'. Grano stayed true to Elizabeth in one regard at least: when he decided to take advantage of a new act to release insolvent debtors from gaol in May 1729, he left his name and hers at the office of the *London Gazette* to have their intention advertised, as by law they must: 'Elizabeth Smith, late of Russel Court, Covent Garden, Widow and Fruitress' immediately follows 'John Baptist Grano, late of Bedfordbury, Covent Garden, Professor of Musick' in the list of hundreds of imprisoned London debtors seeking the same relief.[50]

By then, getting out of the Marshalsea had become an increasingly pressing matter for Grano. The vendetta conducted against him in the early part of 1729 shook his nerve. It added to his awareness of the dangers of the Marshalsea that had been apparent to some extent from the outset. For Grano knew that death was all around him. Woken by some crows squabbling in the Park a few weeks into his imprisonment, he wondered whether 'they was agreeing how to divide the Corps of those unhappy wretches that Dye so briefly in this Place'. A couple of weeks later he was roused by 'a great Cry after the Watch', because Captain Tudman's chum, 'the Major', had died in the night. Next month a man died in a room on the second staircase of Grano's building, and around New Year 1729 he discovered that Wills, the master turnkey, had suddenly died.[51]

Of course, London itself was dangerous. Ironically the nearest Grano came to death during his imprisonment was when he had been let out of the gaol – alone and drunk – one night in May 1729: 'as I was <going> under

Summerset-House-Wall was knockt down by some Street Robbers who after Rifling my Pockets and took what little Silver I had about me Struck me and Left me for Dead'. A good Samaritan put him in a coach and paid for his care at Evans's Bagnio, bathhouse and hotel combined, in Covent Garden. If all this put the Marshalsea's perils in perspective, he still would not have wished to end his days like the 'Dead Carcase [that] was Stop'd for his Living Fees, as they was carrying the same to be Buried', that he heard about a couple of months after his committal.[52]

Yet obtaining a discharge was not easy for him. He could get out of the Marshalsea certainly, but at a price. By a writ of habeas corpus he could remove himself to a prison with comforts and freedoms more in keeping with his status, such as the Fleet or King's Bench. Indeed, he was assured that the passage to either would be made easy for him, but he declined to change one gaol for another more expensive because of the support he was receiving from Acton and the gentlemen of the Borough. In the Marshalsea he saw many fellow prisoners reach an accommodation with their creditors after getting help from their friends, but no one was able or willing to burden themselves with the product of Grano's extravagancies. In fact, these burdens were added to during his imprisonment, for Acton told him in September 1728 that a charge for a further £50 had been delivered to the gaol on behalf of a 'Widdow', probably of his tailor, for he complained that 'I never had any more for all than two Suits of Cloaths'. There was worse. The debtors' gaol has been cast as an asylum from the nagging fear of the bailiff's tap and the dun's knock and to a large extent that was true: many prisoners in the Marshalsea throughout its existence were 'voluntarily' there – they could have discharged themselves through one means or another but did not do so for fear of future arrests. Even in Grano's time there were some who preferred to pay their room rent and the high prison living costs rather than leave, and as long as there was space in the gaol Acton had no reason to remove them, provided that they gave no trouble.[53]

But what if the debtor's creditor was arrested in turn and joined him in prison? Such was the case with the Life Guard man and his imprisoning bawd, we might recall, and so it was with Grano and Samuel Shepherd, a weaver's clerk of St Martin-in-the-Fields, who was brought into the Marshalsea six weeks or so after the great trumpeter. Shepherd had 'a Note of Mine of about 50 Shillings Remaining due to a Brother of his which I had promis'd to discharge at my Conveniency'. Now, Shepherd made plain, that elusive time had arrived. He plagued Grano, even at inconvenient moments, while pissing in the Park, for instance: 'in short I never was us'd so ill by any body in my Life'. And Grano was similarly affronted when, while in his room 'musing' on the neglect of his friends, 'I was interrupted by a Boy who brought me a Letter from his Father (Namely Addams) desiring me to send him a Crown towards a Small Debt I had ye misfortune to contract with him'. He wrote in answer that 'if I had run in Debt beyond my power to pay by any miss Management, I was punish'd severely enough for the same by forfeiting my Liberty'. The crown was not enclosed.[54]

Even more troublesome were the Marshalsea-bred duns, such as Mrs Bradshaw the coffee-house proprietor and McDonnell of the cook shop. McDonnell proved of stern stuff. Unable to squeeze money out of Grano, he took surprising measures. In March 1729, accompanied by Acton to the musical club at Thurtle's coffee house, Grano was approached in the street 'by a rascally Baily [who] told me he had a Writ against me' at the suit of McDonnell. Grano thought it must be a mistake, 'not apprehending 'twas practicable to Arrest any Body all ready a Prisoner &c.', and was at first terrified 'that Treason might have been Swore against me', presumably for his closet Catholicism. But Acton explained that this was 'call'd a Borough writ', answerable at the local court of requests, not in the Marshalsea court. That same night, when Grano returned 'Home' around midnight, he discovered that McDonnell and his wife with another prisoner had broken into his room to remove a table and chair they had loaned him and ripped out the grate and stove from the fireplace. The latter he recovered the next day. These were all undesirable complications of prison life. At first a resentful Grano decided to defend the action by challenging the amount and making a proposal to pay the residue in easy instalments. But Acton, unwilling 'at the present Juncto' to make an enemy of McDonnell, urged him to reach an agreement and pay the demand, which he reluctantly did.[55]

By this time – indeed, from January 1729 – rumours had reached the Marshalsea that Parliament was likely to consider one or more bills for the relief of imprisoned insolvent debtors. By February it became clear that two bills were pending, one in the Commons and one in the Lords. Between them they would release all debtors charged with debts of less than £500, provided that they agreed to hand over their total financial resources for the use of their creditors; debtors could keep clothes, bedding, tools and so on to the value of £10, independently assessed and sworn to on oath. Creditors could object to a prisoner's discharge but by doing so undertook to pay maintenance to the debtor of 4d a day or 2s 4d a week, or 3s 6d for a large debt, during the time the debtor remained in prison. Failure to pay would render the debtor 'supersedable' and able to obtain a discharge as long as the gaoler's fees were paid. All debtors detained only for their fees on the operative date were freed. And there was special relief for debtors owing less than £50 imprisoned in the Marshalsea and Surrey county gaols only. The acts, as they became, persisted for five years after the operative date, applying to all in gaol in the Marshalsea on 29 March 1729.[56]

Information reached Grano about the impending changes in contradictory ways. He heard that he would not be able to take advantage of the act going through the Commons because he had spent so much time outside the gaol during his imprisonment and he combed through his journal to total up the days and parts of days he had been allowed out. Another time he was told by a fellow prisoner that he was actually discharged some seven months earlier than in fact he was. He anxiously took advice from Mr Brown the debtor attorney about how to defend himself from other charges loading further his indebtedness. Declarations against him did come in: 'Mr Harvey one of the Attorneys of this Court told me very Courteously that he was oblig'd to Declare against me and hoped I would excuse the same to which I reply'd all was Fair in Love and Politicks.' In April he received a cautionary word of advice from Alderman Parsons, whom he was then seeing frequently, that the bill would pass the Commons the next day but that 'who ever conceal'd any Effects would certainly be Hang'd'. In May, after dining at his parents', he was in Green Park to see the king and his escort returning from Parliament after giving the royal assent to the acts for the relief of insolvent debtors, among other measures. On 22 May copies of 'ye Act' – presumably that of the Commons – were on sale in the Marshalsea and 'I bought ye same'.[57]

Having advertised his intention to take advantage of the act, he 'Busy'd my Self with Writing of Schedules &c.' for proceedings at the Surrey quarter sessions at Guildford in the middle of July. The poor debtors with debts under £50 were discharged by the justices without the expense of appearing in court, but those like Grano owing significant sums went down, he travelling by morning coach from the White Horse in Piccadilly: he caroused the night before with Elder and others over punch till midnight in the inn's famous Cellar. At Guildford, the evening before the justices began their work he had supper with Justice Ryall of Southwark and others, the company including 'Mr Darby the Keeper of the Marshalsea. we were very Merry.' Next morning at 4.30 he 'took a Turn about the Town', at the George Inn finding 'Mr Elder and one Lockwood of our College very drunk', and advised them to go to bed. It was a holiday time for all the debtors expecting their discharge from the Marshalsea and Grano was as light-hearted as any.[58]

But Grano's joy was premature. Perhaps because of objections, the court could not discharge him. The justices were sympathetic and he was assured that 'I should be releiv'd of ye Lord's Act'. The next night he was requested to play for the justices at their supper, but, though he had stayed in Guildford another night to oblige them, 'they did not present me with one Farthing'. He returned to the Marshalsea, although from then on he stayed many days and nights out of the prison alone. He received his discharge probably under the Lords Act, though the details are obscure, and he spent his last day there on 23 September 1729, more than two months after the trip to Guildford. He seems to have had no thought of moving back home across the river to the expensive streets of St James's. On the day of his discharge he walked Lambeth way to 'Cupid's Gardens' in search of a suitable lodging, 'but found none proper or to my Mind', so came back to the prison for dinner. Later that afternoon he took 'a Lodging at Mr Holmes's in Queen Street within a Place call'd the Park in ye Borough'. The irony of exchanging one Park for another went unremarked, but Queen Street was decent enough, 'a clean, and open Street, with good built Houses'. Grano retired to his room, just north of the Mint, 'about one in ye Morning'.[59]

Perhaps now obscurity suited him. After his sixteen months in the Marshalsea, the once-celebrated John Baptist Grano never recovered the position he had held in the musical life of London. We find him a year later performing his own music not in Hickford's Room, St James's, but 'S. George's Spaw in Southwark', cheap pleasure gardens for the middling and lower sort attached to the Dog and Duck in St George's Fields. Perhaps he played his musical setting of *London, An Ode*, whose author has not come down to us. One verse must surely have had a bitter ring for the composer:

> The distant Sun for *London* shines;
> For *London* teem the golden Mines;
> She thro the Land her Wealth bestows,
> Which to her Bosom daily flows:
> Nor does she rob the foreign Fields,
> But grateful sends what *Britain* yields.
> Hail happyest City on the Ball!
> Enriching, and enrich'd by, all![60]

There was in truth little enrichment for Grano. In 1732 he was playing in Bath and his name was advertised in musical miscellanies of various composers' works for domestic enjoyment. But after 1735 nothing more of him can be discovered in the newspapers. It is not known when this extraordinary man died or where he was buried.

London was, though, to hear a little more of William Acton, Grano's 'Governor', deputy keeper of the Marshalsea.

4

SKINNING THE FLINT: ACTON'S MARSHALSEA, 1728–30

ON the morning of Tuesday 25 March 1729 the committee of MPs enquiring into the state of the gaols of the kingdom – the Gaols Committee – entered the Marshalsea for the first time. They visited prisoners' wards and rooms and, John Grano recorded in his journal, in the courthouse 'Read Petitions and Heard the Complaints of all the Unfortunate in this Direful abode'.[1]

In the 'Common Side', 'inclosed with a strong Brick Wall', they found over 330 prisoners confined, around seventy of whom were women. They were 'divided into particular Rooms called Wards' where they were locked up each winter night at 8 p.m., an hour later in the summer. Most wards 'are excessively Crowded, Thirty, Forty, nay Fifty Persons having been locked up in some of them not Sixteen Foot Square': we will recall the affecting cries on locking up that disturbed Grano that first night of his imprisonment some ten months earlier, and these dreadful numbers tell us why. To accommodate them half the prisoners lay in hammocks suspended above those who had to lie on the bare floor. The 'Air is so wasted' that prisoners had been stifled, 'several having in the Heat of Summer perished for want of Air'.

Unlocking was at 8 a.m. in winter and 5 in summer and until then the prisoners 'cannot upon any Occasion come out, so that they are forced to ease Nature within the Rooms, the Stench of which is noisome beyond Expression'. 'This crowding of prisoners', the committee thought, 'is one great Occasion of the Goal Distemper', or gaol fever – louse-born typhus.[2]

Sickness was endemic and not just because of the distemper. Those prisoners who escaped or survived a fever might well succumb to an even more common complaint, for 'once they have sold everything they have, and if they have not Relief from their Friends, Famine destroys them'. The committee assessed the food coming into the common side for those with nothing else to eat as 'an accidental allowance of Pease given once a Week by a Gentleman, who conceals his Name, and about Thirty Pounds of Beef' provided as a gift of the judges and officers of the Marshalsea court distributed on Mondays, Wednesdays and Fridays. This was cut into portions of 'about an Ounce and an half' and served with a quarter of a penny loaf. The sick received this first, so they had something at least three times a week; the remaining portions could only reach the rest of the prisoners very infrequently, it was thought to each man once a fortnight and each woman weekly.

Once sickening from fever or starvation such that 'he is no longer able to stand, if he can raise 3 d. to pay the Fee of the common Nurse of the Prison, he obtains the Liberty of being carried into the Sick Ward, and lingers on for about a Month or two, by the assistance of the abovementioned Prison Portion of Provision, and then dies'. In the women's sick ward were seven 'miserable Objects lying without Beds on the Floor, perishing with extream Want'. In the men's sick ward they found eleven 'miserable Men', living skeletons as they must have been, in a terrible condition: three or four lay between the legs of trestles on the floor; three or four lay over them on boards resting on the trestles; and over them lay three or four more in hammocks. 'On the giving Food to these poor Wretches (tho' it was done with the utmost Caution, they being only allowed at first the smallest Quantities, and that of liquid Nourishment) one died.' 'Those who were not so far gone, on proper Nourishment given them recovered, so that not above Nine have died since the 25th of *March* last', so in about seven weeks. The committee understood that before this, 'a Day seldom passed without a Death, and upon the advancing of the Spring, not less than Eight or Ten usually died every 24 Hours'. The newspapers reported that the committee members were so moved by what they saw 'that they made a very bountiful Contribution, out of their own Pockets' to support the sick, ordering the attendance of an apothecary and nurses.[3]

How was it possible to make a profit from people as destitute as this? Or, 'how to skin a flint, or to get a shirt off a naked man, as the saying is'? That was the task that fell to William Acton, deputy keeper of the Marshalsea. And in fulfilling it, in the Gaols Committee's clear view, Acton had made the prisoners' plight immeasurably – murderously – worse.[4]

Little is known of '*William Acton* Butcher', as he is described in the Gaols Committee's report, before his sudden notoriety from May 1729. How long butchering had been his trade is unclear, but he had for four years been journeyman to a Hackney master-butcher called Haysey at some point before becoming chief turnkey at the Marshalsea. This he was in 1725, having taken over from one Burleigh; the extent of his previous connections with the prison are unknown. Then or later he also became the clerk of the gaol, responsible for its official records of those brought into the prison and discharged. From May 1727, as we know, he farmed the Marshalsea from John Darby, the deputy marshal. He undertook to pay Darby £140 each year for the lease of the gaol, in return for which Acton received the fees due by law to the gaoler once prisoners were discharged from his custody. He paid Darby a further £260 a year for the right to rent out rooms on the master's side, including the rent of the tap, run by his wife; it seems likely that her late father had been the former tapster, possibly having himself been a prisoner. Acton married Mary Wilson at St Martin-in-the-Fields, Westminster, Mary's home parish, in July 1723; their son Henry was born in November 1724 and baptised at that prestigious church a month later. Acton's age is unknown, though he must have been a youngish man in the full vigour of life. He was literate and sharp-witted, educated or self-taught to an attainment above his journeyman status. He was brought up to a trade needing great strength and nerve in which he was inured to cruelty – butchers then their own slaughtermen. And his talents, supplemented perhaps by a fortunate marriage or family resources, had endowed him with financial means far in excess of anything that could be amassed from a journeyman's customary 15s 6d a week. Acton was, in many respects, a formidable man.[5]

We have seen Acton the genial host to visitors and to select prisoners such as Grano; we have seen his fondness for the acquaintance of grand personages and popular figures; we have seen Acton the family man at home with his wife and boy, maintaining close relations with his wife's mother, keeping family occasions like birthdays and Christmas with fond extravagance. He was a churchgoer, occasionally at least, and kept his Bible on public display in his living quarters. But he also revealed even to Grano a sullenness and an unpredictability of temper that made this favourite prisoner wary of crossing him. Between bouts of accommodation and generosity there were inexplicable changes of mood. Asking permission to step out to the Crown tavern one night in December 1728, a favour generally granted with ease, Grano 'found Him very cool and quite different from his

usual way of Treating me' and 'reply'd very cooly Wills shall
go with you by and by'. A similar occasion recurred after
Christmas, so vexing that Grano vowed privately 'at
revenging the affrontive denyal', but only when 'I was out
of the Lyon's Mouth'; on reflexion he then resolved to make
his peace 'with the Person who exerted so much Tyrany'. A
few days later in the lodge, 'as Mr Acton came down I was
a going to Salute him but he Took no Notice of me'; even
more galling, he received similar treatment from Mrs Acton,
the former prisoner's daughter as he took her to be. And on
the night of the queen's birthday, when Grano had been
slow to put candles in his windows, 'I was very credibly
inform'd Mr Acton was pleas'd to say that He would not
have his Bed Cloaths Spoyl'd for any Son of a Bitch of them
All which in my humble Opinion was not only calling me
a Son of a Bitch but all ye Company I have the Honour to
be admitted in . . .'[6]

Getting money out of his sons of bitches was Acton's
preoccupation. If he failed to get Darby his £400 a year, if
he defaulted on the prison's poor rates of £4 11s a year or
on his brewer's bill, then he risked arrest and imprisonment
in his own gaol. Fees on discharge had been set in 1675 and
totalled a minimum of 6s 2d for each prisoner, with the
possibility of a further 5s if the discharge involved a second
action or more, as many did. But as we have seen, some
prisoners free of their debts remained imprisoned for their
fees; and if they lay on the common side there was no profit
for Acton. How profitable the fees were for Acton is unclear,
though in a good year with large numbers imprisoned they
were likely to be highly so – Acton would have scrutinised
the prison's balance sheets before committing to his investment. Certainly the rents were potentially very profitable
indeed, the rent roll in 1729 totalling £596 14s, of which
£555 2s was from the eighty prisoners then lying on the
master's side, including the few commercial lettings. After

paying Darby his £260 for farming the rents, Acton netted some £309, less the rates and running repairs, or 'Bed Cloaths Spoyl'd' and no doubt much of the same.[7]

Here again, though, a rent roll was one thing, rent pocketed was something else. Acton's Saturday nights were largely spent presiding over the prison's metaphorical genuflexion to the 'Black Book'. This was a Marshalsea tradition pre-dating Acton – it is mentioned in *Hell in Epitome* (1718), as 'a Book as black as that will be/ At Judgment Day':

> Unless the Respites and Reprieves they pay,
> They're forc'd to Dungeons, ne'er to see the Day.[8]

One Saturday in November 1728 Acton had escorted Grano to St James's and returned by coach over London Bridge. When they reached the Marshalsea ''twas just about Black Book Time': 'while we were in the Lodge my Governor call'd for my half Crown for my Black Book which I gave him and said he might expect another by Hanah from me not doubting that my Chum would have paid it'. But Hannah came back empty-handed and Grano paid Elder's half-crown too so 'that Mr Acton should not be baulk'd'.[9]

The Black Book probably did more than account for rent owed. Acton occasionally loaned Grano a crown and that was presumably noted against his name. So no doubt were other little extras that were attached to favours given and not yet made good, like being escorted past the gate on debtors' business, in part for the gaoler's gain. But it was rent that weighed heaviest in the Black Book, and not just for Acton. The terrors of the alternative, the dread common side or sick wards, were unbearable to contemplate and gave every incentive for master's-side debtors to meet their obligations. The Gaols Committee reported on two sick prisoners on the master's side, laying their sad plight at Acton's door. The reality was probably more complex. Mary Trapp shared a bed with two other women, each paying her half-crown, when she took ill with some putrid or ulcerative condition. For the last three weeks of her life she grew 'so Offensive that the others were hardly able to bear the Room' and even the turnkeys couldn't stand to enter it. Her bedfellows pressed repeatedly for Mrs Trapp to be removed, but she still paid her rent and Acton had every reason still to collect it. And among the men lay a prisoner with a fistula leaking bowel contents, also sharing a bed with two others, all having to pay their 2s 6d to Acton; but again, and despite his chums' protests, what man would change his bed for the horrors of the common-side sick ward?[10]

The most terrible accusation against Acton, however, was that he withheld money due to common-side prisoners from charitable endowments and other sources that might have kept them alive: that he deliberately pocketed the money and left men and women to starve to death. No crime could be more heinous. And a crime here made more heinous still by being carried out among all the gluttonous excesses of Acton's groaning table a hundred or so feet away from the common side.

The charities intended for the Marshalsea's poor prisoners were legion, even in 1727 – more would be added in the years that followed. Nearly all bequests were small, many half-forgotten, most difficult to collect. Sir John Peche's Gift of 1533 promised 5s annually; John Marsh's Gift of 1557 and Roper's Gift of 1628 each gave 20s; Peter Symonds's Charities of 1586 sent forty-eight penny white loaves; Garratt's Gift of 1582 sent 6s 8d; Craythorne's Gift of 1586 sent 15s; Margaret Simcott's Charity of 1633 sent 390 penny loaves; and so on. There were perhaps a score and more of these old legacies donating money or victuals to the common side, on parchment at least. There was only one cash endowment of any value, easy to look out for: the Mercers Company sent £10 each year to the prison as part of Sir Thomas

Gresham's famous will of 1575. In addition to all these, every county in England was required to send £1 each year by the Poor Law of Elizabeth I, the so-called 'county money' or 'exhibition money'.[11]

Before Acton's time the charities received in the Marshalsea were managed by the 'steward' chosen by the common side, either from inside or outside the gaol, perhaps from among respected former prisoners. The steward held the 'Common Seal', and he and the six ward constables would sign and seal in wax a receipt for the monies or victuals coming into their wards; these receipts would then be passed to the executors who had forwarded annual donations to the gaol. In 1722, one Matthew Pugh was chosen steward and proved particularly active, discovering 'several Charities which had been before concealed', which shows either that Acton's defalcations were nothing new or that some legacies had been maladministered by the various executors of the old gifts. Pugh alleged the former, specifically that John Darby 'and his Servants in the Lodge' had copied the common seal and were using it to give donors false receipts for gifts that had never been passed to the wards. Whether those servants included Acton is unclear, but the timing is such that they might have done. Accordingly Pugh and the poor-side prisoners commissioned a new common seal stamped 'MARSHALSEA PRISON 1725'. It was kept in a 'Chest' fixed to the wall and locked with seven keys, one each for the six constables and the steward.

Soon after, John Darby moved against Pugh, who, he claimed, had 'behaved himself very turbulently' in both gaol and courtroom, and in July 1725 the Marshalsea judges banished him from both prison and court, requiring the common side to choose a different steward. According to the Gaols Committee, the new steward was chosen 'by those in the Keeper's Interest' and was Darby's own clerk, John Grace. The affronted ward constables refused to relinquish their keys, so Grace and Acton as chief turnkey together broke the chest from its fixings and carried it off with the common seal inside. Around this time, mid-1725, an act for the relief of insolvent debtors freed many of those common-side prisoners acquainted with all this murky history. After that the charity money was distributed only in an irregular fashion by Grace or an official of the court. But once Acton leased the gaol in March 1727 he dispensed with any steward other than himself:

> upon his Examination, he confessed, that from *May* 1728, to *May* 1729, he had received Charity Money for the poor Prisoners, amounting to above 115 *l*. of which he had kept no Account, and took no Notice thereof till this Committee was appointed to Enquire into the State of the Goals, not expecting to have been asked about it. He pretended he had distributed the Money among the prisoners directly, but produced no sort of Vouchers for it.[12]

We have independent verification of the point. On 22 March 1729, while Grano was walking in the Park, 'there was some Charity Money Paid, which the generality of yᵉ People say had been given them a great while a goe and would not have come to light but for fear of yᵉ approaching inspection of yᵉ Committy'.

Acton's control over the charity money did not stop with the legacies and exhibition money. The traditional begging baskets (for broken victuals) and boxes (for loose change) that prisoners were licensed to take out from time to time were also misappropriated by Acton, who let the victuals in but kept the money for his own purposes. It was also said that charities directed to the release of poor prisoners had been used to 'free' voluntary prisoners who acted as his servants, even turnkeys; after a time away they returned to the gaol once Acton had pouched the imaginary prison fees, paid by the charities. The Gaols Committee's conclusion that the charity money properly distributed 'would have prevented the Starving to death many miserable Wretches' seems unimpeachable.[13]

So it must have appeared to the common side too. In their desperation and fury they tried to wreak vengeance on their tormentor. Just two instances have come down to us, both from John Grano's journal. In November 1728, Grano had been at the west end of the town with Wills, returning at night. Arriving 'in the Lodge we heard that the people of the Common Side were rose against my Governor'. It seems to have been an ambush:

> 'twas a very villainous thing in the Main; being Mr Acton went only to do a piece of Justice calling in ye Ward to procure a Man his Coat again which his fellow prisoners had taken from him; instead of giving an account of the same one Anderson of ye Ward cry'd out one & all and immediately they fell upon him but thrô God's Mercy and his own behaviour he came off with the Loss of a little Blood and a torn Shirt . . .[14]

A few days later Grano heard of what seems to have been an earlier incident. At the Crown tavern in the Borough, he was sitting down to pea soup and a steak when Acton arrived unexpectedly and shared some food with him. What happened next is unclear but it seems that Acton was served a summons from 'a fellow that was a Prisoner Here some time agoe who had the audaciousness and inhumanity to endeavour to Stab my Governor in the Dark only because he was a going to send him to his Ward being very Riotous'; he was now acting 'under pretence of his [Acton's] Assaulting Him which gave him some uneasiness notwithstanding the Rascall's Vouchers are a couple of common Women and that M[r] Acton can bring several People of Reputation to Testifye what has been observ'd'. This was a facility that soon proved useful to Acton.[15]

Resistance took other forms. Some prisoners suffering 'Hunger and extreme Want' became 'so desperate, that after having fasted four Days, and seeing no Hope of Relief, they attempted to break thro' the Prison Wall, and were taken in the Attempt'. Had an escape been successful, of course, then Acton's profits would have been dented, possibly significantly, and his standing with Darby would have been shattered. To punish the miscreants and to deter emulation, Acton resorted to those medieval instruments of torture that had survived somewhere in the Marshalsea since 1483 and almost certainly before. He was said to have used thumbscrews and laden men with heavy leg irons 'called sheers'; employed an 'Iron Engine, or Instrument (which appears to be an Iron Scull-Cap)', and an 'Iron Instrument, called a *Collar*, (like a pair of Tongs)', that fixed to one victim's neck and screwed tight made his eyes 'ready to start out of his Head, the Blood gushed out of his Ears and Nose, he foamed at the Mouth, the Slaber run down, and he made several Motions to speak, but could not'. There was also hung up in the lodge 'an *Instrument* . . . for beating the prisoners', the very name of which 'became a Terrour to them'. This was a bull's pizzle, dried hard as teak, some three or four feet long with a swollen end like a knobkerrie, a favoured weapon of butchers who were slaughtermen.[16]

After being tortured, some refractory prisoners were kept in irons and confined in the 'Strong Room', a place with no windows, the 'Common Shore' or sewer running beneath its floorboards or nearby; sometimes with 'Humane Carcasses' awaiting burial. One prisoner, it was said, was locked up with 'two dead Bodies which had lain there Four Days'; he stayed with them 'Six Days longer, in which time the Vermin devoured the Flesh from the Faces, eat the Eyes out of the Heads of the Carcasses, which were bloated, putrifyed, and turned green . . .'[17]

John Grano witnessed none of this, as we know, but we do have an anonymous common-side voice that can testify to some of the conditions there. It comes from a pamphlet published in the glare of the Gaols Committee's reports, but it nevertheless has the piercing ring of truth. It contains a narrative of a King's Bench prisoner sent to the Marshalsea as punishment for assisting in the escape of two of his fellows, a charge he denied. He found himself in Duke's Ward, a room he thought fourteen by eleven feet in which twenty-eight men had to bed down. He had 4s 6d garnish demanded from him by the ward constable 'and the Elders, as they call them'; unable to pay at that moment, he had to hand over some clothes which were pawned – he redeemed them later when his friends sent money. He found the stench from the ward's 'open Tub' intolerable, and noted that the wards 'abound with Lice, Bugs, and other Vermin', so that he was almost 'destroyed with Vermin' before allowed back in the King's Bench:

> the Poverty of the People is so great, that nothing upon Earth can be more miserable; great Numbers of them in Rags, and almost naked, starving for want of Bread. I had a very small Matter with which to maintain my self in this miserable unhappy Place; yet when I was eating my Morsel, so many eager Eyes were always fixed upon me, such a Number of fellow Prisoners constantly hovering about me, like so many Shadows, pale, and faint, without any the least Subsistence, and in all Appearance, perishing for want of Relief, and daily seeing the dead Bodies of others, who were famished, carried out, I could not withhold from parting with some of that which was given me, till I was almost brought to the like Condition my self.[18]

A central allegation of the Gaols Committee was that this whole edifice of appropriation, starvation, repression, torture and even murder rested on an illegality. When Sir Philip Meadows had appointed for life John Darby as deputy marshal and keeper of the Marshalsea in November 1720, the deed stipulated that no part of his office should be 'let to Farm' without Meadows's 'Consent in Writing'. Here, apparently, no consent had been sought, and was plainly not given. But this was a mere technicality. Meadows knew Darby was a prosperous and busy City printer who would never soil his fingers or risk his reputation by daily managing perhaps the most notorious debtors' gaol in the kingdom, a byword for misery up and down the land. The Marshalsea had been farmed to deputy keepers in the past and there is no reason to suppose that Meadows would have withheld consent, although perhaps he preferred not to 'know' of the arrangement to distance himself from any ensuing scandal. Had the unlawful farming of the Marshalsea been the Gaols Committee's main criticism, it would have been laughed from the floor of the House of Commons, many of its members no doubt receiving income from similar arrangements. But it was the morbid injustice that prisoners suffered at the hands of their gaoler that unquestionably moved and vexed the committee's chairman, James Oglethorpe.

It had been a single act of injustice at another debtors' prison, the Fleet, that set Oglethorpe on what would become an obsession for him. As a young man Oglethorpe had served as an officer in the armies of both the Duke of Marlborough and Prince Eugene before he was returned as MP for Haslemere in 1722. He soon became acquainted with the London debtor's world, because in 1723 he had been a member of the committee enquiring into the Mint and the year after that he was one of the committee on the Insolvent Debtors Bill. But it was the fate of a debtor friend that moved this energetic and upright soldier-parliamentarian decisively to action. Robert Castell, a promising architect, was committed to the Fleet for debt during the rapacious regime of keeper Thomas Bambridge. Eventually he was utterly without resources, and we can only think that Oglethorpe found out about his plight when it was all too late to help. Unable to pay the gaoler's fee to get a better berth, he was forced into quarters where 'the Small-Pox then raged'. He had never had the disease and was in great fear of it. Despite his protests, and in an already weakened condition, Castell contracted smallpox and died in November 1728.[19]

Oglethorpe was a Tory and of Jacobite stock. He was, therefore, a political enemy of the ruling administration and its leader, Sir Robert Walpole. The very establishment of the Gaols Committee – for that reason alone – was of concern to the Whig camp. Even so, his allegations against Bambridge and the Fleet were so serious that the Commons found an inquiry irresistible.

The Gaols Committee's membership exemplifies the nuanced and contingent nature of politics in these years. Politics may have been tribal on the surface but underneath they were cross-cut by friendships and family allegiances and obligations of one kind or another. Of course, the committee could be no blunt instrument of anti-government propaganda, if only because the Whig majority in Parliament had a large say in its membership. On the other hand, the committee's Whigs couldn't necessarily be relied on to support the government line. And the danger here was that the committee would trace abuses in the prison wards far higher than Bambridge and his ilk: for questions of place, who was in which office and why, and by what mechanisms they managed their public duties, led directly to the administration of Sir Robert Walpole, and to the ways in which power and purchase were so closely inter-woven.

Some of these complexities emerge when we consider just who was elected to the Gaols Committee. Among its ninety-odd members were the Chancellor of the Exchequer and

Arthur Onslow, the Speaker of the House of Commons, both figures close to government. Others had allegiances less easily fixed. Lord John Perceval, for instance, was a Whig and loyal supporter of Walpole, but he was one of Oglethorpe's closest friends. Sir Edward Knatchbull was nominally a moderate Tory, but he was no Jacobite and was slowly turning Walpole's way. On the other hand, Captain (later Admiral) Vernon, though elected as a Whig, was moving noisily towards the opposition. There were numerous others of interest. Two Whig members, Sir Archibald Grant and Sir Robert Sutton, would later be expelled from the House of Commons for involvement in speculations and frauds on charities – ironically, given the findings in respect of the Marshalsea: in the *History of Parliament* they are two of just twelve members in this period labelled 'rogues'. Sir James Thornhill is best remembered as the greatest history painter of his day and the reluctant father-in-law of William Hogarth, but he was also a Dorset MP and a loyal supporter of government. Alderman Francis Child and Thomas Martin were two hugely rich City bankers, the first a Tory and the second a Whig. And another alderman, Humphrey Parsons, whom we have already met, was an outspoken Jacobite, one of the most notable City opponents of Walpole and all his works; or so it seemed on the surface. We get rather a different perspective from his work on the Gaols Committee. Parsons had been among the committee members surveying the Marshalsea on that first visit of 25 March 1729, for he gratifyingly called on Grano to make his presence known; two other members visited him too, possibly James Oglethorpe himself, for they certainly recognised each other at an accidental meeting some weeks later.[20]

The committee reported on the Fleet on 20 March 1729. Their report contained two resolutions charging the warden of the Fleet, Thomas Bambridge, and a former warden with 'Extortions, cruelties, and other high Crimes and

Misdemeanours'; the House of Commons resolved to ask the king to prosecute both men.[21] When Oglethorpe's committee visited the Marshalsea nine days later they found horrors far worse, and gathered testimony more sinister, than anything they had found in Bambridge's gaol. Acton must have feared the worst from the outset. Unsurprisingly, he sought what help he could. On 11 April Grano called on Alderman Humphrey Parsons in the City, perhaps in pursuit of his own affairs but conceivably at Acton's request, for the conversation turned to Grano's 'Governor'. Parsons

> ask'd me how M[r] Acton did to which I reply'd that his Heart was almost broke for want of His Honour's Presence and that till now the Hon[ble] Committee had done nothing but hearing y[e] Complaints and Accusations of y[e] Prisoners and had not given Him leave to make any Defence not that He question'd their Equitable dispositions and Intentions – the Alderman was so kind in Answer to this, to give me leave to assure M[r] Acton he would attend y[e] rest of the Committee y[e] next time they came and do Him all the Service Justice will admitt of and desir'd me to advise Him to get a few responsable Men and of good Character to appear in his behalf, and some who have been an Eye Witness to his behaviour toward y[e] Prisoners &c.[22]

The Jacobite alderman's assistance to the committee's main target, potentially undermining Oglethorpe's intentions as it did, was a surprising intervention but to no avail, at this stage at least. A month later, on 14 May 1729, the committee's report on the Marshalsea was presented to the House of Commons by James Oglethorpe. The committee resolved that William Acton, 'Clerk of the Prison of the *Marshalsea*, and Farmer of the same Goal . . . hath been guilty of many High Crimes and Misdemeanours'. In particular, it alleged he 'arbitrarily and unlawfully loaded with irons, Tortured and Destroyed, in the most Inhumane, Cruel, and Barbarous Manner, Prisoners for Debt under his Care, in high Violation and Contempt of the Laws of this Kingdom'. John Darby was arraigned for unlawfully farming the gaol to Acton and for neglect of duty. Both men were implicated in the misappropriation of charity monies intended for the prisoners. Oglethorpe moved 'That an humble Address be presented to his Majesty, that he will be graciously pleased to direct his Attorney-general forthwith to prosecute, in the most effectual Manner, the said *William Acton* and *John Darby*, for their said Crimes and Misdemeanours.' The House resolved accordingly.[23]

The published reports on the Fleet and Marshalsea caused a great stir. Hogarth famously painted the examination of Thomas Bambridge, hunted and at bay in the Fleet, where the painter's own father had been prisoner for a time, and a pamphleteering war broke out involving Bambridge himself, his detractors and his supporters. The pamphlets that followed the Marshalsea report, however, tended all one way. Acton seems to have found no defenders in print. The lurid tales of torture by ancient 'engines' fascinated many. Within a month of the report a broadsheet was published illustrating the irons, collar and skullcap, and showing the sick ward. Further illustrations in crude woodcut appeared around the same time in a pamphlet popularising the committee's findings on the Fleet and Marshalsea.[24]

It was a difficult time for the deputy keeper of the Marshalsea. Matters came to a head on 9 June, when the Duke of Newcastle, Secretary of State, received from Queen Caroline her command to the Attorney General 'for the prosecution of William Acton, Clerk of the Prison of the Marshalsea and John Darby Keeper of the said Prison', the proceedings to be conducted at 'His Maj^ty's Expence'. Acton was arrested that day. Darby, that prominent Whig printer so loyal to the crown, seems not to have been proceeded against: if he was, then he never stood his trial. That Monday 9 June, Grano recorded that 'soon after Dinner I was Surpris'd and very much afflicted with the News of My Governor Mr Acton's being taken into Custody and carried to the new Goal assoon as which I dress'd and went to Him . . .' The new gaol was the rebuilt or renovated White Lyon, next to St George the Martyr's churchyard, so Acton did not have far to walk. Grano found him 'in ye Kitching' with several visitors, some Borough tradesmen among them. He made a point of visiting 'the distress'd Mr Acton' frequently in the next few days and it is clear that Acton was still carrying out his clerkly duties for the Marshalsea, signing and administering prisoners' paperwork. Lively on Acton's behalf, on 19 June Grano went to the Swan tavern near the Royal Exchange to perform for Alderman Parsons, who was giving an entertainment for the City's Grand Jury: 'the Conversation was extream good, and I mention'd my poor Governor in his Affliction, with as much Art as I was Master of and found I mov'd the Company to Compassionate His Misfortunes and to beleive He was very much wrong'd and they all hop'd he would surmount his Difficulties with Honour.' This was not Grano's only acquaintance during the summer with members of the Gaols Committee. He saw Parsons a few times more, even staying overnight at his country house in Reigate. And he 'Met Mr Oglethorpe and M^r [Rogers] Holland [Whig barrister and MP for Chippenham] in a Chariot behind Holdbourn: they Stop'd and Spoke to me and ask'd me several Questions in relation to our Castle ye Which I answer'd as a well as I could'. He presumably kept his feelings about his Governor to himself.[25]

After investigations lasting some weeks, the Attorney General brought charges against William Acton on four separate counts of murder. Every victim had been a debtor prisoner in his care: they were Thomas Bliss, John Bromfield,

Robert Newton and James Thompson. Acton was set to stand trial at the Kingston Assizes on 31 July. Grano called on him a few days before. Acton 'made me promise to meet Him at Kingston next Thursday &c.' and Grano went down by coach, arriving at the Lyon and Lamb in Kingston around 11 in the morning. That afternoon Grano heard Acton charged with murder. Acton pleaded not guilty to all the charges and was told the first trial would begin next morning, Friday 1 August 1729. The evening before, in Kingston's marketplace, Grano found 'a great many of my Acquaintances' from the Borough, including Justice Maltys Ryall and other Southwark worthies.[26]

The trial of William Acton for the murder of Thomas Bliss was heard before Mr Baron (Justice) Carter. It took up the whole of 1 August, a long time in the eighteenth-century court of justice. The case of Bliss, a carpenter by trade, had been recounted as especially vicious in the report of the Gaols Committee. Starved, as were so many on the common side, he had attempted to escape but was taken, beaten, put in irons, tortured and kept in 'the Strong Room', 'a dangerous, damp, noisome, filthy and unwholesome Place'. Weak and near death's door, Bliss had been released by Acton but never recovered, dying in St Thomas's Hospital, half a mile or so from the Marshalsea, where he had suffered so much. Such was the charge. These events took place in 1726, so three years before.[27]

The trial began at 9 a.m. in front of a crowded court. There was, a contemporary account reported, 'a very great and extraordinary Audience present', including peers, the Speaker of the Commons, Arthur Onslow, other committee members, such as Oglethorpe and Charles Selwyn, 'and many other Gentlemen of distinction, and a Crowd of Ladies'. The prosecution called many witnesses, several of whom painted a picture of the common-side regime under Acton. An exchange with John Wilson, a prisoner since 1726, bringing out the two sides of Acton's character, was recorded thus by the shorthand writers:

> Mr. *Acton*. Please to ask, my Lord, if he saw my Behaviour to the Prisoners in general.
> Mr. Baron *Carter*. What say you to that?
> Mr. *Wilson*. I have seen People beat, and put in Irons.
> Mr. *Ward* [prosecuting counsel]. By whose Directions?
> Mr. *Wil*. I believe by *Acton*'s.
> Mr. *Ward*. Have you seen Acton strike Prisoners?
> Mr. *Wil*. I have seen him strike prisoners with his Fist.
> Mr. *Ward*. Did you see *Bliss* with an Iron Instrument on?
> Mr. *Wil*. No.
> Mr. Baron *Carter*. What behaviour did *Acton* use towards his Prisoners?
> Mr. *Wil*. He behaved very well to some, and used others ill.[28]

Bliss had been involved with six or seven others in an attempt to escape by breaking through the prison walls into a baker's adjoining in Ax and Bottle Yard. They were all caught and Bliss, who seems not to have been a main instigator, was confined in the strong room and fettered, staying there for some weeks before being sent back to the common side. Two or three months later he made a second escape attempt: 'The Man was almost perished for want,' Mary Gillis swore, 'and with a Rope had attempted to escape, being tied round his Middle; but being discovered, the Rope was cut . . .' Ruth Butler swore she 'saw him going over the House, and he fell off', hurting his ankle; he 'was taken on the other side, and brought in again; and was put in the Strong Room by *Acton, Thomas Nichols, Rogers* and *Page.*' According to Mrs Butler, '*Acton* beat him with a *Bull's-pizzle* there, and stamped upon his Body several Times', 'Betwixt his Belly and his Stomach'.[29]

Next day Mrs Bliss came to visit Thomas, as she did, she said, every morning and night. When she got there:

Nichols said, there is the Bitch his Wife, and *Acton* ordered me to be called into the Lodge; and said, Damn you, Madam, I will have you before Justice *Ladd*, for bringing the Rope to your Husband: Damn you, I will confine you, and he put me into the Place where they put the irons in, adjoining to the Lodge, and kept me there an Hour.

She heard Acton order Bliss into the lodge and instruct the turnkeys to 'put on the Scull-cap, Collar, Thumb-Screws, and Fetters', Acton wanting Bliss to confess how he came by the rope. After a time he was moved to the strong room, where through the hole used to deliver food and drink Mrs Bliss saw him with the skullcap, irons and collar still on; she saw too the marks on his body of a beating from 'the Bull's-pizzle *Acton* kept', as his clothes had to be cut off him to ease his swellings. She saw him bleeding from the mouth, he said from the skullcap, and from under his thumbnails. These instruments of torture were removed the next day or possibly later.

Bliss seems to have been put in the strong room two or three times, once for over a month. While there he was seen by other prisoners. Susannah Dodds swore to carrying him some victuals in the strong room while he still had on thumbscrews, leg irons including the sheers, and the skullcap – all were produced in court. Bliss asked her 'to chew his Victuals, for his Mouth was sore; and I pulled it to Pieces, and fed him'. Other prisoners swore to Bliss's being beaten and ironed, and to his weakened and sickly state while he remained in the Marshalsea. He was finally put in the men's sick ward, where 'he had no Stockings, no Shirt, only a Blanket.'

Brutal mistreatment – though contradicted by Acton's witnesses, among whom were also former prisoners, as well as turnkeys and others dependent on the gaoler's good opinion – was, from the shorthand record at least, convincingly evidenced. Much time was taken up over the condition of the strong room, a place of punishment for many years before Acton, as *Hell in Epitome* recorded. Even the prosecution witnesses disagreed over whether it was damp or not, and various opinions were voiced about how close to the common sewer, and how noisome, it really was. But much of the defence more tellingly went to the critical weakness of the prosecution's case. The charge was of murder. But Bliss had been discharged months before he died in St Thomas's – the timings of his imprisonment and death were, by modern standards, left surprisingly vague – and all agreed that in falling during his escape he had bruised himself and damaged his leg. Evidence about his physical condition at the time of his discharge was wildly at odds, some affirming his near-death-like condition, others that he was sprightly and in good heart. As to the cause of death, Mrs Jane Lapworth, nurse at St Thomas's Hospital, swore that Bliss died of a fever: 'I heard him say no more, than that he had been in the Country, and caught an Ague and an intermitting Fever.' Acton also lined up an impressive list of witnesses who swore to his character as a 'very humane Man': Sir John Darnell, judge of the Marshalsea court; Edmund Halsey, brewer and MP for Southwark, provider of beer to the Marshalsea prison and himself at death's door whether he knew it or not (he would be dead within three weeks); Justice Maltys Ryall of the Surrey bench, one of Grano's patrons; and numerous wealthy tradesmen of the Borough.

There was an especially controversial moment during the trial. One of Acton's witnesses as to facts was Hester Long, married to Mrs Bliss's brother. She had seen Bliss after his discharge and swore he told her that his freedom 'was owing to Mr. *Acton*; and said, God Bless him, he got me out. I asked him, If he was arrested again, what would he do? he said, *Acton* would stand by him.' Long said that Mrs Bliss had told her that her husband 'was as well as ever in his Life'. As if this were not astonishing enough, prompted by Acton she said that Mrs Bliss had lodged with her after her husband's death and that 'a Messenger came, and said, there was Money for Mrs. *Bliss* in *Southwark*'. This would be available for Mrs Bliss if she swore against Acton and that she had already received 'two Guineas given her by one of the Gentlemen of the Committee'. At this point James Oglethorpe rose from his seat and asked for permission to speak. Mr Baron Carter, doubtless taken aback but aware of the MP's special position, replied, 'Sir, you may.' Oglethorpe asked that Mrs Bliss be recalled to confront her sister-in-law. By contrast, Mrs Bliss said that Long had offered to go to Acton on her behalf 'and make it up, and he would give me something'. The two guineas had been a present from her master, with whom she had been in service but had left because 'There were so many came flocking, up and down after me, that I could not live with him. There came two Gentlemen last *Sunday*.' Counsel asked who sent them and she replied, 'They said they came from *Acton*.' At which point Mr Baron Carter pointed out, 'What they said is no Evidence', which was true enough. Oglethorpe rose again:

> My Lord, I must with all humble Submission beg leave to speak. Reputation is a very valuable Thing; and here is an Aspersion thrown out at random against a Member of a Committee, which may affect the Characters of several Gentlemen who are not here present.
>
> Mr. Baron *Carter*. There are many Committees, and I should have taken notice if any thing had been said of any Committee of the House of Commons.[30]

In the end, Mrs Long was unable to identify which member, indeed which committee, she reported Mrs Bliss as mentioning. A telling note from a press report of the trials plainly referred to Hester Long and what many regarded as her suborned evidence: 'We are inform'd, that an Indictment for Perjury was drawn, in order to be preferr'd against some of the Evidences who swore in the Behalf of Mr *Acton*, on his Trial for the Murder of *Bliss*; but before Council could peruse it, the Grand Jury was discharg'd.'[31]

There was then a long summing-up of the evidence by Mr Baron Carter, who picked out, as one trial report had it, 'The Consistency and Inconsistency, the Credibility and Incredility, and the many and various Contrarieties and Contradictions that occurr'd in this long Tryal' involving 'Fifty odd Witnesses'.[32] After retiring, the jury found William Acton not guilty of the murder of Thomas Bliss. John Grano had heard much of the evidence but didn't stay for the verdict, being invited to dine nearby with Borough acquaintances 'on a Hanch of venison a Salmon a Ham and chicken &c.' Later he added a note to his journal entry for 1 August 1729: 'NB. This Day a Tryal came on between His Majesty and William Acton before Baron Carter, for the Murther of Thomas Bliss, and after a full hearing of about 8 Hours He was acquited with General Satisfaction; the whole appearing to be a Malicious Prosecution.'

Next day the court heard the further three charges of murder. Baron Carter once more presided. To the horror of the prosecution the same jury that had heard the case in respect of Bliss was sworn in for the further trials too. The 'Sollicitor for the Crown, three several Times insisted upon a new Pannel', but Carter saw no cause to change the jury after being told by Acton's counsel that 'The other Pannel cannot write; these are Men of Ability and Experience.' The prosecution was merely able to challenge one juror, who was replaced.[33]

The first trial of the day, Acton's second indictment for murder, concerned the death of Captain John Bromfield, who died in the Marshalsea in June 1725. He had stabbed a turnkey with a penknife after a dispute. Evidence was given that he was ironed and put in a place called the Hole, 'under the Stairs; a little bigger than a large Coffin in Width and Length', where he could not stand upright and where the earthen floor was wet. There he stayed three or four days. Released, he was kept in irons on the common side, in George's Ward. The irons were in place some weeks until shortly before he died. Acton's defence was that Darby, as keeper, ordered Bromfield to be ironed because of his violent assault on a turnkey, that he was only in the hole a few hours and that he died of jaundice, unaffected by his treatment in prison.

Acton's third trial was for the murder of Robert Newton, another failed escapee, who also died in 1725. Captain Tudman, Mr Smith and others gave evidence for the crown as to Newton's subsequent treatment: that he was kept ironed in the strong room for about two weeks, lying on the bare floor, and then transferred to the sick ward, where he died. 'He had no Illness before he was put in Irons; he was a hale, strong, young Man.' More evidence was given about the strong room, timber-built against the side of a wall, the common sewer and 'the Soil that comes from the Necessary-house' nearby, and 'Abundance of rats creep into it'. Dead bodies were kept there and seen eaten by rats. Acton's defence was again that Darby had ordered Newton ironed, that he had a bed in the strong room, a healthy place which some prisoners preferred to the common-side wards, and that he died of the 'Gaol-Distemper'. Acton also produced witnesses to swear that a prosecution evidence had 'said he would swear against Mr. Acton, right or wrong, in order to make an Example of him'.

Acton's fourth trial was for the murder of Captain James Thompson, who died in the strong room in 1726 and was found with his face 'disfigured with the Rats'. The prosecution brought evidence to say he was already a sick man and in the strong room had no bed to lie on. William Jennings, at that time 'one of *Acton*'s Watchmen', complained of Thompson's miserable condition during his confinement 'and I desired *Acton* to have him removed, and *Acton* said, What Business have you to meddle with it? Let him die like a Son of a Bitch, and be damned.' Acton's defence had it that Thompson 'had the Diabetes, and his Ward-mates said he stunk' when he made water at night; they 'fined him, and took his Coat from him, and carried it away, and the Man had not Money to redeem it'. He pressed Acton to move him from the ward so he might get some peace; he said he would get none in the sick ward either, but would be fined again. In the strong room he did have a bed – 'A Pillow and a Blanket', a prison bed as it became known during the trial – and one of Acton's witnesses swore Thompson told him, 'God bless Mr. *Acton*, for he had saved his Life by putting him in the Strong Room . . .'

Acton was acquitted of all these charges without the jury leaving their box. Both Acton and his counsel then asked that he be discharged. For reasons that are unclear – perhaps because of the leading role the House of Commons had taken in the prosecution and the prominence of its members watching in the courtroom – Baron Carter demurred. At this moment Acton's counsel turned to Oglethorpe and asked him for his 'Opinion' as to whether Acton could now go free. Oglethorpe rose and replied:

Were I Prosecutor, I should desire the Prisoner might be released; not that I think him innocent, but that every *Englishman*, be him never so unjustly acquitted, hath, by the *Habeas Corpus* Act, on his Acquittal, a Right to be discharged;

nor can any Subornation of Perjury, or any Management of a Jury, prevent it, for they are cognizable at another Time. *(There being then a great Noise in the Court, interrupted his speaking for some Time, and as soon as it ceased, he went on again.)* As I said before, I am not the Prosecutor; if I were, I know what I should have done. The Attorney General was ordered to prosecute by the Crown . . . I have not had anything to do in conducting the Prosecution here, which has appeared evidently . . .[34]

That Saturday afternoon, John Grano was invited to entertain the Surrey Grand Jury at the Sun tavern, Kingston, where the Lord Chancellor, Sir Robert Walpole 'and other Grandee's' were also dining, keen no doubt to know the outcome of the Gaols Committee's prosecutions. Afterwards Grano returned to the court, where he found that Acton had been acquitted. The two went to another inn, where John Darby met them for supper and the three of them drank ''Rack Punch' till past two in the morning. On Sunday, Grano returned to the Marshalsea at Acton's expense, sharing a coach with the gaoler's aunt and mother-in-law, Acton presumably travelling back separately with Mary.[35]

Acton returned as deputy keeper of the Marshalsea. But the questions of subornation, perjury and the malign influence of the judicial bench on the Gaols Committee's activities – for Bambridge was acquitted of all charges too – muttered on into 1730. The most active of the committee members were deeply embarrassed by the prosecutions' failure, 'vilified in the world for proceeding so zealous', as Oglethorpe put it to Lord John Perceval. Perceval, loyal to both Oglethorpe his friend and Walpole his leader, was torn in two ways. He well 'knew the ill will the Administration bore [the Gaols Committee], and the weight of the judges and Court would be against us' should the committee be revived in the new parliamentary session of February 1730. The administration was also said to be undermining the committee, with Walpole's personal role emphasised in the pamphlets: 'it is commonly thought that *Somebody*' – plainly referring to 'Sir R. W.' – 'used all his *Arts* and *Cunning* to *mislead*' the committee, 'and even to *wound* the *Reputation* of those particular Gentlemen who appeared most active'. The judges in particular, 'who had behaved strangely, and used us contemptuously', were especially mistrusted by Oglethorpe and those closest to him. For of course the committee had trespassed on the province of the Marshalsea court and had, by implication, accused its judges of turning their backs on the most monstrous injustice. The judges were thought to be hand in glove with Bambridge in the Fleet and Darby and Acton in the Marshalsea. And as Perceval confided to his diary, any attempt 'to call the judges to account . . . will draw upon our backs the power of the Ministry, who will certainly protect them'.[36]

Nevertheless, friendship outweighed prudence and Perceval voted for the revival of the committee. Oglethorpe had his way and the committee, with an altered membership, began work on the King's Bench and other prisons in February 1730. The investigations of these other gaols revealed none of the flagrant abuses of the Marshalsea or Fleet. But the defeats of the previous summer continued to rankle. Oglethorpe and Perceval both thought 'it could be proved public money was given to support the gaolers we prose-cuted'. In March 1730 the committee heard how Acton had allegedly arranged for a key witness against him to be committed to Newgate on a false charge; it was said he was released after Acton's acquittals. But nothing more was heard of the matter.[37]

At that point, though, it seemed as if justice might still be done to William Acton. For in September 1729 he had been arrested on a fifth murder charge in respect of a Whitechapel baker dying after a spell ironed in the strong room. This time Acton found it harder to mobilise influential friends in his cause. Unable to obtain bail, he spent the winter behind bars. His trial was fixed for 18 March 1730 at the Guildford Assizes. But the Surrey Grand Jury, whom Grano had entertained some seven months before, threw out the bill against him and he was a free man once more.[38]

Acton did not, this time, return to the Marshalsea. He moved temporarily in 1730 to a house in Faulcon Court, 'very handsomely built with a Free-stone Pavement and well-inhabited', on the west side of Borough High Street nearly opposite the King's Bench prison, and then seems to have moved out of the parish of St George the Martyr. But he was back in 1737, publican of the Greyhound inn, just across the road from the prison that had made his name notorious throughout the land. William Acton died there in 1748. He left his copyhold and personal estate to Mary and a separate legacy of £100 to Henry. In February 1732 John Darby farmed the gaol to William Taylor, a Borough undertaker, a useful Marshalsea trade.[39]

What can we make of Acton's trials? The evidence against him of torture and brutality was so circumstantial and attested to by so many as to appear both overwhelming and incontrovertible. But in no case could the prosecution prove that Acton's maltreatment, usually exacted as punishment or revenge for serious infractions of gaol discipline, had led to any of the deaths with which he was charged. Sickness was so rife, in and out of the Marshalsea, that some other cause of death was readily plausible. To make the jury's job even more difficult, perjured or prejudiced evidence on his behalf seems to have been given by a raft of witnesses, often his dependants in the gaol of one kind or another – turnkeys, paid helpers, prisoners who needed his favours or who would sell their word for a shilling or two. Certainly one of his 'evidences', Elizabeth Clayton, called 'an old Bawd' by a fellow prisoner whose testimony she had refuted, tried to

sell concocted 'secret' information about Catholics and
Jacobites (Grano's fears about a charge of treason were not
that far-fetched) to the authorities while she was a prisoner
in late 1728 and again in 1732, for instance.[40]

On the more general findings of the Gaols Committee, of
starvation deliberately engineered by Acton's siphoning the
charity money into his own purse, again the case seems fully
made out. So was the neglect of the sick and dying, though
this must be weighed against contemporary standards in
workhouse sick wards, on shipboard or in most prisons
anywhere. It is impossible to know, however, just how many
deaths were caused by Acton's harsh regime. The Marshalsea
had always been a deadly place. We might recall the hundred
dying there in three months reported to the House of
Commons in 1719, almost certainly caused by an epidemic
of gaol fever. But evidence of more normal times is hard to
come by. Coroners' inquests had not sat on Marshalsea
bodies, it was said in the committee's report and at Acton's
trials, for many years and that seems to have been true as
far as debtors were concerned. But one piece of evidence
has survived about Marshalsea deaths, for inquests *were*
held on 'felons' detained there while it was the local Surrey
county gaol, the White Lyon then being under reconstruction.
From October 1720 John Darby had to pay for these inquests
from his own profits. Before that the costs had been borne
from rent paid to him by a coach-maker, perhaps in a part
of the prison or premises adjoining in Ax and Bottle Yard,
but this had now 'gone from him'. He consequently asked
the Surrey magistrates to reimburse him for these county
expenses totalling £1 3s an inquest, made up of 10s to the
coroner, 2s to the jury, 1s to the jury summoner, and 10s in
all to the searchers (body-washers), coffin-maker, bearers
and burial fees. The list ended in February 1724. Darby
sought £41 for thirty-six inquests in forty-one months.
Deaths were markedly seasonal, especially prevalent from

October to April and probably due to typhus in the main, with men and women equally affected. In 1723, the worst year, there were thirteen inquests. These were on county prisoners only, we must remember, who had allowances of bread from the justices and who can merely have represented a small portion of the Marshalsea's population.[41]

The Acton years can though be put into a broader context. The local churchyard of St George the Martyr buried many prisoners from the Marshalsea over the years. Families and friends who were in a position to do so no doubt removed most bodies to other parts of London to which the dead 'belonged'; and prisoners known to be staunch dissenters or Roman Catholics would generally also have been buried elsewhere. Those bodies with no friends to claim them were taken to lie in St George's churchyard nearby. Burials there from the Marshalsea fluctuated year on year, so that in 1698 we find twelve (including two children), in 1708 twenty-seven and in 1718, the year of *Hell in Epitome*, thirty-two. But in 1728, the year under Acton directly preceding the Gaols Committee's investigation, fifty-three bodies were buried from the Marshalsea in St George's, including one child and seven women prisoners. It is plain from the registers that bodies were held back in the gaol until someone else died and were buried in pairs so that the costs could be minimised. Mortality in London generally was high in the 1720s and St George's was no exception, but in that context 1728 does not stand out; yet in that year Marshalsea burials accounted for one in every eleven interments in the parish churchyard. Whatever view we take of the Gaols Committee's reported numbers of deaths from the prison, this was an exceptional mortality in a population at any one time of around 400 souls. And these deaths can only stand proxy for many more.[42]

Acton's misappropriation of charity money seems likely to have caused some at least of this excess mortality. Yet

charity money had probably never come easily to the
common side and difficulties certainly persisted after Acton's
departure. In August 1735 the six ward constables petitioned
the Surrey justices to assist in 'getting in all the Arrears of
the Legacys which the severall Donors have Respectively
bequeathed to us, And also the Exhibition or High Barr
money' from the county treasurers. The petition was endorsed
by Charles Thornton, clerk of the prison and prothonotary
or chief clerk of the Marshalsea court: he thought the nine
legacies listed by the prisoners were 'in Arrear about 5 Years',
the 'Exhibition money about two Years'. Four years later
and the county money had become an urgent grievance, the
common side producing an elaborate memorial to the justices
and 'to all people of Distinction'. It claimed that the receiver
for the past ten years, Henry Masterman, 'by his Negligence
or Wilfullness', had failed to distribute some £500 to the
prisoners in 'Exobition Mony'. On petition to the Lord Chief
Justice and Sir Philip Meadows sometime before, Masterman
had been replaced. The prisoners had requested that 'their
Agent', John Adams, should be appointed receiver. But
instead Meadows had installed 'one Abraham Odall', whom
the prisoners considered 'one of Mr Masterman's Creatures,
a Dealer in Harps an Established Jury-man of ye Marshalsea
Court, and a Mercinary Tool of ye Goalers, that concerns
himself so much with ye Charitys that belongs to ye poor
prisoners, which causes them to call out Aloud for Justice,
against <those> that endeavours to Starve to Death His
Majestys poor Subjects . . .' The common-side prayed for a
new receiver to be put in Odall's place. We don't know if
that plea was answered. Similar complaints would dog the
Marshalsea throughout its history.[43]

How much, then, did the Oglethorpe committee improve
matters for prisoners of the Marshalsea? There were some
immediate effects, all welcome. A brutal gaoler had been
removed. The medieval torture instruments, kept in the gaol

for centuries, were taken away, never to return. Lives were
saved as money came into the common side to tend the sick
and rescue the starving. Hundreds were released from prison
and helped to reorder their debts by the Insolvent Debtors
Acts directly sponsored by the committee, though such acts
had been passed before and would be again. And the gaol
fees and rents were revised, with charges for bedding and
bed hire reduced, especially for those sharing a bed: they
had previously paid 2s 6d a week each, they would now
pay 1s 2d.[44]

Among wider public opinion the immediate verdict was
high in praise. In part that was because the committee's
exposures were a stick with which to beat Walpole and his
administration. But Oglethorpe and his committee entered
into the conscience of the times and even made a mark on
its literature: the Scottish poet James Thomson, then living
in London, memorably added new lines to the 1730 text of
'Winter' in *The Seasons*, praising the committee as that
'generous band' and condemning the 'little tyrants' who
'Snatch'd the lean morsel from the starving mouth'.[45]

Oglethorpe went on to lead a long, eventful and useful
life, most notably helping to found the state of Georgia in
1732, first envisaged as a sanctuary, almost a Utopia, for
London debtors released from prison by the 1729 acts. The
idea of transplanting failed tradesmen from the Borough and
congested City suburbs to the virgin wilds of a new territory,
among an indigenous population not always friendly to white
settlers, seems to have given Oglethorpe, Perceval and other
philanthropists little uneasiness of mind. A hundred willing
debtors were sought, a charter for the new territory engrossed,
a petition to the king for a grant of lands duly drawn up
and eventually conceded. It all took two years to plan and
implement. In the event some forty able-bodied unemployed
with their families, perhaps an insolvent debtor or two among
them, arrived in Charleston harbour in January 1733. But

any debtors in Georgia would quickly be outnumbered by Protestant refugees and sturdy Highlanders, the two main emigrant groups eventually proving most robust and useful in the new world. Nevertheless the committee members' continuing efforts on behalf of the imprisoned debtors were laudable and impressive for the time, duly remembered and etched in stone for posterity on the monument erected to Oglethorpe in his burial place at Cranham, Essex, soon after his death in 1785.[46]

Oglethorpe and the Gaols Committee are often connected with the work of the prison reformer John Howard in the 1770s and 1780s. But some fifty years separated them and in truth the Gaols Committee, while undoubtedly provoking a momentary spasm of shame and horror at the abuses it uncovered, created no momentum for reform of the way the gaols were run. For the Marshalsea continued to be farmed for profit. It was not invested in by crown or Parliament or its profit-rakers until its ruinous condition made it unfit to be considered a reliable place of custody at all. The ripples made by the Gaols Committee in 1729 were quickly stilled. The Marshalsea would very much go on in the way it always had for some generations to come.

5

'MANSIONS OF MISERY': THE OLD MARSHALSEA, 1730–1811

SOME things did change after 1730, but the changes were not due to reform. The Gaols Committee found 400 or so prisoners there in the spring of 1729. When John Howard, the London-born prison reformer surveyed it in March 1774 he found 167, the numbers creeping up to more than 230 in 1776. For the intervening half-century there are no precise figures but it seems unlikely that the numbers of debtors in the prison on any one day again reached the gaol population under William Acton. A petition to the House of Commons drafted in 1742 spoke of 130 prisoners 'and upwards' and in 1768 there were said to be 'two Hundred and upwards', so the fluctuations reported by Howard seem to have been something like the norm for the decades after 1730. The spare room, if such we can call it, allowed more space than before to accommodate debtors' families: in March 1775, 175 prisoners shared the gaol with forty-six family members, wives or partners and children.[1]

Even so there were periods when the gaol became abnormally crowded. The Admiralty continued to send offenders on the high seas to the Marshalsea, whether king's navy defaulters, merchantmen accused or convicted of crime, or pirates. And the gaol took its share of prisoners during moments of national crisis. Jacobite rebels were sent here once more, this time after 'The '45'. In February 1746 prisoners from Carlisle were marched to the gaol with an escort of foot guards, who were unable to prevent an indignant populace 'pelting them with Dirt, &c.'; and in June shiploads were received in the Thames, 'the common Men, to the Number of about 600', were sent to the Marshalsea, an extraordinary figure if true. Similarly, in March 1762 'a great number of French prisoners of war' were confined there under 'A double guard of soldiers'. This is likely to have been the last overcrowding crisis in the gaol, although some pressure was felt when the Marshalsea received significant numbers of mutineers following the troubles at the Nore in 1797.[2]

One other unlikely instance of an influx, this time of debtors, brought its own pressures on the common side in 1750. Around March that year twenty-one Lascars – Indian seamen – were brought into the Marshalsea for debt. They had been part of the crew of a Royal Navy vessel, the *Medway's Prize*, a French ship captured in the East Indies in early 1744. The *Medway's Prize* seized a Spanish ship, the *Sainta Catherina*, or so it was named in the London newspapers. The *Medway's Prize* was sailed to England by its partly Lascar crew and all its sailors were paid off at Deptford, where the ship was moored to be received by its new owners, in August 1749.

The Lascars, and no doubt others among the crew, expected prize money from taking the Spaniard. They said they were assured of it and on the strength of that promise found it easy to procure board and lodging somewhere along the river. But the prize money never materialised and one of their creditors, almost certainly a publican or lodging-house keeper, lost patience and had twenty-one of them arrested on mesne process and carried to the Marshalsea.

Another ten Lascars from the *Medway's Prize* remained at large, sustaining themselves by begging on the streets.

The Marshalsea Lascars, kept on the common side, were granted a subsistence allowance by the Admiralty of 8d a day – generous compared with what they would have received in charity and even twice the groats that the law would eventually have required the creditor to pay each of them. The Admiralty then made arrangements for them to be taken to India by East India Company ships, offering to clothe and provision them at the navy's expense. But the men, all but one, made the same reply: 'they absolutely say that they would rather be hang'd than go without their Prize Money.' They held to this despite becoming ill in the Marshalsea, where they were treated by a local apothecary with a lengthy schedule of drugs and ointments, including, 'An Antefebrile mixture', 'An Anodine Bolus', 'A purging potion', 'A Cathartick potion', 'A Vomiting potion' and many more. Ships were twice held for them at Gravesend but had to sail when 'these Obstinate Lascars' refused to leave the Marshalsea without their money. In the end, just before Christmas 1750, after the Lascars had spent some nine months in gaol, the Admiralty instituted proceedings in the Palace court to force the creditor to lodge an execution and so render him liable to maintain them all at 4d a day. It seems likely that he failed to do so and the Lascars were discharged when the Admiralty paid their gaol fees, lawyers' costs and apothecary's bills and washed their hands of the men. The twenty-one Marshalsea Lascars, still waiting for their prize money, seem to have joined their ten shipmates in begging about London, where they achieved some notoriety over the next year and more.[3]

They stayed for their prize money and in the end they got it. There were other claims against the *Sainta Catherina*, notably from some Armenian merchants. After some toing and froing in the Admiralty court, the prize was eventually awarded to the officers and men of the *Medway's Prize*,

including the Lascars. They were all paid out at the King's
Arms tavern on Tower Hill in April 1752: 'Each sailor's
share amounted to upwards of 65l. The Lascars, who have
been beggars about the streets of this city, belonged to the
said Medway's prize.' The prize money was secured after
extraordinary efforts and great privation but for one it
proved easier to win than to keep: a Lascar was brought up
for a violent assault on 'one Catherine Brownlow' but was
discharged when he showed she 'had from Time to Time
stript him of almost all his Prize Money, and then deserted
him and married another of the Lascars'. Those who wished
to sail for India – presumably paying or working their
passage – eventually did so in 1753 and 1754.[4]

A quarter-century after these events things changed dras-
tically on the debtors' side so far as numbers in the
Marshalsea were concerned. An act of 1779 increased the
limits for arrests on mesne process from £2 to £10. Debtors
owing less than £10 could not now be arrested unless the
existence of the debt was proved in court, protecting small
debtors from frivolous or vindictive imprisonment. The effect
in the Marshalsea was immediate: on 15 May 1776 there
were 234 debtors, in January 1782 just forty-eight. Howard
reported that creditors were getting round the act by loading
the costs of actions on to the original debt until it exceeded
the £10 limit and then bringing new proceedings and an
arrest for the total sum, but by August 1783 the numbers
in the gaol still totalled only seventy-one. Though the number
on any one day continued to fluctuate, it never again reached
the levels common before 1779.[5]

Even so, these daily numbers are deceptive. At Christmas
1811, for instance, there were fifty debtors in the Marshalsea.
But since 1 January that year 308 had been brought into
custody, most of whom were discharged for one reason or
another during the course of the year. In 1821 there were
416 imprisoned there, in 1831 the figure was 580 and in

1841, when the numbers on any one day were generally fewer than fifty, 242.[6]

These hundreds of debtors in and out of the Marshalsea year after year developed complex survival mechanisms in a gaol where prisoners had to live on their own resources, on whatever help they could get from outside, on the assistance of their fellows or on charity. Never, at any time in its history, did debtors receive an allowance from the Marshalsea of any kind at all.

Thankfully, however, the poorest debtors there were a continuing object of charity. After the scandalous revelations of 1729–30 the old legacies – still, as we have seen, difficult to get – were added to by occasional gifts. Each Christmas the Lord Mayor and City sheriffs collected money for poor prisoners, including the Marshalsea's. Gifts might also be importuned collectively by the prisoners themselves, the plight of the Marshalsea debtors forever on the conscience of Londoners. A benefit night for the 'PRISONERS in the MARSHALSEA PRISON, Southwark, (Being their First Application of this Kind)' was given at Drury Lane Theatre in May 1750, David Garrick leading in Vanbrugh's *The Provok'd Wife* – perhaps an actor was in quod. This seems to have been the only instance of a stage benefit, but in 1759 James Worsdale published his *Gasconado the Great, A Tragical, Comical, Operatical, Farcical, Pantomimical, Political, Burlesque OPERA* for the 'Benefit of the miserable INSOLVENTS in the MARSHALSEA PRISON', which hopefully brought some cheer to both author and prisoners.[7]

Isolated instances of benevolence have also come down to us, though many more must have gone unrecorded. In January 1763 Edward Milbourne of the Strand, 'a wealthy Officer belonging to His Majesty's Palace Court', donated bread and meat for twelve days to help the prisoners through a bitter cold snap; and in the winter of 1772, when meat prices were exceptionally high, the Marshalsea's deputy

keeper bought an ox, had it driven into the Marshalsea and
slaughtered there by a debtor butcher, then sold the meat
to the prisoners below market price, an example of thrifty
philanthropy that the newspapers commended to other
gaolers. But publicity for these acts of generosity gratified
the prisoners too, for it encouraged others to give. Nor were
they shy of using the newspapers for their own ends, buying
space to advertise their thanks for anonymous gifts of three
guineas and periodic donations of beef and bread.[8]

These collective supplications for aid were dwarfed by
the daily stream of begging letters issuing from the rooms
and wards of the gaol. We might recall that John Grano was
a tireless writer of begging letters and so were many more,
the habit generally picked up in the spunging house, that
first point of detention. Grano's seem mainly to have been
addressed to his family and friends, but perhaps also included
casual acquaintances among the great. Wealthy and famous
men and women were notoriously the target of these letters,
especially if they had a reputation for benevolence or
patronage. A connection of some sort, however shadowy,
would serve by way of introduction. Anthony Osborn, a
Marshalsea prisoner for some ten months around 1738,
importuned Sir Hans Sloane, the renowned physician and
collector, to purchase 'an antick which I have had by me for
some considerable time' and which he had refused to part
with – he said – to the Duke of Devonshire; he now offered
it for £40 to free him from prison. Sloane was shown it by
an intermediary but proclaimed it 'of no value'.[9]

In 1742 the Irish writer and adventuress Laetitia Pilkington
was arrested at her lodgings in Duke Street, St James's, at the
suit of her landlady: 'Get up, you *Irish* Papist Bitch', she was
ungallantly ordered by the bailiffs who came for her. In the
Marshalsea she turned her facile pen to account, begging from
Sir Richard Mead, the plutocrat-physician and art connoisseur
of Great Ormond Street. She had visited him previously on

the strength of a connection with the Irish branch of his family. She put her 'plaintive Pray'r' into verse, of a kind, pleading 'Such Affliction, as before/ Never hapless Woman bore.' She struck no gold, or very little, Mead complaining of the many claims on his pocket, 'those from your Country alone are very numerous': 'I have, for the last time, sent you a Guinea'. She was eventually relieved after various applications by Colley Cibber, the playwright and fellow versifier, whose own father had been a prisoner in the Marshalsea many years before; he organised a subscription that included, Laetitia tells us, 'contributions from no less than sixteen Dukes'. She expressed her gratitude in print 'To COLLEY CIBBER, Esq.':

> Lost in a Prison's joyless Gloom,
> Chearless, and dreary as the Tomb, [etc.][10]

Laetitia Pilkington was a character of some notoriety and her name would have been known to many wealthy potential patrons. Even so, and even in the republic of letters, where the bailiff's tap on the shoulder was a daily experience, staunch friends like Cibber were hard to come by. For others of the middling sort and below, wealthy acquaintances must have been more difficult to identify.

That was a burden that only the desperate or the audacious could overcome. Letters to the 2nd Marquess of Rockingham from three Marshalsea debtors in the winter of 1768 illustrate both approaches. Thomas Stephens, who claimed to have been 'brought up a Clergyman, & of a Good Family', had 'labour'd under ye keen Harrows of Affliction's upwards of two years and an half in this place of Confinement': 'I am so much distressed that I am obliged to crave boon from your well known Goodness, & if so fortunate to recieve a small donation, should with a Heart ever full of Gratitude return my sincere thanks for your seasonable relief.'[11]

The other, from Richard Warre and John Penn, made a different sort of plea. Warre was the penman and almost certainly the self-proclaimed 'Son of a Gentleman':

My Lord

As Strangers We are perfectly at a Loss how to approach your Lordship's Dignity, but thro' the Medium of that noble Generosity and benevolent Disposition, which shine so conspicuously thro' every one of your Lordship's Actions: Supported by a Consciousness of this amiable Quality, and urged by the sharp Stings of Adversity, which we now labour under in the Marshalsea prison Southwark. We have presum'd to be thus impertinent. Give us leave to assure your Lordship that 'tis the Treachery of our falsely esteem'd Friends, ungratefully exerted in Consequence of our good Nature, that has been the Cause of this distressful Scene. The one of us, My Lord, is a Clergyman, the other the Son of a Gentleman, both liberally & genteely educated, and therefore render'd more sensible of the Severity of Fortune. To be destitute, My Lord, of bare Necessaries to support Nature, and Coals against the Inclemency of a piercing wintry Season, which, My Lord, is really our Case, are Circumstances painful to the Body, galling to Reflection, and will not we trust fail to meet your Lordship's wonted Compassion for the distress'd. Pray, my Lord, pardon this Presumptuous Freedom, and the Method of conveyance adopted, as Prison Messengers are altogether unfit to appear at your Lordhsip's Door, and demand Pay inadequate to the Barreness of our Pockets
We are
My Lord
        your Lordship's most devoted
                & most obsequious Serv^{ts}
                    Rich: Warre
                        John Penn[12]

Perhaps this was the same Richard Warre whose where-abouts were sought by City tradesmen in the following autumn. A 'table set of very fine nankeen china, and one complete tea set, blue and imaged, with a gold border', together worth near £40, and 'four Carpets of different Sizes', were ordered on Warre's behalf by 'two ladies' who 'came in a coach' to two different warehouses. The goods were dispatched 'to the house of Richard Warre, Esq., in Lower Grosvenor street'. When payment was sought Warre, the ladies, the china and carpets had all disappeared. One of his accomplices was eventually named as 'Ann Warre, otherwise Stewart'.[13]

Stephens, Warre and Penn were strangers to Rockingham with no connection they could lay claim to. But one loose bond, readily exploited, was service in the army or navy, as generals and admirals were viewed as a fruitful source of alms. Lord and Lady Clive received numerous Marshalsea letters, and no doubt every commander on sea or land was similarly besieged. We might let one such stand for many. It is a petition in the third person to Lord Robert Clive from John Callander in the Marshalsea prison, 18 July 1767. And unlike some of its kind, this has a genuine ring about it:

> That Your Lordships Petitioner served his Majesty during the late War, Two Years as Lieutenant by Warrant in the 49th Regt of Foot at Jamaica and Afterwards as Volunteer with the Royal British Artillery in Germany, where he remained 'till the Peace was Concluded without being provided for . . .
>
> That Your Lordships Petitioner, by a long continuance in Town after his Return from Germany, on Promises of being Promoted, unfortunately Contracted some Small Debts, for which he was Arrested and thrown into Prison, where he has remained for these Six Months past, and is now reduced to the lowest degree of Misery, Having suffered every Calamity that Indigence and a prison can Inflict and is now

destitute of Cloaths, and every other Necessary of Life, Not having a single friend in England to grant him the smallest reliefe, Your Lordships Petitioner being a Native of Jamaica, where all his friends now reside.

Your Petitioner, Emboldened by Your Lordships Great, Noble, Generous, and disinterested Conduct and Character in Life, has most humbly Presumed to lay this Petition before your Lordship, Imploring that your Lordship will be pleased to take his unhappy Situation into Consideration. The Amount of the whole Sum for which he is confin'd does not exceed Twenty Pounds. And by granting him the smallest reliefe; will be the Means of Preserving a Life, that may in time be of use to this Country, and the best of Kings: but if not soon relieved, must Terminate in the greatest Misery.[14]

Poor Callander's petition lay unanswered; he wrote again, with some desperation, six weeks later but we do not know how he fared.

Where a supplicant had no great friends, or could conjure none from the vagaries of a career, the newspapers offered an alternative. From around the mid-1760s advertisements seeking aid appeared in the papers on behalf of Marshalsea debtors. 'A Foreign Person of Quality', a debtor prisoner for twenty-three months by the spring of 1765 and owing £120, sought subscribers for a translation into French of Lloyd's *New History of England* to be composed during his imprisonment: patrons were invited to send donations to 'the Colonel at the Marshalsea-Prison', where any subscriber would be acknowledged with 'proper Tickets, with his [the Colonel's] Arms attached'. The common-side prisoners advertised for alms in 1770, as did someone on behalf of a wife, just brought to child, of a Marshalsea prisoner. So did 'A Gentleman' who had been there several months but was now confined merely 'for his fees and lodging, which together amount to about two guineas': he headed his plea '*Libertas*

Auro Pretiorior Est' (freedom is more precious than gold), the Latin tag a sign of his gentle education. Sometime later the *World and Fashionable Advertiser* carried a plea from 'An Industrious Widow, with Seven Children' who was now in the Marshalsea and seeking a benefactor to set her up in 'some small way of business' once more; donors were directed to a goldsmith at 21 Cornhill. Doubtless there were others, for this way of seeking help would remain in fashion till the prison's end.[15]

The wife whose baby had just been delivered, the widow's seven children and every prisoner's dependants left destitute at home or sharing a room with him in the gaol had one other recourse. It was unpalatable yet much resorted to. This was the parish poor law, run by the churchwardens and overseers of the local vestry wherever a destitute person could prove a 'settlement', or legal claim, on the parish. The poor law couldn't help the debtor in prison but was the last safety net for those left behind. Imprisonment in the Marshalsea gave no settlement in the local parish of St George the Martyr, Southwark, but nonetheless the prison added great burdens to the ratepayers of a parish with many poor persons already to be maintained. St George's had to provide immediate relief to sick or starving women and children coming out of the gaol or lodging near to their imprisoned husbands until they could be removed to a parish where they already were settled; it had to bear the cost of enquiries and of requiring another parish to accept responsibility in such cases, disputes sometimes resulting in expensive court cases; and it had to succour those without a settlement elsewhere for as long as they needed it.[16]

In 1783 the House of Commons reported on a petition from St George's praying for aid. A Commons committee concluded that no settlement should be given to families of prisoners in the Marshalsea and the other gaols nearby, even if they were renting for some time in the district, and that some aid should be given to the parish to help pay for those who had no settlement elsewhere. The report gave prominence to 'a Servant to a prisoner in the *Marshalsea* being deprived of her senses' and removed from the gaol to the Southwark workhouse and then to Bedlam in Moorgate, all at the expense of St George's ratepayers. The law was duly changed in St George's favour, though the difficulties for this Southwark parish populated by prisons were never entirely removed.[17]

Certain it is that poor law officers London-wide had always known of the burdens that imprisonment for debt routinely caused them. The ramifications of confinement in the Marshalsea rippled across the capital, and even beyond. So from the parish of St Martin-in-the-Fields, Mrs Acton's parish we might remember, we hear in the 1730s of Mary White, twenty-seven, sleeping on doorsteps with her four children aged eight months to nine years, her stay-maker husband in the Marshalsea; of Mary Rodgers, forty-two and penniless, her husband a shoemaker in the Marshalsea for his fees; Ann Burkett, fifteen, her brother aged five already in the workhouse, her father an alehouse keeper now in the Marshalsea and her mother in lodgings near the gaol; John Bird, sixty-four, a barber and peruke-maker, released after five months in the Marshalsea on the day he sought help from St Martin's, now destitute and unable to help himself; and numerous others whose husbands – more stay-makers, more licensed victuallers, more shoemakers, tailors, bakers, grocers, hatters – were confined in the prison. There are similar tales from St Clement Danes and from St Botolph's, Aldgate, and, were the records before us, we would hear them from every single parish in the metropolis.[18]

The consequences of a Marshalsea confinement extended too into the working world of London. Among the imprisoned tailors, victuallers, shoemakers and others were employers and masters of apprentices who had been paid to teach a boy a trade. What was that boy to do when he found no master to teach him and his parents' or guardians' investment ill spent? The justices' records of the capital are littered with requests from frustrated apprentices to be released from their indentures because their master was now a debtor in the Marshalsea. From the Middlesex quarter sessions we hear of James Topsell, apprenticed to Edward Hall, a tailor in Bloomsbury, who at the best of times had little business to teach him and was eventually arrested and confined in the Marshalsea. Hall's goods were seized for rent, his wife and family evicted along with Topsell, 'very Young and helpless to provide for himselfe without any Manner of Sustenance & not a place to Harbour him, being almost starved with Hunger & Cold' until he was taken in by a 'relation he had in Towne'. Hall had now been in the Marshalsea two months and Topsell sought a new master or to be discharged from his apprenticeship. Similar cases have survived from Marylebone (a coach-maker), two brothers apprenticed to the same Finsbury tailor, and an apprentice carpenter employed by a ship's joiner and cabinet-maker in Shadwell, now in the Marshalsea for seven months. These discharges were not always easily obtained. William Baker was apprenticed to John Poulton, a Clerkenwell plater and founderer who himself foundered; he had been imprisoned for three months in the Marshalsea when Baker first petitioned the justices in December 1797. For some reason the magistrates refused to discharge him at that time, so Baker renewed his petition a month or so later, complaining he had 'continued with his Master several Weeks in the prison and during that time his master frequently played at Cards with him for money and particularly on a Sunday'.[19]

It seems hardly feasible to think that William could have learned much of the plater's trade in the Marshalsea, but with some trades it was possible to continue working on the master's side of the gaol and even on the common side, where the Gaols Committee noted 'a large empty Room kept (as we are informed) for Workmen'. Edward Serjeant, whose shoemaker master near the Strand was imprisoned in the Marshalsea, worked there 'three or four days now and then with him' and no doubt there were others doing the same over the years. Perhaps it was this room too that was used by prisoners employed occasionally 'cutting pegs for the Brewers' at a rate of two shillings per thousand.[20]

One unexpected instance of an artisan continuing his trade in the Marshalsea won some public profile early in the nineteenth century. The prestigious *Gentleman's Magazine*, read wherever English was spoken, carried in September 1803 illustrations of the decaying Marshalsea, its ancient buildings standing only with the aid of timber raking shores. They were printed in the magazine as sent from 'T.P.' A note by 'Mr Urban', John Nichols the editor, described his contributor as 'our ingenious but unfortunate correspondent'. His name would, in fact, have been known to many.[21]

Thomas Prattent (pronounced Pratton it seems, for he was arrested under that spelling of his name) was a well-known engraver, brought up in that part of London just north of the City so familiar to Hogarth, and probably born around 1764. He married Ann Grace in 1787 at the Wren City church of St Michael Paternoster Royal, the burial place of Sir Richard Whittington. The marriage seems to have been childless. Prattent's business was in Cloth Fair, Smithfield, and later on Clerkenwell Green. He was a respected engraver of architectural and other antiquities. His *Virtuoso's Companion and Coin Collector's Guide* was published in eight volumes between 1795 and 1797, and he had engraved illustrations for Nichols since 1792 if not before. He had also made prints from the work of George Morland, the dissolute portraitist and landscape painter. We do not know what brought this respectable and established craftsman into debt and into the Marshalsea, but there he was, taken there by the bailiffs probably on 10 December 1802. Within a week he was writing to Nichols

> from those Mansions of Misery call'd the Marshalsea prison where I am confined for debt since last Friday[.] I am very solicitous for some employ to pass the gloom away & get something to support my wants which are great as I declare when I came to this place I had no more than sixpence in my pocket & there is no allowance whatever[.] for the last year it has pleased god to afflict me or rather illness a nervous fever & an excessive weakness in my Eyes has deprived of following a principal Branch of my Business[.] any thing in the coarser part of Engraving, Copying Sketches or Writing in short any thing tending to pass the weary hours away I should be thankfull & gratefull for[.] there is on the East side of the prison formerly a Palace the remains nearly intire of the Ancient Building which if you should approve would make a tolerable subject for your attention[.] if you please I will make an accurate sketch & send it to you
>
> Dear Sir I am reduced very very low indeed & have been frequently in want of the common necessary's of Life[.] the smallest pecuniary assistance as a loan would be recieved with a gratefull Heart & cheerfully repaid with thankfulness tis not so much for myself as for a beloved Wife whose sufferings is great indeed plunged from happiness to misery it would help to dry her tears & confey a favor which never would be erased from my mind[.] the smallest trifle would be gratefully acknowledged & prudently apply'd nor ever a second application made[.] dire necessity alone urges me to address you & I hope your Goodness will excuse it[.] any communication addressed to me N° 14 Marshalsea will be sure to be received[.] in trembling hope of hearing favourably from you
> > I am Sir
> > Y^r Distressed & Obliged Servt
> > > Thos Prattent[22]

Prattent would be in the Marshalsea for another twenty months or so and he could not keep his promise 'nor ever' to make 'a second application' for a loan, though he was pitifully modest in seeking a few shillings here and there. He sent further pictures from the prison and these were also published in the magazine in May 1804. But that was not before, as he several times reported to Nichols, 'I frequently feel the want of a Meals Victuals' and 'frequently have experienced[,] *fatal Reverse*[,] the want of Hunger'. He had contemplated swearing himself on to the poor side by taking an oath he was not worth forty shillings but couldn't do so truthfully, '& after being used to life in a genteel line to be hearded with the poorest & distrest of manking not to despise them <got 6 or 7 in a room> but the contrast is great'. 'Dʳ Sir The Favor I by most earnestly is I hope youll not be angry is to SEND ME 5ˢ for which I shall be very, very, thankfull!!' Poor Prattent was eventually returned to his 'Amiable and Beloved Partner my Dʳ Wife' around August 1804, though not through Nichols's intervention.[23]

Apart from one drawing of his own, of the elaborate interior of the Jacobean courthouse published subsequently, the Marshalsea views that Prattent engraved were loaned him by John Jenkins, then the prison's 'chum master' and chief turnkey under his father William, the deputy marshal and keeper. The artist of these was identified in the *Gentleman's Magazine* of May 1804 as 'Lieut. Orme', in fact Joseph Boardman Orme, who had been discharged from the Marshalsea in the summer of 1801, so eighteen months or so before Prattent was brought in. Orme probably gave Jenkins the pictures to offset some money still owed in rent, fees or favours, for Orme was a talented amateur watercolourist, though whether his work extended far beyond the walls of the Marshalsea is unclear. Most of all he was an adventurer, a lieutenant in the Lancashire Volunteers, born in Didsbury around 1771 and bred to trade in Manchester.

By the time he entered the Marshalsea, a 'Gentleman', he was young in years but old in debt. His fatal vice seems to have been gambling – he would go on to sue William Crockford, the famous gaming master, for £180,000 in 1824, but it proved an unlucky throw and the court rejected his suit.[24]

There were other adventurers who also had to turn their talents to account in the Marshalsea. A free and easy attitude to matters sexual was always an element of life in debtors' prisons, one of their more cheerful features. So it was in Grano's time and so it remained. We read in the City sessions papers in 1739 of Anne Minchen, who bigamously married two men, both makers of leather breeches; she was unfaithful to her second husband with her first, whom she comforted for a time during his confinement in the Marshalsea. And, some years later, of poor Eleanor Thorneycraft, twenty years old and lying 'now great with child or children' in the St Martin-in-the-Fields workhouse in 1761; she blamed one John Nash for her trouble, having been in his bed 'several times' while he was a prisoner in the Marshalsea some seven months before.[25]

Whether Eleanor was seduced while herself a prisoner is unclear but there is no doubt that seduction was common currency in the Marshalsea. Prostitutes confined there would need to bring money into their purses to survive, just as did tailors and engravers. For instance, William-George Jones was brought before an Old Bailey jury in December 1802 charged with bigamy, marrying his second wife, Frances-Maria Drought, at Paddington some two months earlier while his first wife still lived. Jones was a tradesman of some description and had been a prisoner in the Marshalsea for eighteen months. During his confinement, according to his defence, Frances-Maria was also brought into custody 'for a mantua-maker's bill; she there used all the insinuating manners that a girl of her description could possibly, and I resisted it; she was upon the town a twelvemonth'. Frances-Maria allegedly 'went by a dozen names', one other – 'Miss Hertfont' – coming up at the trial, and she seems to have been well known in the Marylebone area, where there were many brothels for the middling sort. Frances-Maria reached an accommodation with her creditor and was discharged, but she was said to have written to Jones daily, grandiosely claiming she 'had given up the first company, that of the Prince of Wales, Duke of Clarence, and Marquis of Hertford, upon my account'. Jones claimed he was inveigled into marriage by this fascinating girl and her overweening mother, but it seems likely there was infatuation on both sides. He was fined just a shilling, but sentenced to twelve months in Newgate. Perhaps it was characters such as Frances-Maria who had made 'modest women' complain to John Howard around 1775 'of the bad company in which they are confined' at the Marshalsea.[26]

Prostitutes were perhaps all too prone to run into debt. A few years later a 'Miss Meredith', a prostitute lodging 'in the neighbourhood of Fitzroy-square' and paying an exorbitant rent of £2 12s 6d a week for the privilege, owed money probably to her landlord. She was arrested and confined in the Marshalsea, but she compounded with her creditor and was released on signing a bill for £20 under onerous weekly payment terms she didn't meet. Sued in the King's Bench in May 1809 for the money, she was defended by the famous William Garrow on the grounds that 'the original contract of debt was vicious'. The court found against her and she may well have landed in the King's Bench prison as a consequence.[27]

Getting money while in the Marshalsea was a preoccupation for everyone individually but also collectively. The necessity was announced baldly from the outset. New prisoners, still dazed from their grim procession in a bailiff's custody through the prison's gates, would find themselves asked in the lodge for money for a bed or directed to the miserable common side. In room or ward, their first meeting with fellow prisoners involved an immediate demand for money too. In late 1742 Laetitia Pilkington was taken from the lodge 'into a Room, where a Parcel of Wretches seized me, and sung a long Song about Garnish, and were going to pull my Clothes off' because she had no money about her. They relented when she was recognised and 'were kind enough to take my Word for some Drink', much like John Grano's experience fourteen years or so before. Had they not done so her clothes would have been taken and pawned, as happened, we might recall, to common-side debtors in Acton's gaol. In 1737 the papers reported that two men were sent from the Marshalsea to the Surrey county gaol nearby to await trial for robbing a fellow prisoner 'of his Money and Clothes, under Pretence that he refus'd paying his Garnish. To strip a Man in any Prison for his Garnish is a capital Offence', and it was true enough that four men had been sentenced to death at the Old Bailey some seven years earlier for a similar offence at the new prison, Clerkenwell. We do not know how much Pilkington had to pay for garnish but John Howard in the 1780s noted it as 1s 4d and said it was formally known as 'ward-dues for coals, &c.', perhaps to circumvent the strictures of the law.[28]

This collective extraction of garnish was one element in the prisoner-management of the Marshalsea. Allowed within wide limits by the keeper and the turnkeys, a debtor democracy established itself. It developed rules and hierarchies – we have already met the constables and elders – punishments for transgressors and rewards for the favoured, and we shall see the system perfected and codified in later years.

Democracy could, however, turn swiftly to tyranny. No issue was more vexed on the common side than the distribution of charity money. We have already witnessed the difficulties of collecting it and bringing it into the gaol in the first place. Acton had done away with the prisoners' own arrangements for distribution and pocketed for himself the money that should have come to the poor side. Complaints of defalcation by those charged with collecting legacies and county money survived Acton and we might remember the efforts of the ward constables in 1735 to secure for the prisoners all the money due to them. But getting the money in was one thing, sharing it among all those who needed it was another. The common side was riven by jealousies and suspicions. Prisoners suspected of misrepresenting their poverty and falsely swearing they were worth less than forty shillings were enquired into by the common side's friends outside the gaol, unsurprisingly because every mouth fed from charity diminished what was left for everyone else. Thomas Chapman, poor-side steward, wrote around 1810, probably to the clerk of the Marshalsea and Palace courts, that 'it is the opinion of us all that James Dyer & James Godbur is not proper object to take the benefits of the Poor Side James Dyer rents the House his familys lives in and his own furniture, and James Godbur has his own furniture'.[29]

Sometimes the steward himself was mistrusted. Four common-side debtors petitioned the prothonotary of the courts in January 1808 to remove the steward, one Coleman, and two others, Wright and Morgan, who were his favourites. 'Monthly on the Poor side a Steward should be Chosen the said Coleman has for sometime contrived to continue himself in that Office by standing Proxy for Others'. Wright had come into £100 and so should never have been accepted on the common side, but got round Coleman by treating him; 'Morgan is imploy at the Tap And has plenty of Victuals and drink', yet Coleman favoured him when doling out the poor-side provisions. By contrast, two new poor debtors 'have not receivd any Money from the Charity and have not had any Meat for three weeks at a time'. These two were among the four prisoners signing the petition.[30]

Violence was not far beneath the surface of arrangements like these and the disputes they fomented. Debtor power – like power in the living world – could be underpinned by brutality, as in the collection of garnish by violent means. Fights too could erupt at any time, as Grano discovered. In September 1738 a quarrel leading to a fist fight left one man, a butcher, 'dead of the Bruises he received'. The coroner's jury brought in a verdict of accidental death. We don't know what led to that dispute, but certainly sharing out charity money and victuals could provoke blows as well as petitions.[31]

On 2 November 1762 William Dove swore an information on oath to the Surrey magistrates against William Weymouth, a fellow prisoner in the Marshalsea. About 8 that same morning he went to Weymouth's room to complain he had not received his share of charity money distributed the day before. They quarrelled and, Dove swore, Weymouth 'Assaulted and Struck' him. During the row Weymouth's wife 'cryed out Murder' and their son shouted, '"Father knock him down"'. Weymouth then 'took up a Hammer and knocked this Informant's Right Eye quit out'. Had not two soldiers on duty at the prison to guard the French prisoners intervened to protect him, Dove 'believes the said William Weymouth would have Murdered him'.[32]

As William Acton knew, violence could also be turned against the gaolers. It might flare up at any time. There was resistance to locking up one night in August 1734, the hot nights always a terrible oppression for the common-side wards, creating 'a great Disturbance amongst the Debtors', when John Williams, a turnkey, was 'stabbed several Inches in the Groin, by Mr. Hume, a Scotch Gentleman'. Eight years later, also in August, 'an extraordinary Insurrection' led to prisoners breaking up 'the Furniture of the best Apartments'; four prisoners were committed to Southwark new gaol, 'there appearing some Circumstances not a little heinous in the

Conspiracy', though whether against other prisoners or the gaolers is unknown. One object of debtors' resentments in September 1749, however, seems to have concerned the management of the tap. The debtors at that time were said to be 'very numerous' and many were involved in a mutiny that lasted from Saturday night into Sunday morning: doors were broken down, the lives of Jane Nailor the tap-keeper and of several others were threatened, and a guard watched all night to prevent the Marshalsea gates from being forced.[33]

Then in the mid-1760s there was a prolonged period of unrest, culminating in a serious riot. It had many overtones of the Acton years and developed once more from arrangements when farming the gaol for profit. In 1765 John Marson, the deputy marshal, leased the Marshalsea to Thomas Shaw, making him the deputy keeper in daily charge of the prison in return for fees and rents. It seems that Marson had made an error of judgement in choosing Shaw as his deputy. There were quickly complaints against him, including misappropriation of the charity money and an inadequate supply of bedding for prisoners on the master's side. Marson tried to dislodge Shaw from his post, but Shaw refused to relinquish the lease and appointed his own man as clerk of the papers and another, John Hough, as head turnkey. In the latter, at least, Shaw too made the wrong choice, for by all accounts Hough proved a humane and considerate gaoler. In May 1766 we hear of an assault on Shaw by a prisoner, who was committed to the Surrey new gaol; and in February 1767 there was a 'mutiny' when prisoners pulled down a new wall that had been built 'for the greater convenience and security' of the gaol but which had incommoded the prisoners in some way. Perhaps it had something to do with a new entrance to the gaol that Shaw was determined to open into King Street, about which there were prisoner protests at the same time, though it went ahead nonetheless.[34]

Things came to a head in the August of 1768. It was known to the prisoners that the governors of the gaol were sundered in civil strife, the unpopular and rapacious Shaw against Marson, the deputy marshal, allied with Hough the chief turnkey. The spark was struck by Hough. He released some poor prisoners who had been detained only for their fees on the promise they would pay when they were back in the living world. This was on the face of it an extraordinary thing to do, in part because who could trust an imprisoned debtor to pay his debts, and not least because the fees belonged to Shaw by virtue of his lease. When the Black Book came to be balanced on the next Saturday night Hough explained that if the fees were not paid in the next week he would reimburse them himself, by instalments. But the vindictive Shaw had Hough arrested for the debt on a Borough writ and he was only released from the bailiff's custody through the intervention of Marson. Hough promptly returned to the Marshalsea and made mischief by telling some prisoners what had taken place. That night 'several Prisoners assembled together, and in the Heat of Liquor and Resentment, broke several Windows in Mr Shaw's House, and did some other Damage'. It was said that Hough and Marson remonstrated with the prisoners to calm things down, but next day some prisoners set fire to waste timber collected in the gaol in an incident that remains obscure. It was, though, a terribly risky thing to do in a gaol as old and cramped as the Marshalsea. It is impossible to fathom Hough's and Marson's motives here but if they wished to provoke the prison to rise against Shaw they achieved their purpose. No one could have foreseen the consequences.

Fearing a recurrence of the previous night's violence, Shaw and his son Michael summoned friends to the Marshalsea in their aid. They brought with them firearms – two pistols and a blunderbuss that they loaded 'with Shot and broken Glass Bottles'. At 10.30 at night, order having broken down, the prisoners were 'drinking and sitting in the Yard' when a brick and some bottles were thrown at them from Shaw's house. Whether it was now or later that the prisoners responded in kind with bricks and stones is not clear, but soon there was firing from Shaw's windows, gunshots wounding eight prisoners, two seriously. One, 'shot in the belly', was reportedly at the point of death, but his fate is unknown. In the melee the more daring of the prisoners, or 'the most horrible and abandoned Fellows', as they were described, broke free from the gaol and clustered in the narrow passage leading from Borough High Street to the gate, 'threatening Death and Destruction to all who should approach it'. Though some gave themselves up, others stayed out: an arrest warrant against Robert Runyon for his part in breaking through the doors of the Marshalsea court with an axe was issued to all constables metropolis-wide by the Surrey justices in January 1769.[35]

Others absconded too. It soon became clear that Shaw's crew had been the aggressors. An order in council in September 1768 called on the persons guilty 'of wilfully shooting at divers other Persons with Fire Arms, within the Marshalsea Prison' to surrender themselves within forty days to answer the charges against them. They did not appear. In December, Thomas and Michael Shaw and three others were all outlawed, their estates forfeited to the crown.[36]

Marson continued as deputy marshal until his death in August 1778. He was probably more careful in that last decade in his choice of farmers, but 'Substitutes' he continued to have. Marson did not live to see the next great drama in the Marshalsea's violent history. This time the trouble was brewed in the living world and not in the gaol.[37]

The Gordon Riots were a momentary civil war that set London ablaze and Londoners trembling for seven days in June 1780. It had not blown up overnight. For some time there had been a campaign to repeal an act, passed two years before, that gave some rights to Roman Catholics to follow their religion within the law. It culminated in a petition assembled by the Protestant Association, formed to pursue the campaign, and containing tens of thousands of signatures, that was to be delivered to the House of Commons on 2 June. A great demonstration was convened to celebrate the occasion and accompany the sacred document on its journey. Four 'Divisions', from London, Westminster, Southwark and one declaring itself 'Scotch', assembled wearing blue cockades in their hats, flying colours and moving to the beat of the drum, on St George's Fields, a mile or less across Borough High Street from the Marshalsea. Some 50,000 or more marchers approached Parliament over the three bridges, the largest column making its way over London Bridge through the City. They converged in riotous tumult in Palace Yard. Peers and commoners were assailed, injured and put in fear of their lives. That night crowds attacked and burned mass-houses, including those in the houses of Catholic emissaries from foreign courts. Desultory attacks, firing and pillage of prominent Catholics' property continued over the weekend and into Monday.[38]

On that day, 5 June, a change of mood was discernible among the rioters. Those arrested in the troubles of Friday and over the weekend began to be processed through the courts and remanded to the gaols of the City and the northern suburbs. Soldiers escorting them to Newgate and elsewhere were hissed; the house of a justice zealous in apprehending rioters was wrecked in Clare Street, Holborn. This mood altered decisively on Tuesday 6 June. What had begun as an anti-Catholic agitation, provoked and organised by the Protestant Association, a body of the middling sort of people but attaching to it a disorderly fringe looking for trouble and the chance of spoil, turned into a general uprising of the London poor. The rioters' primary target was now not so much the institutions of Catholic London or the homes and businesses of Catholics and their supporters, though cries of 'No Popery' were frequently heard and such attacks continued to be made. Instead the fury of this crowd turned itself most of all against the institutions of justice, cruellest symbols of class oppression in eighteenth-century London. Most prominent among them, most loathed and most feared, were the London prisons.

That night Newgate, a brand-new gaol, was broken into and fired, its interior destroyed. The prisoners were brought out in triumph, some from the condemned cells still in their chains. Prisoners were freed from the Clerkenwell new gaol and the Clerkenwell Bridewell for petty offenders and vagrants: those gaols too would have been burned, but the rioters were said to be reluctant to risk the poor homes that clustered narrowly around. Overnight the keepers of the Fleet prison, in the north of the City, were forced to open the gates and preparations were made to fire it, but the debtors – some of them 'in for life', as the papers had it – begged for time to remove their belongings and were permitted to do so. That same night, the rioters called on the citizens to light up their windows in celebration of Newgate's destruction. Among the drinkers at the Bell public house, St James's Market, Thomas Haycock, a tavern waiter by calling, boasted how he'd been active in breaking and firing the gaol: 'I asked him what could induce him to do all this? He said *the cause*. I said, do you mean a religious cause? He said no; *for he was of no religion*. He said, *there should not be a prison standing on the morrow in London.*'[39]

Next day, 7 June, 'Black Wednesday' as it would be known for many years, saw London burning, it seemed, from end to end. Amidst much violence the prisons again were specially selected for destruction. The Fleet was now put to the torch. And south of the river, where the Gordon Riots had truly begun, the rioters wreaked great destruction. The King's Bench prison, on its new site in St George's Fields, was burned and 'totally destroyed'; the ancient Borough Clink near the south bank was burned to the ground, and so was Southwark Bridewell in Tooley Street; the prisoners were released from all these and from the new gaol close to St George the Martyr, the keepers opening the gates without a struggle. Next morning at dawn 'the new Watch-house near St. George's-church' was pulled down and set alight, and the same was done to the local lock-up or 'roundhouse' opposite the entrance to Kent Street.

Around 11 o'clock that morning, Thursday 8 June, the rioters, 'a great number of people', turned their attention to the Marshalsea. They 'began to pull it down; but before they could set fire to it a military force arrived, and prevented their effecting their purpose. It is said that near 30 persons were killed on this occasion.' This is the fullest report we have, but it is clear that before the soldiers arrived the gates were forced or opened by the turnkeys and that many prisoners made their escape. At least forty-three got out, including two women. One escapee, Edward Ryley, had been in the Marshalsea more than two years and five others for over a year. Steps were quickly taken to indemnify the keepers of civil and other prisons from claims by creditors whose debtors had flown in the general chaos and an amnesty was granted to all prisoners who surrendered themselves by 1 September 1780. Of forty-two Marshalsea escapees for whom we have records, all but ten surrendered in time, including Ryley and both women. The gaol was repaired and once more receiving prisoners in the usual way by the last week in July.[40]

The great escape of 1780 and the impromptu gaol delivery of August 1768 were the most dramatic break-outs from the Marshalsea in modern times, but throughout the eighteenth century its half-derelict condition made it but a leaky receptacle at best. We have seen something of Acton's troubles with escapes, propping up the walls of his gaol with terror to deter future attempts, although it seems certain that a harsh regime was itself productive of prison-breaks. In 1766, for instance, under Thomas Shaw's flint-skinning rule, no fewer than six escaped prisoners were reported in the papers. Two absconded together in February, one an odd-job man from Whitechapel, the other a pipe-maker; Shaw advertised a reward of two guineas each for their return. An army officer imprisoned for debt somehow broke through a wall and got out in July. And three went together in November, a jobbing smith originally from Chatham and two publicans, one from Westminster and the other from Goswell Street (as it then was), north of the City; one of the vintners was worth three guineas to Shaw, the others just a guinea each.[41]

Under draconian management no doubt all sorts of prisoners were tempted to risk an escape, but in normal times it was probably the most desperate and dangerous men having little to lose who forced or tricked their way out of the Marshalsea. One case coming to a climax in 1739 stands out. William Udall was the son of a distiller from a respectable family, brought up in Clerkenwell and bred a watchmaker. But his constancy was undermined by being 'addicted to gaming, drinking and other Vices'. Needing more money than he could earn as an apprentice, he proved dishonest before he was out of his indentures and became a seasoned thief, trickster, even highwayman for a time. Involved in numerous street robberies, he was caught at least twice but managed to save his own skin by turning king's evidence against his accomplices. Udall had become indebted to a thief-taker but was unable to satisfy a bill when due. Arrested, he was taken to the Marshalsea owing £8 for the debt and costs. There, with Thomas Mann, another debtor equally desperate, Udall engineered their escape. A friend of Mann brought in 'a Spring Saw, a Key Hole Saw, and some Gimblets, and I began to *mill it away* at the Chapel, from whence I broke into [an] adjoining Room, and from thence into a Closet, where I cut the Window Bar, and took off the Casement'. Mrs Mann smuggled in a rope and the two men let themselves into a passage or yard adjacent to the gaol around 9 o'clock, 'rather too early in the Evening', for they were disturbed by someone coming out of a house who 'would have stopped us, but *Mann* swore bitterly if he made any Noise he would kill him, which made him quiet'. Soon after escaping they agreed to go 'on the Road'. They borrowed money for horses and robbed coaches and wagons, and they worked as footpads, in these ways roaming over the roads about London near Edmonton, Brentwood, Stratford, Epping Forest and Holloway. Udall was eventually taken by Marshalsea officers or turnkeys with the aid of thief-takers. Mann, in a reversal of fortune for Udall, turned evidence against him. William Udall, just twenty-two, was hanged in early 1739. Other criminal connections were probably never lacking in the Marshalsea. Later that same year, a husband and wife who had committed a robbery at a house in Long Lane, Southwark, fled to the Marshalsea, where they were taken in by a prisoner; they were eventually discovered there by the victim a week later.[42]

Debtors were not usually desperadoes, though some were; but there was another class of prisoner, in the Marshalsea's Admiralty buildings, who were constitutionally reckless men. Pirates captured on the high seas were brought here throughout the eighteenth century. The Gaols Committee in 1729 had complained of 'Pyrates', 'generally a very desperate and abandoned Sort of People', mixing with the common-side debtors and tempting them to lawless living. Two pirates and a debtor broke out of the gaol together early on a September morning in 1744, for instance, and an American mariner charged with piracy and murder escaped in November 1775 with an eighteen-pound shackle still pinioned to his right leg; two pirate captains also got out in 1783.[43]

Desperate or otherwise, escapees seem to have been treated with respect for their cavalier courage by fellow prisoners. Richard Spencer, a resident of King Street, the through-road to Bermondsey that replaced Ax and Bottle Yard to the north of the gaol sometime after the middle of the century, was surprised in his back yard one Saturday night in December 1778 by John Phillips, who was making his escape from the Marshalsea. Spencer went round to the gate and told the turnkeys what he had seen. Next morning, in daylight, he found the place through or over which Phillips had made his exit and again went to the lodge to acquaint the keepers with his discovery. His public-spiritedness or busybody inter-ference, depending on one's point of view, caused resentment among some of the prisoners whom Phillips had left behind; perhaps a few were contemplating a similar route to freedom. As Spencer

> was coming out of the said prison he was seized in the Lodge or Lobby thereof by several persons whose names he has been informed are Thomas fforester John Quarterman John Johnson Cornelius Cassidy John Haytor and several others and dragged into the said prison under a pump, when Johnson and several others pumpt upon for the space of one Minute and upwards in total defiance and inspite of the assistance of James Nowell and Alexander Stanhope two people belonging to the prison in care of the said prison And lastly that the said Thomas fforester struck this Informant several violent blows upon different parts of his body and particularly one under the Ribbs of his left side.[44]

By the 1790s the Marshalsea was becoming so insecure that escapes grew probably even more common. A reward of 100 guineas, a great sum, was offered in January 1797 for the capture of Walter Marsh:

about 35 years old, about 5 feet 7 inches high, dark brown hair, which he wore tied, rather a sallow complexion, what is called a Roman nose, long visage, long chin, with the upper jaw projecting particularly when speaking; had on a dark pepper and salt coloured coat, and nankeen waistcoat and breeches; has been much on the recruiting service at Birmingham (of which place he is a native) and also in London; is well known at Charing Cross and St. George's Fields, and has rather a smart appearance.

Two others who escaped with him, a jeweller and carpenter by trade, were valued at only five guineas each. And in January 1800 two more pirates broke out 'by making a hole through the wall of their room'.[45]

There were other ways out of the Marshalsea, even less palatable than the consequences of punishment, fines and yet more debt incurred by the recaptured debtor. Deaths at the Marshalsea went generally unremarked in the public record, inquest juries in any event rarely recording any verdict other than 'died by the visitation of God'. A very occasional case of prisoners dying 'for want' reached the papers, including in 1799 a ninety-four-year-old imprisoned for £4. One case, though, did arouse great disquiet. An inquest on Thomas Culver in January 1811 concluded that he 'Died for want, &c.' Culver's death was raised in the House of Lords by Lord Holland some six weeks later. He said that Culver had no bed or clothing, slept in a room with no windows – perhaps the strong room – and had been 'reduced even to gnaw the bones which were thrown into the yard'. The coroner's jury had reportedly first wished to bring in a verdict of death by starvation, but finally decided it was through 'want of food and clothing, and of proper attention in his illness'. Holland's intervention provoked much comment and was trumpeted by that growing number who wished to see imprisonment for debt reformed, or abolished altogether. There followed an inquiry by the House of Lords into Culver's death which led to publication of the witness evidence at the inquest. This showed in fact that Culver had suffered from a debilitating bowel disorder, or 'dysentery', and that he had wasted away as a consequence. William Jenkins, the keeper, was exonerated of maltreatment or neglect, Culver receiving treatment from the Marshalsea's surgeon, Mr Phillips, who attended to sick prisoners.[46]

Some debtors, though, could not wait for a release to overtake them. Suicide was one way out of the debtor's despair and out of the Marshalsea's miseries. We hear of prisoners cutting their throats in the gaol in 1739, 1764 and 1792, the last an 'unfortunate young woman, of respectable parents, about 19 years of age'; she was imprisoned with her lover, a 'young gentleman', who received a probably fatal wound to his abdomen in trying to wrest the knife from her. And we hear of a 'Poor Man, a prisoner in the Marshalsea', who hanged himself there in December 1748, and of Anne Elliot, who tried around 1740 to hang herself while a debtor in the gaol 'but was cut down by one of the Turnkeys'; she was only 'reserv'd for a more publick Death', hanged two years later at Tyburn for burglary and robbery. Nor did a debtor's desolation end at the prison gate:

> One James Davis, a Barber, who from his genteel Appearance was known by the Title of Jemmy the King's Barber, lately discharged from the Marshalsea Prison in a miserable manner, where he had been confin'd for Debt, and was after taken into a Parish Workhouse; but having absented himself from thence wander'd about in a starving Condition 'till Monday in the Afternoon, when he went up three Pair of Stairs high, in one of the common Stair-Cases in Fig-Tree Court in the Temple, and threw himself from the Window upon the Pavement in the Court, and was kill'd.[47]

A few debtors were driven to other desperate stratagems to escape the Marshalsea and their burdens. Jacob Stone, a prisoner there in 1752, was accused of forging his dead father's will to his benefit, but the prosecution came to nothing when no evidence appeared against him at the Old Bailey. However, the case of a Marshalsea prisoner forging a bill of exchange to release himself from gaol had been proved some three years before. Thomas Jones, twenty-eight years old, was from Cheshire and apprenticed to a draper in Manchester before going to sea as a clerk in the navy. Discharged at the end of the War of the Austrian Succession, he contracted board and lodging debts in London of £14, though he may have owed more elsewhere. He was arrested and committed to the Marshalsea, where, 'having in a great Measure disobliged my Friends by my former Extravagancies', he lay for over three months 'without the least Support imaginable . . . Not one Friend, or Relation came near me . . . nor had I one Farthing in my Pocket; so that all the Support I really had for that Time was given me by . . . my fellow Prisoners.' He devised an elaborate scheme for defrauding a City bank of £300 on the pretended acceptance of a bill by Sir Watkin Williams Wynn, one of the richest commoners in the land. The forgery was spotted at its first outing and Jones paid for his foolhardy enterprise with his life.[48]

Jones had been abandoned, but for those with wealthy friends there was a quick and painless though costly way out of the Marshalsea. Of the three great debtors' prisons of London the Marshalsea was of the lowest caste. Most who had the capacity to do so would take their chance to move up to the Fleet or, if they could afford it, to the King's Bench. Both those gaols, as we have seen, were considered more comfortable and brought with them the benefit of being able to move out of the prison and take lodgings within the rules in the streets around, with relative freedom of movement and less of the gaol taint. The Marshalsea had none of this. And it was tarnished by the jurisdiction of the Marshalsea and Palace courts bringing in debtors for small sums. Those with access to money – their own or, as it was more likely to be, their friends' – could change gaols by applying for a writ of habeas corpus. It could happen very quickly, within a day or so; some, their feet hardly disturbing the Marshalsea dust, removed themselves on the very day they were brought in. The costs of doing so varied, but Marshalsea prison and court fees generally totalled between 24s and 31s 6d (or a guinea and a half), payable to the keeper in the lodge. Legal expenses would be in addition and further costs were due when the receiving gaol was entered. Even so, despite these burdens, of 308 debtors coming through the lodge between 1 January and 24 December 1811, forty-five were discharged by habeas corpus, twelve to the Fleet and thirty-three to the King's Bench. We have no figures for earlier years, but there is little reason to believe that the proportions differed greatly over time, and nor would they for some years to come. In this way, Hannah Glasse, the famous cookery writer, removed herself from the Marshalsea to the Fleet after a fortnight in the summer of 1757, for instance; and Christopher Smart the poet, after 'a fortnight at a spunging house, one week at the Marshalsea in the want of all things', was helped by his friend Charles Burney to the kinder King's Bench in April 1770.[49]

Other ways of getting a discharge from the Marshalsea took longer, or generally did so. Four out of ten debtors imprisoned there during 1811 made some accommodation with their arresting creditors and were released accordingly, some recognition of the effectiveness of proceeding to impris-onment from the creditor's point of view, and recognition too of the shock the Marshalsea no doubt made on the debtor's system, on first acquaintance with the gaol at least. Some 126 of the debtors coming in during 1811 were released this way, forty of them within a week, all inside six months. Indeed, if a debtor made no acceptable proposals within three months it was unlikely that the creditor would recover much if anything of the debt originally pursued. Of the rest, in this year, fourteen debtors became supersedable because creditors failed to issue a writ of execution in the allotted time, the arrest having been on mesne process without the debt having been proved; most of these prisoners remained in gaol between three and six months. Twenty-six were then released because their creditors had failed to maintain them with an allowance of 6d a day once the debt had been established in court. One debtor was freed this year from the Marshalsea because his creditor, by accident or subterfuge, had substituted a foreign coin which at first glance passed for a sixpence; it was an irregularity that the court ruled vitiated the creditor's claim, the law holding perils for all parties to an action. Discharges of this kind under the Lords Act of 1759, as later amended, took longer to work their way through the system, generally from two months to a year, depending on the creditor's patience and the debtor's capacity to take advantage of a default: in the latter case the Marshalsea gaolers gave every assistance in applying for a debtor's release once the sixpences (formerly groats) ceased.[50]

In 1811 a further sixteen debtors were discharged by resorting to a general settlement with all outstanding creditors, not just the person who had arrested them or who had brought further charges while they were in gaol. From time to time Insolvent Debtors Acts allowed prisoners to regain their freedom while keeping personal property to the value of £10 and releasing everything else to their creditors. The acts were time-limited, giving a deadline by which proceedings had to begin, and debtors had to advertise their intention to take the benefit of an act by publishing three notices in the London Gazette so that creditors could lodge a claim.

The process was overseen by the insolvency court and usually involved multiple appearances there until creditors were satisfied and debtors disencumbered. Creditors could also oppose the release of an imprisoned debtor and if successful had then to pay maintenance of 6d a day. Insolvency became an increasingly popular route out of gaol in the early nineteenth century; in 1816, for instance, when 359 debtors were committed to the Marshalsea, ninety, or one in four, were released in this way. Both Joseph Boardman Orme (1801) and Thomas Prattent (1804) were released through the insolvency route.[51]

The prospect of a new Insolvent Debtors Act always caused intense excitement in the Marshalsea, as in all debtors' prisons throughout the land. It began with drawing up a petition to pray for parliamentary intervention, the prisoners calling on their most fluent wordsmiths to express their collective desire, even though the form of these petitions was less inspiration than tradition. It didn't seem that way, however, to Laetitia Pilkington, who turned her hand to one in 1742: 'I may praise God that I was under him, the happy Instrument of Good to Numbers of my wretched Fellow-creatures, since by one pathetic Memorial I wrote for them, the sorrowful Sighing of the Prisoners reached the Hearts of the Legislative Powers, and obtained an Act of Grace for them.' In fact, petitions on the same lines had already reached Parliament from the Fleet and King's Bench. Those debtors from the Marshalsea advertising their intention to take the benefit of this act ran the full range of prisoners' occupations, from 'gentleman' and widows, through artisans like 'Sive-maker', cutler, watchmaker, jeweller, turner and weaver, to an apothecary, licensed victuallers and a 'Dealer and Chapwoman', though Laetitia herself had been already discharged by her friends compounding with her creditor. These acts were also the opportunity for 'Fugitives for Debt, and beyond the Seas' to come forward and surrender themselves to the keeper of the gaol in order to declare themselves insolvent in court; these were debtors who had escaped their creditors by jumping bail or in some other way, often fleeing abroad.[52]

Once an act was passed it became a cause for celebration in the Marshalsea. In May 1778 the whole prison was said to have 'dined together on tables spread all over the ground, on account of the Insolvent Debtors Act. They had an elegant dinner, with a band of music playing the whole time; after which many loyal toasts were drank. For one day, the whole prison seemed to have forgot distress, and every heart was elated upon the occasion.' There was also no doubt a celebration or two on the road to the Surrey quarter sessions at Guildford, Kingston or Reigate – sixty-seven Marshalsea prisoners travelling to the last in May 1761, for instance. These were collective moments of joy, seen by all or most as a moral victory over the whole clan of vindictive imprisoning creditors.[53]

Occasionally there also arose an opportunity for stalwart debtors of limited means – not many of these in the Marshalsea after a month or so of imprisonment, one imagines – to obtain a release courtesy of the government. In 1778, for instance, during the American Revolutionary War, a recruiting officer visited the debtors' gaols of London 'offering to release all those prisoners whose debts amount to less than ten pounds', provided that they joined 'his Majesty's service either by sea or land'.[54]

Far more useful to the debtors, though, were those philanthropists – dead or living – who devoted their resources to freeing the poorest debtors from their imprisonment. Some of these were occasional bounties. In 1735 'about twenty Debtors' were discharged by an Islington attorney and a clergyman acting under 'a Private Charity from an unknown Hand'; they 'paid not only their Fees and the Debts they were confin'd for, but compounded all their other Debts'.

The following year Samuel Wright, a rich nonconformist from Newington, Southwark, left numerous valuable legacies including £300 to prisoners in the Marshalsea to be distributed to deserving debtors: fifty-three were released whose debts amounted to £108 in all. The Rev. Mr Canham, curate of St Dunstan in the East, among numerous other benefactions, travelled to the Marshalsea to set twelve debtors free in 1751 – it cost him £15. Similarly the Christmas jury for Westminster in 1756 clubbed together to release 'several' poor debtors from the Marshalsea and elsewhere. Publicity for the benevolent was frequently not unwelcome to them: 'if anyone enquires for me', says Dr Cantwell in Isaac Bickerstaffe's *The Hypocrite* of 1769, 'say I am gone to Newgate, and the Marshalsea, to distribute alms'. But individual philanthropists might also assist privately, where a sad and deserving case was brought to their attention. John Wesley found there in 1768 'a Dutchman, a chemist by profession', who had been arrested at his landlord's suit, a countryman of his; the man spoke no English and had 'a wife near her time'. A wealthy supporter of Wesley sent £15, which both set the Dutchman free and helped put him in a way to get his living. That must have been one of many similar interventions over the years.[55]

There were also at least two enduring legacies directed to releasing prisoners year after year who could be freed for small sums of money. Mrs Frances Ashton's legacy in a will of 1727 only obtained probate in 1809 and freed a few Marshalsea prisoners who could compound for debts and fees totalling £5 or less. Similarly, Dr Pelling's charity, a modest £9 per annum, was freeing a handful of prisoners most years, certainly from 1812, when records become available; six were freed, the money laid out by the keeper, William Jenkins. Of greater significance to the prisoners was Henry Allnutt's legacy, generally known as the Oxford Charity. Henry Allnutt, his surname variously spelled, died in 1724.

He had been a Middle Temple barrister and spent some time imprisoned in the Marshalsea, possibly because of a religious or political infraction, possibly because he was then in debt. During his time in gaol or after, he inherited a huge family fortune. Allnutt demised various Oxfordshire estates, notably one at Goring, for charitable purposes, including a grant of £100 a year to release poor debtors from the Marshalsea. That sum appears to have been dutifully paid each year, reaping substantial benefit – some forty to fifty debtors were released most years in this way.[56]

There was then, from 1772, a most useful addition to the debtor's armoury. The mid-century wave of philanthropic sentiment in London that built hospitals, orphanages and refuges for foundlings and prostitutes, and helped rescue homeless boys from the streets, now embraced the plight of those imprisoned for small debts to the cost of their families and of society at large. In February 1772 a sermon was preached on this theme at the Charlotte Chapel in Pimlico and then, influentially, by Dr William Dodd at the prosperous Bedford Chapel in Bloomsbury. Dodd, the so-called 'Macaroni Parson' after his ultra-fashionable dress and deportment, would himself fall precipitately on the slippery slope of extravagant living, unmanageable debts and forgery, suffering for his sins at the rope's end just five years later. But he was an emotional and effective preacher and the Bloomsbury collection brought in over £80 from a crowded congregation. Out of the interest this bred emerged the Society for the Discharge and Relief of Persons Imprisoned for Small Debts throughout England, more conveniently remembered as the Thatched House Society after the fashionable tavern in St James's Street where a committee was formed to take forward the project two months after the sermons. The Bedford Chapel collection freed some thirty-four debtors and that success brought in more funds to set up a charity on a permanent basis. The society was formally established in

May 1773. Its practical driving force was James Neild, a Cheshire-born Quaker and a prosperous London jeweller with premises close to the Thatched House itself. Neild had visited a fellow apprentice in the King's Bench in the 1760s and the experience led him to a lifetime of penal reform, especially of the laws of imprisonment for debt. He was the society's treasurer until his death in 1814. By then he had adopted the mantle of John Howard, surveying the state of the gaols throughout Great Britain and reporting comprehensively on their condition.[57]

The society was exceptional in rousing the charitable instincts of all sorts and conditions of Londoner, although the aristocracy and judiciary were especially well represented on the committee. No one was untouched by the draconian effects of imprisonment for debt and thousands gave what they could afford, gifts and subscriptions duly published in the society's reports. Some made very substantial donations anonymously, like 'D.D. by Mr. Nelme', £200; the elite of the nation gave annually (the Duke and Duchess of Devonshire each subscribing ten guineas); the clubs made impromptu collections ('The Old Club at Le Tellieurs, in Half Moon Street, Piccadilly', £22 1s, or the 'Scavoir Vivre Club', £52 10s); citizens gave princely sums ('A London Tradesman's one Year's Profit', £385 5s); the raffish shelled out when cash was to hand ('A. the Overplus of a Tavern reckoning', 12s 9d, for instance, or 'A Wager concerning the fate of Mr. Wilkes's Election to the Mayoralty, intended to have been spent at a Tavern', £3 13s 6d); wage earners gave what they could ('A Collection by Servants in a Family', £4 8s); and anonymous sums from odd shillings to ten guineas were posted daily through the society's letter box when it moved to an office in Craven Street, Strand. Occasionally a benefactor specified a favoured prison ('Mr. Bowles for the Marshalsea', £148 2s 3d), but this was rare, imprisoned debtors everywhere the object of pity. Indeed, it is likely that some donations that previously might have gone to the Marshalsea now found their way into the coffers of the Thatched House Society for the greater good.[58]

On the other hand, the Marshalsea derived great benefit from the society's work. In 1787–8, for instance, 766 debtors nationwide were released at a cost of just £2 18s for each prisoner; sixty-eight of them were freed from the Marshalsea. We have no comprehensive numbers but in 1789–90 there were sixty-seven, in 1795–6 just four out of 481 and in 1801–2 thirty-three. Over the years from 1773 it seems likely that the Thatched House Society was as effective as the Oxford Charity in helping debtors gain their freedom from the Marshalsea prison.[59]

With all these various legitimate means of securing their freedom, how long did prisoners stay in the Marshalsea after being brought into custody? We have no way of knowing before 1811, because the lodge's earlier day books of commitments and discharges have not survived. But of 239 debtors entering and leaving the gaol between 1 January and 24 December 1811, 128 left inside a month, generally either by writ of habeas corpus or by settling promptly with their creditors; a further seventy-nine were released within three months, so 87 per cent stayed no longer than a quarter of a year. Forty-one were released after three months, thirty-three of them within six months of their confinement. The numbers released after six months were very small, just eight. These figures exclude all those in the gaol on 31 December 1810 and discharged during the coming year; and those brought in during the year and still there on 25 December. An analysis of the day book for 1816 shows a broadly similar picture, though with a marked reduction in the proportion released within three months to 70 per cent, probably because large numbers waited for an Insolvent Debtors Act to come on to the statute book later that year.[60]

These figures understate the numbers staying a longer time in the gaol, but the general picture that this was a highly mobile prisoner population seems true enough. 'There is a constant fluctuation in the Marshalsea', reported Dr William Smith in 1776; 'most of the prisoners are confined for small sums, and seldom remain long.' We should note, however, that some prisoners were back in the gaol soon after release, at the suit of another creditor, and that this was a feature of the Marshalsea and no doubt other debtors' prisons, as we shall see. And some prisoners stuck: a spell in the Marshalsea of longer than a year was unusual but by no means rare. Thomas Prattent was one, and so were the 'Foreign Person of Quality', William-George Jones, Edward Ryley the Gordon Riots escaper and numerous others who have found a place in this chapter. Dr Smith himself claimed for the Marshalsea that 'one prisoner has been eighteen years in gaol'. If true, that was likely to have been a voluntary prisoner who could have taken steps to free himself if desired; we do not know the name of this real-life 'Father of the Marshalsea'.[61]

By 1811 little of substance had changed in the Marshalsea despite the shocking revelations of the Gaols Committee some eighty years before. The brutality of the Acton years, and probably the years before him too, did not return. Yet the system that had permitted him to flourish was unaltered, and prisoners were always vulnerable to the consequences of a grasping deputy keeper installed as farmer of the gaol. Shaw, it seems, was no Acton and the prisoners' collective resistance to his depredations proved successful if bloody. Yet even in small things the Gaols Committee had not been able to affect much in the daily life of the prison. The collection of charity money from legacies and county money proved always problematic and the turnover of prisoners meant that new inmates were frequently unclear just what should be coming to the common side. The committee had criticised the absence of a list of bequests publicly displayed in the gaol, but John Howard found none still when he published his second report on the state of the prisons in 1784, and nor was one put up as a result. By the Health of Prisoners Act 1774, a reform spawned by Howard's revelations, ward and room walls were to be scraped and whitewashed annually, sickrooms were to be provided separately for men and women, a surgeon or apothecary was to attend the sick, and warm and cold baths of some description were to be installed. But baths were never provided and nor was an infirmary in the old gaol, and annual whitewashing was neglected. Local doctors, however, were commissioned to respond to the needs of sick prisoners and by all accounts the gaol was remarkably healthy by the turn of the nineteenth century: just two of the 308 prisoners admitted in 1811 died in the gaol during that year, for instance.[62]

The spiritual needs of prisoners also exercised the gaol reformers, in the Marshalsea as elsewhere. The prison had always had a chapel and its furnishings were listed in the inventory of 1483. It is shown on the first floor of a small medieval building next to the courthouse in the view of 1773. There was no official chaplain until late in the eighteenth century, but it was used occasionally for services in earlier years. John Wesley preached here in March 1739 and visited again in February 1753. He was not favourably impressed: 'a nursery of all manner of wickedness. Oh shame to man that there should be such a place, such a picture of hell upon earth!' Yet even wicked Laetitia Pilkington could be moved by what she heard in the 'Sort of a Chappel belonging to the Jail'. During her stay in 1742 she was edified by the sermons of Dr William Freind, at that time a King's Bench prisoner for debt, the Marshalsea, we might recall, conveniently within the rules, so he could walk there unmolested by bailiffs. It gave him profit of a kind, for he 'was now so low reduced as even to be beholden to such an unfortunate Creature as I for Sixpence', which she 'could not refuse to so fine an Orator'. Whatever spiritual benefits the few conforming prisoners might gain, the material rewards went from the gaol and into the preacher's pockets.[63]

There was one peculiar instance of a flow the other way, though it was probably never repeated. One Sunday in October 1775 music and prayer were brought into the Marshalsea for the benefit of the prisoners with a sermon, an audience from outside the prison, professional singers and 'a select band'. The polite congregation was reassured they would be preserved from embarrassment, 'The Door in King-Street to be opened only, and no Prisoners to be admitted'.[64]

By then it seems, or shortly after, the Marshalsea had an official chaplain, funded in the same way as all those making a living from the debtors. The chaplain received 1s for each debtor discharged, paid out of the gaol fees. It was given him whether debtors sought his counsel or not, and even if they espoused a different religion entirely; the surgeon had a similar slice from every debtor, sick or well. The chaplain in 1776 was a Rev. Mr Cockane, who was expected to preach in the chapel every other Sunday.[65]

It was an unrewarding obligation, or certainly some found it so. There is something of 'the unfortunate Dr Dodd' about a Marshalsea chaplain who inherited Cockane's cassock, the Rev. William Woolley – indeed, even much of the Marshalsea adventurer about him. In a pamphlet war with those notables he thought had disappointed him in his legitimate deserts, Woolley proved disarmingly frank about his own motives. When the chaplaincy became vacant around 1786 he applied and was appointed. 'The perquisites were very trifling', he thought, though whether more trifling than the duties is a matter of judgement. But Woolley had expectations: 'I do not wish to insinuate, that my clerical visits at the Marshalsea for above two years, without any pecuniary reward, were purely disinterested. Though there was no fixed

In St James's Street, a bailiff shows his writ and arrests the spendthrift anti-hero of William Hogarth's *Rake's Progress* (1734); in case of trouble a villainous-looking assistant armed with a club is in close attendance.

A line of washing stretches across the Marshalsea 'park' in Joseph Orme's watercolour of the prison painted around 1801, engraved by Thomas Prattent for *The Gentleman's Magazine* and published in May 1804. Both men were Marshalsea debtor-prisoners.

A broadsheet of 1729 captures conditions found by the Gaols Committee on its visits to the Marshalsea in March that year. Clockwise from top left: the Sick Men's ward, with its three tiers of prisoners, some of them starving and near death; Thomas Bliss is tortured by William Acton with the 'Scull Cap'; and a prisoner is loaded with heavy leg-fetters as punishment for an attempted escape.

Another of Orme's watercolours of the Marshalsea buildings and park, subsequently engraved by Prattent for *The Gentleman's Magazine* in September 1803. The original was in the possession of the deputy marshal, William Jenkins, probably to discharge some debts in the prison's 'black book'.

The old Marshalsea painted by J. Nash, another artist-prisoner, shortly before closure in 1811, showing the ancient buildings propped up with raking shores and, on the right, the new rooms erected around 1802 on the park to replace unusable accommodation.

The north side of the old
Marshalsea captured in 1773,
the common side to the left
at E–J and the seventeenth-
century courtroom on the
right at Y. Beneath is the floor
plan of the new Marshalsea
from 1811, the prison that
held John Dickens for a time
in 1824.

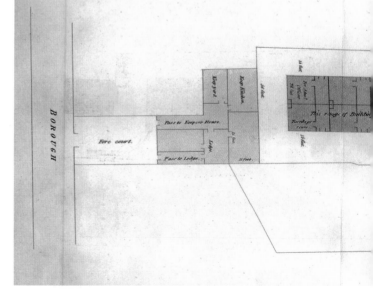

VACANT GROUND

Little Dorrit (1855–57) is Charles Dickens's autobiographical reconstruction of the prison that haunted his memory for so long. The sights he saw there and the people he encountered were formative influences on his writing life. The novel was illustrated by Hablot Knight Browne ('Phiz'), who here imagines William Dorrit released from prison by his inheritance in 'The Marshalsea becomes an Orphan' (*above*), and Little Dorrit in her attic room in the turnkey's house, with Maggy, her dependent (*left*).

Benjamin Haydon's *The Mock Election* of 1827, his famous painting of a riotous day in the King's Bench prison, where Haydon himself was a prisoner. Contemporary comment identified the central figure of the 'high sheriff' doffing his hat as 'Linton of the Marshalsea'.

The new Marshalsea's inner courtyard with the lodge (the dark iron-clad door to the right) and deputy marshal's house facing the painter, George Hassell, himself a debtor in the gaol from September 1831 to March 1832. The gate onto Southwark High Street is behind Hassell.

J. Crowther's view in 1887 of Marshalsea Place, as the back-to-back houses of the new Marshalsea became after closure. The prison's south wall, cut down from the original, is on the right, with the churchyard of St George the Martyr behind it.

salary, yet I had some flattering hopes of being able to procure it from government.' In the interim he supplemented his prison fees with odd livings and odd jobs, for most Anglican clergymen had to be jobbing saviours to save themselves – an Essex living (Widdington) worth a respectable £300 a year in 1790, not mentioned in his subsequent literary effusions and which he probably managed by installing a curate, four guineas a year for (he said) reading prayers twice-weekly at the nearby Surrey Chapel, and 'the thinly scattered *windfalls* of some casual Sundays . . .'[66]

The Surrey Chapel in Blackfriars Road, Southwark, recently opened in 1783, was founded by the Rev. Rowland Hill and it was Hill and his philanthropic brother Sir Richard Hill who became the chief targets of Woolley's ire. Rowland Hill, at Woolley's urging, had tried to get the Marshalsea chaplain a salary from government but failed. In that event, Woolley felt himself due compensation for the small remuneration he had received for his efforts on behalf of the Surrey Chapel: he expected 'a 20l. bank-note' but received just 'nine pounds and a few shillings'. The difference opened a pamphlet war, begun by Woolley in 1792 with *The Benefit of Starving; or the Advantages of Hunger, Cold, and Nakedness; intended as a Cordial for the Poor, and an Apology for the Rich*. At first sight, from the pen of the prison's chaplain, this looked like a plea for the Marshalsea debtors, but the game was given away in a final clause, for the pamphlet was *Addressed to the Rev. Rowland Hill, M.A.* It was poor Woolley who was hungry, shivering and naked, and he was left so by the selfish manoeuvrings of the brothers Hill. Claim and counterclaim over two years led to Woolley defending a suit for libel brought by Sir Richard Hill in the court of King's Bench in front of Lord Kenyon, that judge vehemently unsympathetic to the importunate chaplain. At the end of a bruising trial Woolley changed his plea to guilty on his counsel's advice. In all the toings and froings, however,

Woolley did see his unpredictable Marshalsea fees translated into a salary of £50 a year. He was spared prolonged imprisonment in the King's Bench for his libel by making a public apology and Hill pursued the case against him no further. Predictably, Woolley had the last word, in *Prison Meditations, composed while in confinement in the King's Bench Prison in the Year 1795,* 'price 1s 6d' and published in May 1796.[67]

During the course of these clerical pyrotechnics the ancient Marshalsea was subsiding into its final state of decrepitude. The wonder is that it had survived so very long. Apart from the courthouse, the prison buildings were noted as 'mean and ruinous' in 1761 and 'run to much decay' in 1766. William Smith, surveying the gaol ten years later, found many of the common-side rooms 'with hardly a pane of glass in the windows' and 'the stairs so dark and ruinous, that it is dangerous to go up and down without a candle' even in broad daylight. In the 1760s the story got about 'that the Marshalsea Prison is intended soon to be pulled down, and a new Prison built near the King's Bench in St. George's Fields'. Certainly some were pressing for such a move, 'otherwise many Prisoners must indubitably die every Year, and epidemic, contagious Diseases' could 'destroy Hundreds within, and Thousands without, as the Contagion might spread thro' the whole island, and cause a general Pestilence'. But both the rumours and the fears proved false.[68]

Complaints about the gaol's condition and stories about its impending demise continued to tease the newspapers and perplex reformers for the next forty years and more. In 1775 it was confidently stated that the Marshalsea was to be taken down and rebuilt on its existing site, as the White Lyon or county gaol had been fifty years before. When John Howard visited in the summer of that year he found the prison 'too small and greatly out of repair'. Even so the gaol was 'well supplied with water' and he was alive to a few of the Marshalsea's compensations: in the yard 'the Prisoners play at rackets, missisippi [a form of bagatelle] &c; and in a little back court, the *Park*, at skittles'. But besides the cramped and decrepit state of the gaol other recreations he thought called out for reform. The tap was kept by a prisoner living in the rules of the King's Bench, although his beer proved unpopular: 'I was credibly informed, that one Sunday in the summer of 1775, about 600 pots of beer were brought in from a public house in the neighbourhood.'[69]

Howard also visited the nearby Surrey county gaol in Southwark – the 'New Gaol', as it had been called since the end of the 1720s. At a subsequent inspection in 1783 he found it a place of much sickness, especially among the felons. Some of his concerns were shared by the Surrey justices, the gaol's managers, and in 1791 they procured an act to build a new county gaol on modern lines at Horsemonger Lane, then in the fields half a mile or so south of St George's Church. It was completed and opened in 1798. The old county gaol seems to have stayed empty from that point. Its future purpose, though, was being discussed at least five years before Horsemonger Lane was ready. *Lloyd's Evening Post* reported in April 1793 that 'After the completion of the gaol now building for the county of Surrey, near the beginning of the Kent Road, the prisoners are to be removed thither from the New Gaol in the Borough, and the prisoners in the Marshalsea are to be removed to the New Gaol. The Marshalsea is to be taken down.' This seems to have been the first accurate public inkling that the Marshalsea, probably after some 400 years and more on its old site, was to be moved.[70]

Yet there would still be many more years during which the old Marshalsea dragged on, despite having demonstrably outlived its usefulness. In 1799 William Cruchley, deputy prothonotary of the Marshalsea and Palace courts, pressed the Secretary of State for the Home Department to remove four Admiralty prisoners because of 'The ruinous and insecure state' of the prison, which in any event had no capacity to carry out the sentence of solitary confinement passed on some of them. And James Neild, visiting around the same time, confirmed it to be 'ruinous and insecure': 'the habitations of the debtors are wretched in the extreme'.[71]

Then, in May 1800, the future of the gaol became a little clearer. The 'desirable leasehold estate . . . comprising the Whole of the Marshalsea Prison (the Materials of which are very valuable, and may be re-converted in new Buildings to great Advantage) together with other Premises adjoining' was offered for sale by public advertisement. The vendor wasn't named but he was Thomas Cracklow of Bishopsgate, who had privately acquired a long lease of the gaol from the government in 1795 as a first step to discharge the burden of the old Marshalsea from the public purse. Cracklow had wanted to erect new buildings on his land, which he advertised as suitable for 'Dwellings, or Warehouses for a Hop-Market', or an 'Inn, a Manufactory, or any Public-Building requiring space'. But he was 'thwarted by Government retaining the possession (although only tenants at will)', despite the new gaol becoming empty two years before. The probable reason for this delay was not hard to find. The old county gaol required adaptation and expansion to accommodate the Marshalsea. And these were desperate times for the public finances, the nation in a life-and-death struggle with Revolutionary France under the leadership from 1799 of Napoleon Bonaparte.[72]

Cracklow was able to relieve his own finances because he sold his lease of the prison in September 1802 to Samuel Davis for the purpose of making a 'Manufactory', in fact a cooperage, being very cramped for space on his present site. Davis had been assured that 'Gov^t had purch^d the County gaol on the Borough of South^k for the purpose of a new Mar: Prison' but found himself baulked in the same way as Cracklow. Davis had borrowed his purchase money and the interest on his loan was, by 1807, costing him £500 a year. Unsurprisingly, he petitioned the Treasury for compensation and the prompt removal of the gaol, but he would receive no satisfaction, on the latter point in any event, for nine long years after he bought the lease.[73]

It is from the time of Cracklow and Davis that we have the views of Orme and Prattent showing the unstable condition of the old Marshalsea, some of its buildings propped up to stop them falling. Other undated watercolours from one J. Nash, possibly a prisoner, seem likely to be from around the same time and show similar conditions. Prattent describes one of his views in the *Gentleman's Magazine* of September 1803 as made 'before the new Buildings were erected', and at the end of 1802 Neild found a new wall across the Marshalsea's courtyard 'and twenty new rooms in the centre of the court, about 11 feet by 10, and 7½ feet high, for the better accommodation of the prisoners to live in and also to sleep in, if they *can*'. These new additions either supplemented or replaced other rooms now too bad to use. But they are evidence of the double burden that the Marshalsea was imposing on government over the period from 1802 to 1811, having to spend capital preparing the new prison a couple of hundred yards to the south while in the interim paying for 'repairs absolutely necessary for upholding the present *Marshalsea* Prison'.[74]

Eventually the new Marshalsea was fitted out for use. On Christmas Eve 1811 the old prison, a rare and striking remnant of medieval Southwark, overladen with history, was closed. Fifty debtors imprisoned for debts worth in all some £1,160, among them Jane Turner, Mary Crouch, Mary Bishop, George Wetenall, Joseph Atkins and William Robinson or Robertson, were escorted the 130 yards south along Borough High Street to their new gaol. Alongside them, no doubt taken separately, were eleven Admiralty prisoners in this year of continuing naval warfare. The old prison would be demolished and replaced first by Davis's cooperage and, around 1823–4, by Gainsford and Wicking's five-storey drapery emporium. The Marshalsea would now begin a new life, while importing many of its old ways. And the new gaol would become home for a time to a prisoner and his family who ensured that the Marshalsea will remain remembered worldwide for as long, it seems, as English is spoken or read.[75]

6

THE NEW GAOL: JOHN DICKENS'S MARSHALSEA, 1812–24

JOHN Dickens was 'as kindhearted and generous a man as ever lived in the world', sociable to a fault, meticulous in discharging an employer's obligations. But he had been bred to expect much from a world where his talents and social standing delivered far less, and the gulf between what he wished for and what he could afford could be bridged only at others' expense. To those tradesmen and friends and relatives from whom he borrowed he displayed a streak of unscrupulous disregard that undermined the generosity of which his son spoke. It would bring him in February 1824 through the gates of the Marshalsea prison.[1]

He was born on 25 August 1785, the second son of two upper servants (his father butler, his mother later housekeeper) of the wealthy and well-connected Crewe family. John's father died less than three months after he was born and he was brought up by his stern and rigid mother, Elizabeth. At some time John was likely to have lived in one or more of their three residences: in Cheshire (Crewe Hall, where Mrs Dickens would later preside), Staffordshire (Madeley Manor) and their town house, 18 Lower Grosvenor Street, Mayfair. His life in these houses of the rich proved an unfortunate schooling in the pleasures of tasteful luxury above stairs and bountiful comfort below. The Crewes seem to have provided him with a sound education: he would take pleasure in an eloquent phrase, his own especially, for the rest of his life. And it was the Crewes who probably arranged for Mrs Dickens's younger boy to embark on a career at the Navy Pay Office, courtesy of their friend George Canning, then treasurer to the navy. John Dickens was taken on as a temporary clerk at Somerset House in the spring of 1805, just six months before the Battle of Trafalgar and the death of Nelson. By 1807 he had ascended to the permanent staff, fifteenth assistant clerk in the office.[2]

A fellow clerk was Thomas Barrow, whose father, Charles, was Chief Conductor of Money at the Navy Office. It was Thomas's sister Elizabeth who won the heart of John Dickens. They were married in June 1809 at St Mary le Strand, just outside the entrance of Somerset House. The Barrows' prospects and reputation would be shaken within a year of the marriage: Charles fled the country having spent £5,689 3s 3d of the navy's money on his own needs.

John and Elizabeth were untouched by the scandal, at least as far as their own financial prospects were concerned. John's salary rose steeply, almost doubling to £200 in 1808, when he moved to the Portsmouth office, receiving the 'outpost allowance' of 5s a day. Elizabeth returned there with him on their marriage and in October 1810 the Dickenses began what would be a large family with a daughter, Frances, known as Fanny. On 7 February 1812 Charles was born at Mile End Terrace, Portsmouth, followed by Letitia (1816), Frederick (1820), Alfred Lamert (1822) and Augustus (1827); two others did not survive childhood. The children were born at many different addresses. Charles had fifteen homes in twelve years, some of them due to relocation of his father's office as he moved from Portsmouth to Chatham to London and back again, usually with a consequential fluctuation in his salary. And it was these fluctuations that added to the family's peripatetic, almost Gypsy mobility in these years as John sought half-heartedly to mould his domestic circumstances to the state of his pocket. One big blow fell early when he was brought back to London at Christmas 1814, his salary dropping by at least £40 or more than a sixth. It seems likely that this was the beginning of John Dickens's struggles with debt. It would have been difficult for anyone to cramp a growing family's lifestyle to accommodate a smaller salary among all the expenses of setting up home in London and perhaps he bargained on the cut being temporary – as indeed it proved, when he was posted out of town once more at Christmas 1816.

By 1820, John's prospects seemed to have not just recovered but enlarged. His pay rose by more than a third that year to £403 10s, and then climbed again to £441 in 1821–2. But the damage had already been done. The demands of his family, the need to keep up appearances as a gentleman of some condition, the domestic comforts he had never gone without, and the good fellowship and theatrical and other entertainments he had grown to love all outpaced the steady money coming to him every three months. Bills of every kind were run up till quarter day, as was customary, but then not paid, which was dangerous. To satisfy the clamour, John sought to make a fresh start and restructure his debts. In August 1819 he mortgaged a slice of his salary to borrow £200 from one James Milbourne of Kennington Green, Lambeth, contracting to pay Milbourne £26 a year for the rest of his life; and he borrowed a further sum at the same time from a prosperous retired tailor, a neighbour in Chatham. But Dickens did not pay these debts either and the Milbourne 'deed', as it was known in the family, was shouldered at the cost of £213 by Thomas Barrow, Elizabeth's brother. Poor Barrow would never get his money back.[3]

There was then a disastrous shift in John Dickens's fortunes. In the summer or autumn of 1822 he was summoned back to London, his salary consequently reduced to £350, a cut of more than one fifth. To make the best of it he rented a cheap house in an unfashionable suburb, 16 Bayham Street at Camden Town. The family brought with them a servant girl apprenticed out of the Chatham workhouse, whose name has not come down to us but who has been immortalised nonetheless. But John proved unable to adjust to his reduced circumstances. Debts mounted. He owed the local paving board for rates and had to be summonsed before eventually paying; he owed local tradesmen for provisions – certainly the baker, James Karr or Kerr, and probably others. But some pretensions were kept up. While the education of Charles was neglected, the eldest child, Fanny, a talented musician, was favoured with tuition, bread and board at the Royal Academy of Music near Hanover Square at the cost of thirty-eight guineas a year.[4]

Mired in money worries, the family again sought the means of breaking out that might offer a fresh start. Elizabeth Dickens provided a notional solution. She would set up a school and take in pupils as boarders. The family took a house in Bloomsbury at 4 Gower Street North, where University College Hospital now stands. 'Mrs Dickens's Establishment' was advertised by a brass plate on the door and Charles delivered flyers round neighbouring streets. 'Yet nobody ever came to school, nor do I recollect that anybody ever proposed to come, or that the least preparation was made to receive anybody. But I know that we got on very badly with the butcher and the baker; [and] that very often we had not too much for dinner . . .' It was at this time or a little later that the family's movable possessions made their way to the pawnbrokers and wardrobe dealers round about. John Dickens had a small collection of books, among them

novels of the previous century by Smollett and Fielding. They
had been a great comfort to his neglected son: 'I have
sustained my own idea of Roderick Random for a month
at a stretch, I verily believe', he wrote later. Now Charles
had the task of taking them to a second-hand bookseller in
Hampstead Road for the best price he could get.[5]

Among the debts for which John Dickens was dunned at
Gower Street North were some carried with him from
Camden Town, including £40 or thereabouts owed to James
Karr the baker. It was a tremendous sum, so large one
wonders whether Dickens ever paid for a single crust. Karr,
knowing or suspecting he was not the only creditor, decided
to stake his claim before the rest. He swore an affidavit to
show Dickens owed him £10 'and upwards' and had him
arrested on a Marshalsea writ under mesne process. The
bailiffs took him to a spunging house to discover whether
he could settle the debt or raise bail and so keep himself
out of the Marshalsea. From there, Charles was sent scut-
tling over the town to run hopeful errands for his father,
but to no avail: 'the last words said to him by his father
before he was finally taken to the Marshalsea, were to the
effect that the sun was set upon him for ever'. On Friday
20 February 1824, 'John Dickins' was brought into custody
at the suit of James Karr to recover the debt of £40. The
details were entered into the prison's 'Day Book' while John
waited in the lodge. There he would have undergone the
same scrutiny that would later happen to Samuel Pickwick
in the Fleet prison, for which in general we should read
Marshalsea, 'the ceremony, known to the initiated as "sitting
for your portrait"', or 'an inspection by the different turnkeys, in order that they might know prisoners from visitors'.[6]

Later that day or perhaps the next, Charles called to see
his father. And we have now the first glimpse of John
Dickens's Marshalsea from the inside through the sharp eyes
of this precocious twelve-year-old with a genius for truthful

and whimsical observation. It was the beginning too of Charles Dickens's long preoccupation, perhaps obsession, with the Marshalsea prison, a place he had already met in Tobias Smollett's *Roderick Random* but was now seeing for the first time:

> My father was waiting for me in the lodge, and we went up to his room (on the top story but one), and cried very much. And he told me, I remember, to take warning by the Marshalsea, and to observe that if a man had twenty pounds a-year, and spent nineteen pounds nineteen shillings and sixpence, he would be happy; but that a shilling spent the other way would make him wretched. I see the fire we sat before, now; with two bricks inside the rusted grate, one on each side, to prevent its burning too many coals. Some other debtor shared the room with him, who came in by-and-by; and as the dinner was a joint-stock repast, I was sent up to 'Captain Porter' in the room overhead, with Mr. Dickens's compliments, and I was his son, and could he, Captain P, lend me a knife and fork?
>
> Captain Porter lent the knife and fork, with his compliments in return. There was a very dirty lady in his little room; and too wan girls, his daughters, with shock heads of hair. I thought I should not have liked to borrow Captain Porter's comb. The Captain himself was in the last extremity of shabbiness; and if I could draw at all, I would draw an accurate portrait of the old, old, brown great-coat he wore, with no other coat below it. His whiskers were large. I saw his bed rolled up in a corner; and I knew (God knows how) that the two girls with the shock heads were Captain Porter's natural children, and that the dirty lady was not married to Captain P. My timid, wondering station on his threshold, was not occupied more than a couple of minutes, I dare say; but I came down again to the room below with all this as surely in my knowledge, as the knife and fork were in my hand.[7]

John Dickens found himself in a gaol in the main part barely twelve years old, though no doubt everywhere showing signs of wear and tear. In an era of Treasury parsimony – few eras were not – what could be saved from the old Surrey county gaol was reused in the new Marshalsea. The narrow gateway on to Borough High Street was likely to have been retained from the old gaol. It lay between Ruck the cheesemongers to the left and to the right the ancient Crown inn, kept in 1824 by Bill Moss; that year he hosted a retirement dinner for Ned Turner, the celebrated Borough prize fighter.[8] Past the gate a narrow courtyard led to the eighteenth-century deputy marshal or keeper's house, built for the Surrey gaol, three storeys tall with attics in the roof. On the ground floor was a door either side of a barred window. That to the left led to the keeper's apartments, the heavy iron-clad door to the right opening into the lodge and then to the prison.

The gaol itself was long and narrow, stretching nearly 300 feet to Colliers Rents at the rear, but just fifty-six feet wide between its high walls. The main block of the prison was new, a double-terrace of eight back-to-back four-storey houses, some of them double-fronted with rooms either side of the entrance passage and staircase. The houses gave access to fifty-six rooms. These varied slightly in size but on average were ten feet ten inches square with ceiling heights of eight or nine feet. There was just one window in each room and no through-ventilation because every room had another behind it in the house at the rear. At least one of the top rooms overlooking St George's churchyard to the south had a garret in the roof.

Around this central block was what would now be called the exercise yard. This was no 'Park'. It was little more than four narrow passages, one on each side, deeply shadowed by the tall houses in the middle and the high walls around, and no more than fifteen feet at their widest. The southerly

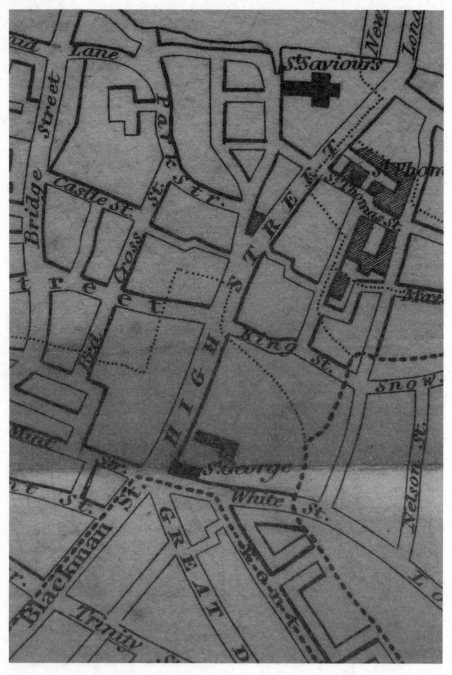

A map of Southwark from 1829 shows the Marshalsea as the
L-shaped building to the north of St George the Martyr Church.

passage contained a pump drawing water from a well close to the graveyard, said to be foul-smelling and chalybeate or iron-rich and so probably purgative, and the cock for the mains of the London Bridge Company's water; by John Dickens's time a cistern had been added that allowed impurities from the unfiltered Thames water to settle before the water was drawn off.[9]

Behind the new houses and further into the gaol were the privies, three in all, one for women and children and two for men. They were a source of nuisance in the new gaol for many years. The privies 'smell very bad', it was said in 1815, largely because the soil was held in a cesspit beneath them which had to be emptied by the nightmen occasionally, ordure inconveniently carted through the passageway of the keeper's house to the street beyond. The debtors petitioned several times for the cesspit to be filled and replaced by a drain flushed by water from the cistern and for more accommodation, as prisoners had to wait outside 'for a considerable time' till a privy became free. The petitions grew increasingly clamant with the approach of the cholera of 1832, when the prison was said to be very crowded, with an average of more than three persons a room, but it seems that nothing was done to remedy either quantity or condition.[10]

In close and perhaps unfortunate proximity to the privies was a building that was the centre of Marshalsea life. It was divided into two: a tap or alehouse at the rear, with a bar and a sitting area called the 'snuggery'; and at the front a public or day room, generally called by the prisoners the 'ale room'. Behind this lay in separate buildings the Admiralty prison, with its own yard: converted from old structures left from the county gaol or even the old White Lyon (it was called 'ancient' in 1833), its ceilings were lined with sheet iron and floors studded with nails to deter escapes. The Admiralty yard was kept nominally separate from the rest of the prison, with its own enclosure and entrance, but there was some mingling with the debtors, except for those few sailors sentenced to solitary confinement who were kept in two 'strong rooms', a name redolent of past crimes. When empty they were used for refractory debtors, as in the old gaol. The final building at the far end of the prison from the lodge was the chapel. It had separate entrances for Admiralty prisoners and debtors and was once more an old building, two-storey and of early-eighteenth-century design if not older, so from the county gaol or before. The Marshalsea's walls were new or perhaps raised on old structures, and in 1818 were not uniformly protected by the crossed iron spikes known as a 'chevaux-de-frize': they had been shoddily built at first, for in early 1813 part of the southern boundary close to St George's churchyard collapsed, killing two prisoners, a tailor and a hackney coachman.[11]

In some respects, especially the lack of exercise space, this new prison was markedly worse than the old: a proposal to extend the yard to the south by incorporating former industrial land cleared to make an extension to St George's churchyard was mooted but proved too expensive or difficult to achieve. But in other ways, notably in the living conditions for debtors in the new houses, this was a big improvement on the old Marshalsea.[12]

The eight houses of the main building were divided among the different classes of debtors. In 1818, seven of the fifty-six rooms were devoted to the poor or common side for those prisoners swearing they were worth no more than 40s. One of these was the chandler's shop for the poor side, probably also used as the shopkeeper's bedroom. A further seven rooms were allocated to women prisoners, enabling a few to have a room to themselves. Two rooms on the master's side were used as a chandler's shop and four by the two turnkeys and their families. The remaining thirty-six rooms were used for male prisoners on the master's side. This number had included four rooms set aside for imprisoned naval officers, but an act of 1816 enabling Marshalsea sentences to be served at other naval establishments made this provision redundant.[13]

There was one other important change in the fabric of the new prison: there was no longer any place for the Marshalsea and Palace courts. The age-old co-location of court and gaol was at last severed, the courts finding a new home on crown land at Great Scotland Yard, off Whitehall.

The numbers confined in the new Marshalsea varied as they always had and the marked turnover of prisoners continued. In 1811 the lower limit for arrests on mesne process was raised from £10 to £15, largely to reflect wartime price inflation; if this led to a reduction in prisoners coming through the gate, as the £10 limit had done at first, it had worked itself through by 1816, when the numbers of imprisoned debtors on any day ranged from around eighty-five to 111, though the new Admiralty law cut naval prisoners there from ten at the start of the year to just two at the end. During those twelve months of 1816 the throughput was considerable, with 465 debtors brought into custody, twenty-nine of them women; in 1821 the numbers were lower at 416, twenty-four of them women. In 1827 the mesne process arrest limit was raised again, to £20, but this had no prolonged effect on the numbers confined, for in 1831 580 debtors were brought in. In 1833 it was said that '170 PERSONS have been confined at *one time* within these walls, making an average of more than *four persons* in each room', possibly due to debtors surrendering to custody in advance of an Insolvent Debtors Act. Such crowding probably left some prisoners sleeping for a time in the day room, tap and chapel.[14]

These large numbers must have made things difficult for the numerous prisoners who brought their families into the prison to make a temporary home there while saving rent and some living costs on the outside. This might not have been tolerated in the busy times but with sixty to eighty prisoners it was manageable: in April 1815, for instance, there were sixty-four debtors who had with them '24 women and 32 children', as the parliamentary committee of inquiry sniffily put it. So when John Dickens procured a single room, like Captain Porter above him, he could bring in Elizabeth and the children. Probably at the end of March or early April 1824 Elizabeth, with Letitia (eight), Harriet (five), Frederick (three) and Alfred (two), moved out of 4 Gower Street North and into John's small room. They brought the Chatham workhouse servant girl to wait on them, though she lived out of the Marshalsea in lodgings they or she found nearby. Fanny was still respectably accommodated at the Royal Academy of Music and a room with board for Charles was found at Little College Street in Camden Town. That was an inconvenient distance from his family in the Marshalsea, and quite a way too for him to get to his work at Warren's blacking factory, at first at Old Hungerford Stairs on the north bank of the river and then in Chandos Street, Covent Garden. He brought these inconveniences home to his father, who had not thought of them before, and a room was found for him by the beginning of May at 1 Lant Street, across Borough High Street from the Marshalsea gate and on the southern border of the old Mint. From the warehouse he crossed the river by means of Southwark Bridge, or 'the Iron Bridge' as it was known, opened just five years earlier. Charles and the orphan servant girl would wait till the gate opened at 8 a.m., when Charles went in for his breakfast; and if he came in the evening he would be locked out at 10 p.m., when all strangers had notionally to leave. He would also spend his Sundays there, taking dinner with his family; occasionally he would walk to meet Fanny at the Academy and she would join them, all in that crowded Marshalsea room.[15]

Alongside the new fabric at the relocated Marshalsea came some new managerial arrangements. The Treasury, which had reluctantly accepted responsibility for building a new gaol before the old one turned finally to dust, now effectively shouldered its running costs. The old gaol had formerly been 'private property' but was now no longer so. The Knight Marshal's age-old position was filled in 1815 by Sir James Bland Burges, Bart, but the deputy marshal or keeper was not now dependent on profits sheared from the debtors. Nor could he farm his duties, as in the past. William Jenkins took up the position just before the old Marshalsea closed in 1811. He was now fundamentally a salaried officer, paid by the Treasury and receiving £300 a year. In addition he kept part of the debtors' discharge fees, worth around £80 a year, the rent from the tap (two guineas a week) and the master's-side chandler's shop (half a guinea). He was also appointed Clerk of the Papers, with annual fees of around £74, but the two posts could be uncoupled and were in the next year or two. In all, then, Jenkins could count on £500 or £600 a year, a more than respectable middle-class salary. Appropriately, Jenkins was plainly an educated and efficient man, as the documentary legacy he left behind of one kind or another testifies. There were then reporting to him two salaried turnkeys, the senior man receiving a slice of the fees worth about £20 to bring his income to around £100 a year and two salaried watchmen. The second turnkey was William Jenkins junior, the keeper's son, not an unusual family connection in the Marshalsea.[16]

This was a welcome improvement on the old farming arrangements, so prone to rapacity and viciousness. Yet the scope for small profits still crept in. John Ewer Poole, a debtor prisoner who published in 1833 a critical pamphlet about the machinery of the Marshalsea and Palace courts and their notorious prison, complained that 'All the *Rooms in No.* 1. *staircase are reserved* by the *turnkeys*, and by *them let out to the* more *wealthy* prisoners, who may desire a room to themselves.' This, Poole reasonably concluded, rendered crowding elsewhere in the prison worse. Perhaps it was one of these traded rooms that John Dickens rented for his family in 1824. In addition, the turnkeys rented out beds to those who had none of their own.[17]

Besides the prison's keeper and others employed to maintain order, the Treasury made arrangements for the spiritual and medical welfare of the debtors. The first, less important by far to the prisoners, was the post of chaplain, in 1815 the sinecure of a Rev. Trollope at the salary of £50 a year – first secured for William Woolley some years before, we might recall – and a slice of the fees worth £10 or £12. There was room for a little farming here too, because Trollope installed a curate, the Rev. Thomas Webster, to carry out his duties, paying him £20 and the fees and keeping £30 to himself for doing precisely nothing at all. Webster conducted Sunday and holy-day services at the chapel, at which the attendance of prisoners was voluntary; the congregation was usually fourteen or fifteen, with no sacrament administered.[18]

The second was the prison's surgeon, Charles Phillips, a local practitioner, who also received £50 a year – the first at the gaol to receive a stipend – and 1s for each debtor discharged, amounting to around a further £9 to £15 a year. Out of his income he provided medicines, but 'linen rag, and lint and trusses, and cupping' or bleeding were 'paid for extra' by Jenkins. These additional costs and any supplementary diet needed by the sick were reimbursed to Jenkins by the Treasury. Phillips or his assistant visited daily. Although Phillips's duties extended solely to the prisoners, he or his assistant treated their wives and children too – 'I should forfeit my reputation if I did not attend them.' He also cared for women in labour, though a baby born to the Marshalsea was a rare event: in 1818 he could remember not more than one in the past five years. In general, he thought, 'we are very healthy'. Fever cases were removed to a sickbay or infirmary, a room over the tap, but most of the diseases to be found in the Marshalsea arose 'from debauchery, dissipations and drinking'. The bad state of the gaol's drains, overflowing at the time of the parliamentary committee's visit in April 1815, and the turbid or smelly water supplies, were considered no worse than in Southwark generally.[19]

Phillips seems to have been able and conscientious, though perhaps a little too ready to side with the keeper, as we shall see, and the authorities took steps to appoint men of standing as his successors. Charles Gaselee, MRCS, 'Surgeon to the Marshalsea Prison', co-authored one of the first treatises on cholera in London during the outbreak of 1832. Southwark was badly hit, and the unusually high number of deaths in the prison that summer and autumn, five in all, seem likely to have been due to the epidemic.[20]

Alongside this public provision, elements of private enterprise persisted, to the benefit of the prisoners. The tap was kept in 1815 by Elizabeth Short, who had run it for some two years past. She had known the old Marshalsea, for her husband had been a turnkey there – perhaps she had been widowed while he was in post. The ale she sold, supplied by Charrington's, was not much liked by the prisoners but, she claimed, the deputy marshal had a contract with the brewer so she had no choice in the matter. Beer could be taken out of the tap or consumed 'in the snuggery'; there was a fire there and 'a great many collegians come in and wish to take their wives and families in there, and we keep the place clean for them, and take a penny a pot for that; it has long been the custom of the place'. Wine was not sold there, but she could have it brought in on a prisoner's orders. Spirits had long been banned by law, but the law had long been sidestepped. It was the custom for the turnkeys to permit gin to be sold surreptitiously from a 'whistling-shop' set up in a prisoner's room – 'for certain lucrative considerations', as

Charles Dickens put it in the 1830s. Outsiders bringing gin
or spirits into the gaol were severely treated in order to maintain the profits of this secret trade. Mary Goodwin, a 'decent
looking young woman', was charged by a turnkey when found
bringing gin to her father there in January 1826; he had no
fire in a freezing winter and the gin was to warm him from
the inside. The court was sympathetic but she still had a day
and a half in the Southwark House of Correction. And in
May 1832 George Eades, 'a man of respectable appearance',
was fined £10 or three months' imprisonment, for trying to
smuggle spirits to 'a prisoner of sporting notoriety'; the turnkeys found the drink 'in a tin case fitted to his stomach'.[21]

The Marshalsea was a complex world. It had many dos
and don'ts, with overlapping jurisdictions of authority and
privilege, and it must all have been new and bewildering to
John Dickens when he entered the gate on 20 February 1824.
Like every other prisoner, he had quickly to be inducted into
its ways. He would discover they involved a complicated
interweaving of official authority and debtor democracy, as
in general they always had.

A number of people were involved in this induction.
Prisoners were met in the lodge by the 'chum master', in
1815 William Jenkins junior, the second turnkey, who
arranged bed-sharing on the master's and common sides. No
fee was taken for a 'chum-ticket', which should have been
issued in 'rotation', but no doubt money might change hands
for a good berth and a clean bedfellow. Once chummed, a
prisoner could negotiate to have his room-mate 'chummed
out', the purchaser paying his ex-chum 2s 6d a week to sleep
somewhere else in the prison, 'the custom of the prison' and
'the settled price'. So John Dickens could have got a room
to himself in this way, too, or just by his chum having been
discharged from the gaol and not replaced.[22]

Besides the chum master, a new debtor would also meet
the 'College Secretary', a prisoner elected by the debtors, in

1815 one George Chump. He demanded garnish – called 'fees' or 'allowance, but such it was – of 8s from each male prisoner and 5s 6d from every woman. It was a hefty sum and would be reduced to 5s 6d for men by 1818. Many found it impossible to raise immediately, so credit was given. Those on the poor side put 'a shilling a time, as they receive the county sixpences' at the rate of 3s 6d a week. The money, for which the college secretary acted as 'accountant', was used to keep the day or ale room in candles and provide coals for the fire at which prisoners dressed 'their victuals' to eat in their rooms. A daily newspaper was also taken in, for it was important for the prisoners to be apprised of the news of the living world that bore directly upon them; in 1815, and perhaps for many years after, this was the *British Press*. Running the ale room was thought to cost around £1 13 4d each week. The 'College Guide', another prisoner, showed newcomers the gaol and instructed them in Marshalsea ways, explaining the two sets of orders and rules that governed their lives there, one official and issued by the deputy marshal, the other the college's own.[23]

Debtors on the poor side had their own 'Steward', who managed and accounted for the charities in cash and kind, chosen by the debtors whom he served 'for such time as I do what is right and just, and satisfy them', as George Nottage, the incumbent for some six months past, put it in 1815. His return was a room to himself – 'I am not chummed on' – and a shilling for the affidavits he wrote for the prisoners so they could swear they were worth 40s or less. The prisoners also paid their own 'scavenger' to collect and remove rubbish and see that the privies were washed out every morning, all at a cost of 4s per week.[24]

The 'College Regulations', or Marshalsea debtors' constitution, had been brought from the ancient gaol by those prisoners moving to the new prison on Christmas Eve 1811. That document was 'an old paper' of uncertain age. When an attorney, Mr Richardson, was imprisoned there in 1814 the collegians took advantage of his expertise to revise the old arrangements for new circumstances. Amendments were 'read over to the prisoners at large, and approved of' and the 'Regulations . . . for maintaining good order in this Prison' were copied in a neat hand, dated 8 August 1814, and carefully kept by the prisoners. They survive still.[25]

The college rules were enforced day to day by a committee of nine with a chairman, all elected monthly by the 'court', a meeting of all male prisoners held on Mondays at noon, non-attenders facing a fine of 3d. Standing on tables or forms at the court or leaving it early were forbidden and prisoners wilfully obstructing college business were fined 9d. The court also elected the secretary month by month and the master of the ale room. Both were paid 7s a week out of the 'allowance' provided by new debtors. Boiling water was to be ready in the ale room from 8.30 to 10.30 each morning and 4.30 till 7 every evening. This room, around which much collective debtor life circulated, was open till 11 p.m. and scrubbed thoroughly every Saturday. On 'club nights' the room was to be ready for a convivial time by 7 p.m. and the master had to ensure that no boys were allowed in and 'to keep the door closed during a song being sung'.

The committee had a judicial function too, deciding 'all matters in dispute which may happen to arise in the college between the members thereof'. Opposing parties and any witnesses were heard and the committee's decisions 'considered final'. Prisoners not abiding by the committee's decision were fined 2s 6d. Those refusing to pay had their names and offences posted 'in the ale-room and other most conspicuous places in the college', chalked on the walls, broadcast loudly in the yard 'by the crier', were sent to Coventry and refused entry to the ale room and its privileges. Any prisoner 'associating with, speaking to, or holding any communication whatever' with the offender was liable to a fine and, finally, the same punishment. The sorts of offences specifically envisioned included theft of another prisoner's property – the committee having the right to search rooms for stolen goods – throwing water over another prisoner, issuing a challenge to fight and 'using obscene, opprobrious or offensive language' against another, preferring a false or frivolous charge, making a disturbance after midnight, pissing in the yard ('excepting the place appropriated for the same'), soiling the privy seats, and so on. Defaulters were met with a fine, backed up by a sentence to Coventry, the ultimate sanction of the rules – physical punishment was not provided for, formally at least, though the committee had discretion to apply further 'articles' as it saw fit. The committee could also turn itself into a 'court of requests' for the settlement of debts between prisoners, exacting payment on pain of rustication from the college and a journey to Coventry. It must, in practice, have been a terrible fate avoided by all except the most stubborn nonconformist, whether in the right or not. The parliamentary committee inquiring into London prisons in 1815 thought these rules 'in many particulars indecorous and improper', especially as prescribing 'festive meetings, in seasons of gaiety and opulence' – presumably the 'club nights'. But plainly these arrangements were necessary and had always been so when maintaining daily order among a constantly shifting population of men and women who had got by in life in part by evading their obligations to others.[26]

This debtor democracy, not merely inviting but requiring active participation in the communal life of the gaol, for men at least, helped create a distinctive subculture. It would have been recognisable to generations of debtors stretching back to the Restoration if not before. In John Dickens's Marshalsea the echoes are as loud as in Grano's.

The old louche morality, for instance, remained much in evidence. Besides the charms of the tap, 'beer is coming in all the day long' from the Borough inns around, potboys in and out for orders. John Ewer Poole, the Marshalsea pamphleteer, complained in 1833 of how innocent or 'novice' debtors were exposed to 'the various methods of time-killing' among their fellows, 'viz. drinking, singing, gambling, fornication, adultery, and, in short, *every kind of debauchery!*' Visitors to the gaol were admitted without hindrance as long as they were well behaved, including 'numbers of the frail sisterhood who visit this place, *some rooms being actually set out for the purpose of PROSTITUTION!*' 'Is it customary for women to sleep in the prison?' the keeper was asked in 1815. 'It always has been the case', he replied. And among the women prisoners themselves, according to Poole, were 'many . . . abandoned women'. A Miss Tomkins, 'an unfortunate female' working in a brothel at Catherine Street, Strand, in 1815 was arrested at the suit of the brothel-keeper for a £20 debt and brought into the Marshalsea, for instance; and a Mrs Arklay, a serial adulteress who perhaps was a courtesan, lived in the prison with her lover for a time in 1817.[27]

We can learn something of the conviviality and mutual support of the ale room from John Sartain, whose *Reminiscences* were published in New York in 1900, many years after his migration from London to Philadelphia. He was taken as a visitor to the Marshalsea by a friend whose employer was imprisoned for debt there, perhaps around 1823, so not long before John Dickens's time. Sartain would then have been about fifteen and, if his memory is to be trusted, he was a sharp-eyed, wide-awake son of London, just like John Dickens's boy was becoming. During one visit he was asked to wait in what was probably the ale room:

A cheerful fire blazed in a grate in one corner of the room and seemed to give more light than the two candles, stuck in the necks of bottles, that stood on a long table of rough

boards. Seated on long, rude benches at each side of the table
were seven or eight persons, two or three of them women,
and some were intent upon a game of cards . . . At the
further end, away from the players and the lights, were three
well-dressed men in conversation across the table.

While Sartain was there, a new debtor arrived whose
presence stopped the play and the conversation. 'A decently
dressed, middle-aged woman had been brought in, looking
most unhappy and forlorn', apparently imprisoned for debts
she had inherited from her husband, now dead. 'A tall man
rose from his seat and spoke to her in kind and soothing
tones, telling her not to grieve, that the Marshalsea was not
the bad place it had the name of being; it was better than
the King's Bench or any of the other places', and guided her
to the seat he had just vacated. Sartain was then taken to
the room of the debtor his friend had come to see. But the
man had no fire and, while he transacted some business or
other, he showed the boys to a better-appointed room, occupied by 'Charlotte', at whose fire a number of prisoners were
gathered. 'I was surprised at the snug comfort of the place,
although the room was small and the ceiling so low that
the four posts of the bedstead, which took up most of the
space, almost touched it.'[28]

And we can see something of the committee at work in
one of Charles Dickens's most remarkable Marshalsea
memories. Sometime during his imprisonment, John Dickens
was elected to the committee of the college and became
eventually its chairman: one imagines his social standing and
sociability, his relish for a florid phrase and his business
experience combined to make him an obvious choice. Whether
it was his idea or another's, the collegians resolved to petition
the king, George IV, for a gift or 'bounty to the prisoners to
drink his majesty's health' on his forthcoming birthday, a
traditional excuse to seek alms from authority. The petition

was duly drawn up and presented for inspection to the college at a ceremony which the young Dickens made special efforts to witness, getting time off work from the blacking warehouse for the occasion. The petition 'was stretched out, I recollect, on a great ironing-board, under the window, which in another part of the room made a bestead at night'. In the room were John Dickens as chairman, supported by as many members of the committee as could be accommodated:

> my old friend Captain Porter (who had washed himself, to do honour to so solemn an occasion) stationed himself close to it, to read it to all who were unacquainted with its contents. The door was then thrown open, and they began to come in, in a long file; several waiting on the landing outside, while one entered, affixed his signature, and went out. To everybody in succession, Captain Porter said, 'Would you like to hear it read?' If he weakly showed the least disposition to hear it, Captain Porter, in a loud sonorous voice, gave him every word of it. I remember a certain luscious roll he gave to such words as 'Majesty – gracious Majesty – your gracious Majesty's unfortunate subjects – your Majesty's well-known munificence,' – as if the words were something real in his mouth, and delicious to taste: my poor father meanwhile listening with a little of an author's vanity, and contemplating (not severely) the spikes on the opposite wall . . . I would rather have seen it than the best play ever played; and I thought about it afterwards, over the pots of paste-blacking, often and often. When I looked, with my mind's eye, into the Fleet-prison during Mr. Pickwick's incarceration, I wonder whether half-a-dozen men were wanting from the Marshalsea crowd that came filing in again, to the sound of Captain Porter's voice![29]

Some years later, in 1837, the pretensions of the collegians won public recognition of a kind. It seems an imprisoned

shoemaker had convincingly argued a point of law in the
Insolvent Debtors' Court. His victory inspired some able
verses by A.D., doubtless one of the many literary characters
who passed through the Marshalsea over the years:

THE MARSHALSEA COLLEGE

Let statesmen and churchmen still boast of their arts,
In preaching of sermons, and making of laws;
Let the poet, too, boast of his genius and parts,
And for a short season obtain some applause.

But what know the statesman, the churchman, or poet?
Ah! how superficial must be all their knowledge;
However they sing, preach, or lecture to show it,
That ne'er took degrees at the Marshalsea College?

There nothing is known of inferiors or betters,
Their laws and religion agree with their knowledge,
'O, pardon our debts, as we pardon our debtors,'
Is the heav'n-taught prayer of the Marshalsea College.

Thus pray'd a poor debtor, but vain was his prayer,
For his duns had resolv'd to exert all their knowledge;
Nor legal advice, nor expenses to spare,
To defeat the poor student of Marshalsea College.

They brought into court, men of wit and discerning,
Well vers'd in the law, and could boast of their knowledge;
But the bold son of Crispin confounded their learning,
And gained a triumph for the Marshalsea College.

Nor were the collegians insensible to it,
They vote a degree for his skill and his knowledge;
A council was call'd, who were proud to bestow it,
And made him a doctor of Marshalsea College.

All hands were alert, and began to prepare,
All famous for genius, for wit, and for knowledge;
To raise the new doctor aloft in the chair,
Who in triumph was borne through the Marshalsea
College.[30]

We do not know what contact the master's-side prisoner John Dickens had with the common-side debtors, but it is likely that they were a little better off than their predecessors in the old Marshalsea, though not by much. At any one time there were probably just a dozen or so debtors with no resources, their worldly goods worth less than 40s in all, and so thrown largely on the mercy of charity and the county money. Such a small number at least meant in theory there was more to go round, but that was never very much, for there remained no allowance. There were in addition the charitable legacies, which had to be petitioned for by the debtors, petitions and answers delivered by a special messenger 'of the name of Smith; we pay him what we can afford, 6d a-piece for bringing them in'. Many of the sixteenth- and seventeenth-century gifts had drained away by 1815, but others had accrued during the course of the eighteenth century, even if they failed to make good all that had been lost. Around ten legacies brought in some £19 each year in cash to the new gaol; there was in addition a rich Christmas bounty of around £23 from fines and donations from judicial officers and court or ecclesiastical officials, including a Christmas dinner most years of roast beef, porter and bread for all the prisoners; gifts in kind for the common side brought in weekly some bread (mainly) and meat. Hunger was never eliminated from the Marshalsea's poor side but starvation to the point of death, unless brought on by some chronic ailment or old age, was a thing of the past.[31]

There was another aid to poor-side prisoners in the Marshalsea from 1812–13. Two acts of those years offered some poor relief for debtors arrested under mesne process and confined in prisons other than county gaols who could not otherwise support themselves. Thees acts applied to Marshalsea prisoners. Debtors on the poor side could apply to the parish of St George the Martyr, Southwark, for relief of 6d a day or 3s 6d a week, in effect advance payment of the monies they could expect to receive from an imprisoning creditor once the debt had been proved in court. There were provisions for the parish to reimburse the costs from wherever the debtor had a settlement, but repayment was complex, difficult and costly to enforce. Debtors applying to the parish were generally, it seems, denied relief. But they could then appeal to the magistrates at Union Hall, just across the road and a few steps down Union Street. Their pleas were frequent enough for the magistrates to have forms printed upholding the prisoner's appeal and ordering the overseers to pay the 6d a day, 'it appearing to me that he is unable to support himself' without relief from the parish. The local burden was such – the King's Bench also no doubt producing similar cases – that the parish petitioned Parliament to have the law repealed, or at least the process of reimbursement simplified. The act was amended and processes streamlined and Marshalsea poor-side debtors seem to have received the parish's sixpences with little interruption thereafter.[32]

These were all improvements, but it would be a mistake to think that extreme want had fled the Marshalsea. In December 1820 the papers reported on 'One most wretched object', a young woman, almost certainly a prostitute, 'turned out of the Marshalsea Prison, and suffering every misery that hunger and nakedness can inflict', taken into the Magdalen Hospital in what had been St George's Fields. And the impact of imprisonment for debt on family poverty across the metropolis continued. In January 1824 the wife of a Covent Garden linen draper now in the Marshalsea was taken up by watchmen near her former home: 'Her age was about thirty, and her appearance altogether that of a foreigner; her eyes and complexion dark, and her costume the remains of what had been genteel; black silk pelisse in rags; black silk bonnet and ostrich feathers, become rusty from age and exposure to all weathers, and almost shoeless feet.' She had been evicted from her lodgings the night before and had walked to the Marshalsea to ask if her husband could take her in. 'He, however, had a chum; and she was sent from thence at a late hour of the night.' The magistrate at Bow Street ordered that she be taken into the workhouse of St Martin-in-the-Fields.[33]

With the statutory or charitable monies coming into the gaol so limited and so unreliable, and then directed only to the very poorest, most debtors fell back on their traditional resources – their 'friends', including relatives and prosperous acquaintances however remote. Thus J. A. McKie, a former naval officer now sunk in debt, wrote to the retired Indian administrator Mountstuart Elphinstone from the Marshalsea on 25 September 1832. He had been paid off from HMS *Meteor* at the beginning of the year, having served under, or at least met, Admiral Charles Elphinstone Fleeming, Mountstuart's elder brother. Fleeming (McKie wrote Fleming) was out of town but his needs were too desperate to wait:

Being only Second Master in the Navy I receive no half pay, and being an entire stranger in England, rendered my situation still worse, and being so long without employment, I consequently incurred a debt for board, washing and lodging to the am^t of £27 – and being unable to pay, my landlord imprisoned me. I am a native of Nassau [in the Bahamas] and came to England with Adm^l Fleming was has [sic] very kindly patronized me, but I am now destitute of clothing or money to purchase any . . . I have very often been obliged to go without a meal since I've been here, and I've principally existed on the Charity of a half pay naval officer who was

in here, but who has left the last two days, however reluctant
or painful to my feelings. I am now through absolute want
obliged to solicit (however small the tribute) some little
pecuniary assistance . . . [F]or the want of money to employ
an attorney I will not even be able to take the benefit of the
Insolvent Act, so that the only prospect before me is to be
in prison as long as my creditor pleases to keep me, so that
away from home and my friends unless some benevolent
Personage assists me God knows what must become of me.
the winter I am sure will be the death of me. No Clothing,
no bedding but a miserable Prison straw one, I feel satisfied
will kill me. I am a member of the Ancient fraternity of Free
Masons, but as there are so many impositions practised in
London, I doubt should I make applications for releif, if it
would be obtain'd[.] [S]hould you be pleased to assist me in
any way you may rely on my repaying you the earliest possible
opportunity of doing so, and that with the most heart felt
feeling of gratitude. your honor may have seen me frequently
at Fentons Hotel when the Admiral was in Town.[34]

The good Elphinstone stumped up, though 'In consequence
of some gross neglect on the part of the 2[dy] Post Man of
this prison' there was a delay in McKie receiving and
acknowledging the grateful news. A couple of weeks later
he applied again. His creditor had offered to commute the
debt of £26 8s if McKie would pay £10. This he could not
raise, and perhaps there were other debts, but just £5 10s
would enable him to benefit from the Insolvent Debtors Act
and that sum he now sought. We do not know the outcome
this time.[35]

With the ever expanding reach of the newspapers more
debtors seem to have advertised for relief, in the absence of
pliant friends one letter reaching many potential benefactors.
Sometimes, very occasionally, a cryptic but urgent message
might appear in the personal columns, like this from 1838:

'F. Is in trouble, and gone to the Marshalsea, and wants to hear of or see L. as soon as possible. – July 9.'; and again, five months later, 'X., as F. is in the Marshalsea, Borough, and in general distress, wishes to hear or see from L. Direct letters to 18, Ernest-street', though which of the three such in the London postal directory was intended was a mystery to all but those in on the secret.[36]

Generally, though, the aim was more promiscuous. In the year John Dickens was committed, the doctor and friends of a newsagent imprisoned for an original debt of just £5, which he was unable to meet through sickness, advertised his predicament to the benevolent. He was now in the Marshalsea on an execution for debt and costs amounting to over £25, where he was bedridden with an agonising rheumatic fever and 'without much hope of recovery'. The advertisers hoped to raise a subscription sufficient to release him from gaol. Some years later the widow of a 'respectable Tradesman, reduced to the greatest distress, and now a prisoner in the Marshalsea', sought donations by advertising in *The Times* in November 1831 to enable her to take advantage of the Insolvent Debtors Act.[37]

Others were even more explicit in their appeal to a wealthy class of benefactors who were pressed to shoulder considerable burdens indeed:

CASE OF DISTRESS. – TO LADIES. – The Advertiser makes this appeal on behalf of his distressed Wife and Five innocent Children, four of whom are girls, the eldest being thirteen years of age, without a prospect of their being educated, or in any way provided for, through the Advertiser, their father, having been reduced from comparative affluence to positive want, and is now in confinement in the Marshalsea prison, for a debt of ten pounds five shillings, and eight pounds ten shillings expenses; having had his furniture and bedding taken from him, his wife and children have nothing to lie upon but the bare boards, with nothing to cover them but their day apparel. The object of this appeal is to obtain, if possible, an education and provision for those helpless children, without the outward sign of charity, their parents in the first instance, through building in the country, sunk gradually their property, until now it is chargeable with upwards of one hundred and forty-eight pounds annually interest for money borrowed upon it; the remaining rental the Mortgagee takes, the Advertiser being further indebted to him. Additional information will be given by applying to Mrs. C., at Mr. Turner's, 34, Great Titchfield-street, Marylebone.[38]

By no means everyone in the Marshalsea was in such a hopeless position. John Dickens, once his family was around him, managed very well, as Charles's biographer recorded: 'They had no want of bodily comforts there. His father's income, still going on, was amply sufficient for that; and in every respect indeed but elbow-room, I have heard him say, the family lived more comfortably in prison than they had done for a long time out of it.' Most of all they were free from duns, from the loud knocking at the street door, the abuse shouted up at them from the pavement for all the neighbours to hear.[39]

This peace of mind, perhaps above all things, was what made some imprisoned debtors reluctant to leave the asylum of the Marshalsea even though they were otherwise free to go. The parliamentary committee of 1815 took evidence from one such 'prisoner', Jonathan Davy, in the Marshalsea for fourteen weeks but now supersedable because his creditor was no longer paying him 6d a day: 'my plaintiff dropped me'. He was now paying the large sum of 2s a night for a room and bedding over the tap, which he shared with his wife; it was offset by the 3s a week he received by renting out to a prisoner another room he had been allocated but did not need. Why then did he stay in? 'Because I cannot

pay my debts, and I expect a detainer as soon as I get out . . .
I am afraid we shall both be sent in again.' He hoped now
to take the benefit of the Insolvent Debtors Act so that he
could settle what he said were all his wife's debts with her
numerous creditors and release himself by paying whatever
could be raised from his effects. In the meantime their creditors' money was seeping away in Marshalsea rent. There
were others in the same position, though those supersedable
were said to be given a chum in preference to prisoners,
'and if riotous we turn them out', at the risk no doubt that
they might soon be back again, at a new suit and in worse
circumstances.[40]

Most prisoners, of course, left as soon as they could.
Nearly all the old ways of doing so remained open to them
in the new Marshalsea. There was a trickle of deaths in the
prison each year from various natural causes ascribed to the
catch-all 'died by visitation of God'. Suicide retained its
attractions as a way out of intractable problems where
tomorrow promised no better than today. An extraordinary
case from the summer of 1829 unsurprisingly won some
public attention. Three German women, the sisters Both, got
into debt and were imprisoned first in Whitecross Street
prison in Finsbury and then in the Marshalsea. A solicitor
who visited them there, John Dickenson, 'found them in the
most deplorable state, without even a change of linen, and
in want of the common necessaries of life'. Only one, the
eldest, had an action against her but the others wouldn't
leave her side, the then deputy marshal, Joseph Rutland,
suffering them to live together. Through Dickenson's efforts
the eldest sister was discharged and all three left vowing to
return to Hanover. But the sisters failed to raise funds for
the journey and were still in London a few weeks later when,
unable to pay for a night's lodging at Greenwich, they hired
a waterman to row them back to London. Opposite Millwall
all three stood up in the boat and jumped into the Thames.

Two were rescued but the youngest, Hermandine, drowned, taking her own life 'under the influence', her sisters testified, 'of extremely oppressive circumstances'.[41]

One other traditional way out of the Marshalsea seems, however, to have dried up in the new gaol. With the more robust modern buildings and walls, escapes were pretty much a thing of the past. There was no escape from the new prison in its first three and a half years, though a prisoner got away from his escort on the lengthened journey from court to gaol. And no escape subsequently seems to have found its way into the newspapers.[42]

The routes to freedom through due process, however, all remained intact. Of 359 prisoners brought in and discharged during 1816, fifty-three transferred to the King's Bench or the Fleet by writ of habeas corpus, forty of them to the former; 121 satisfied their arresting creditors in some way, usually by compromising on the sum owed or claimed; eighty-three were supersedable and discharged because their plaintiffs did not proceed expeditiously or failed to pay the daily 6d once a debt had been proved; ninety took advantage of the most recent Insolvent Debtors Act; and a few were discharged by other means (mainly special bail or by order of the court). Of all these, 70 per cent were released within three months of committal, almost all within six months. The Thatched House Society continued to be active in assisting poor debtors to take one or other of these routes: in 1823–4, for instance, 151 Marshalsea prisoners were helped to their discharge by the society, the largest number of any prison in the country; and the legacies from Allnutt, Ashton and Pelling assisted some fifty or so more to gain their freedom during the year.[43]

Among annual fluctuations there was a steadily rising preference for the insolvent debtor route. A permanent Insolvent Debtors' Court in Portugal Street, to the north of the Strand, was established in 1813, the product of Lord

Redesdale's act of that year. It helped streamline processes and perhaps reduce costs for both sides of an action, and became increasingly used from the beginning of the 1820s. So in 1821, 163 of 341 debtors committed and discharged during the year were freed by insolvency, with a concomitant reduction in the numbers becoming supersedable, though 113, or just shy of one third, still settled with their creditor in some way. That year some 92 per cent of the total were out within three months of committal. In the busy year of 1831, 216 of 433 claimed insolvency, while 162 settled; 77 per cent were freed within three months.[44]

Insolvency, then, was a well-trodden road out of the new Marshalsea. So it proved during the period of John Dickens's imprisonment. The numbers in the Marshalsea in 1824 were unexceptional, with eighty-four debtors in custody on 13 May, for instance. During the fourteen weeks or so of his imprisonment he saw 142 debtors brought into the prison; of these just four were women. In the same period he saw 138 prisoners discharged, some of whom were already in the prison when he arrived, but the large majority (110) were released though in gaol for a shorter period than he. When John Dickens was brought into the lodge on 20 February three others came in that same day: George Giles (owing £50), Francis Turner (£100) and William Cockburn (taken in execution for £26 and costs); Cockburn transferred to the Fleet within a fortnight, Giles was released under insolvency at the end of April and Turner was still in the Marshalsea when Dickens left.[45]

Most debtors that February to May of 1824 left for two main reasons. Of the 138 discharges fifty-two settled with their plaintiffs, among them George Nottage, almost certainly that poor-side steward of 1815, back in a familiar setting. He was now an auctioneer of Kingsland, Hackney, deep in debt from his youth, for he was probably born in the early 1790s at Henham in Essex, where his father followed the same trade: his father would revoke a bequest to him in his will in a few years' time. On this occasion George was able to release himself inside two days by settling his creditor's claim of £18.[46]

Another fifty-nine took advantage of the Insolvent Debtors Act. John Dickens chose this way too. It would release him from the Marshalsea but never from his money worries.

His imprisonment on 20 February had relieved him from many embarrassments but caused him one that was both new and pressing: how to deal with his employer, the Navy Pay Office, from whom each quarter he was receiving his annual salary of £350 while now unable to discharge his duties. For some years Dickens had suffered with a painful and at times disabling urethral stricture restraining urine flow, of which his colleagues at work must have been aware. It seems likely that on his imprisonment, perhaps while at the spunging house, he excused his immediate absence with a sick note. Certainly he now took rapid steps to explore the possibility of early retirement on grounds of ill health. After nineteen years' conscientious service, he felt he was due a permanent pension and commissioned medical evidence to support his case. On 2 March he wrote to the Navy Pay Office from 4 Gower Street North – he was understandably coy about his present whereabouts – enclosing certificates from two surgeons, one of Dover Street, Piccadilly, and the other of the Old Kent Road – confirming that he 'is from infirmity of body, arising from a chronic affection of the Urinary Organs, incapacitated from attending to any public duty'.

While the Navy Pay Office was considering his application, Dickens's 'private Embarrassments' came to light, perhaps because he told them or perhaps through its own enquiries. The combination of ill health and burdensome debt rendered his employers sympathetic to his permanent removal from his post, the prospect of his name and position

'Gazetted' and reported in the newspapers a potential source of disrepute that plainly made his services dispensable. But the cogs of bureaucracy ground only slowly forward and retirement on a pension did not come Dickens's way while he was in the Marshalsea. Instead, and gratifyingly, he continued to receive full pay for the whole period of his confinement.[47]

With money coming in, with his family cramped though cared for, and with his social status recognised and valued by his fellow collegians, there was no pressing need to settle with James Karr. Compromising the baker's suit might have won Dickens his freedom but only to put himself at the mercy of a pack of others eager for a second bite at his person. He was thus in a not dissimilar position to that of superseded debtor Jonathan Davy, who had scandalised the parliamentary committee of 1815. Certainly, John Dickens would have had little difficulty in paying for the legal costs and fees of taking the benefit of an Insolvent Debtors Act when the opportunity arose. Doing so involved him in drawing up a schedule of creditors to identify who was owed what, no doubt a tricky task taxing both memory and honesty. The schedule has not survived but we know that many were owed money and some, like his long-suffering brother-in-law, were owed a great deal. When finally cast, the account reached several hundred pounds, perhaps two or even three years' full salary.

While Dickens was in the Marshalsea he received news that he must have anticipated for some time – though hardly wished for. His mother, Elizabeth, died on 26 April 1824 at her home in Oxford Street. She had made her final will in January that year, and her main legacies were £500 to her elder son, William, and £450 to John: 'The reason that I make this difference between my two Sons,' she explained, 'is, that my son John Dickens having had from me several Sums of Money some years ago –'. The legacies were held in stock, Bank of England 3 per cent Consols. She also shared her 'wearing apparel' equally between the sons.[48]

For many years some of Dickens's biographers interpreted Elizabeth's bequest as the key that unlocked the Marshalsea gate for his father. But even this windfall, substantial and no doubt welcome as it was, could not relieve John Dickens of his debts or offer him anything like a new start. It could not even found an acceptable compromise that might be offered to his many creditors with any chance of success. Neither would the Thatched House Society nor the Marshalsea legacies offer help to a man of his means or, more important, of his profligate weight of debts. In these circumstances, it was less a case of John Dickens choosing the insolvency route than insolvency choosing him.

A new Insolvent Debtors Act was passed in 1824 and through its provisions John Dickens gained his freedom. The schedule of debts and creditors was duly sworn to, his name posted in the notices of the *London Gazette* warning his creditors that he was intending to take the benefit of the act so they could add themselves to the list or challenge the sums declared or show good cause why he should not be released from gaol provided that they contribute to his expenses while there. For all this, legal expenses, court costs and prison fees had to be paid. All monies and possessions that the debtor retained or could gain access to had to be surrendered for the use of his creditors. Elizabeth's legacy duly went into the pot.

At the point of insolvency, the debtor could keep for his own use and the use of his family only cash, clothing and domestic necessaries to a total value of £20, equivalent to John Dickens's salary for three weeks. This sum had to be sworn to and there was an independent valuation to satisfy the creditors that nothing was being held back. The family, too, had to be appraised in this way. Charles Dickens remembered, years later, that

It was necessary, as a matter of form, that the clothes I wore should be seen by the official appraiser. I had a half-holiday to enable me to call upon him, at his own time, at a house somewhere beyond the Obelisk. I recollect his coming out to look at me with his mouth full, and a strong smell of beer upon him, and saying good-naturedly that 'that would do,' and 'it was all right.' Certainly the hardest creditor would not have been disposed (even if he had been legally entitled) to avail himself of my poor white hat, little jacket, or corduroy trowsers. But I had a fat old silver watch in my pocket, which had been given me by my grandmother before the blacking days, and I had entertained my doubts as I went along whether that valuable possession might not bring me over the twenty pounds. So I was greatly relieved, and made him a bow of acknowledgment as I went out.[49]

John Dickens walked free from the Marshalsea on 28 May 1824. He remained in employment at the Navy Pay Office until he retired, at just under forty, on health grounds on 9 March 1825. His pension of £145 16s 8d, just over two-fifths of his previous salary, was paid quarterly there-after. It did not vary in value, though he was to receive it for twenty-six years. Probably from 1831, when further proceedings took place that seem to have made him an insolvent for a second time, £25 a year was paid directly into court for the benefit of his creditors; from 1846 he had to pay income tax of £4 5s a year, so in all his pension paid him in his last years around £116 10s or £2 5s a week.[50]

This was supplemented by what was probably a steadily mounting income from his pen, for which he had ever had a predilection and some facility. He learned shorthand, reporting parliamentary debates for two newspapers, and he contributed articles on marine insurance to the *British Press* – the Marshalsea's daily in 1815, we might recall, so perhaps he made its acquaintance there. When the paper folded, causing him, he complained, 'serious pecuniary inconvenience', he solicited Lloyd's for alms: he had praised the underwriters in his articles and they generously rewarded him with ten guineas. Later, and more fruitfully, John Dickens was appointed from January 1846 manager of the reporters on the *Daily News*, of which his son had been briefly the first editor. This seems to have given him some financial stability in his final years.[51]

Until then, probably for twenty years after John Dickens slipped out of the Marshalsea, its shadow never left him. His pension and his Grub Street earnings proved insufficient either to satisfy his creditors or to stop new debts arising. He borrowed shamelessly from his famous son's friends and even his son's publishers. He fell behind with Fanny's fees and boarding costs at the Royal Academy of Music and in October 1825 sent the governors a letter accompanying a promise to pay at Christmas that presents an instance not just of his verbosity but of the insouciant disregard of any interest other than his own, especially when it came to forking out the rhino:

My dear Sir, Circumstances compel me to seek your friendly aid as on a former occasion by accepting in lieu of *present payment* an order as above [for the outstanding £32 11s 11d, to be deducted from his pension]. I flatter myself you will take some pleasure in forwarding my views in this respect with the Committee when I assure you that I shall consider it a most signal act of friendship. A circumstance of great moment to me will be decided in the ensuing term which I confidently hope will place me in comparative affluence, and by which I shall be enabled to redeem the order before the period of Christmas Day. At any rate it will meet with same attention as before, I shall have the pleasure of expressing to you my sincere obligations . . .

And now, my dear Sir, it only remains for me to assure you of the sense I entertain of your general kindness and attention, and to subscribe myself, Your obliged and obedient servant, JOHN DICKENS.[52]

In fact the 'order' was not honoured, the bill remained unsatisfied, an agreement to pay what was owed in instalments was not adhered to and Fanny had to be withdrawn from the Royal Academy in June 1827. That same year the Dickens family were evicted from their home, presumably because of non-payment of rent. Among a welter of 'pecuniary inconveniences', in November 1834 John Dickens was arrested on a Marshalsea writ by his wine suppliers and taken to Sloman's or Slowman's spunging house at 4 Cursitor Street, but a step from the Insolvent Debtors' Court and so a part of town John knew well. His son, now aged twenty-two, organised legal assistance and raised funds to bail him out or settle the bill to avoid any repeat of the Marshalsea shame, though it seems to have been a narrow escape; indeed, Charles was afraid he would himself be 'taken' at any moment, probably because he had backed a bill for his father that was now due. Somehow the matter was accommodated. But it led again to the Dickens family abandoning their present home in prestigious Bentinck Street, Marylebone, with John taking lodgings away from his wife and daughters for a time. And Charles Dickens too became temporarily dependent on his friends, begging small loans in ways that must have been deeply discomforting to him, and for a time casting a Marshalsea shade over his own future.[53]

John was again arrested sometime before December 1835 and had to find bail to avoid imprisonment in the Marshalsea once more. To remove his parents from the expensive whirl of London life, in March 1839 Charles rented a country cottage just outside Exeter and banished them to birdsong and cowpats. But John could not be stopped from coming up to town and trading on his son's name, by now known to every household in the land. He unashamedly incurred debts in Devon and London by giving notes that promised payment from his son's publishers, 'a moral outrage', the author fumed, 'which words can scarcely censure enough'. In March 1841 Charles took the extraordinary step of repudiating his father's debts by instructing his solicitors to take out an advertisement in all the leading London papers affirming that the only debts he would honour were his own and his wife's: 'certain persons bearing, or purporting to bear, the surname of our said client, have put into circulation . . . certain acceptances made payable at his private residence, or at the offices of his business agents'; now, 'such bills . . . will not be paid'. Charles even tried to make arrangements to ship his father, and mother if she would go, 'to Calais, Boulogne, or Antwerp', but the plans came to nothing. Though small depredations at his father's hands probably continued, there was never the need for a repeat of the 1841 blow-up.[54]

In all this time the Insolvent Debtors' Court continued to be involved in the proceedings begun in 1824. These seemed – indeed, frequently were – endless, as probably most insolvents found: George Nottage the auctioneer was wrapped up similarly in proceedings that drew him back and forth to the insolvency or bankruptcy courts from 1819 to 1848 at least. John Dickens now trod that same weary way. Meetings of his creditors were held in Rochester and London. Dividends were paid but fresh creditors added in that second insolvency of 1831. Further dividends were paid in 1833 and 1834. In November 1846, by which time his finances should have been in better order from his senior responsibilities at the *Daily News*, his income continued to be substantially at the service of his creditors. That month they secured another dividend, this time of 4s 3d for every pound he owed them.[55]

Yet another, perhaps the last and the fourth arising from the second insolvency, reaping 5s 5d, was agreed by the court in January 1852. By then John Dickens's debts were pursuing him even beyond the grave, for he had been dead ten months. His death came while he was surrounded by his family in his surgeon's house at 34 Keppel Street, Bloomsbury, on census night, 31 March 1851. A few days before an emergency operation had been carried out on his penis and scrotum 'without chloroform', as his horrified son related, 'the most terrible operation known in surgery . . . He bore it with astonishing fortitude, and I saw him directly afterwards – his room, a slaughter house of blood. He was wonderfully cheerful and strong-hearted.' Such resilience had borne him, generally buoyant, through an adult lifetime of financial anxiety that would have cast many another into an earlier grave. It would not be those money worries that killed him but that other condition he had lived with so long, now in its final stage: 'Rupture of the Urethra from old standing stricture and consequent mortification of the scrotum from infiltration of urine.'[56]

We know so much about John Dickens and his Marshalsea life because of the celebrity of his eldest son. There was no typical Marshalsea debtor, for each had his or her own story to tell, could we only piece it together. But there was much about John Dickens's lifetime of money troubles, pivoting on the Marshalsea, that will be familiar when we come to consider some other Marshalsea lives that have come down to us through the years. But they hold, too, many surprises. And they take us into many odd byways of London life.

7

BRIEF LIVES: MARSHALSEA
DEBTORS, 1820–42

'You'll find some characters behind other locks, I don't say you won't; but if you want the top sawyer . . . you must come to the Marshalsea.'[1]

AT around 6.15 in the evening of Wednesday 10 June 1840, Queen Victoria and Prince Albert took their 'customary drive in Hyde-park before dinner'. 'Customary' is stretching it a little because they had only been married four months, but certainly on fine evenings that spring and early summer crowds of sightseers had grown accustomed to seeing their young and much-loved sovereign take the London air with her new prince. They drove 'in a very open phaeton, drawn by four bays' and apart from probably two postilions they were alone in the carriage. It left the gates of Buckingham Palace and swept up Constitution Hill, the palace garden wall to the left and Green Park railings on the right. The queen sat on the side of the carriage next to the wall, with Albert on the park side. There were just four escorts, mounted equerries of the palace household cantering behind the carriage and policemen dotted irregularly either side of the road. Crowds of ordinary Londoners watched and applauded. A few jogged alongside the carriage to hold a longer view of the royal couple.

Some 200 yards or so along Constitution Hill a young man, slight and boyish even for his eighteen years, stepped forward from the Green Park railings to the edge of the pavement within a few yards of the carriage, raised a pistol at the queen and fired. The ball or bullet was never found, but a bystander on the wall side of the road claimed it buzzed past his face. The postilions pulled on the reins and Victoria rose in her seat, but Albert shouted to drive on.

Across the road, close to the wall, Joshua Reeve Lowe had been running to keep pace with the royal carriage and gain a better view of the queen. He was accompanied by his nephew Albert. They both heard the shot, as did many others in the crowd. They looked across and saw the man who had fired standing about three yards or so from the carriage. His right hand holding the pistol had dropped but Joshua saw him raise a second pistol in his left hand, level it across his right arm to take aim at the carriage now in front of him and fire again. Once more the shot, if such it was, did not strike home. Joshua ran across the road with Albert at his heels and was the first to seize the man, while Albert disarmed him. Seeing the pistols in Albert's hands, some of the crowd took hold of him as the potential assassin, but the man who had fired 'cried out, "I did it," or "It was me that did it."' Two policemen then arrived and took him to the nearest station house, accompanied by a posse of eager witnesses, including the Lowes.

The gunman was Edward Oxford, then lodging at West Street, Lambeth. He was born in Birmingham and his pistols too were Birmingham-made. Oxford was an out-of-work barman – some reports described him as a 'pot-boy' but more truly he had taken on supervisory functions in various public houses, some education compensating for his youth and boyish looks. He had a lengthy history of bizarre and violent behaviour. At his trial for high treason at the Old Bailey on 6–10 July 1840, Oxford was declared insane and sentenced to be detained at her majesty's pleasure. He was committed to Bethlem Hospital in Lambeth, just a hop from his last lodgings. There for the next twenty-four years he lived quietly, busying himself learning languages, for which he discovered a flair. When he was transferred to Broadmoor in 1864 the doctors there thought him sane and three years later he was released but exiled, choosing Australia as his new home and taking a new name, John Freeman. He died in Melbourne in 1900.[2]

The assassination attempt unsurprisingly caused a sensation. The royal couple had sought refuge at the queen mother's house in Belgrave Square. When Victoria and Albert returned that same evening to Hyde Park on their way to the palace, they found 'an immense concourse of persons of all ranks and both sexes' cheering themselves hoarse. 'God Save the Queen' was sung at all the London theatres, at public dinners and at the opera house that Wednesday night; next day, out again for their airing but now accompanied by platoons of horse guards, huge crowds greeted the couple in the park; and on the Friday a great procession of peers and commoners in their coaches, watched again by cheering crowds, paid their respects at the palace.[3]

This mood of monarchical enthusiasm no doubt lit up Copthall Court, a narrow turning off Throgmorton Street just north of the Bank of England. No. 2 was the shop of Joshua Reeve Lowe, the first man to lay hold of Edward Oxford and briefly the hero of the hour, his name in every metropolitan newspaper and beyond. As far as we know, he was a respectable City artisan, a 'Working Optician' or 'spectacle-maker' as he described himself in the various proceedings arising from the assassination attempt. He was then living at London Wall and had been City-born, in December 1810, so was not yet thirty at the time of his unanticipated moment of fame on Constitution Hill. By then he was married to Elizabeth Mucklow, with five young children, the eldest not eight years old; the children must have been born at a variety of City addresses, for there was something about the Lowes reminiscent of the peripatetic wanderings of the Dickens family, though on a smaller pitch, with homes and shops recorded at Aldersgate Street, London Wall, Cherry Tree Court, Princes Street and Beech Street over perhaps a decade since Lowe's marriage in 1831. Whether that domestic mobility owed something to indebtedness is uncertain but it is a possibility, because in subsequent actions debts stretching back to 1833 were brought to the attention of the Insolvent Debtors' Court. Even so, Joshua seems successfully to have juggled the calls on his purse, both commercial and domestic, and to have remained in business as a City optician and maker of spectacles to the day of his fleeting celebrity.[4]

This, for surely the first time in his life, brought Joshua Reeve Lowe in touch with some of the greatest in the land – even, in person or more probably through agents, with the queen mother and Prince Albert himself. It must have seemed a stroke of good fortune heralding a new and more prosperous life for himself and his family. Celebrity induced a fateful decision. Within a year of the drama on Constitution Hill, Lowe had moved west from the London he had known all his life, setting up home in hardly extravagant lodgings in part of a densely occupied house in Dartmouth Street, not far from Westminster Abbey. Domestic frugality contrasted oddly with commercial extravagance, for Dartmouth Street was but a short walk from his new shop. He was no longer pandering to City tradesmen and shopmen but was setting out his stall in the midst of the richest clientele in the land, at St James's Street in the heart of the West End. In the summer of 1841 he advertised his intention to set his sights high. He made all he could of his new royal connections, though his grammar must have provoked the odd aristocratic snigger:

Joshua Reeve Lowe, Optician, by Special Appointment to HRH Prince Albert, and under the immediate patronage of

the Queen Dowager and HRH the Duchess of Kent, 34, St.
James's-street, London, begs to solicit an inspection by the
Nobility, Gentry, &c., of his highly finished assortment of
Articles in the above business, being fully convinced of their
superiority and workmanship.

J.R.L. especially requests the favour of an examination
of his stock of Spectacles, Eye and opera Glasses. From his
thorough knowledge of this branch, and having been prac-
tically engaged as a manufacturer 15 years, he is enabled
to make that selection of Pebbles which possess the desired
object without fear of injury to the most sensitive organ
of the eye. He, therefore, respectfully ventures to anticipate
in addition to his high and distinguished Appointment and
Patronage; the favours of the Nobility, Gentry, &c., of
which it will be his chief study to merit and ensure a
continuance of.[5]

Lowe's move from the City was a disaster for him. The
'Nobility, Gentry, &c.' failed to call, his expansive wares
stayed unsold, his suppliers' bills went unpaid and in his
desperation he pawned stock for ready money rather than
returning it. Within weeks he closed the St James's Street
premises, saved what he could from the wreck and tried to
make a go of things as an optician at Hatfield Street, south
of the river near Waterloo Road, but could mount no
recovery. By December he had accumulated huge and unmanageable debts and was arrested for a niggling amount of
£21 plus costs that he was unable to discharge. On
13 December 1841 he was brought into custody at the
Marshalsea prison. He remained there for over nine months
until he was able to ship out via a writ of habeas corpus to
the more comfortable Queen's Bench on 16 September 1842.[6]

Three months or so later, in his schedule of liabilities
lodged at the Insolvent Debtors' Court, Lowe acknowledged
debts of nearly £4,000, with just £85 owed to him. He was

in debt to no fewer than 170 creditors. In an accompanying statement he sought to explain his business collapse, with a bitter side-swipe at an ungrateful monarch.

'I ascribe my insolvency to the heavy expenses incurred in opening a shop and premises in St. James's-street, Piccadilly, which I was induced to do upon obtaining the highest patronage in the realm, and afterwards to my inability to dispose of goods to enable me to meet my engagements, and to losses sustained in consequence thereon.' He expected, he said, to be made a Court tradesman, as in the case of the person who saved the life of George the Third from the hand of an assassin; but his expectations were not realised. He received 70*l*. from Prince Albert for a telescope which his Royal Highness purchased. Being unable to sell his goods, the insolvent was obliged, at various times, to pawn a portion of them.[7]

Joshua Reeve Lowe was at last discharged from the Queen's prison, as it had become, probably in January 1843, after more than a year in gaol. His discharge had been opposed by one creditor whose goods he had pawned, but that was overcome with the help of some sympathetic solicitors who had taken up his case: pawning in these circumstances was a risky business that might have landed Lowe in the criminal courts had a harsher view been taken of his behaviour. Whether his many creditors received any part of their money back is unknown, but unlikely: certainly no dividends were reported in the *London Gazette*. By 1845 Lowe was still living south of the river and trading as an optician, his home and shop now at 15 Broadway, just east of Borough High Street. He did not trade there long. Joshua Reeve Lowe died at home on 25 January 1848. He was just thirty-seven. The cause of death was given as 'Phthisis', probably chronic pulmonary tuberculosis; if so, it can't have been helped by so many months in Southwark's prisons. Sometime before his death he gave up all pretensions to business, his occupation noted on his death certificate as 'Railway Clerk'.[8]

As we have seen, tradesmen like Lowe made up a significant portion of the Marshalsea's population. They were not the largest element but they were among the most visible: journeymen working for employers, craftsmen working on their own account, wage labourers, seamen and poor widows have left far fewer records of their lives in or out of prison. Men and women in trade generally had more resources on which their creditors could batten, so a little of their lives can be pieced together from the notices arising from their insolvency proceedings, dry stuff hiding many tearful anxieties and desperate shifts. There the twists and turns of their working lives can be plotted in the social geography etched on the London street maps. Most frequently there was a tendency downhill; many of these debtors' careers did indeed 'go south' or at least south of the river. Yet despite these markers we know very little of what these men and women felt of their predicament. Debtors rarely speak directly to us and we must infer what we reasonably can from the few sentences from Joshua Reeve Lowe and some others whose court appearances were occasionally reported in the newspapers.[9] Two Marshalsea debtors, though, who did seize a right to speak, even if in very different ways, were John Ewer Poole and Giles Hemens.

Poole, we might recall, was the author of *An Expose* [sic] *of the Practice of the Palace, or Marshalsea Court; with a Description of the Prison, the Secrets of the Prison-House, its Regulations, Fees, &c. &c* . . ., published anonymously and probably at his own expense in 1833. It sold for a shilling. Poole called the author 'An Eye-Witness', as indeed he was, for he had been a Marshalsea prisoner that very year, brought into custody for a debt of £30 on 12 March and released by the Insolvent Debtors Acts on 10 May.[10]

Despite that intimacy, the *Expose* pretended a detached view of the imprisoned debtor's world: 'Having been an *eye-witness* of the baneful effects of *imprisonment for debt*, through the misfortunes of others', gave the reader more than an impression that no such misfortune had happened to the author. But the case of 'A.B.', which immediately followed, spoke directly to his own experience, at least in timescale, for he described A.B. as taken in execution on a Marshalsea writ 'In the month of March last'. 'A.B. had met with some heavy losses in trade, and had solicited and obtained *time* of all his creditors, with the exception of a few *small* claimants', one of whom now had him arrested on a debt originally less than £5 but which was subsequently loaded with costs. This total A.B. could not pay. Here 'was a man (who had for years supported himself and family by honest industry – respectable in himself, and respected by all who *knew* him – and by whose exertions every creditor would have been paid)', now prevented from doing so by a creditor who exploited a vicious system and sent his debtor to the Marshalsea. 'I could not desert such a man *in prison*', and indeed he could not, for Poole and A.B. were one and the same.[11]

There follows an able exposé of the oppressions of the Palace and Marshalsea courts, their intrinsic bias in favour of creditors and attorneys, and the counterproductive burdens on society when respectable and industrious debtors such as A.B. are imprisoned and can no longer support their families. And Eye-Witness rages with biblical fervour against the iniquities of the Marshalsea prison and its moral dangers for honest traders and female virtue, tempted beyond endurance by crushing poverty and the need for ready money inside the gaol:

> Look on this picture, ye who would make us religious by Act of Parliament! Ye advocates of *Negro* Emancipation! Ye who condemn the Factory System! Ye Bible Societies! Ye dispensers of Religious Tracts! Ye Societies for promoting Christian Knowledge! and for the Suppression of Vice! I call on ye in

the name of Religion! I call on ye in the name of Morality!
I call on ye in the name of *all* that is dear to the character
of a Christian! to unite in the good cause of obtaining *abolition of imprisonment for debt*. View the Metropolitan Debtors'
Prisons – visit the prisions of the King's Bench, the Fleet, and,
though last, not least in iniquity, the 'Palace or Marshalsea!'
Here you will find imprisonment for debt has been, and is
productive of more vice, than almost any other cause! Here,
then, you will find employ *worthy* a Christian Legislator.[12]

Poole had at least one Christian Legislator in mind. On
8 July 1833 he wrote from temporary lodgings at 3 Union
Row, New Kent Road, enclosing a copy of his *Expose* to
Joseph Hume, the radical MP for Middlesex, recently one
of the successful parliamentary movers of the Great Reform
Act and an advocate of prison reform among many other
progressive causes. Poole made clear in his letter that
'Eye-Witness' was rather more than a disinterested observer
of the misfortunes of others: 'I take the liberty of enclosing
a Pamphlet, which I have published, as the only means of
obtaining Bread, for a sick wife & a large Family who have
been reduced to beggary by my <u>imprisonment for debt</u>.'[13]

We know little of John Ewer Poole, not when he was
born or when he married, though the large family was
attested to in 1825 when he claimed 'a family of eight
dependants on him'. He did, though, leave an eloquent paper
trail in court and prison records of one kind or another. Far
from the honest and industrious and respectable A.B., whose
exertions would have satisfied every creditor had he been
left free to do so, John Ewer Poole was a serial insolvent,
constantly shifting his address to avoid creditors, in and out
of debtors' gaols across London, prosecuted and imprisoned
for unlawfully pawning goods that did not belong to him;
and, as his Marshalsea pamphlet eloquently testifies, an
arch-hypocrite and dissembler. On the other hand, for such

there usually was in the debtor's world, he was intelligent, imaginative, venturesome, irrepressible and humorous.[14]

John Ewer Poole's first appearance in the London courts was not as a defendant but a witness, indeed a prosecutor. In 1814 he was a tobacconist, the *Post Office Directory* that year noting him at 203 Strand, a respectable address indeed. Five years later he had moved home and shop to prestigious 74 New Bond Street, for in January 1819 a seventeen-year-old boy, John Johnson, was prosecuted by Poole for stealing a brass moulding he had broken away from the tobacconist's shop window – Johnson received six months in prison and a whipping.[15]

Poole's upward rise in the tobacco trade did not continue long. By the end of 1820 he had moved again, to 2 Jermyn Street, St James's, another wealthy shopping street, where he was trading as 'Auctioneer and Appraiser'; but now he was laden with debt and must have had his first taste of a debtor's prison, for he was declaring himself insolvent as a way of satisfying his creditors. He can't have been free long, for in February 1821 he was imprisoned in the Fleet by order of the Insolvent Debtors' Court at the suit of four men, perhaps more of those '*small* claimants' that it was so easy to neglect in an insolvency schedule. By September 1825 he had moved to a newly built but quickly disreputable suburb of north-west Marylebone at 53 Lisson Grove, continuing the trade of auctioneer. It was from here that he unlawfully pawned goods entrusted to him to sell for an undischarged bankrupt who never got his money for them. He was given three months' hard labour in Coldbath Fields House of Correction at Clerkenwell. Despite a petition from sixteen people whom Poole had enlisted to give him a character reference, and despite a verbose plea to Sir Robert Peel, Home Secretary, detailing how he had informed on a publisher of blasphemous books and how his honourable motives had been misunderstood, he appears to have served his full sentence at 'The Steel'.[16]

Between 1826 and 1833, when he was imprisoned in the Marshalsea, Poole racked up a great number of addresses, both business and residential. He had a preference for the West End but was frequently pushed back to the margins, sometimes the suburbs, always a moving target: from Mount Street (Mayfair) to Lower Sloane Street (Chelsea) while carrying on business as auctioneer and other things for part of the time at Park Street (Grosvenor Square); then living in Praed Street (Paddington) while in business at Fitzroy Square and at Old Jewry in the City; then living in Harrow Road (Paddington), Castle Street (Leicester Square), Hart Street (Bloomsbury) and Collumpton Place (Kentish Town) while carrying on business at Mortimer Street (Fitzroy Square); when he was arrested in 1833 he was living at low-class Robert Street (Hampstead Road). In all, this was twelve addresses for home or business in six or seven years, one more instance of the debtor's necessarily itchy feet. His trade proved as flexible as his lodgings. While he was in the Marshalsea he was described as 'Appraiser, House-Agent, and Accountant, and for a short-time Plasterer, Painter, and Paper-Hanger', testimony to the speculative attractions of the London property market in these years of seemingly endless suburban expansion.[17]

For the next five years Poole's movements are not known, but he was back in the Marshalsea again in September 1838 for a debt of just under £10 that he was able to discharge and so free himself within a week or two. From there and for the next four years or so new debts seem steadily to have accumulated alongside his peripatetic adventures round all points of the London compass, now including the Surrey side of the river: back to the Strand, No. 337, where he added 'Licensed Victualler's Agent, and proprietor of the Hall of Information' to his professional portfolio; and living at Beresford Street (Walworth), Half Moon Street (Islington), West Square (Lambeth, where Edward Oxford was a near neighbour if the dates coincided, either at West Street or Bethlem Hospital), Cherry Tree Cottage (St John's Wood), Bridge Street (Westminster), Hercules Buildings (Lambeth, where William Blake had once lived) and finally Princes Road (Kennington); he also had offices in Gerrard Street (Soho) and Basinghall Street (City). In between times he had spent 'a few days a prisoner for Debt in the County Gaol of Surrey, Horsemonger-lane' and another 'few days' in the Debtors' Prison for London and Middlesex at Whitecross Street in the City, new-built in 1815.[18]

On 12 August 1842, once again in front of the Insolvent Debtors' Court, where he had been an inveterate, refractory and slippery petitioner for over twenty years, John Ewer Poole was discharged for what seems to have been the last time, having satisfied the chief commissioner that he had taken what steps he could to meet his creditors' just demands. Here was a man who would never succumb to a knock-out blow:

> The insolvent, who had previously been discharged, had been an auctioneer, &c. He kept a 'Hall of Information,' in the Strand, and could have supplied a good deal of information if he had communicated one half of his troubles.
>
> The Chief Commissioner asked when he begun to instruct the rising generation?
>
> The insolvent said in 1834. He had brought up a family of 14 children.
>
> The Court ordered him to be discharged.[19]

And the Hall of Information? In fact it seems to have been Poole's salvation. Whether it was his idea or not is unclear, but it might well have been because it was founded just two years before he was described as its 'Proprietor'. It was an information exchange, offering a poste restante to hold 'letters for persons from the country who had no town address, and people advertising in the newspapers, who did not wish their

ordinary address to appear'. By 1844 it was advertising its
services as a City employment exchange for 'Commercial
Assistants, male and female', so clerks and shop assistants
in general. Anyone wanting an engagement paid to have their
names and employment details registered so that employers
could find suitable candidates. The assistants paid 'is to 2s
6d' to join the register in 1844, though by 1849 it was firmly
2s 6d. Employers inspected the lists free of charge. Assistants
contacted by employers through the agency were charged a
further is. By 1844 the Hall of Information had moved to
8 Fore Street, Moorgate, where it was still trading in 1849
and probably after. Poole was still the proprietor in 1848,
and perhaps throughout, for that February he complained
to the City magistrate of a swindler using the office to receive
articles for which he had no intention of paying. He was
thanked by the sitting alderman for the warning, which would
be widely communicated to the City's traders: 'Mr. Poole
considered he had only done his duty towards the public,
and, having thanked Alderman Salomons for his attention
to his application, retired.' The case no doubt raised an
eyebrow or two among his acquaintances.[20]

Perhaps the Hall of Information kept Poole's many creditors if not satisfied at least at bay. From 1845 the *Post
Office Directory* had him, still auctioneer and accountant,
living at 9 Spital Square, a respectable address on the eastern
edge of the City, and his peripatetic days were gratifyingly
over. For it was there that he died on 18 March 1854.
Probate was granted to his widow, Elizabeth Theodora Poole,
but it took four years for her husband's complicated affairs
to be settled, by which time she had moved to Sidney Street
in eminently respectable Brompton; she would receive effects
valued in all at less than £20.[21]

Oddly, Giles Hemens also described himself as auctioneer
and appraiser, although he did not share Poole's wandering
ways and nor did he achieve much public profile outside the

Marshalsea itself. Indeed, he operated on a far humbler scale. He was born probably in 1764 and was first married in 1789 to Sarah Holwell at St Dunstan in the West, Fleet Street. Sarah died in 1814 and six weeks later Hemens was married again to Elizabeth (often called Eliza) Clark at St George the Martyr, Southwark, near neighbour to the Marshalsea prison, whose gate he must have glimpsed on his wedding day. Giles and Eliza already had two children together and Eliza had adopted the surname Hemens by 1809.[22]

Giles Hemens had been in business as an auctioneer, appraiser and undertaker at Frith Street, Soho, and then in Stacey Street, St Giles, a mixed parish though one notorious for the slum 'Holy Land' or 'Rookery' in the west; Hemens would spend most of the rest of his life in the better-off parts of St Giles. Here he dissolved his partnership with one Low Westwood to trade on his own account, for a time at least. Hemens believed in advertising, and we have glimpses of his business accordingly. He took out a notice in *The Times* in January 1802 to herald a forthcoming auction he was holding of china, Staffordshire ware and glass. Around 1811, now trading at Portugal Street, Lincoln's Inn Fields, he had a card printed promising 'Most Money for Household Furniture', which he adopted as a slogan, and showing a dapper Hemens with blond wavy hair, gavel in hand, gentlemen customers in ranks beneath him. And in August 1814, now at 5 Denmark Street, St Giles, he advertised his business with tickets entitling the bearer to a free pint of beer at the Hand and Hammer drinking booth in the premature peace celebrations at 'Hyde Park Fair' in August 1814.[23]

Advertising proved a costly business. Hemens was arrested and imprisoned in November 1812 in the King's Bench for a debt of nearly £72, while confessing to owing £489 3s 1d to all his creditors. These were large sums and Hemens petitioned to take advantage of the Insolvent Debtors Acts of 1813 and 1814 to settle with his creditors. This action he abandoned, possibly because he took on a new partner, Charles Robertson, who brought capital into the business. They traded for a time as Hemens and Co., but partners seem not to have sat easily with Giles and the firm was dissolved, Hemens buying out Robertson's share in December 1816. Hemens's creditors may have been placated for a time but not for long. By 1818 and perhaps before, he was taking in lodgers to swell his business earnings at 5 Denmark Street and probably doing everything else he could to keep out of trouble – he seems in all to have been an honest man. But in early 1820 he was arrested again and this time brought into custody at the Marshalsea on 18 February.[24]

Hemens would have a terrible time there. He refused to suffer in silence. His case exposes the dark side of debtor democracy and the undercurrent of violence flowing beneath that neat copperplate script of the 'College Regulations'. And his exposé had serious consequences for those nominally in charge of the gaol.[25]

When Hemens was committed to the Marshalsea he was on his beam ends, as the contemporary phrase had it. He told the Palace court's deputy prothonotary that 'he was very poor & could barely procure what was necessary for him, his friends assisted him with trifling sums . . .' Soon after he arrived he sent out to a particular friend, a Mr Bacon in New Compton Street, Soho, and asked Bacon to visit him, 'but having a debtor here of the name of Dolman he was Afraid to come'. Hemens had a tendency to involve himself in the affairs of others. It was a quality that had a positive side: he appeared as a witness in an Old Bailey trial in 1816 where he had found an eight-year-old girl crying in the street, rightly suspected she had been robbed, saw a man running away and promptly pursued him. But in the Marshalsea, with its myriad secret sensitivities, inquisitiveness could be a dangerous virtue.[26]

Hemens met Dolman, accidentally he said, 'on the parade of this place'. Hemens presumably mentioned that they shared a common acquaintance, Mr Bacon, Dolman's creditor. Hemens understood Dolman to say that Bacon's attorney was at fault for not distinguishing the debt from costs: were they to be separated, then Dolman might settle the debt and so release himself from the Marshalsea. Hemens promptly wrote to Bacon to tell him so, thinking that if Dolman were out of the gaol, then Bacon would be free to visit his friend. Sometime later Dolman asked Hemens if he had written to anyone about his affairs, 'to which I replyed I had he said I am very much oblidge to you Sir for your candour. will you call round to my room as there is a person there who will speak to you on the subject'. Hemens shortly did so, finding Dolman and his friend, who accused him of interfering in a way that had in fact prevented Dolman settling with his plaintiff. There was a row, Dolman called Hemens 'a d—d raskle took his stick with intent to strike me, but I left the room'.

There things seemed to stand. But indignation was hardening into a plot to exact revenge, and four or five weeks later it was ready to hatch. According to Hemens's sworn statement, he was with some visitors in the snuggery when a prisoner whose name he took to be McMoles publicly abused him for being 'the ruin of Mr Dolman'. Later, in the yard, Hemens remonstrated with McMoles but quickly found himself 'surrounded by a number of the Lower order of Prisoners'. Disentangling himself, he went to return to his room but on the staircase McMoles caught him by the leg and dragged him to the door. Hemens, who was in his midfifties by this time, was seized by several men, a filthy sack used as a doormat was flung over his head and he was dragged about thirty yards to the pump, where he was methodically soaked: his clothes were torn and he lost his hat and one shoe, perhaps 'stoln'.

Next morning 'two of the prisoners called Constables here with Constables Staves in their hands' ordered Hemens to report to the college committee. There he was charged with interfering in the affairs of Dolman to his serious detriment; he defended himself by explaining why he had written to Bacon, but was found guilty and sent to Coventry for a month. On his way out of the ale room he discerned that some prisoners were getting ready to exact further punishment. He implored the committee to protect him, but they broke up and scuttled out before him. Leaving the ale room, he sought help from the lodge, where a turnkey told him to say nothing and the prisoners would leave him alone. But on the way to his staircase he was assailed with pails of 'slush' from upper windows and in the passage and on the stairs to his room. Once there he gained some relief and wrote to John Cruchley, the deputy marshal and keeper, to say his life was in danger; a turnkey brought him answer that he could be locked up in the Admiralty block, where he would have his own yard and no one could get to him. But Hemens would have been utterly alone there and instead he decided to keep to his room for the period of the college's sentence.

Hemens did so for about three weeks, visited only by Eliza, it seems, and perhaps some friends from outside. Then on Wednesday 7 June, after 11 at night, there was a loud banging at his door. It was broken open and a number of men, apparently in disguise or masked, rushed in and in the darkness seized him by his arms and legs and dragged him from his room and down the stairs. When he cried out 'Murder' they stopped his mouth as best they could with their hands. At the bottom of two pairs of stairs there was talk of putting him down the privy, but instead they beat him where he lay about the head and body. After, Hemens called for the watch and was taken to the Admiralty prison and locked in for his own protection.

Either Hemens or Eliza or both made urgent representations to the authorities about these abuses in the Marshalsea prison. Eliza summoned Dr Phillips at his local surgery on 8 June when she discovered her husband's plight, but he did not see Hemens till the next day, when he bled him and examined the bruises, which he declared were not dangerous. But on that 9 June it seems that Hemens's complaint had reached the Palace court at Great Scotland Yard, where Cruchley was confronted about the matter 'in open Court'. He sought to cover his back with Sir Bland Burges, the Knight Marshal from whom he had received his appointment, but had to confess that he had spent some nights away from the gaol, contrary to his contract – he said because his house at the prison was under repair and uninhabitable. He blamed Hemens's bad treatment on a malevolent debtor prisoner, Mortimer Madden, 'a dreadfull bad Character' and a violent man, and had him removed by habeas corpus to the Surrey county gaol to await trial for the assault.

But Hemens's complaint was received with the utmost seriousness. In different circumstances it might have been treated more lightly, but one gets the impression that here was an opportunity to be rid of an unsatisfactory agent in John Cruchley. Even the Knight Marshal, who made a public virtue of never interfering in the running of the gaol, was moved to visit Hemens with J. C. Hewlitt, the deputy protho-notary, on 12 June. They found much to complain about. Hemens was lying in a cell nine feet by six, with no fireplace and empty apart from his prison bed laid on the floor; he still had several bruises, 'particularly a very large one on the left side of his body', was thought to have hearing problems from being beaten about the head and to be urinating blood. In three places on walls about the gaol in letters over a foot high was chalked 'Hemmins sent to Coventry' or something like it, which the Knight Marshal publicly reprimanded Cruchley for tolerating and ordered their immediate removal. The Hemens affair had drastic consequences for John Cruchley. He was dismissed on 28

June and a more trustworthy replacement, Joseph Rutland, was installed next day.[27]

Giles Hemens remained in the Marshalsea until 23 June 1820, when he was discharged under the Insolvent Debtors Acts. He didn't trouble the Marshalsea again. Although he seems to have suffered no long-term problems from his ill-treatment, he failed to prosper. His old age must have been racked by poverty, for he died in St Giles workhouse, Short's Gardens, just a step from Denmark Street, aged seventy-three, on 27 June 1837.[28]

Giles Hemens's case is known to us because he had the courage to make a fuss and because of its weighty sequel. Though hardly learned or well connected, he was an articulate and enterprising man of some education who was keen to foster a public presence and could use his voice to effect. Most Marshalsea debtors made no such mark in the public record, were often of no learning at all, and remain silent to us. But one strange case of a debtor who had no desire to be heard by the authorities – indeed, quite the contrary – but whose voice nonetheless survived for a moment arose during Hemens's confinement, when they were fellow prisoners, for a time at least.

For London 1820 was a troubled year in the midst of troubled times. The end of the Napoleonic Wars five years earlier led to unemployment, high food prices, ultra-radical agitation and riots. A small group of metropolitan ultras, desiring the overthrow of government by violent means and its replacement by a democratic parliament and equal distribution of land and property, sought to revive causes actively stifled by years of wartime repression. Their agitation was penetrated, indeed partly fostered, by a network of spies working directly to the Home Office, often through the chief metropolitan magistrate at Bow Street, Sir Richard Birnie. He was aided by the small squad of plain-clothes police officers or runners distributed at magistrates' offices across the capital, including the one at Union Hall, just across the road from the Marshalsea.

The coming of peace encouraged the extreme radicals to try to foment a more popular opposition to the government. Great meetings of radicals and their supporters at Spa Fields, Clerkenwell, were held in November and December 1816. The latter ended in a half-drunken raid on gunsmiths' shops and an armed attack on the Tower of London. The assault was led by Arthur Thistlewood, bred to the Lincolnshire gentry and an army officer for a time, who had been active in metropolitan radicalism for many years. Further great though peaceful demonstrations took place in London in 1817 and 1818. The mood shifted with the Peterloo Massacre in Manchester in August 1819, when unarmed workers were cut down by militia cavalry formed from the local gentry; this provoked fury among radicals and many working people in London and breathed new life into conspiracies to bring down the government with exemplary violence.

In late February 1820 one desperate plot was thought ready to hatch. Once more Arthur Thistlewood was leader and chief planner. With a motley band of supporters he planned to assassinate simultaneously members of the Cabinet at their homes late at night. The very night had been chosen when it was learned from the newspapers that a Cabinet dinner was to be held at Grosvenor Square that same evening, Wednesday 23 February 1820. Now it could all be done in a single massacre. The heads of Viscounts Sidmouth (Home Secretary) and Castlereagh (the government's leader in the House of Commons) 'were to be brought away in a bag' to encourage others to revolt.

One of Thistlewood's fellow conspirators was 'Edwards', a government spy, and the plot's every twist was in the hands of ministers. As Thistlewood and nearly thirty others gathered over a stable at Cato Street, Marylebone, just east of the Edgware Road, the place was raided by Bow Street runners and a party of Coldstream Guards. The police officers were first in the room, where 'cutlasses, bayonets, pistols, sword-belts, pistol-balls in great quantities, ball-cartridges, &c' lay on tables. In the melee, Thistlewood, 'armed with a cut-and-thrust sword of unusual length', stabbed a runner named Richard Smithers through the heart: "'Oh God! I am –"' were Smithers's last words. In the confusion most conspirators got away from Cato Street. Nine were arrested that night, Thistlewood and a few others were apprehended over the next day or two, and some escaped scot free. Besides Thistlewood the ringleaders included James Ings, a butcher, Richard Tidd and John Brunt, both shoemakers, and 'a man of colour', William Davidson, a cabinetmaker and son of the attorney general in Kingston, Jamaica.

On 1 May 1820 all five were hanged outside Newgate. An enormous crowd, held well back from the scaffold because of fear of a rescue, greeted the men with cheers. There were cries of "'God bless you, Thistlewood!"' After the hangings a medical man in a black mask cut off their heads and the executioner held up each in turn to the crowd: "'This is the head of Arthur Thistlewood, the traitor!"' The decapitations were greeted with 'exclamations of horror and of reproach', with 'hissings and hootings'.[29]

The thought prevailed in government that there were many other traitors implicated in the Cato Street events who had not yet been brought to book. These were frantically anxious times for those in power and it was in the interests of the network of spies that such anxieties were kept alive. At this fevered moment it was not surprising that agitators of former times – survivors of the London Corresponding Society (LCS) of the 1790s, old English Jacobins sympathetic to revolutionary France, followers of Thomas Spence the land reformer, frequenters of out-of-the-way ale houses where radicals clustered, congregations of back-street chapels espoused by strange sectlets with millenarian ideas – should all be tracked down to discover whether they were active in any current seditious movement.

One of these was Robert Moggridge. He was a tailor and had lived for many years in Bloomsbury. In 1794–5 he had been active in the LCS, a member of its general committee, even chairing it from time to time, and founder with others of a 'Division' that met in a house or pub 'at the corner of Francis & Thornhaugh Street', close to what would soon become Russell Square. He was a committed believer in the land equalisation policy of Thomas Spence and had played a part in hiding and then smuggling to America James Watson the younger, implicated in the violent Spa Fields riot of December 1816. Thereafter, Moggridge became a follower of the more moderate Spencian Thomas Evans, eschewing thoughts of revolutionary conspiracy and believing that popular radical upheaval would come from the North of England and not from the fractious radical movements of the metropolis. Among those who met at the Archer Street dissenting chapel in the seedy north-east corner of St James's, established by Evans in 1818, were Robert Moggridge and William Carr, a house painter.[30]

We know little about Robert Moggridge's public life, necessarily secretive as it was, and even less of his person and family. His first wife died and he was married again, in 1817, to Sarah Whittington. He had a number of children by his first wife, at least four – John and Mary Ann, both baptised in 1804, Eliza baptised in 1808 and Ann Julia born in 1814. Robert signed Ann Julia's marriage certificate in 1833, when she was just nineteen. We do not know when Robert was born or when he died, but he continued a radical for some years after Cato Street: he was active in the agitation in favour of Queen Caroline, in that unhappy monarch's struggle to share the crown of George IV, in late 1820 to early 1821, and he was a member of a radical debating club meeting in Long Acre at the end of the 1820s.[31]

Moggridge also struggled with debt over many years. He was imprisoned in the King's Bench for debt in 1809, from where he was discharged after obtaining the benefit of an Insolvent Debtors Act, but insolvency could not keep him permanently out of trouble. On 19 December 1819 he was brought into custody in the Marshalsea at the suit of William Crosse for a debt of £13 18s 4d. The Marshalsea was certainly a cast-iron alibi – had he needed one – for the Cato Street conspiracy, for he was still there when the drama of 23 February 1820 was played out at Marylebone. At that time Moggridge was contemplating insolvency again and was working on his schedule for the court proceedings. An old radical friend, William Carr, was also a debtor, very similarly circumstanced in the Debtors' Prison for London and Middlesex at Whitecross Street. Indeed, they seem to have owed each other money, though whom the balance favoured is unknown. Either Carr or Moggridge was being watched by the authorities, for when the latter wrote from 'Marshalsea Prison/N° 3 in 2' on 24 February, his letter was intercepted at Whitecross Street next day and taken directly to the Home Office.

From Citizzen Moggridge in the Marshalsea prison to Citizen Carr in White Cross Street Prison
has wee have been Politically engaged together it will not appear Radical to schedule each other, I therefore request of you note to send me a Notice, has I shall not schedule you, I suppose you are frequently Visited by your Radical Friends, while you are in Durance Vile, I can assure you on my part it will be an easy thing for me to return the Compliment to my Old friends, neither the wants of my family nor their being forced from the home they have Occupied for Ten Years, has made any Impression on their flinty Hearts, but an honest heart, Patiense, and a good Conscience, is a sure remedy, for as Mr Hunt has justly Observed, save a Man from the Gallows he will turn round and Cut your throat,

and from the treatment I have received the Observation is
verified, you will hardly Credit it, excepting Mr Hall has been
with me twice I have seen nor heard from any of them, nor
my family, for they could not offend, but we must expect to
be scourged and to receive evil for good
with my best wishes for you and your familys health and
welfare
    I remain yours truly
    Citizen Moggridge[32]

If Mr Hall was Abel Hall, Moggridge's fellow tailor, who
was active in the Cato Street conspiracy but evaded arrest,
then it might explain how Moggridge's letter came into
Home Office hands; in later years he was known to be a
government spy, but perhaps his informing had begun earlier.
In any event, such was the state of the official mind in these
hectic days that the Home Office instructed John Cruchley,
then still deputy marshal, to search the Marshalsea for arms.
On 29 February Cruchley could report that 'I have searched
every room in the prison for the purpose of detecting Arms
of any description And have every reason to believe that
there are no Arms in possession of the prisoners in this
Prison.' Robert Moggridge seems to have been spied on no
more in gaol. He was discharged from the Marshalsea on
8 June 1820 under the Insolvent Debtors Act. No doubt
other debtor radicals moved in and out of its lodge over the
years, but no other case has so far come down to us.[33]
    Certain it is, though, that all sorts and conditions of
Londoner were to be found in the Marshalsea prison. Some
were public characters, and we might recall James Spiller
the actor, Mrs Pilkington the poetaster and Grano the trumpeter, with others along the way, in the old Marshalsea. So
too they cropped up in the new gaol. There was, for instance,
that 'prisoner of sporting notoriety' for whom George Eades
had risked his own liberty with a friendly nip of gin in May

1832. But probably the most celebrated of all the sporting characters gracing the Marshalsea at this period was Bishop Sharpe the bare-knuckle fighter, known as the Bold Smuggler by the 'fancy' but most commonly as just 'The Bishop'.

Bishop Sharpe was born in 1796 at Woolwich and all his life was spent in the riverside towns on the south-east of the metropolis. He served in the Royal Navy, though his fighting sobriquet indicated he had other interests on sea and shore. They could not have lasted long, though, for by 1817 he had become a prizefighter of 'the *third-rate*', too light to be a 'Champion of England' for he stood some five feet seven with a fighting weight around eleven stone. Nevertheless he won fame, many fights and heavy purses against the Deptford Carrier, Gypsy Jack Cooper, Young Dutch Sam and others at prize rings all over south-east London from Blackheath to Plumstead, at Epping Forest by the Fairlop Oak, at No Man's Land in Hertfordshire and elsewhere, from 1817 till his retirement in 1828 or 1830. On the strength of his success he became a family man, marrying Ann Cowen at St Paul's, Deptford, in 1821; they had a daughter, Hannah, in 1824 and a son, the third generation of Bishops, in 1824. Sadly the boy died when he was just three.[34]

A sporting career was generally short, and sure enough the Bishop met his nemesis in Alec Reid, the Chelsea Snob. Sharpe beat Reid at No Man's Land over twenty rounds for a purse of £100 in 1826, but two years later Reid had his revenge at the same venue, over a gruelling ninety-one rounds that lasted near an hour and a half. It was thought by seasoned scribes of the fancy to be 'one of the hardest contested battles we have ever witnessed'. When it was over poor Sharpe

remained stretched on a heap of straw in the ring, quite insensible; and on being bled, was carried off to his quarters, where he remained last night in a dangerous state. His punishment both on the body and on the head was dreadful, and nothing but the most determined game and unshrinking courage could have enabled him so long to stand against its appalling effects.[35]

This defeat marked the end of Bishop Sharpe's fleeting prosperity. His earnings had been large but chancy, and the temptations to high living had no doubt proved irresistible. But on retirement he was now fitted only for this irregular world and unsuited to anything more prosaic or mundane. He earned a little by sparring in benefit matches and acting as a second to the ring's coming generation; and he was generally recognised and no doubt applauded at the ringside of big fights for some years to come. But he lived mainly as a 'boothkeeper', selling beer from a tent or van at fights and fairs, trading on his fading celebrity. It didn't pay. In 1831 he was arrested for a debt of £100 and on 13 July found himself a prisoner for the first time in the Marshalsea. Unable to pay such a large sum, he quickly headed for the Insolvent Debtors' Court, where his petition was heard on 15 September and he was discharged from prison. In court he blamed his indebtedness in part on the high cost of his training 'in 1830', perhaps for a comeback; or perhaps he was just confused over dates for when the court asked, 'Pray, did not some persons pay those expenses or a part of them?' 'The Bishop looked crestfallen, and sorrowfully replied, "No, Sir, I got LICKED by Alic Reid, the Chelsea Snob." This reply caused a roar of laughter, in which the Learned Commissioner heartily joined.' Let's hope that Sharpe saw the funny side too.[36]

On his release Bishop Sharpe persisted with his booth, landing a £15 fine when an informer prosecuted him for selling 'exciseable liquors' at Greenwich Fair in May 1834; he was one of several traders in court for the same offence that day. Three years later, in November 1837, he was back in the Marshalsea, on a suit of John Merryweather for a debt of £50. Sharpe petitioned for insolvency a second time, giving the hacks of the metropolis the chance of laboured amusement at his expense.

> Bishop Sharpe, the far-famed ex-pugilist, applied on his peti-
> tion to be discharged, and was unopposed. It appeared that
> poor Sharpe had been twice on the floor of the court as an
> insolvent debtor, and each time had been awarded to be
> entitled to the benefit of the Act. He took his last benefit on
> the stage of the Insolvent Court in September, 1831, and
> since then he had retired from the glory of the prize ring,
> putting up with the humble cognomen of the keeper of a
> booth at races and fairs; finding, however, that this wandering
> sort of life was stale and unprofitable, he assumed several
> names, for the purpose of keeping body and soul together,
> but all would not do; he was floored for the second time,
> and, horrid to relate, was again in durance vile, at the suit
> of a brother pall of his own wandering tribe, yclept a booth
> keeper, who rejoiced in the happy cognomen of Merryweather.
> Since he had taken proceedings against poor Sharpe some
> compunction had smote the heart of the conscientious
> Merryweather, and he determined not to come to the scratch
> to oppose one with whom he had spent so many hours on
> the turf, and at fairs and wakes.
>
>   The Court ordered the insolvent to be discharged, and
> thereby again enabled him to pursue his worthy calling.[37]

There would be a third time in the Marshalsea for Sharpe. In May 1842 he joined Joshua Reeve Lowe and others in the gaol, this time for a debt of over £55. Again he took the insolvency route to compound with his creditors and free himself and was discharged on 1 August. He was then still living in Greenwich and still doggedly attached to his booth. He was in Greenwich too in 1851, sharing a house at a place called Cold Bath with Ann and with Hannah and her husband. Bishop Sharpe died sometime in the first quarter of 1861.[38]

Not all the Marshalsea's public figures followed callings so haphazard or disreputable as Bishop Sharpe's. Musicians, for instance, continued to turn up in the prison as they had in John Baptist Grano's time. Their careers inevitably involved much that was freelance, peripatetic between orchestral stage and theatre pit, and though there were growing opportunities for professional musicians in these years times were often hard. Most professionals supplemented their earnings with teaching, generally unrewarding in both senses of the word. It was a fortunate or highly skilled and ambitious performer who could put something away for a comfortable old age – indeed, retirement perforce preceded much ripeness of years as bodily and mental strains took their toll on a performer's abilities.

We might cite William Parke, born in Westminster in 1761. His much older brother was a musician too and William, after experimenting with several instruments, finally settled on the oboe. He was in the Vauxhall Gardens orchestra as second oboe from 1777, so aged only sixteen, and then from 1783 a principal in the theatre orchestra at Covent Garden – all theatrical evenings involving music of one sort or another. He was to hold that post for forty years and was one of the most celebrated wind soloists in London; composers wrote works for him and, like Grano, he played his own compositions. Parke had two sons by his mistress, a professional singer who died in 1807, and in 1822 he married for the first time, at St James, Clerkenwell; he was sixty-one and about to retire from the Covent Garden orchestra. A son was born to the couple just over a year later, and it is possible that his wife had children from a previous marriage.

Perhaps these two events, marriage and retirement, conspired against him financially. He had sought to bolster his old age by joining in 1783 the Society for Decay'd Musicians and their Families, from 1790 the Royal Society of Musicians. Less than eighteen months after his marriage he was in dire money trouble and it was to the society he turned. His tale will be familiar to us, but pitiable nonetheless. His letter was addressed from the 'Marshalsea Prison, Decr 6th 1823':

> Gentlemen. Having been arrested and brought to this place on Tuesday the 25th of last month with only one pound in my pocket (seven shillings and sixpence of which was immediately paid for fees) I have had no other means of subsisting myself, my Wife, and five young children but the remains of that and the County allowance, three and sixpence per week. I have not receiv'd a shilling from the theatre although two nights pay are due to me. I therefore am depriv'd of the common comforts of life, proper food, fire and candle, added to which, I am now labouring under a bilious attack, and am totally without the means of procuring either medicine or medical assistance. I therefore am compell'd to sollicit of you such temporary relief as shall be in your liberal feelings appear to be necessary, and I at the same time take the liberty to sollicit that if you should determine to commiserate my case, that it may be kindly convey'd to me as soon as possible, as I have not otherwise, the means of recovering my health, or of obtaining a meal. I must remain here five or six weeks in order to take the benefit of the Insolvent Act, and as I trust that I have been 'more sinn'd against, than having sinn'd' I feel no doubt of an honourable acquital. I remain Gentlemen yr most sincere, & very Obet Sert.
> W. T. Parke.

The society granted him £7, which must have been a relief to him. He was discharged from the Marshalsea under an Insolvent Debtors Act on 31 January 1824, so a month or so before John Dickens was brought in. Parke's finances then just kept him afloat, it seems, although another child was born in 1826, the lively pensioner then sixty-five years old and still apparently strong in wind. He was also moving house frequently, perhaps to keep costs low or to hoodwink his landlords, with known addresses in a court off Ossulston Street in lowly Somers Town, in Popham Street, Islington, at three houses in a plebeian street, and finally at 38 Bridport Place, Hoxton. He received a quarterly allowance from the society, though his illegitimate children seem to have been an impediment to the additional aid he occasionally sought. His income was significantly boosted in 1829 with a respectable £30 advance on his autobiography, *Musical Memories*, a sum repeated in 1830 when his publisher persuaded Parke to write a second volume. Some years later he was also being supported by allowances from his grown-up children. He died in 1847 at the good age of eighty-six; his widow and a married son, also now in debt, sought the society's aid into the 1860s.[39]

That William Parke was not alone among contemporary musicians in paying the Marshalsea an obligatory visit we know from the case of Charles James Griesbach, one of a well-known musical family with some links to royal patronage. Griesbach was a music master teaching violin and piano, an overstocked trade, in the smarter parts of Chelsea and elsewhere in comfortably situated districts of London. He was forty-four when he was arrested for a debt of just £17 or so and brought into the Marshalsea in April 1841; he was discharged inside a fortnight, securing bail under the Judgments Act of 1838, which made it easier for debtors to give security for their freedom after being imprisoned as well as before.[40]

Indeed the debt laws were constantly shifting in this period. Debt was a tricky business, plagued by law and lawyers, who could have a field day and frequently did. But they too could smash and we might recall the debtor lawyer Mr Brown, who gave Grano advice in the Marshalsea, or Mr Richardson, who helped the collegians modernise their rules in 1814. Not every lawyer could get his costs or pay his creditors and one such was Jabez Pelham, an attorney of Old Gravel Lane, Ratcliffe, close to the East End riverside. That was hardly the epicentre of legal London, but he was the solicitor chosen to manage the defence of Edward Oxford, the failed regicide, in July 1840 on the charge of high treason. Within six months of that success Pelham was arrested and imprisoned in the Queen's Bench, petitioning for relief from his creditors in the Insolvent Debtors' Court. He owed £738 but claimed he was owed in turn £2,414 10s 3d; of the debts owing to him £247 'were good' and £385 'doubtful', which left a hefty whack worth nothing at all. Among those owing him money was Hannah Oxford, Edward's mother, who had not paid her son's costs of £510; the sum was entered as a bad debt.[41]

Jabez Pelham avoided the Marshalsea, but one attorney who surprisingly did not was John de la Mare, brother of James de la Mare, whose son Walter, born in 1873, would become the famous poet and storyteller. John was the eldest of the family, some eighteen years older than James, and was born around 1794 into an eminently respectable Essex household with Huguenot merchant roots. He was inducted into the legal profession and articled to an attorney living in Romford near the Delamares (as the name was then most frequently written) but with a practice in Westminster. John was sixteen when articled and a fully fledged attorney from 1817. That year he married Mary Churchill in Barking and over the next six years the couple had four children surviving infancy, the first three born in Essex and the last, Eliza, probably in Clapham, the family moving there by 1823. There they kept 'a large establishment, two carriages and horses'. Besides his City practice John came into a sizeable private income from his marriage settlement.[42]

By this time, however, things had gone badly wrong for John de la Mare. He struck up what would be a fateful acquaintance with another Mary, the wife of Captain Benjamin Laing, a wealthy trader with South America who both owned and sailed his own valuable vessel. Mr and Mrs Laing lived in Charles Street, Northumberland Avenue, in the heart of Westminster, and had between them seven children, of whom five survived. Mrs Laing and de la Mare had apparently met through her brother, a friend of John's. An affair developed while a lengthy voyage was being undertaken by Captain Laing. Mrs Laing 'was a woman of great personal beauty' and 'still . . . of that age to excite the desires of a man'. John de la Mare proved not only excitable but indiscreet. By the summer of 1823 the affair was discovered and Mrs Laing left her children and the family home and moved 'under the protection of Mr. Delamare'. His family at Clapham were said to be 'in a state of unspeakable distress'.[43]

That autumn de la Mare and Mrs Laing moved precipitately to France. John's business affairs were left in the hands of John Delamare the elder, his father, but despite a pursuit to Paris the errant attorney's whereabouts remained hidden. In his absence he was sued by Captain Laing for 'criminal conversation' and damages of £10,000 were awarded against him. These were subsequently reduced to £2,000 at a hearing at which he was represented but did not appear. The proceedings were extensively reported in the London papers and repeated in many in the provinces, including in Essex. From this time it seems the Delamares of Romford obliterated John from the family record. He seems not to have been spoken about or acknowledged, and to Walter and the other numerous nephews and nieces it was as though their eldest uncle had never existed. Contact, though, was dutifully maintained with Mary and the children, especially by John's younger brothers Abraham, rector of St Thomas, Woolwich, born about 1804, and Walter's father, James, born in 1811. It has been accepted by Walter's biographer that the one 'unsteady Huguenot Delamare' was Abraham's twin brother, Henry, who fathered an illegitimate child. Now we know there was another.[44]

John de la Mare stayed on the Continent, it seems, for much of the next six years. His wanderings were sketched, as far as they were known, in the *London Gazette* during the autumn of 1829:

De La Mare, John, the younger, heretofore of Frederick's Place, Old Jewry, London, and of Clapham-Common, Surry, Attorney at Law, since of Calais, and then of Paris, both in France, afterwards of Brussels, and then of Ostend, both in the Kingdom of the Netherlands, afterwards of Havre de Grace, in France, since residing at the Four Swans Inn, Bishopsgate-Street, London, then at No. 6, Haberdasher's-Place East, Hoxton, Middlesex, and lastly residing at the York Hotel, Bridge-Street, Blackfriars, London, in no profession or business, (sued and committed, and commonly known, as John Delamare).[45]

At the York Hotel or nearby he was arrested for debt and imprisoned in the King's Bench. There he sought to take advantage of the Insolvent Debtors Act to accommodate his creditors and free himself from gaol. His application was opposed from a predictable quarter. Captain Laing's costs in the various hearings had been over £150 and he had received not a penny of his damages, though he had offered to settle for £500 down and to accept security for £500 more. But de la Mare's problems had multiplied and effectively he was now a man of straw. He owed debts of £3,856, his wife had separated from him and had sued him in Chancery for steps he had taken to secure her property to himself; he had lost the case and was now in contempt of court. The Commissioner of Insolvency, rather than consign him to an unlimited time in gaol because of Laing's opposition to his discharge, prolonged de la Mare's stay in the King's Bench by a further six months.[46]

That would have taken him to the end of May 1830. Once out he accrued new debts. He was arrested on mesne process and on 14 October 1831 he was brought into custody at the lodge of the Marshalsea prison for a debt of just £22. He seems to have stayed there, improbable as it sounds, until June 1836, when he was released at the suit of John Bartholomew, the arresting creditor; perhaps he had been a 'voluntary prisoner', keeping out of further harm's (and Captain Laing's) way. His troubles were not over, though, and perhaps never would be. He and 'Mary de la Mare', formerly Laing, were living in Child's Place, Fleet Street, in 1841, but in September 1844 he was in gaol again, at the Debtors' Prison for London and Middlesex; that was followed or accompanied by bankruptcy proceedings and he was there still in August 1845. It is unclear when he freed himself. By the time of the 1851 census there had been some move up in the world, for John and Mary were lodging at Royal Avenue Terrace, south Chelsea; even so they lived without servants in a mixed street of multi-occupied houses. In 1861 John was alone, a widower, lodging over a coffee shop at 65 Princes Street, Soho. John de la Mare died at the very end of 1867 or early in the new year, aged seventy-three: he had been living in Pimlico, but the good Abraham arranged to bury his elder brother at St Thomas, Woolwich, on 6 January 1868.[47]

Lawyers, musicians, artisans, tradesmen, all had bulked out the Marshalsea's population over many generations; but one other category had also been especially prominent – those in his majesty's service in either the navy or, more commonly, the army. The Marshalsea records are littered with military ranks, though only rarely above the ubiquitous captain, from Captain Tudman, such a nuisance to John Grano, to the young Dickens's orotund Captain Porter a century later, with forgotten regiments of others in between.

They crop up in unlikely and unpropitious circumstances. Take Lieutenant Frederick Cox, for example, nabbed by bailiffs for debt in January 1830 and swiftly lodged in the

Marshalsea. It was a most unlucky arrest, for without it Cox must surely have been making his way to France: earlier that day he had been a fellow officer's second at a duel with pistols in Battersea Fields in which Oliver Clayton, a publisher, was shot dead. Cox was charged with wilful murder, brought up from the Marshalsea and committed to the Surrey county gaol. Cox and Lieutenant Lambrecht, whose second he had been, were acquitted of murder at Kingston Assizes on 2 April and discharged. The next day he settled his debts, perhaps with the help of his friends, and was freed from the Marshalsea too.[48]

Cox's case was unusual in its details, but few army officers in the eighteenth and early nineteenth centuries could avoid the expensive temptations of the officers' mess, of the gaming house and the brothel. For many, a commission was probably a surer means of losing a fortune than of gaining one. Such was the case of Lieutenant Mathew Arnot Stewart. He was born into a landowning family in Ayrshire, among their assets a fine large house, Lochrigg, property of his mother, and with significant holdings in land on his own account. Stewart's downfall was gambling. A weighty inheritance near Lockwood, Edinburgh, was intact when he joined the army in 1822. Three years later Stewart 'began mortgaging it very heavily'. His debts were staggering and were recounted to the Insolvent Debtors' Court in April 1829: they 'amounted to upwards of 78,000*l*., and his general and special expenses, including his losses at gaming, on the Turf, (and from 1822 to 1828 he had lost about 15,000*l*.) amounted to about 10,000*l*. a year'. Although his officer's pay was irrelevant to such encumbrances, his position cannot have been helped when he was put 'on the unattached half-pay list' in April 1826. On 1 February he was arrested for debt and, unable to free himself, confined in the King's Bench prison. In April 1829 he was living in the rules of the Bench and his addresses chart the geography of failure from 'Lochridge, in the County of Ayr,

Scotland, then of Dorchester, Dorsetshire, afterwards of Long's Hotel, Bond-Street', known for its fast living among smart-set gamblers; but then south of the river at Temple-Place, Blackfriars Road, and Portland Place, Borough Road. While a prisoner his portable property drained away – his 'four valuable horses', his phaeton, his sword and his gun, all sold for the ready. Whether connected or not to her son's desperate position, his mother sold Lochrigg in 1830. That year Stewart, presumably now free from prison, was able to buy a full commission and remove himself from the half-pay list.[49]

It was merely a temporary respite. In April 1831 he was arrested and on the 22nd brought into the Marshalsea prison; not taking to his lodgings, he was there just a month until he transferred to the Fleet on a writ of habeas corpus. Four months later he traded down to the half-pay list, exchanging his commission for cash. Finally his luck seems to have turned. Well connected still, he was reported to have been posted to the West Indies as a stipendiary magistrate – his experience of law-court procedure, though mainly in Portugal Street, no doubt standing him in good stead. He is said to have died unmarried, though when or where that was we do not know.[50]

Mathew Arnot Stewart was not, of course, the only gambling man to have found his way into the Marshalsea. A celebrated case arose a few years before Stewart entered the lodge. In October 1822 Thomas Erskine Grant brought an unusual suit into the court of King's Bench. Grant was a young man 'bred in military life in India', who had arrived in London shortly before he came of age. He had inherited 'a considerable property', but had been unluckily introduced to a notorious gaming house in Bennett (now Bennet) Street, off St James's Street, where he lost money very heavily, playing at the 'Rouge et Noir table three nights in the week' from October 1819. 'Sunk in the vortex of dissipation', as his counsel put it, 'he lost every shilling he possessed in the world'. Grant was duly arrested for debt and on 10 December 1819 brought into the Marshalsea owing the imprisoning creditor £60. Once there he applied to the two gaming-house keepers for financial help, 'reminding them that he had been ruined by the practices allowed in their house'. They refused him, claiming not to have known him during the period of his 'downfall'.[51]

His plight became known 'to his friends', who agreed to settle his debts on the condition that he sued the proprietors of 9 Bennett Street for bringing about his ruin – he was duly released after settling with his arresting creditor on 7 April 1820, where he had shared the prison with Giles Hemens and Robert Moggridge, among others. His lawyers presented his case as one fought in the public interest; success in his action, the court was told, 'could not fail of benefiting society'. The defence alleged on the contrary that the case was brought 'merely for the purpose of extorting money'; indeed, one of the defendants had given Grant £50 to settle the case, which he had then used to fund the prosecution. Both proprietors were found guilty, but further cross-petitions and trials followed and it is unclear how much Grant actually netted from it, if anything. He also successfully prosecuted a second gaming house in St James's, likely to have been 71 Pall Mall, in May 1823, probably for the informer's reward. A month later Grant married Elizabeth Hunt Howell at St Clement Danes, Westminster; Elizabeth was pregnant at the time but their son William Henry, and another son born in 1829, unluckily did not survive infancy. Elizabeth herself died in 1833 and at that time they had a daughter living, Emma Louisa, born probably in 1825. Thomas Erskine Grant was married again, to Harriet Hurst, also at St Clement Danes, in March 1846, but there were no children from the marriage.[52]

Grant's later career is lost in obscurity, perhaps gratefully, for when he next appeared in a court of law it was in

September 1849 to answer a charge of indecent exposure, showing himself to 'two little girls' in the dark arches under the Adelphi. Grant claimed he had gone there to relieve himself. Described as 'a well-dressed middle-aged man', married 'and passionately attached to his wife – a lady much younger than himself', Grant was convicted on the confident evidence of a lighterman and sentenced at Bow Street to three months' hard labour. He wriggled out of it, appealing on a technicality that the offence was not committed in a place of 'public resort', and the conviction was quashed. Grant died of phthisis in Whitecross Street in 1851.[53]

If we were to catalogue some of the errors and flaws of the lives in this brief prosopography of the Marshalsea debtors' world in the twenty years or so before the gaol closed, then what would they amount to? Over-optimism or recklessness in business, dissembling and economy with the truth when it came to taking on debt without the ability to pay, a weakness for high living, gaming tables and other men's wives, all were sins to which many of their metropolitan contemporaries might plead guilty but which would not, in luckier circumstances, take them through the lodge of the Marshalsea prison.

Some, though, were of a different mark. We have glimpsed instances of a darker seam among the debtors, desperate thieves, violent men who would stop at nothing, confidence tricksters and swindlers who traded on appearance not just to mislead but to rob. These too were present in the new Marshalsea and we might conclude our portrait gallery with one case of some contemporary notoriety. It was an extraordinary tale.[54]

On Saturday 27 December 1828, James Stamp Sutton Cooke 'Died by the Visitation of God' in the Marshalsea prison. A few days later the fact was noted in brief paragraphs in many newspapers, not just in the metropolis. For Cooke had been known by reputation throughout England.

He had long "'lived on his wits'", as a newspaper reported at the time, 'or, more correctly speaking, by duping the credulous part of the community'. It was a career he had shared in part with his second wife, Sophia, though at the beginning it seems that she too was one of his dupes. To be fair to Sophia, Cooke's victims were legion, for the 'credulous part of the community' included at times even the royal household itself.[55]

James Stamp Sutton Cooke was born in April 1780 in Clerkenwell. He came from a Gloucestershire family of the middling sort or above and around 1799 was 'a military man', he said in the Royal South Gloucestershire Militia. In that year, not yet nineteen but swearing before the clerk in Doctors' Commons that he was over twenty-one, he married at St James's, Piccadilly, Jane Browning, a farmer's daughter from Kent. Cooke described himself as 'gentleman'. Jane was also a minor but her father consented to the union and provided the couple with their first home at the farm in Kent, keeping Cooke in funds. But Cooke proved a feckless husband, and after a few disappearances finally deserted Jane, leaving her penniless, even pawning her spare clothes, after some three years of fractious marriage.[56]

In September 1808 Cooke met Sophia Sanders. She was a young woman 'of colour', her father 'a man of property in the West Indies', in fact Jamaica. In October they married at St Luke's, Old Street, at which time Sophia was a minor, just under nineteen. They had two children, only one of whom was living in 1812. By that time there had been a falling-out and the couple were no longer living together. Sophia was staying with her mother, who supported her daughter and baby. Things were tense between Cooke and his mother-in-law, so tense that she prosecuted him for assault and around 1811 he spent time in Clerkenwell Bridewell as a result. Sophia, perhaps at her mother's prompting, now brought a charge of bigamy against Cooke, who was

prosecuted at the Old Bailey in April 1812, convicted and
sentenced to seven years' transportation. That sentence was
never carried out for 'the Royal Clemency was extended to
him by proving that his first marriage was null and void',
probably on the grounds that his father had opposed the
marriage and that Cooke had lied about his age.[57]

At some point after the Old Bailey proceedings, conceivably before, James Stamp Sutton Cooke adopted the full-time
career of swindler. His enterprises were various and imaginative. Sometimes they made money and sometimes they lost
money, but it was all one because Cooke never paid anyone
what he owed. It was a high-wire balancing act that had
him in and out of the country's law courts and prisons, so
much so that he was fortunate to escape a lifetime banishment. Sophia, soon reconciled to him after the Old Bailey
drama – they had a son together in 1814 – and generally
going under the name of Mrs Cooke, pursued a similar
career but would not be so lucky.

Many of Cooke's early ventures centred on the metropolis.
They remain obscure but involved what later generations
would know as a long-firm fraud – opening up a shop,
trading apparently prosperously for a time, then disappearing
after disposing of the goods while owing suppliers large
sums of money. Certainly he traded in the unlikely guise of
a cheesemonger – the Gloucestershire connection perhaps –
in Golden Lane in the City, but we hear of him running a
hosiery shop in Oxford Street, a hatter's in High Holborn
and a billiard saloon in Fleet Street. His addresses, where
he lived the high life, were said to include Orchard Street
and Manchester Square in Marylebone, Brick Court in the
Temple, Upper Berkeley Street, Mayfair, and Duke Street, St
James's, and for a time he lived in France, no doubt keeping
out of harm's way. Sophia worked alongside him and independently, reportedly passing herself off to hoteliers as the
Countess of Ogilby.[58]

Cooke was investigated at police offices across London but no charge of fraud could be made to stick. He was less lucky with bailiffs. In 1816 he was arrested for a debt of £50 and brought into custody in the Marshalsea on 30 August; dissatisfied with the accommodation, he transferred by habeas corpus to the Fleet the next day. In 1818 he was bankrupted as that City cheesemonger but satisfied the commissioners he could be discharged. Despite that he was back in the Fleet for a time in the summer of 1820.[59]

Through all his inventive trickery, in which sharp wits, cool nerve and bottomless bravado must all have had a hand, Cooke never lost sight of the bigger prize. Early on in his career, perhaps from birth and education, he learned to move effortlessly among men and women of the highest rank. His pretensions were inexhaustible, his audacity breathtaking.

By the time Cooke was being bankrupted as a cheese-monger in Golden Lane he had hatched the greatest plan of his extraordinary career. His late mother had been, before her marriage to John Cooke in 1768, Catherine Stafford of Marlwood Park, Thornbury, Gloucestershire. She was descended from Sir William Stafford, a Tudor courtier, who had married into the family of the first Baron Stafford while never being entitled to the barony itself, which descended to the Jerningham family. The barony was unjustly forfeited in 1680 during the aftermath of the Titus Oates plot, but in the early 1820s Sir George Jerningham, then seventh baronet and in possession of the ruinous Stafford Castle and its prosperous estates, petitioned the House of Lords to have the 1680 attainder (or forfeiture) reversed. It was while these proceedings were afoot that Cooke developed a scheme to steal the putative barony from under Sir George's very nose. He determined to claim the restored barony for his older brother, Richard, reportedly an insolvent second-hand furniture dealer at Wisbech in Cambridgeshire. In all of the subsequent dealings Richard seems to have been a dumb cipher for his younger, but far more enterprising, brother James.[60]

The ground was painstakingly laid by Cooke. Early in 1818 he had set out 'the proofs of his descent' in 'a Book called the "Stafford Peerage"'. Somehow he procured a presentation at the Prince Regent's levee at Carlton House in June 1818, when George 'was most graciously pleased to accept' the 'Book' from the importunate Cooke. After extricating himself from the Fleet, Cooke was then presented to the new king in March 1821, again at Carlton House, when the Cabinet and all officers of state were in attendance. He petitioned for an invitation to George's coronation in July 1821 as being 'lawfully descended in the Protestant Line from the Royal House of Plantagenet' and although we do not know the outcome he was presented at Buckingham Palace to the king on his official birthday on St George's Day 1822. One further step in gilding the Cooke lily was taken by James that same year: he had his and Sophia's son, now eight years old, baptised at Old St Pancras Church as George Plantagenet Stafford Cooke.[61]

Jerningham would eventually secure his reversal of attainder in 1824. But by then Cooke had already moved on the ground to implement Richard's claim. From James's lodgings in deeply unfashionable Clarendon Street, Somers Town, 'a conspiracy to defraud' the Jerninghams was evolved in late 1822. On 30 December a party of visitors was being shown around the ancient castle and the new restoration works then under way. Among them were Cooke, his brother and a local sheriff's officer they had managed to get on their side. At the end of the visit these three refused to leave the castle and asserted that Richard was the new owner of the Stafford estates; they had to be ejected by force. Undeterred, Cooke issued notices to all the Jerningham tenants, explaining that the estate had passed into Richard Cooke's possession, and ordering that all rents should be paid to James as his agent; they had timber felled on the estates and sold it, pocketing the proceeds; they sought to evict Sir George's agent and solicitor from his offices, though without success. Soon after this excitement, the *Morning Post* announced in its society pages the arrival in town at the Blenheim Hotel, Bond Street, of 'the Hon. James Stamp Sutton Cooke, from Stafford Castle, the lately acquired seat belonging to (his brother, Stafford Cooke) Lord Stafford, pursuant to the Act of the 1st of King Edward the Sixth, that Nobleman being the lawful heir of Henry the restored Baron, son of Edward Duke of Buckingham'.[62]

The farce ran and ran, playing to packed audiences in law courts up and down the country: in Derby in July 1823, when Cooke brought a libel case against a local paper that had exposed his London swindles and where he won a farthing damages as not every claim could be substantiated (perhaps about his bigamous marriage); at Gloucester in April 1824, when Cooke was convicted of conspiracy to obtain money under false pretences from Sir George Jerningham; at the court of King's Bench in July 1824, when Cooke sued again for libel, this time against the author of a pamphlet, *The Stafford Peerage; or, The Imposture Unmasked*, winning a further farthing; and at the same court, where, after desperate delaying tactics by Cooke, he was sentenced in May 1826 to nine months in Coldbath Fields prison for the Stafford conspiracy and required to give sureties for his good behaviour for the following three years. Even this did not still the irrepressible Cooke: in spring 1827 he served notices to quit once more on over 150 of Jerningham's tenants, who provokingly refused to pay their rents to the true baron's agent, James Stamp Sutton Cooke. His reluctant tenantry once more left him 'down on his uppers': in September 1828 he was reported to be an imprisoned debtor again, living in the rules of the Fleet.[63]

By this time 'the notorious Mrs. Cooke', alias Stamp, alias Saunders, alias Sanders, alias Sutton, had seized the limelight from her fading star of a husband. She had inevitably experienced her own entanglements with bailiffs and debtors' prisons. In December 1824 the marshal of the King's Bench was successfully sued for £110 damages when the slippery Sophia vanished from the rules; she had apparently shared her humble lodgings in what had been St George's Fields, now a great cluster of cheap housing, with a town house in Bayswater, where she kept a carriage, useful for plundering West End tradesmen.[64]

Her final clash with the criminal law began at Bow Street in September 1828. She appeared in the dock, heavily pregnant. There seems to have been some confusion in the court reporter's mind over the paternity of the child who accompanied her, or perhaps Sophia varnished the tale for sympathy's sake:

> She had with her a very beautiful girl, about four years of age, and a servant maid. The child has for her reputed father a Noble Baron, whose ancestor's blood was attainted. Mrs. Cooke was dressed in a black bombazine gown, with black bonnet and veil. She, though evidently an accomplished woman, and lady-like in her manners, was but meanly attired. Her child was dressed very elegantly. The servant girl wept incessantly.[65]

After a long search, Sophia had finally been arrested and brought up on a charge of defrauding Messrs Rathnacker of Soho Square of a pianoforte. While on remand at Newgate she gave birth 'to a thumping boy'. At the Old Bailey she was convicted with her accomplice William Barrett, alias Godfrey: both were sentenced to be transported for seven years. Poor Sophia died on board the *Lucy Davidson* on the journey to Australia, it was said of a burst blood vessel, in October 1829. She was about thirty-eight years old.[66]

By then, her husband, James Stamp Sutton Cooke, was ten months dead. He had been brought into the Marshalsea

a second and final time on 24 November 1828 for a debt
of £50 – 'a small sum' he was 'unable to pay', as the papers
had it; 'but a short time ago', it was reported that he 'was
living at No. 5 Euston-place, Euston-square, where he kept
his carriage and two livery servants', but perhaps that was
before he moved into the rules of the Fleet. Now Cooke
could not afford a transfer to 'the Farringdon Hotel' and
had to bed down in the Marshalsea. A month later he was
dead, aged forty-eight. He was buried, like numerous
prisoners dying there, in the adjacent graveyard of St George
the Martyr. The flamboyant career of one of the most sensa-
tional swindlers of the late Georgian period had come to a
shabby and sordid end.[67]

James Stamp Sutton Cooke was a shooting star of what
would be the last generation of Marshalsea debtors. The
injustices and overall ineffectiveness of the laws of imprisonment for debt had long been apparent and had led directly
to the formation of the Thatched House Society half a century
earlier. Even before the old enemy abroad was finally laid
to rest at Waterloo, there was a growing appetite to identify
and deal with the enemies that had long been left to suppurate
at home: irreligion, ignorance, the savageries of the penal
justice system and the prison house, the ever-rising cost of
the poor, the corruption and iniquity of parliamentary administration. Much of the nation's public life needed reform and
modernisation and in a large agenda the medieval monstrosity
(as many saw it) of imprisonment for debt was not neglected.
The inquiries into conditions in the Marshalsea and other
debtors' prisons in London from 1815 to 1818 were part
of this awakening. So were the increasing hurdles put in the
way of arresting under mesne process in 1811 and 1827.
And so were the modernised arrangements for managing
the Marshalsea in place for the new prison in 1812. Not all
of this spirit of reform was on the side of the debtor;
the protection of the honest creditor from fraudulent

exploitation was uppermost in the minds of numerous pamphleteers and of parliamentary committees looking into the operation of the debt laws in 1819 and 1823, for instance. But everything tended to scrutiny in which the fitness for purpose of the existing legal framework came in for close attention.[68]

Movements for social improvements of all kinds gathered pace after the new reformed parliament was chosen at the general election of 1832. Calls for the abolition of all arrests on mesne process had been in the air for some time before – they had been voiced, for instance, in 1827 by Joseph Hume, the MP to whom John Ewer Poole had sent his *Expose*, and slightly after by Henry Brougham, MP for Winchester, a Scottish barrister and famous law and education reformer. Bills for this purpose were introduced and driven forward by Hume, Brougham and others in every parliamentary session from 1834. One bill eventually became law in 1838 (Lord Cottenham's Act). It removed the ability to proceed against the person of the debtor without proving the debt and obtaining an order of the court, at the same time making it easier to take action against the debtor's property.[69]

The effect of the new law on the Marshalsea and the other debtors' prisons of London was dramatic. At Christmas 1838 it was reported that 'the new act has diminished the business of the Insolvent Debtors' Court beyond what was anticipated, and at the present period the various prisons are comparatively deserted'. There were fifty-five prisoners in the Marshalsea, 'which is considered a very small amount', but the reductions in the other gaols were more drastic still. In midsummer 1839 the number had fallen to thirty-four, including three Admiralty prisoners, while the cost of running the prison, according to a radical paper, the *Charter*, was £3,000 per annum. A year later, in June 1840, the number of prisoners was just twenty-two, 'being the lowest number ever known to have been confined within the walls'; it was also noted in explanation that the abolition of arrest on mesne process had now led, 'by some beneficial working of the system', to fewer arrests on execution too. Later that year it was noted that one of the Marshalsea debtors was said to have been confined 'about four years', though able to release himself through the Insolvent Debtors' Court had he chosen to do so – one more argument for abolishing imprisonment for debtors who could exploit the system to hide from their creditors.[70]

In fact, once more, an analysis of the Marshalsea day books shows a fluid number within the walls. During the course of 1841, 242 debtors were brought into custody, just nine of them women, all arrested on execution in furtherance of an order of the Palace court. The highest number in the prison on any one day was around sixty and the lowest thirty-two; we do not know how many of these were accompanied by family members but presumably some were for that had always been the case. The Marshalsea, then, still had its uses. But the costs of keeping it open were increasingly disproportionate; and gains were to be had for the public purse if the gaol could be sold on the private market, ever buoyant in respect of land in central London.[71]

In the meantime, as far as we know, things went on in the college pretty much as they always had. Queen Victoria's marriage in February 1840 brought a familiar bounty, the debtors 'regaled . . . with good old English fare' in honour of the occasion. Christmas was more than ever a feast-time of plenty as the number of mouths to feed reduced: in 1841 the Marshalsea debtors were said each to have received '5 lbs. of beef, the same quantity of bread, a plentiful supply of malt liquor, and in addition 1s. and 6d. in cash'.[72]

Yet the closure of the Marshalsea was palpably not far off. A rationalisation of prison space was overdue with prisoner numbers falling everywhere. The closure of the Fleet and Marshalsea was mooted in the papers in the summer

of 1839, when it was said that the prisons' marshals had
been put on notice that all prisoners were to be concentrated
in the Queen's Bench. But official wheels turned slowly and
it was not till March 1842 that Parliament resolved to close
both gaols and consolidate the London debtors' prisons
outside the City in the Queen's Bench, to be renamed the
Queen's prison. It was said in the newspapers that the
Marshalsea was to be pulled down, perhaps the origin of
later confusion in the public mind over just what did happen
to the prison after it was closed. The confusion would persist
for many years.[73]

From 1 January 1842 a further 107 debtors were brought
into custody. The last, James Edward Yates, entered the lodge
on 24 May. Over the next few months almost all the debtors
were discharged through the normal avenues, most commonly
under the Insolvent Debtors Acts. When the prison closed,
on 9 November 1842, there were just three prisoners
remaining. All were taken that day to the Queen's prison, a
short walk away across Borough High Street, or Blackman
Street as it had become. They included Judith Avery, the only
woman among them, who was a widow from Marylebone,
already in the Marshalsea for fifteen months for a debt of
£36. She would eventually be released from the Queen's
prison four months later in March 1843 but would die after
just two years of freedom, aged sixty-five.[74]

By then the prison's remains had been sold at auction.
The Marshalsea would have some sort of afterlife on the
ground, as we shall see. But it would have an afterlife too,
more vivid and memorable by far, in the minds of subsequent generations. For the Marshalsea achieved worldwide
immortality as a most powerful muse for the London novelist's pen.

8

THE MARSHALSEA MUSE
AND OTHER SURVIVALS

'Top sawyers' or just plain 'characters', debtors and debtors' locks were everywhere in the eighteenth- and early-nineteenth-century novel: in Daniel Defoe, where Moll Flanders follows her debtor 'husband' into the Mint for a time (1722); in Samuel Richardson, who has Clarissa imprisoned in a spunging house at the suit of wicked Mrs Sinclair (1747–8); in Henry Fielding's *Amelia* (1751), where Captain Booth shares a similar fate though with less dire consequences; in Tobias Smollett, who seems to have coined in 1753 'mansions of misery' for a debtors' prison, the phrase used so effortlessly fifty years later, we might recall, by Thomas Prattent in the Marshalsea; in Oliver Goldsmith, whose good Vicar of Wakefield is imprisoned for his unpaid rent (1766); and so on. Debtors abound for a century to come. We meet them in the Fleet in Pierce Egan's *Life in London* (1821) and all over the metropolis in *Real Life in London* (1824) by an 'Amateur'; whole novels were written about them, by John Mills in *D'Horsay*, an extravagantly libellous satire on the real-life prodigal Count Alfred D'Orsay (1844), and by Charles Rowcroft in his fictional *Recollections of the Fleet Prison* (1847), where he'd been a prisoner himself; debtors populate the novels of Blanchard Jerrold, Anthony Trollope

and a host of others; readers of *Vanity Fair* (1847–8) can
see Mathew Arnot Stewart in Thackeray's Colonel Rawdon
Crawley and there is much of James Stamp Sutton Cooke
in Montague Tigg, or Tigg Montague as he becomes, in
Charles Dickens's *The Adventures of Martin Chuzzlewit*
(1843–4): '"Still the same name, I suppose?"' asks the pawnbroker's clerk, taking in a shirt pledged so many times it
'has grown yellow in the service'. '"Still the same name,"
said Mr Tigg, "my claim to the dormant peerage not being
yet established by the House of Lords."'[1]

It is not hard to see why debtors and their enemies –
malicious creditors, abusing duns, extortionate bailiffs,
grasping gaolers – offered novelists such graphic fare. For
the world of debt was the writer's world too. Most had
struggled to pay their way and the rest had known, frequently
helped, those struggling friends who turned to them in their
troubles. Some had found themselves prisoners in one or
more of the metropolitan debtors' gaols and even more
frequently in bailiffs' spunging houses. In the eighteenth
century a minor galaxy of writers had passed through the
Marshalsea lodge: Laetitia Pilkington, the poet and memoirist,
in 1742; Hannah Glasse, a well-known cookery writer, in
1757; Charlotte Forman, the journalist and translator, in
1766; Christopher Smart, the poet, in 1770. Others visited
friends or acquaintances there. But whether prisoners or
visitors, many literary characters had no doubt met some
'top sawyers' in debtors' prisons and heard their stories from
them or from others, sometimes using them for copy. And
all would have been struck by the peculiar intensity of existence within the walls of prisons such as the Marshalsea, the
Fleet and the King's Bench.[2]

It was Smollett who also seems to have first identified the
debtors' prison as a '*microcosm*' of the 'great world'. Here,
in miniature, as under a gardener's glass frame, was every
gradation of the living world but on a stunted stage. In a

debtors' gaol 'several small communities' would form and re-form, 'consisting of people who are attracted by the manners and dispositions of each other'. '"For my own part, Sir, I have always made it a maxim to associate with the best company I can find,"' a debtor tells the newly imprisoned Ferdinand Count Fathom in what Smollett probably intended as the King's Bench. The prisoners' 'club' there, just like society beyond the walls, could even boast as 'head or chairman' a 'sovereign prince', the 'celebrated Theodore king of Corsica', in fact a German adventurer who was indeed imprisoned for debt in the King's Bench in the 1750s.[3]

For writers such as Smollett the debtors' prison was a living satire on the pretensions, the dubious appearances, the calculated lies, dissimulations and meretriciousness of 'London Society', from St James's Palace all the way to the Southwark Mint. It was the acme of stage fakery, where the players were all in on the secret and where the masquerade of the wider world was in plain sight. It was captured in one striking image early in the nineteenth century by the history-painter Benjamin Haydon, himself a frequent debtor prisoner, in *The Mock Election* (1827), in which the 'Election of Two Members for the Borough of Tenterden' at the King's Bench offered the chance to catch every stage of anxious sorrow and reckless riot among the debtors and for them to satirise the civil and court ceremonies of the living world. Its large array of characters included, the *Morning Post* explained, at centre stage 'the High Sheriff, the "mute" yet not now "inglorious" LINTON of the Marshalsea, with a mopstick for a wand of office, gracefully tipped with a strawberry pottle – his curtain rings for a gold chain – striving with gravity, the more laughable from its earnestness, to keep the peace between the Honourable Candidates'.[4]

The debtors' prison as microcosm, as symbol of the wider metropolitan social relationships that had spawned it and exposing society's frailties to a truthful gaze, could offer writers a fertile inspiration. Inevitably the Marshalsea was part of the territory. Its best-known earliest manifestation in fiction was in *Roderick Random*, Tobias Smollett's popular picaresque novel of 1748. It was his first writing success, with more than a touch of autobiography in its account of Random, a Scottish surgeon who comes to London, struggles to make his way and gets employment as a naval sawbones. Smollett later attested that 'The low Situations in which I have exhibited Roderick I never experienced in my own Person', and as far as we know Smollett was never a prisoner in the Marshalsea or for debt anywhere else, though he would later be gaoled for three months in the King's Bench for a libel in 1760–61. It seems likely, though, that he knew the London debtors' prisons, through friendship or benevolence or both.[5]

Certainly the Marshalsea figures largely in *Random*. Miss Nancy Williams, a prostitute whose life Roderick saves when he discovers her starving in a St Giles garret, is later arrested for debt and taken to the Marshalsea; but there she is shown not to be the notorious debtor named in the Palace court writ and so gains her freedom. Later, however, it is Roderick himself who passes through the Marshalsea lodge, when he is arrested at the suit (so to speak) of his tailor. He hires 'a small paultry bed-chamber for a crown a week'. He soon discovers a friend fallen on hard times whom he'd not recently seen and learns from him 'the oeconomy of the place'. Roderick orders in from 'a cook's shop in the neighbourhood' some 'boiled beef and greens' and a bottle of wine, and after dinner accompanies his friend to 'the common side, where I saw a number of naked miserable wretches assembled together'.

We had not been here many minutes, when a figure appeared, wrapt in a dirty rug, tied about his loins with two pieces of list, of different colours, knotted together; having a black

bushy beard, and his head covered with a huge mass of
brown periwig, which seemed to have been ravished from
the crown of some scare-crow. – This apparition, stalking in
with great solemnity, made a profound bow to the audience
who signified their approbation by a general response of
'How d'ye do, doctor?'[6]

This was Mr Melopoyn, a learned but unsuccessful playwright, his talents stifled by the rapacity and fickleness of
the London theatre managers and their leading actors, and
whose lengthy tale of woe mirrored Smollett's own disap-
pointments with his play *The Regicide*. There is much in the
Melopoyn chapters of Smollett paying back old grievances,
but many of the incidentals of the Marshalsea episodes ring
true, especially so in one regard where it is hard to believe
that Smollett had not witnessed such a thing himself. For
Roderick gives up hope in the Marshalsea, as 'a train of
melancholy thoughts took possession of my soul':

> I, seeing my money melt away, without any certainty of
> deliverance, and in short, all my hopes frustrated; grew negli-
> gent of life, lost all appetite, and degenerated into such a
> sloven, that during the space of two months, I was neither
> washed, shifted, nor shaved; so that my face, rendered meagre
> with abstinence, was obscured with dirt, and overshadowed
> with hair, and my whole appearance squalid and even
> frightful . . .[7]

Poor Roderick is eventually relieved by his generous Uncle
Bowling, a naval officer made wealthy by taking a rich prize,
who settled with the unforgiving tailor and released his
distressed nephew. The Marshalsea chapters of *Roderick
Random* are memorable episodes in even this vivid and fast-
paced novel, so sharply observant of London life in the
1740s. The prison is made to symbolise here one specific

element in the microcosm of metropolitan mores, the injustice met by unrecognised genius, honest talent suppressed by duplicitous self-interest and thus left at the mercy of clamorous creditors. This Marshalsea is the graveyard of worthy endeavour, the final resting place of merit trounced by knavery.

This portrait of the Marshalsea as a prison for society's victims was perpetuated in an anonymous sentimental novel produced some twenty-five years later, *The Triumph of Benevolence; or, the History of Francis Wills* (1772). The susceptible Wills, incapable of ignoring others' unhappiness though himself recently disappointed in love, finds himself in Birdcage Walk at dusk. In St James's Park he spies a young woman 'superior to the generality of the unhappy wretches that ply there continually, and earn a wretched and precarious subsistence by the most abandoned prostitution'. She is poorly dressed but 'clean'. Near the edge of Rosamond's Pond, once a place of frequent suicides, he addresses her and she confesses her poverty is driving her to contemplate killing herself. For she is alone in the world apart from her father, who is '"Confined in a loathsome jail . . . His name is Belton, and he is confined in the Marshalsea prison in the borough of Southwark . . . it is so dreadful a place —"'.[8]

In Smollett the Marshalsea's appearance and most of its arrangements are invisible, but here the reader follows Wills through the 'dirty court', 'large gates' and high walls with their '*chevaux de frize*' mentioned in a passage already cited that accurately describes the approach to the gaol. Within, the prisoners are generally of the Melopoyn variety. 'There may be some, who, pursuing fraudulent methods, have drawn this heavy vengeance upon themselves: but they are few in comparison of the unfortunate.' These many were 'A set of miserable creatures, meagre through want, squalid and pale with confinement, perhaps the object of pique and malevolence, and imprisoned at the suit of some relentless creditor . . .'[9]

Belton is one such. He lies starving in a 'very small' room bare of furniture except a bed without curtains, two chairs and 'a little table'. At first he fears that Wills has come to trick him and seduce his lovely daughter Sophy, but the benevolent Francis – '"Misery is sacred with me, Sir"' – retrieves Belton's clothes from a neighbouring pawnbroker and pays for Sophy to order in from a local tavern 'broth, and other things fit for a weak stomach'. Once refreshed, Belton tells his story – of an evil aristocratic patron, Lord Cotswold, to whom he was first tutor and then land agent. The beautiful Sophia, when little more than a child, catches the eye of the lustful lord. Cotswold's efforts to seduce her fail, so he schemes to blackmail her into submission. On a fateful day, Belton is tricked into putting his name to a bill. The bill is called in but Belton cannot fulfil his acceptance, is arrested and imprisoned. Sophia and Belton are made to understand that her virtue is the only key that will unlock the Marshalsea gates. Despite all Wills's efforts to intercede with Lord Cotswold, he proves adamant. Wills has to raise the value of the full debt with interest and costs, now some £270, by mortgaging his own property and settling the bill through the Palace court to relieve the hapless Belton.[10]

In 1772, with sentimental benevolence all the rage in the novel, in the very year those influential sermons were preached that led to the formation of the Society for the Discharge and Relief of Persons Imprisoned for Small Debts throughout England, it seemed fitting to present the Marshalsea as a symbol of unjust imprisonment, a dungeon for the meek and maligned. But a different trope had already begun to emerge that uncomfortably disconnected the worlds of Melopoyn and Belton.

Eight years earlier another anonymous novel, probably from a female hand, painted an intimate picture of the gaol but from an entirely different angle. In *The History of Miss Charlotte Seymour* (1764) the Marshalsea's reputation for misery is reinforced. But now the misery is not just largely self-imposed but richly deserved, due reward for reckless profligacy with other people's money and for wilful rejection of society's moral compass. In general the prisoners are merely reaping the fruits of flagrant misbehaviour, of selfishness, lust, indiscipline and deceit. Now the 'real object of charity', the innocent victims of injustice or misfortune in trade, are a rarity.[11]

They exist, of course, because Charlotte Seymour is one herself. Her father was a City hosier, a prosperous citizen with his 'box' on the Essex and Hertfordshire border, where Charlotte was born. He has liberal views on a girl's need for education and she is sent to a boarding school. Charlotte's subsequent journey into the world is beset by assaults on her virtue by scheming men aided by complaisant women, for like Sophy Belton she is a lovely girl. These she fends off, but worse befalls her. For Mr Seymour expands his business but overreaches himself, breaks and is bankrupted, plunging Charlotte into poverty or something near it. By then she has fallen out with her father for not accepting the husband he has chosen for her, and on his failure she is left to fend for herself. Dependent on the self-interested friendships of designing young rakes, whose support is guaranteed only at the cost of her modesty, she falls into debt with dress shops and her landlady, who importunes Charlotte to take up prostitution as an answer to her money worries, but this was 'a course of life, which to her was worse than death'. Thinking an older man, whom she admires, is in love with her, she invests in finery, expecting to satisfy the bill once he declares himself. In fact, he has no amatory intentions and she is arrested at her mercer's suit. After some troublesome days and restless nights in a spunging house 'in a street near the Hay-market', she is committed to the Marshalsea.[12]

'Here was a new world for Charlotte — Such a scene opened to her view as she was before entirely unacquainted with. Here were several she before had known in the gay world, some of whom were said to be dead, others gone abroad, and others gone in the country.' Such as Tom Dapperwit, the beau of Ranelagh and Vauxhall, 'a constant dangler', 'the terror of fops, and the scourge of coquettes', but now 'a very wretch indeed! whose garments could scarce cover his nakedness, and whose odoriferous scent, was scarce supportable, whose intimates . . . were cutaneous animals, and voracious vermin'. The kindly Charlotte gives him half a crown, though he promptly 'drank it out' in gin in 'the tap room'. And like the celebrated 'Miss Lucy C— [Cooper]', 'who, from being a common prostitute, had been cried up for a woman of great wit and reading, because, she had a smattering of common place quibbles, extracted from jest books and brothels, and had got a few sentences of Latin . . .' Lucy was not alone, for

as to the female inmates, they were for the most part ladies of pleasure, of very dissolute morals, and very disagreeable conversation, who having in general exhausted their credit with their landladies, were thrown in here, in hopes that some men, with more money than wit, would take pity of them, by releasing them from their confinement, and discharge their debt . . . Besides this early acquaintance with Miss Lucy C—, Charlotte found invitations from several other ladies, who, from various misfortunes, incident to the sex, (when *their stars are more in fault than they*) were obliged to take up their lodging under the same roof; but none of their cards obtained any notice, except that of Miss Brilliant. They were indeed for the most part, so sadly scrawled, and so deformed with pseudo orthography, that it required good decyphering to unriddle their meaning.[13]

Miss Brilliant's story – of a not unwilling seduction through the false promises of a rich man, ensuing dissipation and extravagance all laid at the door of '*vanity*' – was of a piece with those of the other debtors Charlotte meets in the Marshalsea. Here it is not the creditor who is at fault – after all, her mercer's claim is a just one – but the debtor. In *Charlotte Seymour* the arcane mechanics of debtor law, familiar to so many contemporary Londoners, become unlikely grist to the novelist's mill. And here the lure of an impending Insolvent Debtors Act, the advantages of which were spelled out to her by her fellow prisoners, becomes a statutory charter of deceit:

> She was informed, that an officer was just arrived, who was a man of great fortune, but being ill used and imposed upon, by some of his creditors, he was resolved to punish them, and take the benefit of the act of grace. Charlotte, who was entirely ignorant of these proceedings, was greatly surprized to think, that a man of fortune should descend to such low subterfuges, to evade the payment of his just debts, and that he should consider the loss of his reputation, and the publication of his name to all the world, as a common cheat, not more than equivalent to the saving of a few pounds. However, she had reason to find afterwards, there were many of this way of thinking . . .[14]

Rejecting the insolvency route, Charlotte is advised to tell her creditor that he should now pursue an execution against her in the Palace court, but the costs and potential frustrations deter him. After she has spent three eventful weeks in the Marshalsea, he frees her 'upon condition of giving him a note for the money; which she readily consented to, as it was her intention to pay him honestly the debt if ever it should be in her power'.[15] Despite the temptations that assailed both her virtue and her honour as a responsible citizen who knows she should pay her way when she can, Charlotte leaves the prison unblemished by the Marshalsea stain. It is an intriguing and well-observed novel that reconstructs the Marshalsea more as temple of idleness than as mansion of misery. It was a dichotomy that would resonate powerfully in the years to come.

But not immediately. After Roderick Random, Charlotte Seymour and Sophy Belton, the Marshalsea's muse dimmed. Its light might indeed have gone out for ever, the gaol passing with little notice from the culture and leaving nothing more than a footnote. When other writers, as they often did over the following half-century and more, spotlighted the debtors' prison as a microcosm of London life, a biting satire on metropolitan manners, it was now the Fleet and the King's Bench to which they turned, as had Smollett in his later novels.

It was of course Charles Dickens, greatest of all English novelists, who revived the Marshalsea as a symbol of society's ills in new, shifting and complex ways. Why he did so is no mystery: for the prison haunted him. It was indelibly associated with his deepest humiliation – the fact of not just his father's imprisonment but the poverty that accompanied it, worst of all the demeaning drudgery in the blacking factory to which he was unfeelingly consigned by father and mother both. For over twenty years he never spoke about this period of his life and he might never have spoken of it at all had not an accident brought it to light. In 'the March or April of 1847', John Forster, Dickens's greatest friend and chosen biographer, happened to relay something a mutual friend, 'old Mr. Dilke', had said to him: that Dilke, a colleague of John Dickens, had seen the young Charles at work in the blacking warehouse near the Strand, 'had noticed him, and received, in return for the gift of a half-crown, a very low bow'. Dickens made no response to Forster, indeed 'was silent for several minutes; I felt that I had immediately touched a painful place in the memory; and to Mr. Dilke I never spoke of the subject again'.[16]

It was only 'some weeks later' that Dickens referred to
the memories Forster had unconsciously refreshed of a time
that 'haunted him and made him miserable, even to that
hour'. It was sometime in mid-1847 that Dickens gave Forster
the autobiographical fragment on which our understanding
of his early years relies. Extensively quoted by Forster, it has
sadly not survived. Dickens's time at the blacking factory
and, by implication, the time his family spent in the
Marshalsea were seared into his mind and scarred it for ever.
The fragment, as cited by Forster, ended thus:

> From that hour until this at which I write, no word of that
> part of my childhood which I have now gladly brought to
> a close, has passed my lips to any human being. I have no
> idea how long it lasted; whether for a year, or much more,
> or less. From that hour, until this, my father and mother
> have been stricken dumb upon it. I have never heard the
> least allusion to it, however far off and remote, from either
> of them. I have never, until I now impart it to this paper, in
> any burst of confidence with any one, my own wife not
> excepted, raised the curtain I then dropped, thank God.
>
> Until old Hungerford-market was pulled down, until old
> Hungerford-stairs were destroyed, and the very nature of the
> ground changed, I never had the courage to go back to the
> place where my servitude began. I never saw it. I could not
> endure to go near it. For many years, when I came near to
> Robert Warren's in the Strand, I crossed over to the opposite
> side of the way, to avoid a certain smell of the cement they
> put upon the blacking-corks, which reminded me of what I
> was once. It was a very long time before I liked to go up
> Chandos-street. My old way home by the borough made me
> cry, after my eldest child could speak.[17]

It seems that writing this, even though not 'a tithe of what
I might have written, or of what I meant to write', or at

least the act of sharing it with Forster, prompted a lengthy process for Dickens of coming to terms with his own past. That autumn of 1847 he began work on one of his Christmas books, a series of seasonal ghost stories that had begun some four years before with *A Christmas Carol*. As he was busy on other projects, not least *Dombey and Son*, Forster persuaded him to put it aside till the next Christmas but one, 1848. *The Haunted Man*, as it became, surely had a deeper personal resonance than was usual, even with him. Redlaw, we never know his full name, is a respected professor of chemistry, revered for his charitable kindness. Yet he is melancholy and lonely, his face hollow, his eyes sunken, his looks shrivelled by a lifetime of disappointment, grieving for a dead and lamented sister won but betrayed by the man Redlaw thought to be his best friend. His sorrow haunts him, but a spectral Redlaw offers to remove all miserable memories of his life's great tragedy. The penalty exacted is that all who come into contact with him will be similarly affected. Redlaw accepts the ghost's bargain. But now his forgotten sorrows have the effect of rendering him unfeeling to all in need around him. His charity disappears and so does that of all those he subsequently meets, except Milly, the wife of the landlord with whom he lodges. Recognising her power to restore goodness, he seeks her out, casts off the ghost's curse and recovers his benevolence. It is an unsatisfying tale on any level, but its meaning for the author is plain enough: that his past sorrows in the blacking factory and the Marshalsea had been instrumental in making Dickens the man he was.[18]

Perhaps he had already begun to come to terms with them, at least with the Marshalsea. Given his father's history, debt, debtors and debtors' locks had an indelible fascination for him – it has been truly said that 'Debtors are everywhere in Dickens' fiction' and the same might be said for debtors' prisons too. 'We have never outgrown the rugged walls of

Newgate, or any other prison on the outside,' he remarked in an autobiographical essay of 1853. 'All within, is still the same blank of remorse and misery.' One way of dealing with it was to write the prison out of his system, endlessly reworking the meaning of prisons, for those within and those on the outside, and the peculiar world of the debtors' gaol in particular.[19]

The Marshalsea's first appearance in his full-length fiction – the Fleet and King's Bench are given earlier outings in newspaper pieces in 1834, later collected in *Sketches by Boz* – came early in the *Pickwick Papers* (1836–7). 'The Old Man's Tale About the Queer Client', while horribly bleak, had much popular appeal and achieved something of an independent existence when adapted for the Adelphi's stage in April 1837. As always, Dickens precisely renders the London he knew so well, but he cannot avoid a shudder as he does so:

> In the Borough High Street, near Saint George's Church, and on the same side of the way, stands, as most people know, the smallest of our debtors' prisons, the Marshalsea. Although in later times it has been a very different place from the sink of filth and dirt it once was, even its improved condition holds out but little temptation to the extravagant, or consolation to the improvident. The condemned felon has as good a yard for air and exercise in Newgate, as the insolvent debtor in the Marshalsea Prison.
>
> It may be my fancy, or it may be that I cannot separate the place from the old recollections associated with it, but this part of London I cannot bear. The street is broad, the shops are spacious, the noise of passing vehicles, the footsteps of a perpetual stream of people – all the busy sounds of traffic, resound in it from morn to midnight, but the streets around are mean and close; poverty and debauchery lie festering in the crowded alleys; want and misfortune are pent

up in the narrow prison; an air of gloom and dreariness
seems, in my eyes at least, to hang about the scene, and to
impart to it a squalid and sickly hue.[20]

Dickens relates a story very much in the mould of
Melopoyn, at least in so far as the debtor was at the mercy
of a malignant creditor through no fault of his own. We
might remember that Smollett had provided Dickens with a
favourite literary escape from humdrum reality when he was
a boy. It is odd to think that Roderick Random gave him
his first glimpse inside the Marshalsea, that it was in his
imagination that pictures were first conjured of life inside
the gaol he was later to know so well.[21]

Dickens's Melopoyn is George Heyling, the Queer Client,
whose wife and child die while Heyling is imprisoned long
years in the Marshalsea. Freed by an inheritance, he instructs
a lawyer to ruin his vindictive creditor, who is his dead wife's
father. Heyling harvests the old man's outstanding bills and
has his attorney plague him with threats of arrest and imprisonment. When his father-in-law, harassed and almost worried
to death, goes into hiding, Heyling ferrets him out and
confronts him to say his arrest is imminent, but the old man
dies before the bailiffs arrive. It is a grim tale of implacable
cruelty breeding merciless revenge in its wake, with the debtors'
prison – here a nursery of oppression – as the fatal weapon.

But the other side of the debtors' prison, as temple of
idleness, appears in full feather later in the book, when Mr
Pickwick undergoes voluntary imprisonment in the Fleet for
a debt he could pay but won't. He can easily afford the
damages and lawyers' fees loaded on him by his trial for
breach of promise, but the suit was unjust and he denies his
creditors their due by consenting to his arrest and imprisonment. If the Marshalsea is allowed to stand as a symbol for
the victimised debtor, then the Fleet represents all that is
morally corrupting about the debtors' gaol, casting its

inmates beyond redemption. Except that this is and is not the Fleet. It is true that Dickens describes the physical realities of 'the Farringdon Hotel' faithfully and in detail; but the prisoners are those same Marshalsea debtors that he remembered from his youth, as he confessed to John Forster a decade or so later:

> There were many classes of people here, from the labouring man in his fustian jacket, to the broken-down spendthrift in his shawl dressing-gown, most appropriately out at elbows; but there was the same air about them all – a listless jail-bird careless swagger, a vagabondish who's-afraid sort of bearing, which is wholly indescribable in words, but which any man can understand in one moment if he wish, by setting foot in the nearest debtors' prison, and looking at the very first group of people he sees there, with the same interest as Mr. Pickwick did.
>
> 'It strikes me, Sam,' said Mr. Pickwick, leaning over the iron-rail at the stairhead, 'It strikes me, Sam, that imprisonment for debt is scarcely any punishment at all.'
>
> 'Think not, sir?' inquired Mr. Weller.
>
> 'You see how these fellows drink, and smoke, and roar,' replied Mr. Pickwick. 'It's quite impossible that they can mind it much.'
>
> 'Ah, that's just the wery thing, sir,' rejoined Sam, '*they* don't mind it; it's a regular holiday to them – all porter and skittles. It's the t'other vuns as gets done over, vith this sort o' thing; them down-hearted fellers as can't svig away at the beer, nor play at skittles neither; them as vould pay if they could, and gets low by being boxed up. I'll tell you wot it is, sir; them as is always a idlin' in public houses it don't damage at all, and them as is alvays a workin' wen they can, it damages too much. "It's unekal," as my father used to say wen his grog worn't made half-and-half; "It's unekal, and that's the fault on it."'[22]

Dickens's two-edged critique, first explored in *Pickwick Papers*, of the debtor's prison as fostering vindictiveness and idleness both, fed into the agitation for the reform of the debt laws going on at this very time. But debtors and their plight had a more personal and long-standing resonance for him. It was reflected especially in his ambivalence towards the whole breed of debtors. His feelings would harden against them in his later work, but the ability to see both good and bad sides of the chronic sponger is there from the beginning. All stemmed from his own unforgettable memories of the Marshalsea and from his conflicted emotions about his father's feckless though lovable character. Appealing debtors, like Dick Swiveller in *The Old Curiosity Shop* (1840–41) – rescued from a dangerous fever by the 'Marchioness', the tiny servant girl whose title, given to her by Dick, is so resonant of the Marshalsea days, from which the author remembered her as skivvy for the imprisoned Dickens family – become fewer, but they are there even towards the end, in the Plornishes, for instance, in *Little Dorrit* (1855–7). Even Montague Tigg, deplorable though he is in so many ways and fittingly punished with a very sticky end, has an energy, inventiveness, wit and charisma that make him among the most memorable of Dickens's minor characters.[23]

Though debtors abound, and though the Marchioness would have echoes for those who later learned Dickens's life story, the Marshalsea was allowed to lie fallow until after the author's revelations to Forster. It then reappeared to stunning effect, not long after he did so, in *David Copperfield* (1849–50), the most autobiographical of his novels to that time. Here the Marshalsea plays a notable role, again not under its own name but this time in disguise as the nearby King's Bench. It is here that Dickens's own circumstances were graphically laid bare, his father translated into Wilkins Micawber, with whom David had lodged while he worked at the blacking warehouse north of the river. Like John

Dickens, Mr Micawber's wife and children join him in his room in the gaol. Even the Marchioness is resurrected as the 'Orfling' servant girl who lives outside the gaol nearby, as does David (and of course as had the boy Dickens in reality). Captain Porter now becomes Captain Hopkins and the scene of reading and signing the memorial is precisely rendered, almost word for word, from the autobiographical fragment given to his friend two years or so before. Unlike the Fleet, which Dickens must have had cause to visit and closely observe, the King's Bench is hardly realised as a physical presence. But the Marshalsea debtors are all there. And their ghosts haunt still the successful author, now thirty-eight years old, and form a chorus in Copperfield's paean of pity for the boy he had been.

As I walked to and fro daily between Southwark and Blackfriars, and lounged about at meal-times in obscure streets, the stones of which may, for anything I know, be worn at this moment by my childish feet, I wonder how many of these people were wanting in the crowd that used to come filing before me in review again, to the echo of Captain Hopkins's voice! When my thoughts go back now, to that slow agony of my youth, I wonder how much of the histories I invented for such people hangs like a mist of fancy over well-remembered facts! When I tread the old ground, I do not wonder that I seem to see and pity, going on before me, an innocent romantic boy, making his imaginative world out of such strange experiences and sordid things.[24]

Why did Dickens not 'name names' in *David Copperfield* and identify Micawber's prison as the Marshalsea rather than disguise it as the King's Bench, by the time the book was written reinvented in reality as the Queen's prison? John Dickens was alive, of course, but it is doubtful whether the true identification of the gaol and its inmates could have mattered to him, or have caused any further offence, given the accuracy of the Marshalsea incidents. Those he must have recognised even if he failed to identify himself completely in Wilkins Micawber.

Nor was there any risk that anyone could associate these parts of *David Copperfield* with the author's own life. Dickens's Marshalsea (and blacking-factory) secret was so closely kept that no one could have interpreted the book in that way. Indeed, the Marshalsea passages in John Forster's life of Dickens (1872) shocked the reviewers, who received their advance copies just before Christmas 1871, and all who read it subsequently. 'Few secrets', the *Graphic* confirmed, 'have been better kept than that which Mr. John Forster has now disclosed . . . By the light of this revelation we re-read the works of our greatest modern humorist with a new and personal interest.' And the *Pall Mall Gazette* agreed that 'No biography has ever taken its readers so much by surprise . . .' It came as a revelation even to Dickens's children, now all adults. So there was no risk to himself in 1849 and any offence to his father could not have been aggravated by giving Micawber's prison its true name. In the end, it seems that to have done so would have been a step too far for Dickens himself, the very name of the Marshalsea something that he could not bear to speak or to hear spoken of, much as he had avoided the way to it for so long.[25]

It would take some years yet for him to confront it completely. The Marshalsea would finally find its apotheosis in the story of *Little Dorrit*, perhaps Dickens's most complex, controversial and personal novel. Dickens expands Smollett's notion of microcosm and makes the prison – both the Marshalsea and imprisonment in general – stand for the iron girdles of money and power binding the whole of contemporary society in a straitjacket that stifles initiative, creativity, mutual affection, even humanity itself. Here the

symbol of the prison is pervasive. Even the Marseilles sun –
Marseilles and Marshalsea are places connected to one
another here by more than name – is so fierce that it locks
people indoors at noonday. And Marseilles, like London, is
a city of prisons, with gaol-birds rotting in its dungeons and
even respectable British travellers like Arthur Clennam held
in quarantine because they might be bringing plague from
the east. The prison trope is so pervasive – Mrs Clennam,
Arthur's mother, is imprisoned in her crumbling City mansion
by disability, by money and by puritanism, and there are
many other instances – that Little Dorrit's prison could have
been anywhere or even nowhere.

But now the Marshalsea is conclusively written out, named
and described in all the crystal detail that had never deserted
the author's mind since he was twelve years old. Here we
can see that nothing had been forgotten, almost nothing
misremembered, over the intervening years – the novel's first
words are 'Thirty years ago', virtually placing it in 1824,
the year of his father's imprisonment – though he had never
revisited the gaol or its location in the meantime. It was
here that he chose to place his central characters, William
Dorrit, 'Father of the Marshalsea', a prisoner there time out
of mind, and Amy, his daughter, born in the prison twenty-
two years before, so slight and childlike in face and form
that she was known to all, including to Mrs Clennam, her
employer, as Little Dorrit. She did not know, but Arthur
Clennam suspects, that her father is kept in prison at the
suit of the pitiless and revengeful Mrs Clennam: 'Smite
though my debtors, Lord, wither them, crush them; do Thou
as I would do, and Thou shalt have my worship: this was
the impious tower of stone she had built up to scale
Heaven.'[26]

If this is the vindictiveness of Pickwick's 'Queer Client'
resurrected, then William Dorrit is the other side of the
debtor's coin. The Marshalsea stain is so deeply engrained

that it has passed to his older children, born before he entered the lodge. And despite his status in the Marshalsea as '"Father of this place"', and the 'wonderful air of benignity and patronage' endowed by his position, he is nothing more now than king of the beggars. On Clennam's first visit to the Marshalsea, Dorrit acquaints him with the '"handsome and delicate action"' of a '"gentleman from Camberwell"' who had also paid him a visit and desired '"to offer some little – Testimonial – to the Father of the place"':

> 'Sometimes,' he went on in a low, soft voice, agitated, and clearing his throat every now and then; 'sometimes – hem – it takes one shape and sometimes another; but it is generally – ha – Money. And it is, I cannot but confess it, it is too often – hem – acceptable. This gentleman that I refer to, was presented to me, Mr. Clennam, in a manner highly gratifying to my feelings, and conversed not only with great politeness, but with great – ahem – information . . . It appeared from his conversation that he had a garden, though he was delicate of mentioning it at first, as gardens are – hem – are not accessible to me. But it came out, through my admiring a very fine cluster of geranium – beautiful cluster of geranium to be sure – which he had brought from his conservatory. On my taking notice of its rich colour, he showed me a piece of paper round it, on which was written, "For the Father of the Marshalsea," and presented it to me. But this was – hem – not all. He made a particular request, on taking leave, that I would remove the paper in half an hour. I – ha – I did so; and I found that it contained – ahem – two guineas. I assure you, Mr. Clennam, I have received – hem – Testimonials in many ways, and of many degrees of value, and they have always been – ha – unfortunately acceptable; but I never was more pleased than with this – ahem – this particular Testimonial.'[27]

Dorrit's Marshalsea indeed was a sanctuary of beggary, a breeding place of beggars. Its influence spread even beyond its walls and gates, for it bred its own reserve army of labour who hung around the gaol before the gates opened each morning for the chance to earn a pittance from the prisoners:

There was a string of people already straggling in, whom it was not difficult to identify as the nondescript messengers, go-betweens, and errand bearers of the place. Some of them had been lounging in the rain till the gate should open; others, who had timed their arrival with greater nicety, were coming up now, and passing in with damp whitey-brown paper bags from the grocers, loaves of bread, lumps of butter, eggs, milk, and the like. The shabbiness of these attendants on shabbiness, the poverty of these insolvent waiters upon insolvency, was a sight to see. Such threadbare coats and trousers, such fusty gowns and shawls, such squashed hats and bonnets, such boots and shoes, such umbrellas and walking-sticks, never were seen in Rag Fair. All of them were the cast-off clothes of other men and women; were made up of patches and pieces of other people's individuality, and had no sartorial existence of their own proper. Their walk was the walk of a race apart. They had a peculiar way of doggedly slinking round the corner, as if they were eternally going to the pawnbroker's. When they coughed, they coughed like people accustomed to be forgotten on door-steps and in draughty passages, waiting for answers to letters in faded ink, which gave the recipients of those manuscripts great mental disturbance and no satisfaction. As they eyed the stranger in passing, they eyed him with borrowing eyes – hungry, sharp, speculative as to his softness if they were accredited to him, and the likelihood of his standing something handsome. Mendicity on commission stooped in their high shoulders, shambled in their unsteady legs, buttoned and pinned and darned and dragged their clothes, frayed their buttonholes, leaked out of their figures in dirty little ends of tape, and issued from their mouths in alcoholic breathings.[28]

Dorrit and all about him are incapable of rescuing themselves through their own efforts. Fittingly then, William Dorrit is eventually released from the Marshalsea by a great bequest – much larger than came the way of John Dickens – that he had never known existed and that others had discovered for him. The event caused great celebration in the gaol. Dickens teases out for us the meaning of the moment for the Marshalsea debtors left behind, and left supine to their fate:

> The Collegians were not envious. Besides that they had a personal and traditional regard for a Collegian of so many years' standing, the event was creditable to the College, and made it famous in the newspapers. Perhaps more of them thought, too, than were quite aware of it, that the thing might in the lottery of chances have happened to themselves, or that something of the sort might yet happen to themselves, some day or other. They took it very well. A few were low at the thought of being left behind, and being left poor; but even these did not grudge the family their brilliant reverse. There might have been much more envy in politer places. It seems probable that mediocrity of fortune would have been disposed to be less magnanimous than the Collegians, who lived from hand to mouth – from the pawnbroker's hand to the day's dinner.[29]

In fact, though gaining his freedom, William Dorrit would never be free from the Marshalsea. He would be haunted by its memory until the day he died; and the shame of the prison and the beggary it induced would haunt his older children too. Even Amy Dorrit cannot quite escape the prison's baneful influence. Before Dorrit is freed, Amy asks

Clennam whether her father will have to repay the original debt for which he had been imprisoned and Clennam confirmed that he would:

> 'It seems to me hard,' said Little Dorrit, 'that he should have lost so many years and suffered so much, and at last pay all the debts as well. It seems to me hard that he should pay in life and money both.'
>
>   'My dear child —' Clennam was beginning.
>
>   'Yes, I know I am wrong,' she pleaded timidly, 'don't think any worse of me; it has grown up with me here.'
>
>   The prison, which could spoil so many things, had tainted Little Dorrit's mind no more than this. Engendered as the confusion was, in compassion for the poor prisoner, her father, it was the first speck Clennam had ever seen, it was the last speck Clennam ever saw, of the prison atmosphere upon her.[30]

So Amy Dorrit, the epitome of selfless love, cannot evade the debtors' prison stain. But the stain seeps wider. Almost every character in the novel, and there are scores of them, is flawed. For the stain of the Marshalsea is nothing less than the contamination of money and the society that worships it; that imprisons, perhaps for life, those who transgress against its laws.

Little Dorrit was the darkest of Dickens's novels so far published, one of the darkest of the whole canon. It was in general not well received by his contemporaries, one reviewer calling it 'the worst' of his fictions. Even in 1911 G. K. Chesterton could dismiss it as Dickens's 'one collapse'. It remained generally unloved until the wholesale re-evaluation of Dickens and his work that took place especially from the 1960s on the approach to the centenary of his death. In that year, 1970, F. R. Leavis acclaimed *Little Dorrit* as Dickens's 'greatest book' and though by no means everyone would endorse this judgement the all-encompassing critique it offers of mid-Victorian Britain retains its brutally vivid force to this day. An immortal work, it incidentally rendered the Marshalsea immortal too.[31]

Whether, in some sort of catharsis, *Little Dorrit* finally relieved Dickens from his own Marshalsea ghost is a moot point. But on the face of things it seems greatly to have eased the burden. On finishing the book, issued in monthly parts over a lengthy period, Dickens came to prepare it for publication in volume form and composed a preface for the purpose. To write it, curiosity at last took him back to the scene of so many momentous events in his painful early years. After a gap of thirty-three years, on 6 May 1857 he retraced his steps to the site of the Marshalsea. That he did so at all, and that the result of his visit is generally so sunny, surely indicate a reconciliation of sorts:

Some of my readers may have an interest in being informed whether or no any portions of the Marshalsea Prison are yet standing. I myself did not know, until I was approaching the end of this story, when I went to look. I found the outer front court-yard, often mentioned here, metamorphosed into a butter shop; and then I almost gave up every brick of the jail for lost. Wandering, however, down a certain adjacent 'Angel Court, leading to Bermondsey,' I came to 'Marshalsea Place;' the houses in which I recognised, not only as the great block of the former prison, but as preserving the rooms that arose in my mind's-eye when I became Little Dorrit's Biographer. The smallest boy I ever conversed with, carrying the largest baby I ever saw, offered a supernaturally intelligent explanation of the locality in its old uses, and was very nearly correct. How this young Newton (for such I judge him to be) came to his information, I don't know; he was a quarter of a century too young to know anything about it of himself. I pointed to the window of the room where Little Dorrit was born, and where her father had lived so long, and asked him what was the name of the lodger who tenanted that apartment at present? He said, 'Tom Pythick.' I asked him who was Tom Pythick? and he said, 'Joe Pythick's uncle.'

A little further on, I found the older and smaller wall, which used to enclose the pent-up inner prison where nobody was put, except for ceremony. Whosoever goes into Marshalsea Place, turning out of Angel Court, leading to Bermondsey, will find his feet on the very paving-stones of the extinct Marshalsea jail; will see its narrow yard to the right and to the left, very little altered if at all, except that the walls were lowered when the place got free; will look upon the rooms in which the debtors lived; will stand among the crowding ghosts of many miserable years.[32]

The fate of the Marshalsea after its closure on 9 November 1842 is difficult to unravel, partly because so many mistaken assertions were made about it over the years. What Dickens described in 1857 remained for a long time. Marshalsea Place continued to provide lodgings for very poor and needy families: in one room there, shortly before Dickens died, were found a man and wife and their five children, three of whom were dead of typhus and one other sick from the same complaint. The buildings of the Admiralty prison, remnants of the old White Lyon that were used for punishing refractory debtors, where Giles Hemens took refuge for a time, lived on for some years too. At Christmas 1886 some of these older buildings were reportedly 'condemned and would shortly be destroyed', and certainly some part of Angel Place, as Angel Court had become, was rebuilt for commercial use by George Harding and Co., hardware suppliers, in that year or the next. But some old buildings of the Admiralty gaol, and the old Marshalsea chapel, were there still in 1897, used as a common lodging house for vagrants and poor labourers. One building retained ceilings 'covered with sheet-iron; the floors studded with nails. Some prisoners' names are cut in the stones of the yard' and were reportedly carved 'on the panels' of the chapel. These old places were then threatened again with demolition, this time for a road widening, but just when they were cleared has not been discovered.[33]

The 'great block of the former prison', where John Dickens had been confined, continued as 'mean houses' offering 'frowsy shelter' for the poor into the 1890s, yet many Dickensians failed to spot what would have been in front of their eyes had they taken the trouble to follow Dickens's own directions. Charles Dickens the Younger claimed of the Marshalsea in 1893 that 'no trace of it is now to be found', despite 'local tradition – unaccompanied by any sort of proof' asserting that something could still be seen of it north of St George's churchyard. But Percy Fitzgerald, one of Dickens's 'young men' on *Household Words* in the 1850s, retraced his master's footsteps around 1900 and faithfully recorded what he found:

> On a late visit to this place it was a surprise to me to find a great portion of it still standing. Turning out of the High Street, and entering a little flagged lane, or court, close to St. George's Church, we find the old high brick wall of the place, with its buttresses, overshadowing us on the right. Over the wall peep rows of windows – the top story of such houses as remained of the old buildings – all forlorn, dingy, and gloomy. There is an inscription in large letters stating that the place was described in 'Little Dorrit.' A portion is now used as a place of business.[34]

These industrial uses – 'partly a factory', it was said a few years later – would steadily encroach, though we can't identify just when the residential use of Marshalsea Place gave way entirely. And local confusion over the whereabouts

of the Marshalsea continued. On 2 January 1902, Little
Dorrit's Playground was laid out on what was thought to
have been the old gaol's site. It was soon considered 'one of
the most charming little gardens to be seen anywhere', but
in fact it lay nearly opposite the Marshalsea on the other
side of the High Street. On the correct site, some years later,
the Marshalsea wall adjoining the churchyard was marked
with a plaque:

> This Site was originally the
> Marshalsea Prison,
> made famous by the late
> Charles Dickens,
> in his well-known work,
> 'Little Dorrit'[35]

A more recent plaque identifying the Marshalsea wall and its
connection with Dickens remains there still, and Little Dorrit's
Playground continues to commemorate the prison's most
famous fictional character, though in the wrong location.

By 1923 the Marshalsea debtors' main quarters had been
turned over entirely to industry, as had much of the land
and buildings around. They were a printing works of some
repute, the Marshalsea Press of J. J. Keliher and Co. Ltd,
producing high-quality colour printing and letterpress. The
press glazed over the space between the building and the
Marshalsea wall, effectively abolishing Marshalsea Place.
Aware of its heritage, the press made a virtue of it in more
than name, producing in 1926 a publicity pamphlet, *Where
Dickens Dreamed of Little Dorrit*, full of inaccuracies but
showing the top storey of Marshalsea Place knocked through
the four pairs of back-to-back houses and stacked with
printing machinery; Little Dorrit's 'sky parlour' window, at
the top of what had been the turnkey's house, remained
intact. At least the press had its topography right; others

who should have known better thought around this time that nothing was left 'to recall the structure except the name of Marshalsea Road . . . on the opposite side of the way'.[36]

From the late 1920s through the 1930s, Dickensians pursued further the lead given them by the hospitable printers of the Marshalsea Press. An extensive though still-inaccurate survey of the prison's remains, with the eighteenth-century lodge now identified as remaining recognisably intact, was undertaken in 1932 by George F. Young, who arranged for the photography of much that remained. The results were published in the *Dickensian* and provide an invaluable record, though Young misidentified the garret window that Dickens had in mind for Little Dorrit's room as an attic in the keeper's old house, rather than the turnkey's in the main Marshalsea block. Young's was a timely intervention. That part of Southwark was very badly bombed in the Second World War, with the virtual obliteration of the rebuilt site of the old Marshalsea between Newcomen Street and Mermaid Court. But despite similar destruction at eighteenth-century Layton's Buildings and the north side of Angel Place, John Dickens's gaol escaped pretty much unscathed. Though the Marshalsea Press had closed by 1955 the main block of the gaol was still standing, now absorbed into Messrs Harding's warehouse; and in 1968, though Harding's had now closed too some five years before, it remained intact.[37]

Between 1968 and the end of the 1970s, municipal offices for the newly created London Borough of Southwark were built in Angel Place, and during this period the main Marshalsea prison block was demolished. The site was incorporated into a public library fronting Borough High Street, with associated offices to the rear. In the twenty-first century these council buildings underwent extensive renovation and enlargement. With fitting irony the new John Harvard Library, reopened in November 2009, incorporates the Southwark Local Studies Library at the rear, just where

John Dickens's Marshalsea had stood since it opened on Christmas Eve 1811. Next to the library on its south side, across a passageway no wider than the debtors would have known, is part of the prison wall shared with the extended churchyard of St George the Martyr, Southwark. It has long lost its spikes and perhaps has come down a little in the world, but it remains a tangible memory of the Marshalsea and what it once stood for.

Now, whoever visits the local history collection of this most fascinating part of London, or who walks along Angel Place to the old wall on the right-hand side of the way, can retrace a few of Charles Dickens's footsteps – and can still be privileged to 'stand among the crowding ghosts of many miserable years'.

NOTES

Abbreviations

BL   British Library
HCJ   *House of Commons Journals*
HLD   *House of Lords Debates*
HMC   Historical Manuscripts Commission
HO   Home Office Papers
LCC   London County Council
LG   *London Gazette*
LMA   London Metropolitan Archives
OBP   Old Bailey Proceedings Online
ODNB   *Oxford Dictionary of National Biography*, online
           editions
TNA   The National Archives

1: The Debtor's World

1. Charles Dickens, *The Old Curiosity Shop*, 1840–41, ch. VIII. His address is given in ch. VII.
2. See generally Craig Muldrew, *The Economy of Obligation: The Culture of Credit and Social Relations in Early Modern England*, Basingstoke, 1998, especially ch. 4; Margot C. Finn, *The Character of Credit: Personal Debt in English Culture, 1740–1914*, Cambridge, 2003, pp. 95–8; for tradesmen's practice see Anthony Trollope, *London Tradesmen*, 1927, pp. 8–9.

3. Anon., *The Cries of the Poor Prisoners, Humbly offer'd to the Serious Consideration of the King and Parliament*, 1716, p. 22.

4. Surrey Quarter Sessions Papers, QS2/6/1725/Mid/68–71, 83.

5. Cited in Jerry White, *London in the Eighteenth Century: A Great and Monstrous Thing*, 2012, p. 190.

6. *Morning Post and Gazetteer*, 22 August 1801. *Report from the Committee Appointed to Enquire into the Practice and Effects of Imprisonment for Debt*, 1792, pp. 89, 25. See also the grouping of occupations of 500 imprisoned debtors in Ian P. H. Duffy, *Bankruptcy and Insolvency in London during the Industrial Revolution*, New York, 1985, pp. 56ff., 371.

7. Anon., *The Cries of the Poor Prisoners*, p. 5.

8. Anon [An Amateur], *Real Life in London . . . .*, 1821–2, Vol. I, pp. 44–5.

9. John Trusler, *The London Adviser and Guide: containing every instruction and information useful and necessary to Persons living in London, and coming to reside there . . . .*, 1786, p. 157.

10. Society for the Discharge and Relief of Persons Imprisoned for Small Debts, *An Account of the Rise, Progress, and Present State, of the Society for the Discharge and Relief of Persons Imprisoned for Small Debts throughout England*, 1794, p. 35.

11. For absconders see Society for the Discharge and Relief of Persons Imprisoned for Small Debts, *An Account of the Rise, Progress, and Present State, of the Society for the Discharge and Relief of Persons Imprisoned for Small Debts throughout England*, 1799, pp. 35–6. Diocese of Winchester, Probate, Archdeaconry Court of Surrey, DW/PA/05/1750/079; PROB/11/1022/141; Railton's 'estates' may have been an expectation of inheritance, whether realistic or not I don't know.

12. *HLD*, 1st Series, Vol. 27, col. 611, 2 May 1814. For the popularity of arrests under mesne process see Duffy, *Bankruptcy and Insolvency in London during the Industrial Revolution*, p. 64.

13. Debtors Imprisonment Act, 32 Geo. II, c. 28; Robert Dorset Neale, *The Prisoner's Guide, or Every Debtor his own Lawyer*, 1800, p. 12.

14. Neale, *The Prisoner's Guide*, p. 5.

15. Dickens, *The Old Curiosity Shop*, ch. XXXIII. See the very useful flow charts in Joanna Innes, 'The King's Bench in the Later Eighteenth Century: Law, Authority and Order in a London Debtors' Prison', in John Brewer and John Styles (eds.), *An Ungovernable People: The English and Their Law in the Seventeenth and Eighteenth Centuries*, 1980, pp. 251–61; Duffy, *Bankruptcy and Insolvency in London during the Industrial Revolution*, ch. II; V. Markham Lester, *Victorian Insolvency: Bankruptcy,*

Imprisonment for Debt, and Company Winding-up in Nineteenth-Century England, Oxford, 1995, ch. 3; Finn, *The Character of Credit*, pp. 109–12.

16. Anon., *The Cries of the Poor Prisoners*, p. 5. Innes in Brewer and Styles (eds.), *An Ungovernable People*, p. 254.

17. For the malice see James Neild, *An Account of the Rise, Progress, and Present State, of the Society for the Discharge and Relief of Persons Imprisoned for Small Debts throughout England and Wales*, 1802, p. 19. Surrey Quarter Sessions Papers, QS2/6/1735/Mid/1.

18. *HLD*, 1st Series, Vol. 27, col. 611, 2 May 1814. OBP, t17740706-74, 6 July 1774, trial of Sarah Dodd for perjury, guilty, transportation.

19. John Ewer Poole ('An Eye-Witness'), *An Expose of the Practice of the Palace, or Marshalsea Court; with a Description of the Prison, the Secrets of the Prison-House, its Regulations, Fees, &c. &c . . .,* 1833, pp. 10–11; though anonymously published, the Senate House Library copy has a letter from Poole tipped in showing that he wrote and published it. Middlesex Justices, Sessions Papers, MJ/SP/1696/04/006 (April 1696), 07/023 (July 1696), 09/019 and 020 (September 1696); W. J. Hardy (ed.), *Middlesex County Records: Calendar of Sessions Books 1689–1709*, 1905, p. 26 (Sessions Book 540, January 1697).

20. Middlesex Justices, Sessions Papers, Justices' Working Documents, LMSMPS500840034, October 1702; *Middlesex County Records*, pp. 279–94 (Sessions Book 625, January 1705). *Weekly Journal or British Gazetteer*, 1 and 29 March 1718; *Weekly Packet*, 29 March–5 April 1718; *Weekly Journal or Saturday's Post*, 12 April 1718; *St James's Evening Post*, 26 June 1718.

21. *Gentleman's Magazine*, 22 June 1733, p. 325; the Quaker was non-suited as he was not 'bred a regular Surgeon'. *Read's Weekly Journal or British Gazetteer*, 31 March 1750.

22. [Society for the Discharge and Relief of Persons Imprisoned for Small Debts], *An Account of the Rise, Progress, and Present State of the Society for the Discharge and Relief of Persons Imprisoned for Small Debts*, 1783, p. 8n. The Gatehouse was the prison for the City of Westminster Liberties, sited near Dean's Yard at the west end of the Abbey.

23. Ibid. Poole, *An Expose of the Practice of the Palace*, pp. 3–4. The mention of nearly £12 is in James Neild, *An Account of the Rise, Progress, and Present State, of the Society for the Discharge and Relief of Persons Imprisoned for Small Debts throughout England and Wales*, 1808, pp. 27–8.

24. Dickens, *The Old Curiosity Shop*, ch. XXXVI. For this aspect of Dickens's life and work see David Sugarman, 'Law and Legal

Institutions', in Paul Schlicke (ed.), *The Oxford Companion to Charles Dickens*, Oxford, 2011.

25. Dickens, *The Old Curiosity Shop*, ch. XXXIII. Letter from A. Grant of Southwark relating to a bill paid to an 'Attorney in the neighbourhood of Soho-square'; *Oracle and Public Advertiser*, 26 June 1799.

26. For Hart see the *Satirist; or the Censor of the Times*, 16 October 1831. For Marshalsea attorneys see the letter by 'Truth' ibid., 27 November 1831. Charles Dickens, *Bleak House*, 1852–3, ch. XXXIX.

27. Surrey Quarter Sessions Papers, QS2/6/1768/Mic/29–30. *Oracle and Public Advertiser*, 9 September 1797. *London Evening Post*, 15–17 May 1739.

28. Dickens, *The Old Curiosity Shop*, ch. XXXIV. For professional bail see Duffy, *Bankruptcy and Insolvency in London during the Industrial Revolution*, p. 62n. John Gifford, *Complete English Lawyer; or Every Man his own Lawyer* 2nd edn, n.d., *c.* 1817, p. 310.

29. Angus Easson, 'Dickens and the Marshalsea', University of Oxford PhD, 1967, pp. 75–7.

30. 'Body-snatcher' is in George Parker, *A View of Society and Manners in High and Low Life*, 2 vols., 1781, Vol. II, p. 70. Anon., *A Companion for Debtors and Prisoners, and Advice to Creditors in Ten Letters: From a Gentleman in Prison, to a Member of Parliament . . .*, 1699, pp. 3, 18–20. 'Cadee' was the early form of cadet. *Morning Post and Daily Advertiser*, 29 November 1776.

31. *Old Whig or the Consistent Protestant*, 29 May 1735. A case in the Court of King's Bench involving trespass by bailiffs, Lewis v. Wood and Another, received much attention, for instance; *Morning Post*, 20 December 1820. The Hoxton incident is in Edward Wedlake Brayley and Others, *London and Middlesex; or, an Historical, Commercial, and Descriptive Survey of the Metropolis of Great Britain . . .*, 4 vols., 1810–1816, Vol. III, part I, p. 45. It was perhaps this case that Thackeray had in mind in writing of Becky Sharp's father in *Vanity Fair*, 1847–8, ch. 2.

32. Parker, *A View of Society and Manners*, Vol. II, pp. 70ff. Charlotte Charke, *A Narrative of the Life of Mrs Charlotte Charke*, 1755 (edited and with an introduction by Robert Rehder, 1999), pp. 47–51, 70. Charlotte Lennox, *The Life of Harriet Stuart, Written by Herself*, 1750 (1995 edn), pp. 236–40.

33. Restrictions on spunging houses were nominally set down by 32 Geo. II, c. 28. Basil Cozens-Hardy (ed.), *The Diary of Sylas Neville 1767–1788*, 1950, p. 65, 18 March 1769.

34. Mary Thale (ed.), *The Autobiography of Francis Place (1771–1854)*, Cambridge, 1972, pp. 24–33. Readers of *Bleak House* will

recall 'Coavinses', the spunging house behind Cursitor Street, also 'a house with barred windows' (ch. XV).

35. *Daily Advertiser,* 25 September 1772.

36. Alexander Smith, *The Comical and Tragical History of the Lives and Adventures of the Most Noted Bayliffs in and about London and Westminster . . .,* 1723, pp. 64–6 (64–56 in the original). Boyte is given as Nathaniel in the press: *Weekly Journal or British Gazetteer,* 11 August 1722.

37. OBP, 22 October 1760, t17601022–17; see also Ordinary's Account, OA17601025.

38. Isobel D. Thornley, 'Sanctuary in Medieval London', *Journal of the British Archaeological Association,* New Series, Vol. 38, 1932, pp. 293–315; Finn, *The Character of Credit,* p. 110.

39. The list is in John Noorthouck, *A New History of London, including Westminster and Southwark,* 1773, p. 284; the act was 8 & 9 Wm. III, c. 27.

40. Victoria County History, *The Victoria History of the County of Surrey: Vol. IV,* 1912, pp. 143–5; Survey of London, *Vol. XXV: St George's Fields (The Parishes of St George the Martyr, Southwark and St Mary Newington),* 1955, pp. 23–5; Nigel Stirk, 'Arresting Ambiguity: The Shifting Geographies of a London Debtors' Sanctuary in the Eighteenth Century', *Social History,* Vol. 25, No. 3, October 2000, pp. 316–29.

41. Victoria County History, *Surrey: Vol. IV,* p. 145; a map of the Rules of the King's Bench, 1760, shows these and dozens of other places, WORKS 6/131/2, f. 73. Anon., *A True description of the Mint,* 1710, pp. 7–13; M. Smith, *Memoirs of the Mint and Queen's-Bench or, A true Account of the Government, Politics, Customs, Humours, and other Surprizing Curiosities of those Inchanted Provinces Never publish'd before. With a Character of the Marshall. In Several Letters to a Person of Quality,* 1713.

42. HCJ, Vol. 20, pp. 155–6, 27 February 1723.

43. Ibid., p. 155; the report is at pp. 154–7; see also p. 132, 11 February 1723, and p. 208, 4 May 1723, for petitions from Mint residents.

44. *British Journal,* 8 June 1723; *Weekly Journal or Saturday's Post,* 20 July 1723. See also Stirk, 'Arresting Ambiguity', p. 325.

45. Daniel Defoe, *A Tour Through the Whole Island of Great Britain,* 2 vols., 1724–6, Vol. I, pp. 355–6.

46. The numbers of debtors in Newgate fluctuated greatly, fifty-one debtors and 141 felons on one day in 1779, and three debtors and 291 felons on another in 1782, for instance, the latter following changes in the minimum debt for arrest on mesne process: John Howard, *The State of the Prisons in England and Wales, with Preliminary Observations, and an Account of Some Foreign Prisons*

and Hospitals, Warrington, 1784, pp. 488–9. For Wood Street see Richard King, *The Complete Modern London Spy . . .*, 1781, pp. 38–42.

47. See John Ashton, *The Fleet. Its River, Prison, and Marriages*, popular edn, 1889, chs. XIX–XXX, which is still valuable; Roger Lee Brown, *A History of the Fleet Prison, London: The Anatomy of the Fleet*, Lampeter, 1996, which is indispensable for the eighteenth-century prison; and Roger Lee Brown, *The Fleet Marriages: A History of Clandestine Marriages with Particular Reference to the Marriages Performed in and around the Fleet Prison, London*, Welshpool, 2007.

48. For the early history of the King's Bench in Southwark see Martha Carlin, *Medieval Southwark*, 1996, p. 103.

49. See Duffy, *Bankruptcy and Insolvency in London during the Industrial Revolution*, pp. 69ff., 372.

50. Henry Hunt, *Memoirs of Henry Hunt, Esq., Written by Himself, In His Majesty's Jail at Ilchester, in the County of Somerset*, 3 vols., 1820–22, Vol. I, pp. 442–3.

2: 'The Worst Prison in the Nation'

1. Burton Morice, *An Essay towards an History of the Ancient Jurisdiction of the Marshalsea of the King's House. To which is subjoined an account of the Court of the Palace of the King at Westminster, created by Letters Patent of King Charles II*, 1812, passim: this is the key authority for all subsequent accounts.

2. Owen Manning and William Bray, *The History and Antiquities of the County of Surrey*, 3 vols., 1804–14, Vol. III, App., pp. xxiv–v.

3. David J. Johnson, *Southwark and the City*, 1969, p. 69, for the 1330s; Martha Carlin, *Medieval Southwark*, 1996, p. 49, for the 1360s and 1370s.

4. Johnson, *Southwark and the City*, p. 43, for 'unruly and unruled', and p. 85, for the date of Southwark Fair – 1462 is also given by some authorities, but it seems erroneously; see also Carlin, *Medieval Southwark*, ch. 4. For aliens see ibid., ch. 6; T. Fairman Ordish, *Early London Theatres*, 1894, chs. IV–VIII.

5. John Stow, *A Survey of London*, 1603 (2 vols., edited by Charles Lethbridge Kingsford, Oxford, 1908), Vol. II, p. 61.

6. Ibid., pp. 61–2; Carlin, *Medieval Southwark*, pp. 105–6, 158–9. Both Tyler's and Cade's revolts involved contingents from Essex and elsewhere, but it was the Kentish rebels who attacked Southwark.

7. For the Admiralty prison see *Survey of London, Vol. XXV: St. George's Fields (The Parishes of St George the Martyr, Southwark and St Mary*

Newington), 1955, p. 14. The inventory is in Carlin, *Medieval Southwark*, pp. 270–71. Stow, *A Survey of London*, Vol. I, p. 246.

8. Ibid., Vol. II, p. 62; John Strype, *A Survey of the Cities of London and Westminster*, 2 vols., 1720, Vol. II, pp. 19–20, has a long circumstantial account of this riot. Johnson, *Southwark and the City*, pp. 227–8.

9. *ODNB*, George Bucker, d. 1543, religious radical; Thomas Mountain, *c.* 1520–73, religious activist – neither St Pancras nor Soper Lane survived the Great Fire; Thomas Raynold, d. 1559, Dean of Exeter; Seth Holland, d. 1561, Dean of Worcester; John Cornelius, *c.* 1557–94, Roman Catholic priest; James Fenn, *c.* 1540–84, Roman Catholic priest and martyr; Richard Topcliffe, 1531–1604, interrogator and torturer (all accessed 25 March 2015).

10. *ODNB*, Edmund Bonner, d. 1569, Bishop of London (accessed 19 March 2015); see also Angus Easson, 'Dickens and the Marshalsea', University of Oxford PhD, 1967, pp. 16–20.

11. The full story of the early-seventeenth-century court is given by Douglas G. Greene, 'The Court of the Marshalsea in Late Tudor and Stuart England', *American Journal of Legal History*, Vol. 20, No. 4, October 1976, pp. 267–81; see also Morice, *An Essay towards an History of the Ancient Jurisdiction of the Marshalsea*, pp. 27–32; Manning and Bray, *The History and Antiquities of the County of Surrey*, Vol. III, App., pp. xxiv–v; Easson, 'Dickens and the Marshalsea', pp. 27–8. Anon., *A True Narrative of the Great and Terrible Fire in Southwark, on Fryday the 26th of May, 1676*, 1676, passim.

12. For the Marshalsea as a Surrey county gaol see J. M. Beattie, *Crime and the Courts in England, 1660–1800*, Oxford, 1986, pp. 291–4; Victoria County History, *The Victoria History of the County of Surrey: Vol. IV*, 1912, p. 141, gives 1695 as the date of agreement between the Marshalsea and the magistrates, though the Survey of London, *Vol. XXV: St George's Fields*, p. 15, says county prisoners were lodged there from 1666. *Weekly Journal or Saturday's Post*, 12 October 1717; 23 September 1721. Elkanah Settle, *The Siege of Troy: A Dramatick Performance, Presented in Mrs. MYNNS's Great Booth, in the Queens-Arms Yard near the Marshalsea Gate in Southwark, during the Time of the Fair*, 1715; see also *Daily Post*, 21 September 1724, when Mr Fawks the conjuror performed there. Southwark Fair was finally suppressed in 1763. For the compter see Victoria County History, *The Victoria History of the County of Surrey: Vol. IV*, p. 141; R. M. Wingent, *Historical Notes on the Borough and the Borough Hospitals*, 1913, p. 18.

13. The old jurisdiction is in Easson, 'Dickens and the Marshalsea', pp. 28–9. *Daily Courant*, 10 December 1715; *Historical Register. Containing an Impartial Relation of all Transactions, Foreign and*

Domestick. Vol. I. For the Year 1716, p. 361, 16 September 1716.
William Tunstall, *St Cyprian's Discourse to Donatus. Done into
English Metre, by W—T— in the Marshalsea*, 1716; *Ballads and
some other Occasional Poems: by W—T— in the Marshalsea*,
1716; Tunstall's date of death is given by the National Portrait
Gallery as 1717, so he may have died in the Marshalsea.

14. The Knight Marshal is occasionally confused, both in the archives
and by subsequent authorities, with the marshal of the Marshalsea
of the King's Bench, the full title of the keeper of the King's Bench
prison; this person had no authority over the Marshalsea prison itself.

15. *ODNB*, Sir Philip Meadows, c. 1662–1757, diplomat and politician (accessed 12 September 2008); we know he sent a steward
to the court from Anon., *Hell in Epitome: or, A Description of the
M—SH—SEA. A Poem*, 1718, p. 18n. For Darby father and son
see John Nichols, *Literary Anecdotes of the Eighteenth Century . . .*,
9 vols., 1812–16, Vol. I, p. 290 and n. The details of Darby's and
Acton's appointment are in *Report from the Committee Appointed
to Enquire into the State of the Goals of this Kingdom: Relating
to the Marshalsea Prison; And farther Relating to the Fleet Prison*,
1729, p. 2. Such an arrangement for a deputy keeper must have
been in place under the elder Darby, given his busy duties in
Bartholomew Close, and probably long before.

16. For the eighteenth-century purchase values see ibid., p. 7, and
Easson, 'Dickens and the Marshalsea', pp. 31–5. *The Satirist; or the
Censor of the Times*, 16 October 1831, 'The Black Sheep of the
Law: The Marshalsea Court'. John Ewer Poole ('An Eye-Witness'),
*An Expose of the Practice of the Palace, or Marshalsea Court; with
a Description of the Prison, the Secrets of the Prison-House, its
Regulations, Fees, &c. &c . . .*, 1833, p. 5. *The Satirist*, 25 November
1832, letter on 'The Palace Court' from 'A Friend to the Six'.

17. CRES 2/932, 'Mem^um of Information rec^d from Mr Monk, one of
the Attorneys of the Marshalsea Court . . .', 15 May 1781; this
widow was perhaps the 'Sarah Mason' mentioned in WORK
6/131/2, f2, 8 April 1791.

18. Strype, *A Survey of the Cities of London and Westminster*, Vol. II,
p. 30. Anon., *The Triumph of Benevolence; or, the History of
Francis Wills*, 2 vols., 1772, Vol. I, pp. 200–201.

19. Survey of London, *Vol. XXV: St George's Fields*, p. 15.

20. *Report from the Committee Appointed to Enquire into the State
of the Goals of this Kingdom: Relating to the Marshalsea Prison*,
pp. 3, 12–13.

21. Survey of London, *Vol. XXV: St George's Fields*, p. 14.

22. Anon., *A Companion for Debtors and Prisoners, and Advice to
Creditors in Ten Letters: From a Gentleman in Prison, to a Member
of Parliament . . .*, 1699, p. 24.

23. Blenheim Papers, Vol. DLII, Add. MS 61652, f29b, from the Earl of Sunderland to the Keeper of the Marshalsea Prison, 2 August 1707; DXIII, Add. MS 61613, f. 8 [n.d., ?1709], to the Earl of Sunderland; Aslaby seems to have been one of a family of recusants from Hull and nearby. State Paper Office MSS, SP/34/17, ff. 11, 3 December 1711, and 144, 15 February 1712.

24. *HCJ*, Vol. 17, p. 602, 28 April 1714. Anon., *The Piercing Cryes of the Poor and Miserable Prisoners for Debt, in all Parts of England . . .*, 1714, p. 5; I can find no trace of this baronetage, though a later one dates from 1839.

25. Anon., *Hell in Epitome*, pp. 3, 10n., 11, 14, 28. The strong room is described as '*A strong Place for condemn'd Criminals*', the prison in 1718 still doubling as a county gaol.

26. *HCJ*, Vol. 19, p. 63, 21 January 1719; Vol. 20, p. 36, 19 December 1722; p. 360, 12 December 1724.

27. M. Smith, *Memoirs of the Mint and Queen's-Bench or, A true Account of the Government, Politics, Customs, Humours, and other Surprizing Curiosities of those Inchanted Provinces Never publish'd before. With a Character of the Marshall. In Several Letters to a Person of Quality*, 1713, pp. 10, 15; 'the Basket' was used to collect broken victuals for the prisoners from nearby shops; 'Punks' were cheaply priced prostitutes, generally young. Anon., *The Arbitrary Punishments and Cruel Tortures Inflicted on Prisoners for Debt Represented and Described . . .*, 1729, pp. 31 and n., 42, 51. *Evening Post*, 29 February–3 March 1724.

3: 'Hardly Any One But Vilains': Grano's Marshalsea, 1728–9

1. John Baptist (Giovanni Battista) Grano, 'A Journal of My Life Inside the Marshalsea' (May 1728–September 1729), MS Rawlinson d.34, 30 May 1728. The 510-page journal was edited and partly transcribed by John Ginger and published in New York as *Handel's Trumpeter: The Diary of John Grano*, in 1998. Anyone interested in the journal is indebted to John Ginger for the little that is known of Grano's life and origins, and for his energetic excavation of persons mentioned in the text. The journal begins and ends with Grano's 480 days in the Marshalsea and is around a quarter of a million words in length. It seems to have been kept for his own amusement, though it is plain that from time to time parts of it were shown to others in the gaol; perhaps it was an aid to survival, a means of affirming his self-worth in dehumanising circumstances. When citing from the journal I have referred in

every case to the original manuscript, retaining original spellings and capitalisation, eccentric though those are, and in general the original punctuation. I have elongated the abbreviations then commonly used within a word, such as writing 'mm' as 'm' with a horizontal line over the letter. To avoid a plethora of references I have usually given in the notes the date of an entry only where I have cited the text directly. Interpolations by Grano are put between <>. I have replaced Grano's square brackets with round ones, reserving the former to any insertions made by me.

2. For this and much of what follows see Ginger (ed.), *Handel's Trumpeter*, pp. 1–26; and the article on Grano by John Ginger and Maurice Byrne in Stanley Sadie (ed.), *The New Grove Dictionary of Music and Musicians*, 29 vols., 2nd edn, 2001, Vol. 10, pp. 298–9.

3. For the quality of Grano's ear see John Hawkins, *A General History of the Science and Practice of Music*, 5 vols., 1776, Vol. V, p. 197n. *Daily Courant*, 4 March 1718 and 30 March 1721, for these last two instances.

4. For some published works advertised either side of his committal see *Country Journal, or The Craftsman*, 4 May and 8 June 1728. For the trumpet march see Charles Burney, *A General History of Music, from the Earliest Ages to the Present Period*, 4 vols., 1776–89, Vol. IV, p. 646n. For Douglas advertised as Grano's student see *Daily Courant*, 10 March 1719. For the Opera House see Ginger (ed), *Handel's Trumpeter*, pp. 12–13.

5. Burney, *A General History of Music*, Vol. IV, p. 646n.

6. For his debt to Turner see Ginger (ed.), *Handel's Trumpeter*, p. 25, citing a list of prisoners in the gaol from February 1729 seen in the then House of Lords Record Office, now the Parliamentary Archives. Sadly the list cannot now be discovered in the catalogue and so is irretrievable to researchers. In Grano, 'A Journal', he gives his address as Shelton's Court, 30 May 1728.

7. 2 June 1728; for the rents see *Report from the Committee Appointed to Enquire into the State of the Goals of this Kingdom: Relating to the Marshalsea Prison; And farther Relating to the Fleet Prison*, 1729, pp. 12–13.

8. Grano, 'A Journal', 3, 6 and 8 June and 29 July 1728, 9 February 1729; he called the prison 'our College' only once, on 18 July 1729, and 'Collegians' not at all, though the term was in use.

9. Elder is thus described ibid., 5 June 1728; the washing, 8 August 1728, the only reference to washing, I think, in the journal; much was of course left unrecorded.

10. For the fittings, ibid., 1 and 26 November 1728; the nymphs, 17 June 1728.

11. Ibid., 21 July and 16 September 1728.

12. Ibid., 1 March 1729 and 5 August 1728.
13. For Mrs Acton's reputed origins see ibid., 19 June 1729; the pots, 13 January 1729. For Cary and Bradshaw see Ginger (ed.), *Handel's Trumpeter*, pp. 338–9, and for the rents and common side cook shop see *Report from the Committee Appointed to Enquire into the State of the Goals of this Kingdom: Relating to the Marshalsea Prison*, pp. 12–13.
14. For Tiddy-Doll the gingerbread man see Charles Hindley, *A History of the Cries of London, Ancient and Modern*, 1881, pp. 108–9; for McDonnell see Ginger (ed.), *Handel's Trumpeter*, p. 346; the fish vendor is in Grano, 'A Journal', 12 September 1728, and a cook in 1 December 1728.
15. Scrutiny in the lodge, recalled so vividly by Dickens in later years, is ibid., 1 September 1728. The troubles with Mrs Bradshaw are ibid., 25 July, 7 and 9 September and 28 November 1728.
16. Martha Carlin, *Medieval Southwark*, 1996, p. 271. 15 August 1728.
17. Grano, 'A Journal', 1–5 October 1728.
18. Ibid., 22 October 1728.
19. Ibid., 10 and 27 October and 3, 14 and 22 November 1728.
20. Ibid., 24 July 1728.
21. For Hannah see Ginger (ed.), *Handel's Trumpeter*, p. 350.
22. For old Hand see ibid., p. 344, and for Nathaniel Bailey p. 337. Grano, 'A Journal', 1 June and 30 November 1728; 12 February and 26 May 1729. For the constables see Anon., *The Miseries of Goals, and the Cruelty of Goalers. Being a Narrative of Several Persons now under Confinement*, 1729, pp. 51–2 and 52n.
23. For the common side garnish see *Report from the Committee Appointed to Enquire into the State of the Goals of this Kingdom: Relating to the Marshalsea Prison*, p. 2. 22 June, 12 September, 13 October and 8 December 1728.
24. Grano, 'A Journal', 28 September and 30 December 1728.
25. Ibid., 10 September 1728 for Yeates, for whom see Sybil Rosenfeld, *The Theatre of the London Fairs in the Eighteenth Century*, Cambridge, 1960, pp. 36–7.
26. Grano, 'A Journal', 27 December 1728 and 21 March 1729. For Lewis Grano or Granom see the article by Maurice Byrne in Sadie (ed.), *The New Grove Dictionary of Music and Musicians*, Vol. 10, p. 299.
27. Anon., *Hell in Epitome: or, A Description of the M—SH—SEA. A Poem*, 1718, p. 8n.
28. Grano, 'A Journal', 23 June, 19 July and 5 and 28 September 1728.
29. Ibid., 20 October 1728; both Nichols and his wife were heavy drinkers and Grano calls Thom 'the Reputed father'.
30. Ibid., 26 November and 24 December 1728, 29 March 1729.
31. For Parsons see *ODNB*, Humphrey Parsons, *c.* 1676–1741, brewer and politician (accessed 9 June 2010); Romney Sedgwick, *The*

House of Commons 1715–1754, 2 vols., 1970, Vol. II, pp. 326–7; Tim Blanning, *The Pursuit of Glory: Europe 1648–1815*, 2007, p. 409.

32. Grano, 'A Journal', 24 October–1 November 1728. Ginger, in Sadie (ed.), *The New Grove Dictionary of Music and Musicians*, Vol. 10, pp. 298–9, credits Parsons with being instrumental in Grano's discharge, but the evidence for that is flimsy.

33. Grano, 'A Journal', 15 October 1728.

34. For Tudman see Ginger (ed.), *Handel's Trumpeter*, p. 351; his will can be found at PROB 11/653/84 (TNA). 2 and 13 February 1729.

35. Grano, 'A Journal', 20 January and 15 February 1729.

36. Ibid., 15 and 29 April and 1 and 10 May 1729.

37. Ibid., 1 May 1729, 6 September and 30 October 1728, 8 August 1728.

38. Ibid., 22 June 1728. Fortune-telling for new gentleman-prisoners was a tradition, it seems: Anon., *Hell in Epitome*, p. 16n.

39. Grano, 'A Journal', 27 November 1728.

40. Ibid., 9 October 1728.

41. Ibid., 11 July, 8 August, 13 September and 15 October 1728.

42. *Gentleman's Magazine*, September 1743, p. 495. For the Bowling Green see John Strype, *A Survey of the Cities of London and Westminster*, 2 vols., 1720, Vol. II, p. 30.

43. Grano, 'A Journal', 14 and 20 September 1728; *Daily Post*, 9 September 1728.

44. Ibid., 17 and 19 September 1728; for Fielding's booth see *Country Journal, or The Craftsman*, 7 September 1728; for the *Quaker's Opera*, see *Daily Post*, 10 September 1728.

45. George Akerby, *The Life of Mr James Spiller, the Late Famous Comedian. In which is Interspers'd much of the Poetical History of His Own Times*, 1729 [old style, i.e. 1730], pp. 38–9.

46. Grano, 'A Journal', 6 September 1728. For Spiller's demise see Akerby, *Life*, p. 47; for Spiller more generally see Charles E. Pearce, *'Polly Peachum'. Being the Story of Lavinia Fenton (Duchess of Bolton) and 'The Beggar's Opera'*, 1913, pp. 117–21, the ticket is opp. p. 64; and *ODNB*, James Spiller, 1692–1730, actor and dancer (accessed 2 December 2013).

47. Grano, 'A Journal', 5 and 24 June and 30 November 1728, 15 February 1729.

48. Ibid., 22 July and 27 August 1728; for Mrs Myngs and her family see Ginger (ed.), *Handel's Trumpeter*, p. 347.

49. Grano, 'A Journal', 8 October 1728.

50. Acton's letter of 11 January 1729 is tipped into the journal. Ibid., 26 May 1729; *LG*, 24–27 May 1729.

51. Grano, 'A Journal', 21 July and 2 August 1728.

52. Ibid., 14 May 1729, 30 July 1728.

53. Ibid., 11 September 1728.

54. For Shepherd see Ginger (ed.), *Handel's Trumpeter*, p. 350; 8 and 20 September 1728; see also Grano, 'A Journal', 1 December 1728. Addams is from 28 September 1728.

55. Ibid., 4 and 28 March 1729.

56. 2 Geo. II, c. 20 (Lords) and c. 22 (Commons). The Lords Act of 1759 introduced the daily groat at an earlier stage in the process.

57. Grano, 'A Journal', 14 February, 11 April and 22 May 1729.

58. Ibid., 17 and 18 July 1729.

59. Ibid., 19 July 1729. Cuper's Gardens frequently went under the name of Cupid in popular parlance. There was another Queen Street in the Mint itself, but this seems more likely: Strype, *A Survey of the Cities of London and Westminster*, Vol. II, p. 29.

60. For Grano in the Spaw see *Grub Street Journal*, 1 October 1730; for the Spaw more generally see Warwick Wroth, *The London Pleasure Gardens of the Eighteenth Century*, 1896, pp. 271–7. For the ode see *British Journal*, 7 November 1730.

4: *Skinning the Flint: Acton's Marshalsea, 1728–30*

1. John Baptist (Giovanni Battista) Grano, 'A Journal of My Life Inside the Marshalsea' (May 1728–September 1729), MS Rawlinson d.34, 25 March 1729. He was visited in his room around 10 a.m. The chairman and several other committee members revisited the gaol on 28 March. No other visits are mentioned in the journal.

2. For the numbers of prisoners see *Report from the Committee Appointed to Enquire into the State of the Goals of this Kingdom: Relating to the Marshalsea Prison; And farther Relating to the Fleet Prison*, 1729, pp. 3–4. The report's appendix, pp. 12–13, gives 319 prisoners, of whom sixty-eight were women. The report was published in May and says, 'now Confined upwards of 330 Prisoners', and possibly the appendix gives the numbers found in March.

3. Ibid., pp. 3–5, 12. *Brice's Weekly Journal*, 4 April 1729; *Flying Post or The Weekly Medley*, 19 April 1729.

4. The 'saying' is in William Rendle, *Old Southwark and Its People*, 1878, p. 100.

5. *Report from the Committee Appointed to Enquire into the State of the Goals of this Kingdom: Relating to the Marshalsea Prison*, p. 2. Haysey and his role as chief turnkey is in Francis Hargrave (ed.), *A Complete Collection of State-Trials, and Proceedings for High-Treason, and other Crimes and Misdemeanours*, 11 vols., 4th

edn, 1778, Vol. IX, cols. 184, 199, 204; *The Tryal of William Acton, Deputy-Keeper and Turnkey of the Marshalsea Prison in Southwark, at Kingston Assizes; on Friday the 1ˢᵗ of August 1729. Upon an Indictment for the Murder of Thomas Bliss, a Prisoner in the said Prison*, 1729, p. 27. For Mary's father as tapster see Hargrave (ed.), *A Complete Collection of State-Trials*, Vol. IX, col. 193. Records taken from the parish register of St Martin-in-the-Fields, Westminster, index accessible at Ancestry.com England, FHL 56155, Select Marriages; FHL 560372–3, Births and Christenings.

6.   Grano, 'A Journal', 14 December 1728, 17 and 21 January, 28 February and 1 March 1729.

7.   Fees and rents are in *Report from the Committee Appointed to Enquire into the State of the Goals of this Kingdom: Relating to the Marshalsea Prison*, pp. 11–13; these included the porter's fee. There were fees to the Knight Marshal (Sir Philip Meadows) of 1s 8d and to his deputy (Darby) of 3d, which it seems unlikely that Acton would have received. St George the Martyr Overseers Accounts, 1727–9, GM 3/1/5, Ax and Bottle Yard. Acton paid the rates from the first quarter of 1728 to the first quarter of 1729; at the beginning of this period the rates were lower, 15s 2d a quarter as against £1 2s 9d.

8.   Anon., *Hell in Epitome: or, A Description of the M—SH—SEA. A Poem*, 1718, pp. 2n., 13–14.

9.   Grano, 'A Journal', 9 November 1728.

10.   *Report from the Committee Appointed to Enquire into the State of the Goals of this Kingdom: Relating to the Marshalsea Prison*, p. 3.

11.   *Further Report[s] of the Commissioners appointed in Pursuance of Two Several Acts of Parliament . . . to inquire concerning Charities in England for the Education of The Poor . . .*, Report 6, 1822, pp. 267–8, 289–90, 294, 297, 331; Report 8, 1823, pp. 317–18; Report 10, 1824, pp. 182–3; see also the lists in Burton Morice, *An Essay towards an History of the Ancient Jurisdiction of the Marshalsea of the King's House. To which is subjoined an account of the Court of the Palace of the King at Westminster, created by Letters Patent of King Charles II*, 1812, pp. 44–6; *Report of the Commissioners appointed in Pursuance of an Act of Parliament . . . to continue the inquiries concerning Charities in England and Wales . . .*, 1840, pp. 858–9.

12.   *Report from the Committee Appointed to Enquire into the State of the Goals of this Kingdom: Relating to the Marshalsea Prison*, p. 6.

13.   Ibid., pp. 5–8.

14.   Grano, 'A Journal', 18 November 1728.

15.   Ibid., 23 November 1728.

16.   *Report from the Committee Appointed to Enquire into the State of the Goals of this Kingdom: Relating to the Marshalsea Prison*,

pp. 8–9. The report does not describe the pizzle but see *The Tryal of William Acton . . . for the Murder of Thomas Bliss*, p. 5; the dimensions are mine, having seen a similar object at a Dorset slaughterhouse in the late 1960s.

17. *Report from the Committee Appointed to Enquire into the State of the Goals of this Kingdom: Relating to the Marshalsea Prison*, p. 9.

18. Anon., *The Miseries of Goals, and the Cruelty of Goalers. Being a Narrative of Several Persons now under Confinement*, 1729, pp. 49–56.

19. St George the Martyr, Southwark, Composite Registers of Weddings, Baptisms and Burials, P92/GEO/143–4, 1695–1757. The Marshalsea burials for 1738 were five, 1748 eighteen, 1758 three; the figures were comparably low thereafter (P92/GEO/145–7, 1758–1820). For London mortality (or at least, parochial burials) generally see Anon., *A Collection of the Yearly Bills of Mortality, from 1657 to 1758 inclusive . . .*, 1759 [n.p.]; St George's had its highest proportions of London burials (2.1 per cent) during this period in 1721, 1722, 1726 and 1728. I am grateful to Professor Vanessa Harding at Birkbeck for this reference.

20. Leslie F. Church, *Oglethorpe: A Study of Philanthropy in England and Georgia*, 1932, pp. 6–8. *Report from the Committee Appointed to Enquire into the State of the Goals of this Kingdom: Relating to the Fleet Prison*, 1729, p. 8; *ODNB*, James Oglethorpe, 1696–1785, army officer and founder of the colony of Georgia (accessed 13 September 2008); *Historical Register . . . For the Year 1729*, p. 127.

21. A list of the committee's members is in Church, *Oglethorpe*, p. 12n. Romney Sedgwick, *The House of Commons 1715–1754*, 2 vols., 1970, Vol. I, p. 153.

22. *HCJ*, Vol. 21, pp. 273–83, 20 March 1729. For the full story of the Fleet at this time see Roger Lee Brown, *A History of the Fleet Prison, London: The Anatomy of the Fleet*, Lampeter, 1996, pp. 57–94.

23. Grano, 'A Journal', 11 April 1729.

24. *Report from the Committee Appointed to Enquire into the State of the Goals of this Kingdom: Relating to the Marshalsea Prison*, p. 10. *HCJ*, Vol. 21, pp. 376–87, 14 May 1729.

25. *Fog's Weekly Journal*, 14 June 1729; *The Representations of the Several Fetters, Irons, and Ingines of Torture that were taken from the Marshalsea Prison . . .*, 1729; Anon., *The Arbitrary Punishments and Cruel Tortures Inflicted on Prisoners for Debt Represented and Described . . .*, 1729, pp. 2, 31.

26. Hardwicke Papers, Add. MS 36,137, f. 242. Grano, 'A Journal', 9, 10, 15, 16 and 19 June and 5 and 21 July 1729.

27. Ibid., 31 July 1729.

28. *Report from the Committee Appointed to Enquire into the State of the Goals of this Kingdom: Relating to the Marshalsea Prison*, p. 9; *The Tryal of William Acton . . . for the Murder of Thomas Bliss*, p. 4.

29. Hargrave (ed.), *A Complete Collection of State-Trials*, Vol. IX, col. 184.

30. Ibid., cols. 181–204 for this and subsequent evidence in the Bliss trial.

31. Ibid., col. 196.

32. *Universal Spectator and Weekly Journal*, 9 August 1729.

33. *The Tryal of William Acton . . . for the Murder of Thomas Bliss*, pp. 29–30.

34. See Hargrave (ed.), *A Complete Collection of State-Trials*, Vol. IX, cols. 203–226 for the last three trials.

35. Ibid., col. 226.

36. Grano, 'A Journal', 2–3 August 1729.

37. Historical Manuscripts Commission, *Diary of Viscount Percival, Afterwards First Earl of Egmont*, 3 vols., 1920–23, Vol. I, pp. 46, 49–50. Eustace Budgell, *A Letter to Cleomenes King of Sparta . . .*, 1731, p. 25; see also his *A Letter to the Craftsman from Eustace Budgell, Esq; occasion'd by his late Presenting an Humble Complaint to His Majesty against the Right Honourable Sir Robert Walpole*, 1730, pp. 28–9; Budgell was a Fleet debtor at this time.

38. HMC, *Diary of Viscount Percival*, p. 78.

39. *Daily Journal*, 18 March 1730; Hargrave (ed.), *A Complete Collection of State-Trials*, Vol. IX, col. 226.

40. John Ginger (ed.), *Handel's Trumpeter: The Diary of John Grano*, New York, 1998, p. 333n. For Faulcon Court and the Greyhound see John Strype, *A Survey of the Cities of London and Westminster*, 2 vols., 1720, Vol. II, p. 30. The Greyhound was a carriers' inn and had long associations with Southwark Fair: see William Rendle and Philip Norman, *The Inns of Old Southwark and their Associations*, 1888, pp. 243, 287, 414. For Acton's will see PROB/11, Prerogative Court of Canterbury, Will Registers, piece 765. For Taylor see *Daily Journal*, 3 February 1732.

41. Hargrave (ed.), *A Complete Collection of State-Trials*, Vol. IX, col. 216; State Paper Office MSS, SP 36/8, f196; SP 36/28, f. 133.

42. Surrey Quarter Sessions Papers, QS 2/6/1724/Eas/7; there were seventeen women and nineteen men.

43. Ibid., QS 2/6/1735/Mid/23; 2/6/1739/Mid/6.

44. *Historical Register . . . For the Year 1730*, p. 71.

45. There is useful commentary in Alan Dugald McKillop, 'Thomson and the Jail Committee', *Studies in Philology*, Vol. 47, No. 1, January 1950, pp. 62–71.

46. Church, *Oglethorpe*, ch. VII; for the memorial see John Nichols, *Literary Anecdotes of the Eighteenth Century . . .*, 9 vols., 1812–16, Vol. II, pp. 21–2n. The search for British migrant debtors in

Georgia has proved unfruitful: see E. Merton Coulter, 'Was Georgia Settled by Debtors?', *Georgia Historical Quarterly*, Savannah, Vol. 53, No. 4, December 1969, pp. 442–54. African slaves were not part of the original settlement: Georgia banned slavery in 1735 but legalised it from 1751.

5: 'Mansions of Misery': The Old Marshalsea, 1730–1811

1. *Report from the Committee Appointed to Enquire into the State of the Goals of this Kingdom: Relating to the Fleet Prison*, 1729, pp. 11–12, enumerated 399 in March 1729, including 319 on the common side; at the time of the report, May 1729, the figure was over 330 on the common side. John Howard, *The State of the Prisons in England and Wales, with Preliminary Observations, and an Account of Some Foreign Prisons and Hospitals*, Warrington, 1784, pp. 250–51. For 1742 see *HCJ*, Vol. 24, p. 377, 13 January 1743. For 1768 see Surrey Quarter Sessions Papers, QS 2/6/1769/Eph/43.

2. *General Advertiser*, 11 February and 23 June 1746. *Lloyd's Evening Post and British Chronicle*, 24–26 March 1762. For the mutiny of the fleet at the Nore in the Thames estuary and the impact on the Marshalsea see, for example, *Oracle and Public Advertiser*, 3 July 1797; *London Evening Post*, 7–9 September 1797.

3. ADM/L/M/125, W. French, 'A Journal of the proceedings of His Majesty's Ship Medways Prize under my Command Commencing the 14th of December 1747 Ending . . . the 25th of August 1749 . . .'. The Admiralty correspondence concerning the Lascars is in ADM/B/142 (9 March 1749/50); 143 (31 October, 7, 20 and 24 November and 8 and 24 December 1750).

4. *Old England or the National Gazette*, 2 May 1752. See also *General Evening Post*, 17–19 January and 15–17 October 1751; *Whitehall Evening Post or London Intelligencer*, 2–4 July 1751; *London Evening Post*, 11–13 February 1752; *Covent-Garden Journal*, 2 March 1752. For the court case see *Covent-Garden Journal*, 18 July 1752. For their departure see *Old England's Journal*, 17 March 1753; *Whitehall Evening Post or London Intelligencer*, 3–5 January 1754.

5. The Inferior Courts Act 1779, 19 Geo. III, c. 70. Howard, *The State of the Prisons in England and Wales*, p. 250; James Neild, *An Account of the Rise, Progress, and Present State, of the Society for the Discharge and Relief of Persons Imprisoned for Small Debts throughout England and Wales*, 1802, p. 206; James Neild, *State of the Prisons in England, Scotland, and Wales . . .*, 1812, p. 386.

6. Calculated from PRIS 11/1A, 11/6, 11/10, 11/13.
7. *General Advertiser*, 7 May 1750; *Public Advertiser*, 8 May 1759.
8. *Public Advertiser*, 31 January 1763; *Middlesex Journal or Chronicle of Liberty*, 26–28 March 1772; this was probably John Marson, who died in post in August 1778. *Public Advertiser*, 26 January, 7 February 1758.
9. For Osborn see Sloane MS 4060, f. 82, dated 29 March but no year (probably *c*. 1738).
10. A. C. Elias, Jr (ed.), *Memoirs of Laetitia Pilkington*, 2 vols., Athens, Georgia, 1997, Vol. I, pp. 202–8; see also Norma Clarke, *Queen of the Wits: A Life of Laetitia Pilkington*, 2008, pp. 197–200.
11. Rockingham Correspondence, WWM/R/1/1136, 17 December 1768.
12. Ibid., WWM/R/1/1133, 14 December 1768.
13. *Gazetteer and New Daily Advertiser*, 27 September 1769; *Public Advertiser*, 26 March 1770.
14. Clive MSS, G/37/45/3 f. 19; see also G/37/94/2 ff. 22–3 (Callander again); G/37/56/3 f. 17 (a Mr Simonton); G/37/57/1 f. 47 (William Henry Pitt).
15. *Lloyd's Evening Post*, 29 April–1 May 1765. I have been unable to trace this publication. *Gazetteer and New Daily Advertiser*, 5 and 20 January 1770. *World and Fashionable Advertiser*, 4 October 1787.
16. For one such court case see *Sun*, 29 January 1798, St George's overseers losing a case brought against them by St Martin-in-the-Fields.
17. *HCJ*, Vol. 39, cols. 137–8, 255–7, 4 and 28 February 1783; King's Bench prison: Poor Relief Act 1783, 23 Geo. III, c. 23.
18. London Lives 1690–1800, St Martin's Settlements, smdsset_24_2431, 15 June 1737 (White); smdsset_115_58954, 29 September 1739 (Rodgers); smdsset_115_58960, 6 October 1739 (Burkett); smdsset_115_59003, 15 November 1739 (Bird).
19. Middlesex Justices, Sessions Papers, Justices' Working Documents (London Lives 1690–1800), LMSMPS503190069, October 1736 (Topsell); LMSMPS506260053, December 1772 (coach-maker); LMSMPS509580076, 21 February 1799, James Gates (carpenter); LMSMPS509460067 and 0066, December 1797, January 1798 (Baker). Middlesex Justices, Sessions Papers (LMA), MJ/SP/1783/10/058 i–iii, Henry and Charles Harrow (Finsbury tailor).
20. *Report from the Committee Appointed to Enquire into the State of the Goals of this Kingdom: Relating to the Fleet Prison*, p. 12. St Martin's Settlements, smdsset_107_58230, 25 November 1741, recalling some years before. For the pegs see Neild, *State of the Prisons in England, Scotland, and Wales . . .*, p. 389.

21. *Gentleman's Magazine*, September 1803, p. 805; May 1804, p. 401.
22. For the pronunciation see *LG*, 11 August 1804 (Issue 15727, p. 983). Ancestry.com England, London and Surrey, England, Marriage Bonds and Allegations, 1597–1921, MS 10091/158. T. Prattent and M. Denton, *The Virtuoso's Companion and Coin Collector's Guide, etc.*, 8 vols., 1795–7. Nichols MSS, MSS Eng. Let. C.362/2, ff. 223–4. Prattent's Marshalsea engravings are not among his works listed in the BL catalogue. The story of the Marshalsea or part of it having once been a royal palace was an old and persistent one but seems to have no foundation.
23. Nichols MSS, ff. 225, 228, 231a–b. Prattent died on 18 February 1841 at 21 Clerkenwell Close, aged seventy-six; Ann died on 8 November 1846 at Jerusalem Court, Clerkenwell, aged eighty-two.
24. For Prattent's drawing of the court interior see Owen Manning and William Bray, *The History and Antiquities of the County of Surrey*, 3 vols., 1804–14, Vol. III, appendix opp. p. xxv. *LG*, 30 June 1801 (Issue 15381, p. 744). *Morning Chronicle*, 16 December 1824.
25. London Lives 1690–1800, City of London Sessions Papers, Justices' Working Documents, 12 December 1738–21 January 1740, LMSLPS 150500017, 28 April 1739. St Martin's Settlements, smdsset_74_54851, 25 June 1761.
26. OBP, t18021201-3, 1 December 1802. John Howard, *The State of the Prisons in England and Wales, with Preliminary Observations, and an Account of Some Foreign Prisons*, Warrington, 1777, p. 206.
27. *Morning Chronicle*, 30 May 1809.
28. Elias (ed.), *Memoirs of Laetitia Pilkington*, Vol. I, p. 203. *London Evening Post*, 11–13 January 1737; OBP, t17300828–85, 28 August 1730. Howard, *The State of the Prisons in England and Wales*, 1784, p. 250.
29. PALA 9/8, Prisoner Petitions bundle, n.d.
30. PALA 9/8, Prisoner Petitions bundle, 'To Mr Chrichley Prothonotary of the Marshalsea Court Southwark', 29 January 1808.
31. *Read's Weekly Journal or British Gazetteer*, 23 September 1738.
32. Surrey Quarter Sessions Papers, QS 2/6/1763/Eph/40.
33. *London Journal*, 17 August 1734; *London Evening Post*, 17 August 1742; *Gentleman's Magazine*, September 1749, p. 427; *Whitehall Evening Post or London Intelligencer*, 23–26 September 1749.
34. For the background see Anon., *A Narrative of the Late Disturbances in the Marshalsea-Prison . . .*, 1768, passim. *Public Advertiser*, 2 May 1766; *London Evening Post*, 26–28 February 1767.

35. *Public Advertiser*, 25 August 1768; *Annual Register for the Year 1768*, p. 157. Surrey Quarter Sessions Papers, QS 2/6/1769/Eph/43.

36. *Public Advertiser*, 12 September and 6 December 1768.

37. For substitutes from 1774 see Howard, *The State of the Prisons in England and Wales*, 1784, p. 250.

38. See Jerry White, *London in the Eighteenth Century: A Great and Monstrous Thing*, 2012, pp. 534–44.

39. For the Fleet see *London Chronicle*, 6–8 June 1780. For Haycock, OBP, t17800628-34, 28 June 1780.

40. *London Chronicle*, 8–10 June 1780; *Whitehall Evening Post*, 6–8 June 1780. The list of prisoners escaping is at Surrey Quarter Sessions Papers, QS 3/2/37; the column recording whether prisoners had surrendered is blank in one case. A story much repeated, including by this author, averred that Teresa Cornelys, the famous impresario of concerts and masquerades of 1760s London, had escaped from the Marshalsea during the riots and had lived anonymously in the capital until she was nabbed again fifteen years or so later: given the list sent to the Surrey magistrates by the keeper of the gaol, the story seems not to be true. For the Marshalsea open for business see *Public Advertiser*, 24 July 1780. No person seems to have been tried for the attack on the Marshalsea.

41. *Gazetteer and New Daily Advertiser*, 10 February and 13 November 1766; *Public Ledger*, 22 July 1766.

42. His name was also spelled Udal: OBP, t17390221-2, 21 February 1739, trial of William Udal, highway robbery, death; Ordinary's Account, 14 March 1739, OA17390314. OBP, 6 September 1739, trial of Catherine Goodyere (her husband, Richard, was implicated but not tried), robbery, transportation.

43. *Report from the Committee Appointed to Enquire into the State of the Goals of this Kingdom: Relating to the Fleet Prison*, p. 8. *London Evening Post*, 27–29 September 1744 and 21–23 November 1775; *Parker's General Advertiser and Morning Intelligencer*, 26 March 1783.

44. Surrey Quarter Sessions Papers, QS 2/6/1779/Eas/93, Information of Richard Spencer, 8 December 1778.

45. *Observer*, 15 January 1797; *Morning Post and Gazetteer*, 13 January 1800. James Neild was wrong to report that no pirates were held in the Marshalsea after July 1789: Neild, *An Account of the Rise, Progress, and Present State . . .*, 1802, p. 207n.

46. *Oracle and Daily Advertiser*, 31 December 1799. Lord Holland early on gave Culver's name as Cullum. See *The Times*, 14 January and 1 March 1811; *Examiner*, 20 January 1811; *Morning Chronicle*, 1 March and 16 April 1811; *Morning Post*, 8 March 1811; *HLD*, 1st Series, Vol. 19, cols.109–110, 444–5.

47. *London and Country Journal*, 13 March 1739; *Lloyd's Evening Post*, 24–26 October 1764; *Public Advertiser*, 12 January 1792; *Whitehall Evening Post or London Intelligencer*, 13–15 December 1748; *Universal Spectator and Weekly Journal*, 17 April 1742; *Read's Weekly Journal or British Gazetteer*, 24 March 1739.

48. City Sessions Working Documents, 26 September 1751–8 December 1752, LMSLPS 150630056–8; OBP, t17520625–57, 25 June 1752, trial of Jacob Stone and George Anderson, forgery, no evidence, not guilty. OBP, t17481207–52, 7 December 1748; OA 17490220.

49. PRIS 11/1A. *ODNB*, Hannah Glasse, *c.* 1708–70 (accessed December 2013). Betty Rizzo, 'Christopher Smart: A Letter and Lines from a Prisoner of the King's Bench', *Review of English Studies*, New Series, Vol. 35, No. 140 (November 1984), pp. 510–16.

50. For the dodgy sixpence see *Cobbett's Weekly Political Register*, 24 April 1811.

51. On the increasing numbers resorting to insolvency see Ian P. H. Duffy, *Bankruptcy and Insolvency in London during the Industrial Revolution*, New York, 1985, p. 374. Figures for 1816 calculated from PRIS 11/4.

52. Elias (ed.), *Memoirs of Laetitia Pilkington*, Vol. I, p. 206; petitions from the King's Bench (March 1742), Fleet (December 1742) and the Marshalsea (January 1743) are in *HCJ*, Vol. 24, pp. 121, 366–7, 377. *LG*, 14–17, 17–21 May 1743.

53. *General Advertiser and Morning Intelligencer*, 20 May 1778; *London Evening Post*, 12–14 and 19–21 May 1761.

54. *London Chronicle*, 29–31 January 1778.

55. *Old Whig or the Consistent Protestant*, 15 May 1735; for Wright see *Old Whig or the Consistent Protestant*, 12 August 1736 and *Common Sense or the Englishman's Journal*, 5 February 1737. *London Morning Penny Post*, 3–5 June 1751. *Read's Weekly Journal or British Gazetteer*, 17 January 1756. Isaac Bickerstaffe, *The Hypocrite*, 1769, Act I, Sc. V. Nehemiah Curnock (ed.), *The Journal of the Rev. John Wesley, AM*, 8 vols., 1909, Vol. V, p. 247, 2 January 1768.

56. For Mrs Ashton see Neild, *State of the Prisons in England, Scotland, and Wales . . .*, pp. 367–8, 390. PALA 9/8, List of prisoners discharged by Dr Pelling's Charity, 1812; Dr Pelling seems likely to have been the Rector of St Anne's, Soho, who died in 1750; there is no record of the legacy in his will but it's conceivable he demised a sum for this purpose before his death. For Allnutt see *Further Report[s] of the Commissioners appointed in Pursuance of Two Several Acts of Parliament . . . to inquire concerning Charities in England for the Education of The Poor . . .,1823*, Further Report No. 8, pp. 516ff. For examples of reports of the

legacy in practice see *General Evening Post*, 4–7 May 1751 and 22–25 January 1774; PALA 9/8, List of Debtors Discharged by the Oxford Charity, 1812. Allnutt is sometimes cited as the original model for Dickens's William Dorrit, though there seems to be no evidence for the claim.

57. *Daily Advertiser*, 15 February 1772; *Gazetteer and New Daily Advertiser*, 18 February 1772. ODNB, James Neild, 1744–1814, penal reformer and philanthropist (accessed 4 June 2015). This article credits the sermon raising £81 to the Rev. Weeden Butler but the newspapers show this to be wrong; Butler may have preached the first sermon at Charlotte Chapel, a speculative venture of Dodd; Butler had a position there, but in all it seems more likely that Dodd preached both. See also David Owen, *English Philanthropy 1660–1960*, Cambridge, Mass., 1960, pp. 63–5.

58. Society for the Discharge and Relief of Persons Imprisoned for Small Debts, *An Account of the Rise, Progress, and Present State, of the Society for the Discharge and Relief of Persons Imprisoned for Small Debts throughout England*, 1794, the list of benefactions at the end (n.p.).

59. *World*, 11 October 1788; *Oracle*, 19 April 1790; *True Briton*, 21 April 1796; Neild, *An Account of the Rise, Progress, and Present State . . .*, 1802, p. 323.

60. Calculated from PRIS 11/1A and 11/4.

61. William Smith, *State of the Gaols in London and Westminster, and Borough of Southwark. To which is added an Account of the Present State of the Convicts sentenced to Hard Labour on Board the Justitia upon the River Thames*, 1776, pp. 27–9.

62. Howard, *The State of the Prisons in England and Wales*, 1784, p251–2. The act was 14 Geo. III, c. 59. For conditions after the act see Smith, *State of the Gaols in London and Westminster, and Borough of Southwark*, pp. 22–3; Neild, *An Account of the Rise, Progress, and Present State . . .*, 1802, p. 207; PALA 11/1A.

63. Curnock (ed.), *The Journal of the Rev. John Wesley, AM*, Vol. II, p. 155, Sunday 25 March 1739; Vol. IV, Saturday 3 February 1753. Elias (ed.), *Memoirs of Laetitia Pilkington*, Vol. I, p. 206, Vol. II, p. 589.

64. *Daily Advertiser*, 20 October 1775.

65. Howard, *The State of the Prisons in England and Wales*, 1777, p. 205.

66. William Woolley, *The Benefit of Starving; or the Advantages of Hunger, Cold, and Nakedness; intended as a Cordial for the Poor, and an Apology for the Rich. Addressed to the Rev. Rowland Hill, M.A.*, 1792, pp. 26ff.

67. See ibid.; William Woolley, *A Cure for Canting; or, The Grand Impostors of St. Stephen's and of Surrey Chapels Unmasked . . .*,

1794; William Woolley, *The Trials of the Rev. William Woolley, Clerk, For Publishing a Libel on Sir Richard Hill, Baronet . . .,* 1794. Sir Richard Hill, *A Detection of Gross Falsehood, and a Display of Black Ingratitude; being an Answer to a Pamphlet lately Published by some Evil-Minded Person, under the name of the Rev*^d *William Woolley, striking himself A.M . . .,* 1794. The trial and its aftermath are in *True Briton,* 12 December 1794; *Sun,* 18 December 1794 and 25 May 1795; *The Times,* 10 February and 29 April 1795; the apology is in *Morning Chronicle,* 23 June 1795. The BL does not have a copy of the meditations, which were advertised in the *Morning Post and Fashionable World,* 13 May 1796.

68. Robert Dodsley (publisher), *London and Its Environs Described . . .,* 6 vols., 1761, Vol. IV, pp. 265–6; John Entick, *A New and Accurate History and Survey of London, Westminster, Southwark, and Places Adjacent . . .,* 4 vols., 1766, Vol. IV, p. 385; Smith, *State of the Gaols in London and Westminster, and Borough of Southwark,* pp. 27–9. *London Evening Post,* 26–28 June 1766; *Public Advertiser,* 29 May 1767.

69. *London Evening Post,* 11–13 May 1775. Howard, *The State of the Prisons in England and Wales,* 1777, p. 206.

70. *Lloyd's Evening Post,* 10–12 April 1793.

71. HO 42/46/153, ff. 325–6; 42/46/154, ff. 327–8. James Neild, *Account of Persons Confined for Debt, in the Various Prisons of England and Wales . . .,* 1800, p. 29.

72. *St James's Chronicle or the British Evening Post,* 10 May 1800. Liverpool Papers, Vol. LIX, Official Correspondence of Second Earl, June, July 1812, Add MS 38248; this printed circular to members of the House of Commons was wrongly dated 1811, amended by hand here to 1 July 1812.

73. CRES 2/932, transcript of a petition of 1807 from Samuel Davis to HM Lords Commissioners of the Treasury. See Survey of London, *Vol. XXV: St George's Fields (The Parishes of St George the Martyr, Southwark and St Mary Newington),* 1955, pp. 15–16n.; according to this source the rear part of the Marshalsea remained in the ownership of the Gosling family until their interest was finally acquired by the LCC in 1950–51, which contradicts Cracklow's claim to be selling 'the Whole of the Marshalsea Prison'.

74. James Neild, *An Account of the Rise, Progress, and Present State, of the Society for the Discharge and Relief of Persons Imprisoned for Small Debts throughout England and Wales,* 1808, p. 367. *HCJ,* Vol. 65, p. 310, 30 April, and p. 322, 3 May 1810; Vol. 66, pp. 396, 408, 5 and 8 June 1811.

75. For the industrial buildings on the site see Survey of London, *Vol. XXV,* pp. 15–16.

6: The New Gaol: John Dickens's
Marshalsea, 1812–24

1. The encomium is in John Forster, *The Life of Charles Dickens*, 3 vols., 1872–74, Vol. I, pp. 17–18.

2. For this and much that follows see Michael Allen, *Charles Dickens' Childhood*, Basingstoke, 1988, pp. 11–14; Leslie C. Staples, 'The Dickens Ancestry, Some New Discoveries', *Dickensian*, Vol. LXV, No. 290, Spring 1949, pp. 64–73; Angus Easson, 'John Dickens and the Navy Pay Office', *Dickensian*, Vol. 70, No. 372, January 1974, pp. 35–45; Michael Slater, *Charles Dickens*, 2009, pp. 3–8; Paul Schlicke (ed.), *The Oxford Companion to Charles Dickens*, Oxford, 2011, 'John Dickens', pp. 172–5; John was baptised in Marylebone in November 1785: see Michael Allen, 'New Evidence on Dickens's Grandparents', *Dickensian*, Vol. 109, No. 489, Spring 2013, pp. 5–20. I am grateful to Michael Allen for sharing with me some of the fruits of his latest research.

3. See Allen, *Charles Dickens' Childhood*, pp. 60–61; William J. Carlton, '"The Deed" in *David Copperfield*', *Dickensian*, Vol. 48, No. 303, June 1952, pp. 101–6.

4. Allen, *Charles Dickens' Childhood*, p. 78; the Chatham servant was model for the Marchioness – her very name an echo of Marshalsea – in *Martin Chuzzlewit* and the Orfling in *David Copperfield*.

5. Forster, *The Life of Charles Dickens*, Vol. I, pp. 9, 23–6.

6. Charles Dickens, *The Posthumous Papers of the Pickwick Club*, 1836–7, ch. XL.

7. Forster, *The Life of Charles Dickens*, Vol. I, pp. 24–5.

8. William Rendle and Philip Norman, *The Inns of Old Southwark and their Associations*, 1888, p. 253.

9. *Report from the Committee on the King's Bench, Fleet, and Marshalsea Prisons; &c.*, 1815, pp. 23–4, 185; *Report from the Commissioners appointed to inquire into the state, conduct and management of the Prison and Gaol of . . . the Court of the Marshalsea of His Majesty's honourable Household; and of the Prisoners in the said respective Prisons confined*, 1818, p. 93 and folding plan. For the garret see George F. Young, 'The Marshalsea Re-visited', *Dickensian*, Vol. XXVIII, No. 223, Summer 1932, pp. 219–27. The height of the main block has caused some confusion. The 1818 report, p. 12, says the building 'consists of three stories' but this probably implied the common parlance of three above the ground floor; it is later clear from the detailed measurements (p. 93) that there were four floors and so it is described in James Neild, *State of the Prisons in England, Scotland, and*

Wales . . ., 1812, p. 393, and is clear from later illustrations, especially by Emslie in 1887 of what was then Marshalsea Place. Trey Philpotts, 'The Real Marshalsea', *Dickensian*, Vol. 87, No. 425, Autumn 1991, pp. 133–45, the most authoritative description of Dickens's Marshalsea, mistakenly calls the building three-storeyed, as he does in *The Companion to Little Dorrit*, Mountfield, 2003, p. 92.

10. *Report from the Committee on the King's Bench, Fleet, and Marshalsea Prisons; &c.*, pp. 24–5, 188; WORK 6/131/2, ff. 35–6 (1827), 41–2 (1829), 54–8 (1830–31), 61–6 (1832).

11. See the descriptions of the prison in *Report from the Committee on the King's Bench, Fleet, and Marshalsea Prisons; &c.*, pp. 22–7; *Report from the Commissioners appointed to inquire into the state, conduct and management of the Prison and Gaol of . . . the Court of the Marshalsea . . .*, pp. 10–16. For 'ancient' see John Ewer Poole ('An Eye-Witness'), *An Expose of the Practice of the Palace, or Marshalsea Court; with a Description of the Prison, the Secrets of the Prison-House, its Regulations, Fees, &c. &c. . . .*, 1833, p. 6. There is a useful article in the *Builder*, 13 November 1897, when the former prison's old buildings were used as a common lodging house. For the wall see *Examiner*, 6 June 1813.

12. Criticism of the lack of space is in *Report from the Commissioners appointed to inquire into the state, conduct and management of the Prison and Gaol of . . . the Court of the Marshalsea . . .*, p. 11; for the cost of the work, which seems to have also involved the potential clearance of the Crown, see WORK 6/131/2 Office of Works and Successor: Miscellanea, ff. 8–10; for the previous industrial users see the plan in State Paper Office MS, SP112/87.

13. *Report from the Committee on the King's Bench, Fleet, and Marshalsea Prisons; &c.*, pp. 23, 185; *Report from the Commissioners appointed to inquire into the state, conduct and management of the Prison and Gaol of . . . the Court of the Marshalsea . . .*, pp. 12, 63.

14. For limits on arrest under mesne process see Ian P. H. Duffy, *Bankruptcy and Insolvency in London during the Industrial Revolution*, New York, 1985, pp. 106–7. Prison numbers are calculated from PRIS 11, Day Books of Commitments and Discharges, Marshalsea Prison, 11/4 (1816), 11/6 (1821), 11/10 (1833). Poole, *An Expose of the Practice of the Palace, or Marshalsea Court*, pp. 6–7.

15. Allen, *Charles Dickens' Childhood*, pp. 87–8; Slater, *Charles Dickens*, pp. 21–3; Forster, *The Life of Charles Dickens*, Vol. I, pp. 38–40. For the opening times of the prison see *Report from the Committee on the King's Bench, Fleet, and Marshalsea Prisons; &c.*, p. 262. Harriet Dickens died in 1827, aged nine.

16. Ibid., pp. 23, 186, 263. *Report from the Commissioners appointed to inquire into the state, conduct and management of the Prison and Gaol of . . . the Court of the Marshalsea . . .*, p. 53.

17. Poole, *An Expose of the Practice of the Palace, or Marshalsea Court*, p. 6.

18. *Report from the Committee on the King's Bench, Fleet, and Marshalsea Prisons; &c.*, pp. 23, 200–201.

19. Ibid., pp. 23, 194–7. *Report from the Commissioners appointed to inquire into the state, conduct and management of the Prison and Gaol of . . . the Court of the Marshalsea . . .*, pp. 14–15.

20. Alexander Tweedie and Charles Gaselee, *A Practical Treatise on Cholera, as it has appeared in Various Parts of the Metropolis,* 1832; Poole, *An Expose of the Practice of the Palace, or Marshalsea Court*, p. 7, makes no complaint of the 'medical gentleman' who attended the prison. *Return of all Coroners' Inquests held within the King's Bench Prison and other Prisons in and near the Metropolis . . . from the 1st May 1832 to . . . 1834 . . .*, 1834, p. 2.

21. *Report from the Committee on the King's Bench, Fleet, and Marshalsea Prisons; &c.*, pp. 194, 262. Dickens, *The Posthumous Papers of the Pickwick Club*, ch. XLV. *Examiner*, 22 January 1826; *Bell's Life in London and Sporting Chronicle*, 6 May 1832.

22. *Report from the Committee on the King's Bench, Fleet, and Marshalsea Prisons; &c.*, pp. 23–4.

23. Ibid., pp. 25–6, 202–4; *Report from the Commissioners appointed to inquire into the state, conduct and management of the Prison and Gaol of . . . the Court of the Marshalsea . . .*, p. 53.

24. *Report from the Committee on the King's Bench, Fleet, and Marshalsea Prisons; &c.*, pp. 204–5.

25. Ibid., p. 203. They can be found in PALA 9/8, Miscellaneous papers related to the prison of the Marshalsea and Palace Courts, 1812–42; they were printed in *Report from the Committee on the King's Bench, Fleet, and Marshalsea Prisons; &c.*, pp. 267–8.

26. For the college crier see Poole, *An Expose of the Practice of the Palace, or Marshalsea Court*, pp. 7–8; *Report from the Committee on the King's Bench, Fleet, and Marshalsea Prisons; &c.*, p. 25.

27. Poole, *An Expose of the Practice of the Palace, or Marshalsea Court*, p. 8 and n.; *Report from the Committee on the King's Bench, Fleet, and Marshalsea Prisons; &c.*, pp. 190, 199; *Morning Chronicle*, 9 September 1815 (Tomkins) and 30 July 1821 (Arklay).

28. John Sartain, *The Reminiscences of a Very Old Man 1808–1897*, New York, 1900, pp. 74–9: the room was remembered as just a few paces from the lodge, while in fact it was further into the gaol and past the main building; it could only have been the ale room or possibly the snuggery.

29. Forster, *The Life of Charles Dickens*, Vol. I, pp. 45–6. In May 1837 the prisoners petitioned for funds for a public dinner on the birthday of William IV: letter from ?J. Dixon, 23 or 25 May 1837, PALA 9/8.

30. *Penny Satirist*, 28 October 1837.

31. The annual gifts are listed in *Report from the Committee on the King's Bench, Fleet, and Marshalsea Prisons; &c.*, pp. 264–5; for the Christmas bounties see, for example, *Morning Chronicle*, 28 December 1816; *Morning Post*, 28 December 1827.

32. Southwark Deeds, 1343, 1346. *HCJ*, Vol. 68, pp. 158–9, 15 February 1813 for the petition; 52 Geo. III, c. 160 and 53 Geo. III, c. 113, for the act and its amendment. For the continuation of payments see *Morning Post*, 17 November 1818.

33. *Morning Post*, 14 December 1820; *Morning Chronicle*, 27 January 1824.

34. Elphinstone Papers, MSS EUR F88/83, ff. 64–5. Fenton's Hotel was 63 St James's Street.

35. Ibid., ff. 66–7, 74–5; I cannot find McKie in subsequent issues of the *LG*.

36. *Morning Post*, 14 July and 31 December 1838.

37. *Morning Post*, 8 October 1824; *The Times*, 14 November 1831.

38. *Morning Post*, 10 August 1833.

39. Forster, *The Life of Charles Dickens*, Vol. I, p. 39.

40. *Report from the Committee on the King's Bench, Fleet, and Marshalsea Prisons; &c.*, pp. 201–2; *Report from the Commissioners appointed to inquire into the state, conduct and management of the Prison and Gaol of . . . the Court of the Marshalsea . . .*, p. 66.

41. *Morning Post*, 24 June 1829; *Standard*, 24 June 1829, which gives the lawyer's name as Dickinson.

42. *Report from the Committee on the King's Bench, Fleet, and Marshalsea Prisons; &c.*, p. 188.

43. Calculated from PRIS 11/4; *The Times*, 17 April 1824; returns of debtors released by the legacies are in PALA 9/8.

44. 53 Geo. III, c. 102; for the increasing popularity of insolvency see Duffy, *Bankruptcy and Insolvency in London during the Industrial Revolution*, pp. 87ff., 374. Calculated from PRIS 11/6 and 11/10.

45. Calculated from PRIS 11/7.

46. Ibid. The will of Thomas Nottage, who died in 1828, is at PROB 11, piece 1742. In the 1861 census for Gloucester Street, Finsbury, where Nottage was living in reduced circumstances, he gave his age as sixty-six, which may have been over-optimistic.

47. Easson, 'John Dickens and the Navy Pay Office', pp. 40–42; Michael Allen, *Charles Dickens and the Blacking Factory*, St Leonards, Hants, 2011, p. 14.

48. Angus Easson, '"I, Elizabeth Dickens"', *Dickensian*, Vol. 67, No. 363, January 1971, pp. 35–40.

49. Forster, *The Life of Charles Dickens*, Vol. I, p. 42. On the operation of the Insolvent Debtors Acts in this period see V. Markham Lester, *Victorian Insolvency: Bankruptcy, Imprisonment for Debt, and Company Winding-up in Nineteenth-Century England*, Oxford, 1995, pp. 88–116.

50. Easson, 'John Dickens and the Navy Pay Office', p. 42.

51. William J. Carlton, 'John Dickens, Journalist', *Dickensian*, Vol. 53, No. 321, January 1957, pp. 5–11.

52. Cited in Allen, *Charles Dickens' Childhood*, pp. 110–11.

53. Madeline House and Graham Storey (eds.), *The Letters of Charles Dickens Vol. 1 1820–1839*, Oxford, 1965, p. 44n., says the eviction was for non-payment of rates, but that can't be right; see pp. 43–7 for the 1834 troubles and Dickens's own fears.

54. Ibid., p. 104n. Slater, *Charles Dickens*, p. 164. The advertisement foreshadows the public statement that Dickens would make about his marriage in June 1858. Madeline House and Graham Storey (eds.), *The Letters of Charles Dickens Vol. 2 1840–1841*, Oxford, 1969, pp. 224–5 and n.

55. For Nottage see, for instance, *LG*, 25 September 1819, p. 1713; 12 March 1833, p. 506; 16 June 1843, p. 2027; 11 July 1848, p. 2637. For John Dickens see Easson, 'John Dickens and the Navy Pay Office', p. 42; *LG*, 21 December 1824, p. 2140; 31 October 1826, p. 2890; 24 November 1846, p. 5255.

56. *LG*, 9 January 1852, p. 101. Graham Storey, Kathleen Tillotson and Nina Burgis (eds.), *The Letters of Charles Dickens Vol. 6 1850–1852*, Oxford, 1988, pp. 333n., 342–3.

7: *Brief Lives: Marshalsea Debtors, 1820–42*

1. Charles Dickens, *Little Dorrit*, 1855–7, Book I, ch. VI.

2. *Annual Register for the Year 1840*, Appendix to Chronicle, pp. 245–63; for the committal proceedings see, for example, *Standard*, 18 June 1840; for the trial see OBP, t18400706–1877; his later life is described in a referenced Wikipedia article, 'Edward Oxford' (accessed 31 July 2015). Oxford's Bethlem is now the Imperial War Museum.

3. *Annual Register for the Year 1840*, Appendix to Chronicle, p. 248.

4. For his addresses and debts see *LG*, 22 November 1842, p3345; *Morning Post*, 19 December 1842. Family history sources are available online at Ancestry.com England, from St Katharine's by the Tower, baptisms and burials, 1770–1812, SKT/C/01/MS9668;

St Botolph, Bishopsgate, register of marriages, 1825–32, P69/BOT4/A/01/MS4520/11.

5. *Argus*, 26 June and 7 August 1841.

6. PRIS 11/13–14.

7. *Morning Post*, 19 December 1842.

8. *Morning Post*, 14 January 1843. Copy death certificate, DAZ094810.

9. 'South Jeopardy' was apparently fear of insolvency: John S. Farmer and W. E. Henley, *Slang and its Analogues, Past and Present*, 7 vols., 1890–1904, Vol. VI, p. 300.

10. PRIS 11/10.

11. John Ewer Poole ('An Eye-Witness'), *An Expose of the Practice of the Palace, or Marshalsea Court; with a Description of the Prison, the Secrets of the Prison-House, its Regulations, Fees, &c. &c. . . .*, 1833, pp. 3–4.

12. Ibid., pp. 9–10. 'Prision' is an early rendition of the modern term.

13. *ODNB*, Joseph Hume, 1777–1855, radical and politician (accessed 5 March 2015). Letter tipped into the Senate House Library copy of *An Expose of the Practice of the Palace, or Marshalsea Court*.

14. The claim is in Home Office Criminal Petitions, Series 1, HO 17/30/133.

15. OBP, t18190113–95.

16. *LG*, 16 January 1821, p. 133; PRIS 10/25, 'Condensed version of Fleet prison Commitment Book', 1810–36; HO 17/30/133.

17. *LG*, 12 April 1833, p. 726.

18. PRIS 11/12; *LG*, 22 July 1842, p. 2042.

19. *Morning Post*, 13 August 1842.

20. *Morning Post*, 22 February 1848. See also the advertisements in *Morning Chronicle*, 22 October 1844, and in John Dickens's paper, the *Daily News*, 28 June 1849.

21. Ancestry.com England, England and Wales, National Probate Calendar, Probate Administrations 1858, p. 155.

22. Ancestry.com England, St Dunstan in the West, Register of Marriages, 1779–96, P69/DUN2/A/01/MS10354/3; St George the Martyr, Southwark, Composite Register, Marriages, July 1800–June 1820, P92/GEO047.

23. *The Times*, 29 January 1802; British Museum Image Gallery Online, Heal 5.16; the ticket is reproduced in Henry B. Wheatley, *Round about Piccadilly and Pall Mall; or, a ramble from The Haymarket to Hyde Park*, 1870, p. 237.

24. PRIS 10/28 (King's Bench prison, 1812–13); *Account of the Names, Trades, and Descriptions of the several persons, who have applied to be discharged under the acts of Parliament of the 53rd and 54th years of His Present Majesty's reign . . .*, 1814–15, p. 30; *LG*, 14

December 1816, p. 2367. For the lodger see OBP, t18180909–186, 9 September 1818, trial of Mary Brown, for stealing a bucket from Hemens's open doorway and two loaves, the property of his lodger. PRIS 11/6.

25. The documents in Giles Hemens's case can be found at PALA 9/8, unsorted. They were carefully transcribed and printed in Angus Easson, 'Dickens and the Marshalsea', University of Oxford PhD, 1967, and I have cited his transcriptions here: he gave the Marshalsea side of Hemens's story at pp. 125–34 and the documents at pp. 353–71.

26. OBP, t18160110–111, 10 January 1816, trial of George White, aka Armstrong.

27. For Bland Burges's disavowal of any role in managing the prison see *Report from the Committee on the King's Bench, Fleet, and Marshalsea Prisons; &c.*, 1815, p. 23.

28. Ancestry.com England, *London, England, Deaths and Burials, 1813–1980*, DL/T/36/89.

29. See Jerry White, *London in the Nineteenth Century: 'A Human Awful Wonder of God'*, 2007, pp. 351–3, 357–8.

30. Mary Thale (ed.), *Selections from the Papers of the London Corresponding Society 1792–1799*, Cambridge, 1983, pp. 228n., 257–8, 268, 312; Iain McCalman, *Radical Underworld: Prophets, Revolutionaries and Pornographers in London, 1795–1840*, Oxford, 1988 (paperback edn, 2002), pp. 108–9, 111, 128–32.

31. Ancestry.com England, St James, Paddington, Register of Marriages, P87/JS/014 (marriage with Sarah, 1817, and of Ann Julia, 1833); *London, England, Marriages and Banns, 1754–1921*, St James, Pentonville, Composite Register: Baptisms, Burials – Rough Book, January 1798–June 1810, P76/JS2/001; St Pancras, Register of Baptism, P90/PAN1/014 (Ann Julia). I. J. Prothero, *Artisans and Politics in Early Nineteenth-Century London: John Gast and His Times*, 1979 (paperback edn, 1981), p. 145; McCalman, *Radical Underworld*, p. 197.

32. HO 44/4/60 ff. 223–4. Henry 'Orator' Hunt, MP, of Peterloo fame, had moved away from the metropolitan ultra-radicals.

33. HO 44/4/101 ff. 330–31. For Hall see Prothero, *Artisans and Politics in Early Nineteenth-Century London*, pp. 131, 262–1; McCalman, *Radical Underworld*, pp.133, 181–2, 195–8, 232–3.

34. For Sharpe's ring career see Mick Hill, *Famous Pugilists of the English Prize Ring*, Peterborough, 2013, pp. 121–3; some of the biographical details given there are incorrect. Ancestry.com England, St Mary Magdalene, Woolwich, Composite Register, January 1779–December 1799, P97/MRY/009 (birth); St Paul,

Deptford, Register of Marriages, P75/PAU/039; St Mary Magdalene, Woolwich, Register of Baptisms, July 1819–June 1823, P97/MRY/013; June 1823–July 1827, P97/MRY/014; Deaths and Burials, P97/MRY/037.

35. *Morning Chronicle*, 16 July 1828.

36. PRIS 11/10; *Bell's Life in London and Sporting Chronicle*, 18 September 1831.

37. PRIS 11/12; *Morning Post*, 10 January 1838.

38. PRIS 11/14; *LG*, 8 July 1842, p. 1899; 1851 Census, HO 107/1586/550, p. 19; Ancestry.com England, Greenwich Registry of Births, Marriages and Deaths, Vol. 1d, p. 412, January–March 1861.

39. Letter cited in Betty Matthews, 'William Parke and the Royal Society of Musicians', *Musical Times*, Vol. 129, No. 1746, August 1988, pp. 400–401; all the other information about his assistance comes from this article. See also *ODNB*, William Thomas Parke, 1761–1847, oboist (accessed 4 August 2015). PRIS 11/7.

40. PRIS 11/13.

41. *LG*, 6 November 1840, p. 2468; *Standard*, 16 December 1840 and 29 January 1841.

42. *Morning Chronicle*, 30 January 1824, for the marriage settlement and Clapham home. Ancestry.com England, UK Articles of Clerkship, 1756–1874; England, Select Marriages, 1538–1973; England, Select Births and Christenings, 1538–1973; St Leonard, Streatham, Register of Baptisms, P95/LEN/065 (Eliza).

43. For this and much of the accompanying detail see *Morning Post*, 22 November 1823; *Morning Chronicle*, 30 January 1824.

44. Theresa Whistler, *Imagination of the Heart: The Life of Walter de La Mare*, 1993, pp. 3–14; see also *ODNB*, Walter John de la Mare, 1873–1956, poet and writer (accessed 4 August 2015); neither mentions Uncle John. James signed Eliza's marriage certificate and Abraham performed the wedding ceremony as a guest clergyman at St Pancras in 1859: Ancestry.com England, St Pancras Parish Church, Register of Marriages, P90/PAN1/124.

45. *LG*, 3 November 1829, p. 2031.

46. *Morning Chronicle*, 26 November 1829.

47. Ancestry.com England, 1841 Census, HO107/726/10/St Dunstan in the West, ED6, f. 8; 1851 Census, HO107/1472, f. 392, p. 25; 1861 Census, *RG* 9/56, f. 98, p. 18; *London, England, Deaths and Burials, 1813–1980*, St Thomas, Woolwich, Kent, 1868, No. 1738.

48. *Morning Chronicle*, 13 January and 3 April 1830; PRIS 11/9–10.

49. *LG*, 31 March 1829, p. 616; *Morning Chronicle*, 22 April 1829; *LG*, 21 September 1830, p. 1996; *Standard*, 22 September 1830. For Long's see Captain Donald Shaw, (One of the Old Brigade), *London in the Sixties (With a Few Digressions)*, 3rd edn, 1909, pp. 140ff., writing of a time thirty years after Stewart but these traditions, like the play, ran deep.

50. PRIS 11/10; *LG*, 6 September 1831, p. 1814; *Morning Post*, 7 September 1831. For the history of the estate and Stewart's last years see James Paterson, *History of the Counties of Ayr and Wigton, Vol. III, Cunninghame, Part II*, Edinburgh, 1866, pp. 603–4.

51. PRIS 11/5–6.

52. The original court case and a little of Grant's background are in *Morning Chronicle*, 21 October 1822, and some of the aftershocks in *Morning Post*, 26 November 1823; *Morning Chronicle*, 8 July 1825. For the prosecution of 71 Pall Mall (71 St James's Street is also mentioned but I think in error) see *Morning Post*, 26 May 1823. For 9 Bennett Street, 71 Pall Mall and others at this time see John Ashton, *The History of Gambling in England*, 1898, pp. 109–17. Ancestry.com England; the children were baptised at St Andrew, Holborn, St Sepulchre, Holborn, and Old St Pancras (St Pancras).

53. *Lloyd's Weekly Newspaper*, 23 September 1849; *Morning Post*, 11 December 1849. Grant's copy death certificate is reference DYD 898943.

54. There were others: see *Morning Post*, 2 November 1837, 'Conviction of Three Swindlers for Conspiracy and Fraud'.

55. *Morning Post*, 5 January 1829, reporting on the death of Cooke; *Morning Chronicle*, 2 January 1829, reporting the prosecution of Sophia.

56. Ancestry.com England, *London and Surrey, England, Marriage Bonds and Allegations, 1597–1921*, DL/A/D/24/MS10091E/112. Much of the circumstantial detail comes from Cooke's subsequent Old Bailey trial for bigamy, OBP, t18120408–65, 8 April 1812.

57. For Sophia's Jamaican roots see *LG*, 26 April 1817, pp. 1012–13. OBP, t18120408–65, 8 April 1812; *Morning Post*, 24 July 1824.

58. *LG*, 12 May 1818, p. 877; for the Countess see *Morning Chronicle*, 26 July 1823, case of Cooke v. Smith.

59. PRIS 11/4; PRIS 10/31, Fleet prison discharges etc. 1819–21. *LG*, 12 May 1818, p. 877.

60. For the Stafford barony see *Burke's Peerage, Baronetage, & Knightage*, 69th edn, 1907, pp. 1562–3. Richard's description is in *Bury and Norwich Post; or Suffolk, Essex, Cambridge, Ely and Norfolk Telegraph*, 12 February 1823.

61. *Morning Post*, 6 June 1818, 22 March 1821 and 24 April 1822. The petition and the story of 'the Book' are in the National

Archives, C 195/8, ff. 100–101. Ancestry.com England, Old St Pancras (St Pancras), Register of Baptism, P90/1/013.

62. The Somers Town conspiracy is in *Morning Chronicle*, 6 April 1824; Clarendon Street is the address on George's baptism entry. *Morning Post*, 1 March 1823.

63. For Derby see *Morning Chronicle*, 26 July 1823. For the conspiracy case see *Morning Chronicle*, 6 April 1824; *Annual Register for the Year 1824*, Appendix to Chronicle, pp. 26*–28*. For the pamphlet libel see *Morning Post*, 24 July 1824. The sentence was reported in *Bury and Norwich Post; or Suffolk, Essex, Cambridge, Ely and Norfolk Telegraph*, and no doubt elsewhere, 17 May 1826. The 1827 notices to quit are in *Lancaster Gazette and General Advertiser for Lancashire, Westmorland &c*, 26 May 1827, and *Morning Chronicle*, 3 July 1827. For Cooke in the rules of the Fleet see *Morning Chronicle*, 4 September 1828.

64. *Morning Post*, 15 December 1824.

65. *Morning Chronicle*, 4 September 1828.

66. *Morning Chronicle*, 24 October 1828. OBP, t18281023-225, 23 October 1828; Ancestry.com England, Archives NSW, Series NRS 12188/4/4014, microfiche 673.

67. *Morning Post*, 5 January 1829; *Manchester Times*, 10 January 1829; PRIS 11/9.

68. On concern for the creditor see, for instance, *Report from the Select Committee on Acts Respecting Insolvent Debtors*, 1819, and *Report from the Select Committee on the Recovery of Small Debts in England and Wales*, 1823; see generally Margot C. Finn, *The Character of Credit: Personal Debt in English Culture, 1740–1914*, Cambridge, 2003, ch. 4; Gustav Peebles, 'Washing Away the Sins of Debt: The Nineteenth-Century Eradication of the Debtors' Prison', *Comparative Studies in Society and History*, Vol. 55, No. 3, Cambridge, 2013, pp. 701–24.

69. See Finn, *Character of Credit*, pp. 172–4; V. Markham Lester, *Victorian Insolvency: Bankruptcy, Imprisonment for Debt, and Company Winding-up in Nineteenth-Century England*, Oxford, 1995, pp. 110–14.

70. *Examiner*, 23 December 1838; *Morning Post*, 13 June 1839; *Charter*, 18 August 1839; *Standard*, 6 June and 12 November 1840.

71. PRIS 11/13.

72. *Morning Post*, 10 February 1840; *Standard*, 22 December 1841.

73. *Charter*, 18 August 1839; *John Bull*, 7 March 1842; *Standard*, 29 March 1842.

74. PRIS 11/13–14; PALA 9/7/4, Marshal's Commitment Books, f. 94. For Avery see *LG*, 23 December 1842, p. 3858; Ancestry.com

England, *London, England, Deaths and Burials, 1813–1980*, P89/
MRY1/348, 15 October 1845, No. 1739.

8: *The Marshalsea Muse and Other Survivals*

1. Daniel Defoe, *The Fortunes and Misfortunes of the Famous Moll
    Flanders . . .*, 1722 (Folio Society edn, 1965), pp. 61ff. Samuel
    Richardson, *Clarissa; or, The History of a Young Lady*, 5 vols.,
    1747–8 (1883 edn), Vol. IV, Letters LXXXI–VII. Henry Fielding,
    Amelia, 1751, Books XI–II. Tobias Smollett, *The Adventures of
    Ferdinand Count Fathom*, 1753, ch. XXXIX. Oliver Goldsmith,
    The Vicar of Wakefield, 1766, chs. XXIV–XXX. John Mills,
    D'Horsay, or Follies of the Day, 1844. Charles Dickens, *The
    Adventures of Martin Chuzzlewit*, 1843–4, ch. XIII.
2. *ODNB*, Hannah Glasse, *c.* 1708–70 (accessed December 2013);
    Charlotte Forman, 1715–87 (accessed December 2013).
3. Smollett, *Ferdinand Count Fathom*, ch. XXXIX; the adventurer
    was Theodor von Neuhoff, 1694–1756.
4. *Morning Post*, 28 January 1828. The painting was bought by George
    IV, that veritable king of debtors, and is in the Royal Collection.
    For the painting and its meanings see Gregory Dart, 'A World within
    Walls: Haydon, *The Mock Election*, and the 1820s Debtors' Prisons',
    in Philip Connell and Nigel Leask, *Romanticism and Popular
    Culture in Britain and Ireland*, Cambridge, 2009, pp. 214–35.
5. Lewis M. Knapp (ed.), *The Letters of Tobias Smollett*, Oxford,
    1970, p. 112, Smollett to Richard Smith, 8 May 1763; see also
    pp. 7–8. In addition, see Alice Parker, 'Tobias Smollett and the
    Law', *Studies in Philology*, Vol. 39, No. 3, Chapel Hill, North
    Carolina, July 1942, pp. 545–58.
6. Tobias Smollett, *The Adventures of Roderick Random*, 2 vols.,
    1748, chs. XXIII, LXI–IV. There were earlier references to the
    Marshalsea in verse, among them Thomas Brown, *The Mourning
    Poet: or the Unknown Comforts of Imprisonment, Calculated for
    the Meridian of the Three Populous Universities of the Queen's
    Bench, the Marshalsea, and Fleet . . . Written by a Poor Brother
    in Durance*, 1703; and·William Tunstall, *St Cyprian's Discourse to
    Donatus. Done into English Metre, By W—T— in the Marshalsea*,
    and *Ballads and some other Occasional Poems: By W—T— in the
    Marshalsea*, both 1716.
7. For Smollett and the theatre managers see Lewis Melville, *The Life
    and Letters of Tobias Smollett (1721–1771)*, 1926, p. 27; *ODNB*,
    Tobias Smollett, 1721–71 (accessed September 2015). Smollett,
    Roderick Random, ch. LXIV.

8. Anon., *The Triumph of Benevolence*, Vol. I, pp. 189–96; the novel has been variously attributed to Oliver Goldsmith and Arthur Murphy, though neither seems likely. Rosamond's Pond had in fact been filled during 1770, so shortly before the novel was published.

9. Ibid., pp. 200–201.

10. Ibid., chs. XVIII–XIX.

11. Anon., *The History of Miss Charlotte Seymour*, 2 vols., 1764, Vol. I, p. 215.

12. Ibid., pp. 156–7, chs. XVIII, XXIV–V.

13. Ibid., pp. 218, 225–6. For Lucy Cooper see Julie Peakman, *Lascivious Bodies: A Sexual History of the Eighteenth Century*, 2004, pp. 112–13, 123–4; and Hallie Rubenhold, *The Covent Garden Ladies: Pimp General Jack & the Extraordinary Story of Harris's List*, 2005, pp. 128–9. Cooper died in 1772, allegedly of the pox, shortly after being released from imprisonment in the King's Bench, where she was in a very bad way: see William Hickey, *Memoirs*, 4 vols., 1913–25, Vol. I, p. 126. Her confinement in the Marshalsea is unconfirmed by other sources but not unlikely.

14. Ibid., pp. 231–2.

15. Ibid., chs. XXVI–VII.

16. John Forster, *The Life of Charles Dickens*, 3 vols., 1872–4, Vol. I, pp. 27–8.

17. Ibid., pp. 49–50. Robert Warren's was the blacking factory of a famous competitor of Dickens's employer. Chandos Street, Charing Cross, was where his employer moved after quitting Hungerford Stairs.

18. Charles Dickens, *The Haunted Man and the Ghost's Bargain. A Fancy for Christmas Time*, 1848. See Stanley Tick, 'Autobiographical Impulses in *The Haunted Man* (1848)', *Dickens Quarterly*, Vol. 18, No. 2, pp. 62–9, Baltimore, June 2001.

19. C. R. B. Dunlop, 'Debtors and Creditors in Dickens' Fiction', *Dickens Studies Annual*, Vol. 19, New York, 1990. Charles Dickens, 'When We Stopped Growing', *Household Words*, Vol. VI, No. 145, 1 January 1853, pp. 361–3.

20. 'Brokers' and Marine-Store Shops' (King's Bench) and 'The Boarding House' (Fleet): see Michael Slater (ed.), *Dickens' Journalism: Sketches by Boz and Other Early Papers 1833–39*, 1994, pp. 179, 287. *Morning Post*, 4 April 1837; the story provided the 'main part' of *The Peregrinations of Pickwick*. Charles Dickens, *The Posthumous Papers of the Pickwick Club*, 1836–7, ch. XXI.

21. It is possible that Dickens heard of the Marshalsea even before reading *Roderick Random*: from his father, as the Admiralty prison for truculent sailors.

22. Ibid., ch. XLI.

23. For a useful discussion of the debtor in Dickens's works see Dunlop, 'Debtors and Creditors in Dickens' Fiction', passim.
24. Charles Dickens, *The Personal History of David Copperfield*, 1849–50, ch. XI.
25. *Graphic*, 28 December 1871; *Pall Mall Gazette*, 13 December 1871.
26. Charles Dickens, *Little Dorrit*, 1855–7, Book I, ch. V.
27. Ibid., ch. VIII.
28. Ibid., ch. IX.
29. Ibid., ch. XXXVI.
30. Ibid., ch. XXXV. The moment has aroused some controversy: see Graham Mott, 'Was There a Stain upon Little Dorrit?', *Dickensian*, Vol. 76, No. 390, Spring 1980, pp. 31–5.
31. For the novel's reception see Charlotte Rotkin, 'The *Athenaeum* Reviews *Little Dorrit*', *Victorian Periodicals Review*, Baltimore, Vol. 23, No. 1, Spring 1990, pp. 25–8. G. K. Chesterton, *Appreciations and Criticisms of the Works of Charles Dickens*, 1911, pp. 184–5; see also, for example, R. Brinley Johnson, 'Little Dorrit, An Unpopular Classic', *Dickensian*, Vol. XXVIII, No. 224, Autumn 1932, pp. 283–7. F. R. and Q. D. Leavis, *Dickens the Novelist*, 1970, p. 221. To show that the prison retains its resonance in the culture, see the popular historical novel by Antonia Hodgson, *The Devil in the Marshalsea: Murder Stalks the Debtors' Prison*, 2014.
32. Dickens, *Little Dorrit*, Preface. For the date see Graham Storey and Kathleen Tillotson (eds.), *The Letters of Charles Dickens Vol. VIII 1856–1858*, Oxford, 1995, p. 321 and n.
33. *Examiner*, 29 January 1870. *Globe*, 24 December 1886; the Goad Fire Insurance Maps for 1887–9, Vol. IV, sheet 94, show Messrs Harding part-built with some still under construction. *Builder*, 13 November 1897; see also E. Beresford Chancellor, *Lost London: Being a Description of Landmarks Which Have Disappeared Pictured by J. Crowther circa 1879–87 . . .*, 1926, pp. 80–88, showing some of the buildings in Marshalsea Place. Alan Stapleton, *London Alleys, Byways and Courts*, 1924, p. 135, exaggerated when he wrote that Marshalsea Place was transformed into a warehouse in 1887, though he must have had Harding and Co. in mind.
34. Sir Walter Besant, *South London*, 1898, p. 280; Alfred Trumble, *In Jail with Charles Dickens*, 1896, p. 106. Charles Dickens the Younger, 'Disappearing Dickensland', *North American Review*, Vol. 156, No. 439, June 1893, p. 682; see also, for a similar mistake, Francis Miltoun, *Dickens' London*, 1904, p. 13; Percy

Fitzgerald, *The Pickwickian Dictionary and Cyclopedia*, 1900, p. 157.

35. *Illustrated London News*, 8 February 1902; Sir Walter Besant, *London in the Nineteenth Century*, 1909, p. 236 (a posthumous work, finished by other hands). The plaque is reproduced in Walter Dexter, *The London of Dickens*, 1923, pp. 117–18.

36. Chancellor, *Lost London*, p. 88.

37. George F. Young, 'The Marshalsea Re-visited', *Dickensian*, Vol. XXVIII, No. 223, Summer 1932, pp. 219–27; see also No. 224, Autumn 1932, p. 321; XXXV, No. 249, Winter 1938/9, pp. 58–60. Laurence Ward, *The London County Council Bomb Damage Maps 1939–1945*, 2015, sheets 76–7; *Dickensian*, Vol. LXII, No. 279, Summer 1946, p. 127. Survey of London, *Vol. XXV: St George's Fields (The Parishes of St George the Martyr, Southwark and St Mary Newington)*, 1955, p. 16; Angus Easson, 'Dickens and the Marshalsea', University of Oxford PhD, 1967, p. 74; *Dickensian*, Vol. LXIV, No. 355, May 1968, p. 115. In a revision of the Goad Fire Maps made in July 1966 and held in Southwark Local Studies Library, the premises are shown as 'Vacant May 1963' (sheet 94).

BIBLIOGRAPHY

The place of publication is London unless indicated otherwise.

Manuscripts

ADM (Admiralty Papers), Caird Library, National Maritime Museum

Blenheim Papers, British Library

C195/8, Court of Claims: Coronation Proceedings, The National Archives

Clive MSS, British Library

Correspondence and Papers, London and Middlesex, Miscellaneous. Marshalsea Prison and Court-house, The National Archives

CRES 2/932, Office of Woods, Forests and Land Revenues and Predecessors: Unfiled, The National Archives

Diocese of Winchester, Probate, Archdeaconry Court of Surrey, London Metropolitan Archives

Elphinstone Papers, British Library

Grano, John Baptist (Giovanni Battista), 'A Journal of My Life Inside the Marshalsea' (May 1728–September 1729), MS Rawlinson d.34, Bodleian Library

Hardwicke Papers, British Library

Home Office Papers, The National Archives

Liverpool Papers, British Library

Middlesex Justices, Sessions Papers, London Metropolitan Archives
Nichols MSS, Bodleian Library
PALA 9/8, Miscellaneous papers related to the prison of the Marshalsea and Palace Courts (1812–42), The National Archives
PRIS 11 etc., Day Books of Commitments and Discharges, Marshalsea Prison, The National Archives
PROB/11, The National Archives
Rockingham Correspondence, Sheffield City Archives
St George the Martyr, Southwark, Composite Registers of Weddings, Baptisms and Burials, P92/GEO, London Metropolitan Archives
St George the Martyr Overseers Accounts, GM 3/1/4–6, Southwark Local History Library and Archive Collections
Sloane MSS, British Library
Southwark Deeds, Southwark Local History Library and Archive Collections
State Paper Office MS, The National Archives
Surrey Quarter Sessions Papers, Surrey History Centre
WORK 6/131/2, Office of Works and Successor: Miscellanea, The National Archives

Online Primary Sources

Ancestry.com England (http://www.ancestry.co.uk)
British Museum Image Gallery Online (https://www.britishmuseum.org/research/collection)
London Lives 1690–1800 (http://www.londonlives.org/)
Old Bailey Proceedings Online, London's Central Criminal Court, 1674–1913 (http://www.oldbaileyonline.org/)

Newspapers etc.

Argus
Bell's Life in London and Sporting Chronicle
Brice's Weekly Journal
British Journal
Builder

Bury and Norwich Post; or Suffolk, Essex, Cambridge, Ely and Norfolk Telegraph
Charter
Cobbett's Weekly Political Register
Common Sense or the Englishman's Journal
Country Journal, or The Craftsman
Covent-Garden Journal
Daily Advertiser
Daily Courant
Daily Journal
Daily News
Daily Post
Evening Post
Examiner
Flying Post or The Weekly Medley
Fog's Weekly Journal
Gazetteer and New Daily Advertiser
General Advertiser
General Advertiser and Morning Intelligencer
General Evening Post
Gentleman's Magazine
Globe
Graphic
Grub Street Journal
Illustrated London News
John Bull
Lancaster Gazette and General Advertiser for Lancashire, Westmorland &c
Lloyd's Evening Post
Lloyd's Evening Post and British Chronicle
Lloyd's Weekly Newspaper
London and Country Journal
London Chronicle
London Evening Post
London Gazette
London Journal
London Morning Penny Post
Manchester Times
Middlesex Journal or Chronicle of Liberty

Morning Chronicle
Morning Post
Morning Post and Daily Advertiser
Morning Post and Fashionable World
Morning Post and Gazetteer
Observer
Old England or the National Gazette
Old England's Journal
Old Whig or the Consistent Protestant
Oracle
Oracle and Daily Advertiser
Oracle and Public Advertiser
Pall Mall Gazette
Parker's General Advertiser and Morning Intelligencer
Penny Satirist
Public Advertiser
Public Ledger
Read's Weekly Journal or British Gazetteer
St James's Chronicle or the British Evening Post
St James's Evening Post
The Satirist; or the Censor of the Times
Standard
Sun
The Times
True Briton
Universal Spectator and Weekly Journal
Weekly Journal or British Gazetteer
Weekly Journal or Saturday's Post
Weekly Packet
Whitehall Evening Post or London Intelligencer
World
World and Fashionable Advertiser

Parliamentary Papers

Account of the Names, Trades, and Descriptions of the several persons, who have applied to be discharged under the acts

of Parliament of the 53rd and 54th years of His Present
Majesty's reign . . ., 1814–15

Further Report[s] of the Commissioners appointed in Pursuance of
Two Several Acts of Parliament . . . to inquire concerning Charities
in England for the Education of The Poor . . .,1821–1831

House of Commons Journals

House of Lords Debates, 1st Series

Report from the Commissioners appointed to inquire into the
state, conduct and management of the Prison and Gaol
of . . . the Court of the Marshalsea of His Majesty's honourable Household; and of the Prisoners in the said respective
Prisons confined, 1818

Report from the Committee Appointed to Enquire into the
Practice and Effects of Imprisonment for Debt, 1792

Report from the Committee Appointed to Enquire into the
State of the Goals of this Kingdom: Relating to the Fleet
Prison, 1729

Report from the Committee Appointed to Enquire into the
State of the Goals of this Kingdom: Relating to the Marshalsea
Prison; And farther Relating to the Fleet Prison, 1729

Report from the Committee on the King's Bench, Fleet, and
Marshalsea Prisons; &c., 1815

Report from the Select Committee on Acts Respecting Insolvent
Debtors, 1819

Report from the Select Committee on the Recovery of Small
Debts in England and Wales, 1823

Report of the Commissioners appointed in Pursuance of an Act
of Parliament . . . to continue the inquiries concerning
Charities in England and Wales . . ., 1840

Return of all Coroners' Inquests held within the King's Bench
Prison and other Prisons in and near the Metropolis . . .
from the 1st May 1832 to . . . 1834 . . ., 1834

Primary Printed Sources

Akerby, George, The Life of Mr James Spiller, the Late Famous
Comedian. In which is Interspers'd much of the Poetical
History of His Own Times, 1729

Annual Register for the Year . . .

Anon., *A Collection of the Yearly Bills of Mortality, from 1657 to 1758 inclusive* . . ., 1759

Anon., *A Companion for Debtors and Prisoners, and Advice to Creditors in Ten Letters: From a Gentleman in Prison, to a Member of Parliament* . . ., 1699

Anon., *A Narrative of the Late Disturbances in the Marshalsea-Prison* . . ., 1768

Anon., *A True description of the Mint*, 1710

Anon., *A True Narrative of the Great and Terrible Fire in Southwark, on Fryday the 26th of May, 1676*, 1676

Anon., *Hell in Epitome: or, A Description of the M—SH—SEA. A Poem*, 1718

Anon. [An Amateur], *Real Life in London....*, 2 Vols., 1821–2

Anon., *The Arbitrary Punishments and Cruel Tortures Inflicted on Prisoners for Debt Represented and Described* . . ., 1729

Anon., *The Cries of the Poor Prisoners, Humbly offer'd to the Serious Consideration of the King and Parliament*, 1716

Anon., *The History of Miss Charlotte Seymour*, 2 vols., 1764

Anon., *The Miseries of Goals, and the Cruelty of Goalers. Being a Narrative of Several Persons now under Confinement*, 1729

Anon., *The Piercing Cryes of the Poor and Miserable Prisoners for Debt, in all Parts of England* . . ., 1714

Anon., *The Triumph of Benevolence; or, the History of Francis Wills*, 2 vols., 1772

Besant, Sir Walter, *London in the Nineteenth Century*, 1909

Besant, Sir Walter, *South London*, 1898

Bickerstaffe, Isaac, *The Hypocrite*, 1769

Brayley, Edward Wedlake, and others, *London and Middlesex; or, an Historical, Commercial, and Descriptive Survey of the Metropolis of Great Britain* . . ., 4 vols., 1810–16

Brown, Thomas, *The Mourning Poet: or the Unknown Comforts of Imprisonment, Calculated for the Meridian of the Three Populous Universities of the Queen's Bench, the Marshalsea, and Fleet* . . . *Written by a Poor Brother in Durance*, 1703

Budgell, Eustace, *A Letter to Cleomenes King of Sparta* . . ., 1731

Budgell, Eustace, *A Letter to the Craftsman from Eustace Budgell, Esq; occasion'd by his late Presenting an Humble*

Complaint to His Majesty against the Right Honourable Sir Robert Walpole, 1730

Burney, Charles, *A General History of Music, from the Earliest Ages to the Present Period*, 4 vols., 1776–89

Chancellor, E. Beresford, *Lost London: Being a Description of Landmarks Which Have Disappeared Pictured by J. Crowther circa 1879–87 . . .*, 1926

Charke, Charlotte, *A Narrative of the Life of Mrs Charlotte Charke*, 1755 (edited and with an introduction by Robert Rehder, 1999)

Cozens-Hardy, Basil (ed.), *The Diary of Sylas Neville 1767–1788*, 1950

Curnock, Nehemiah (ed.), *The Journal of the Rev. John Wesley, AM*, 8 vols., 1909

Defoe, Daniel, *A Tour Through the Whole Island of Great Britain*, 2 vols., 1724–6

Defoe, Daniel *The Fortunes and Misfortunes of the Famous Moll Flanders . . .*, 1722 (Folio Society edn, 1965)

Dexter, Walter, *The London of Dickens*, 1923

Dickens, Charles, *Bleak House*, 1852–3

Dickens, Charles, *Little Dorrit*, 1855–7

Dickens, Charles, *The Adventures of Martin Chuzzlewit*, 1843–4

Dickens, Charles, *The Haunted Man and the Ghost's Bargain. A Fancy for Christmas Time*, 1848

Dickens, Charles, *The Old Curiosity Shop*, 1840–41

Dickens, Charles, *The Personal History of David Copperfield*, 1849–50

Dickens, Charles, *The Posthumous Papers of the Pickwick Club*, 1836–7

Dickens, Charles, 'When We Stopped Growing', *Household Words*, Vol. VI, No. 145, 1 January 1853

Dickens, Charles the Younger, 'Disappearing Dickensland', *North American Review*, Vol. 156, No. 439, June 1893

Dodsley, Robert (publisher), *London and Its Environs Described . . .*, 6 vols., 1761

Elias, A. C. Jr (ed.), *Memoirs of Laetitia Pilkington*, 2 vols., Athens, Georgia, 1997

Entick, John, *A New and Accurate History and Survey of London, Westminster, Southwark, and Places Adjacent . . .*, 4 vols., 1766

Farmer, John S., and Henley, W. E., *Slang and its Analogues, Past and Present*, 7 vols., 1890–1904

Fielding, Henry, *Amelia*, 1751

Fitzgerald, Percy, *The Pickwickian Dictionary and Cyclopedia*, 1900

Forster, John, *The Life of Charles Dickens*, 3 vols., 1872–4

Gifford, John, *Complete English Lawyer; or Every Man his own Lawyer*, 2nd edn, n.d., *c.* 1817

Ginger, John (ed.), *Handel's Trumpeter: The Diary of John Grano*, New York, 1998

Goad Fire Insurance Maps, 1887–9

Goldsmith, Oliver, *The Vicar of Wakefield*, 1766

Hardy, W. J. (ed.), *Middlesex County Records: Calendar of Sessions Books 1689–1709*, 1905

Hargrave, Francis (ed.), *A Complete Collection of State-Trials, and Proceedings for High-Treason, and other Crimes and Misdemeanours*, 11 vols., 4th edn, 1778

Hawkins, John, *A General History of the Science and Practice of Music*, 5 vols., 1776

Hickey, William, *Memoirs*, 4 vols., 1913–25

Hill, Sir Richard, *A Detection of Gross Falsehood, and a Display of Black Ingratitude; being an Answer to a Pamphlet lately Published by some Evil-Minded Person, under the name of the Revd William Woolley, striking himself A.M . . .*, 1794

Historical Manuscripts Commission, *Diary of Viscount Percival, Afterwards First Earl of Egmont*, 3 vols., 1920–23

Historical Register. Containing an Impartial Relation of all Transactions, Foreign and Domestick . . . For the Year . . .

House, Madeline, and Storey, Graham (eds.), *The Letters of Charles Dickens Vol. 1 1820–1839*, Oxford, 1965

House, Madeline, and Storey, Graham (eds.), *The Letters of Charles Dickens Vol. 2 1840–1841*, Oxford, 1969

Howard, John, *The State of the Prisons in England and Wales, with Preliminary Observations, and an Account of Some Foreign Prisons*, Warrington, 1777

Howard, John, *The State of the Prisons in England and Wales, with Preliminary Observations, and an Account of Some Foreign Prisons and Hospitals*, Warrington, 1784

Hunt, Henry, *Memoirs of Henry Hunt, Esq., Written by Himself, In His Majesty's Jail at Ilchester, in the County of Somerset*, 3 vols., 1820–22

King, Richard (A Gentleman of Fortune, Revised, corrected and improved by), *The Complete Modern London Spy . . .*, 1781

Knapp, Lewis M. (ed.), *The Letters of Tobias Smollett*, Oxford, 1970

Lennox, Charlotte, *The Life of Harriet Stuart, Written by Herself*, 1750 (1995 edn)

Manning, Owen, and Bray, William, *The History and Antiquities of the County of Surrey*, 3 vols., 1804–14

Mills, John, *D'Horsay, or Follies of the Day*, 1844

Miltoun, Francis, *Dickens' London*, 1904

Morice, Burton, *An Essay towards an History of the Ancient Jurisdiction of the Marshalsea of the King's House. To which is subjoined an account of the Court of the Palace of the King at Westminster, created by Letters Patent of King Charles II*, 1812

Neale, Robert Dorset, *The Prisoner's Guide, or Every Debtor his own Lawyer*, 1800

Neild, James, *Account of Persons Confined for Debt, in the Various Prisons of England and Wales . . .*, 1800

Neild, James, *An Account of the Rise, Progress, and Present State, of the Society for the Discharge and Relief of Persons Imprisoned for Small Debts throughout England and Wales*, 1802

Neild, James, *An Account of the Rise, Progress, and Present State, of the Society for the Discharge and Relief of Persons Imprisoned for Small Debts throughout England and Wales*, 1808

Neild, James, *State of the Prisons in England, Scotland, and Wales . . .*, 1812

Nichols, John, *Literary Anecdotes of the Eighteenth Century . . .*, 9 vols., 1812–16

Noorthouck, John, *A New History of London, including Westminster and Southwark*, 1773

Parker, George, *A View of Society and Manners in High and Low Life*, 2 vols., 1781

Paterson, James, *History of the Counties of Ayr and Wigton, Vol. III, Cunninghame, Part II*, Edinburgh, 1866

Poole, John Ewer ('An Eye-Witness'), *An Expose of the Practice of the Palace, or Marshalsea Court; with a Description of the Prison, the Secrets of the Prison-House, its Regulations, Fees, &c. &c. . . .*, 1833

Prattent, Thomas, and Denton, M., *The Virtuoso's Companion and Coin Collector's Guide, etc.*, 8 vols., 1795–7

Richardson, Samuel, *Clarissa; or, The History of a Young Lady*, 5 vols., 1747–8 (1883 edn)

Sartain, John, *The Reminiscences of a Very Old Man 1808–1897*, New York, 1900

Settle, Elkanah, *The Siege of Troy: A Dramatick Performance, Presented in Mrs. MYNNS's Great Booth, in the Queens-Arms Yard near the Marshalsea Gate in Southwark, during the Time of the Fair*, 1715

Shaw, Captain Donald (One of the Old Brigade), *London in the Sixties (With a Few Digressions)*, 3rd edn, 1909

Slater, Michael (ed.), *Dickens' Journalism: Sketches by Boz and Other Early Papers 1833–39*, 1994

Smith, Alexander, *The Comical and Tragical History of the Lives and Adventures of the Most Noted Bayliffs in and about London and Westminster . . .*, 1723

Smith, M., *Memoirs of the Mint and Queen's-Bench or, A true Account of the Government, Politics, Customs, Humours, and other Surprizing Curiosities of those Inchanted Provinces Never publish'd before. With a Character of the Marshall. In Several Letters to a Person of Quality*, 1713

Smith, William, *State of the Gaols in London and Westminster, and Borough of Southwark. To which is added an Account of the Present State of the Convicts sentenced to Hard Labour on Board the Justitia upon the River Thames*, 1776

Smollett, Tobias, *The Adventures of Ferdinand Count Fathom*, 1753

Smollett, Tobias, *The Adventures of Roderick Random*, 2 vols., 1748

[Society for the Discharge and Relief of Persons Imprisoned for Small Debts], *An Account of the Rise, Progress, and Present State of the Society for the Discharge and Relief of Persons Imprisoned for Small Debts*, 1783

Society for the Discharge and Relief of Persons Imprisoned for Small Debts, *An Account of the Rise, Progress, and Present State, of the Society for the Discharge and Relief of Persons Imprisoned for Small Debts throughout England*, 1794

Society for the Discharge and Relief of Persons Imprisoned for Small Debts, *An Account of the Rise, Progress, and Present State, of the Society for the Discharge and Relief of Persons Imprisoned for Small Debts throughout England*, 1799

Stapleton, Alan, *London Alleys, Byways and Courts*, 1924

Storey, Graham and Tillotson, Kathleen (eds.), *The Letters of Charles Dickens Vol. VIII 1856–1858*, Oxford, 1995

Storey, Graham, Tillotson, Kathleen, and Burgis, Nina (eds.), *The Letters of Charles Dickens Vol. 6 1850–1852*, Oxford, 1988

Stow, John, *A Survey of London*, 1603 (2 vols., edited by Charles Lethbridge Kingsford, Oxford, 1908)

Strype, John, *A Survey of the Cities of London and Westminster*, 2 vols., 1720

Thackeray, William Makepeace, *Vanity Fair. A Novel Without a Hero*, 1847–8

Thale, Mary (ed.), *The Autobiography of Francis Place (1771–1854)*, Cambridge, 1972

Thale, Mary (ed.), *Selections from the Papers of the London Corresponding Society 1792–1799*, Cambridge, 1983

The Representations of the Several Fetters, Irons, and Ingines of Torture that were taken from the Marshalsea Prison . . ., 1729

The Tryal of William Acton, Deputy-Keeper and Lessee of the Marshalsea Prison in Southwark, at Kingston Assizes; on Saturday the 2d of August 1729. Upon three several Indictments, for the several Murders of Capt. John Bromfield, Robert Newton, and Capt. James Thompson, Three Prisoners in the said Prison, 1729

The Tryal of William Acton, Deputy-Keeper and Turnkey of the Marshalsea Prison in Southwark, at Kingston Assizes; on

Friday the 1st of August 1729. Upon an Indictment for the Murder of Thomas Bliss, a Prisoner in the said Prison, 1729

Trollope, Anthony, *London Tradesmen*, 1927

Trumble, Alfred, *In Jail with Charles Dickens*, 1896

Trusler, John, *The London Adviser and Guide: containing every instruction and information useful and necessary to Persons living in London, and coming to reside there....*, 1786

Tunstall, William, *Ballads and some other Occasional Poems: By W—T— in the Marshalsea*, 1716

Tunstall, William, *St Cyprian's Discourse to Donatus. Done into English Metre, By W—T— in the Marshalsea*, 1716

Tweedie, Alexander, and Gaselee, Charles, *A Practical Treatise on Cholera, as it has appeared in Various Parts of the Metropolis*, 1832

Ward, Laurence, *The London County Council Bomb Damage Maps 1939–1945*, 2015

Wheatley, Henry B., *Round about Piccadilly and Pall Mall; or, a ramble from The Haymarket to Hyde Park*, 1870

Woolley, William, *A Cure for Canting; or, The Grand Impostors of St. Stephen's and of Surrey Chapels Unmasked . . .*, 1794

Woolley, William, *The Benefit of Starving; or the Advantages of Hunger, Cold, and Nakedness; intended as a Cordial for the Poor, and an Apology for the Rich. Addressed to the Rev. Rowland Hill, M.A.*, 1792

Woolley, William, *Prison Meditations, composed while in confinement in the King's Bench Prison in the Year 1795*, 1796

Woolley, William, *The Trials of the Rev. William Woolley, Clerk, For Publishing a Libel on Sir Richard Hill, Baronet . . .*, 1794

Secondary Sources

Allen, Michael, *Charles Dickens and the Blacking Factory*, St Leonards, Hants, 2011

Allen, Michael, *Charles Dickens' Childhood*, Basingstoke, 1988

Allen, Michael, 'New Evidence on Dickens's Grandparents', *Dickensian*, Vol. 109, No. 489, Spring 2013

Ashton, John, *The Fleet. Its River, Prison, and Marriages*, popular edn, 1889

Ashton, John, *The History of Gambling in England*, 1898

Beattie, J. M., *Crime and the Courts in England, 1660–1800*, Oxford, 1986

Blanning, Tim, *The Pursuit of Glory: Europe 1648–1815*, 2007

Brewer, John, and Styles, John (eds.), *An Ungovernable People: The English and Their Law in the Seventeenth and Eighteenth Centuries*, 1980

Brinley Johnson, R., 'Little Dorrit, An Unpopular Classic', *Dickensian*, Vol. XXVIII, No. 224, Autumn 1932

Brown, Roger Lee, *A History of the Fleet Prison, London: The Anatomy of the Fleet*, Lampeter, 1996

Brown, Roger Lee, *The Fleet Marriages: A History of Clandestine Marriages with Particular Reference to the Marriages Performed in and around the Fleet Prison, London*, Welshpool, 2007

Burke's Peerage, Baronetage, & Knightage, 69th edn, 1907

Carlin, Martha, *Medieval Southwark*, 1996

Carlton, William J., 'John Dickens, Journalist', *Dickensian*, Vol. 53, No. 321, January 1957

Carlton, William J., '"The Deed" in *David Copperfield*', *Dickensian*, Vol. 48, No. 303, June 1952

Chesterton, G. K., *Appreciations and Criticisms of the Works of Charles Dickens*, 1911

Church, Leslie F., *Oglethorpe: A Study of Philanthropy in England and Georgia*, 1932

Clarke, Norma, *Queen of the Wits: A Life of Laetitia Pilkington*, 2008

Connell, Philip, and Leask, Nigel, *Romanticism and Popular Culture in Britain and Ireland*, Cambridge, 2009

Coulter, E. Merton, 'Was Georgia Settled by Debtors?', *Georgia Historical Quarterly*, Savannah, Vol. 53, No. 4, December 1969

Duffy, Ian P. H., *Bankruptcy and Insolvency in London during the Industrial Revolution*, New York, 1985

Dunlop, C. R. B., 'Debtors and Creditors in Dickens' Fiction', *Dickens Studies Annual*, Vol. 19, New York, 1990

Easson, Angus, 'Dickens and the Marshalsea', University of Oxford PhD, 1967 (Bodleian MS, D. Phil, d, 4231)

Easson, Angus, '"I, Elizabeth Dickens"', *Dickensian*, Vol. 67, No. 363, January 1971

Easson, Angus, 'John Dickens and the Navy Pay Office', *Dickensian*, Vol. 70, No. 372, January 1974

Finn, Margot C., *The Character of Credit: Personal Debt in English Culture, 1740–1914*, Cambridge, 2003

Greene, Douglas G., 'The Court of the Marshalsea in Late Tudor and Stuart England', *American Journal of Legal History*, Vol. 20, No. 4, October 1976

Hill, Mick, *Famous Pugilists of the English Prize Ring*, Peterborough, 2013

Hindley, Charles, *A History of the Cries of London, Ancient and Modern*, 1881

Hodgson, Antonia, *The Devil in the Marshalsea: Murder Stalks the Debtors' Prison*, 2014

Johnson, David J., *Southwark and the City*, 1969

Leavis, F. R. and Q. D., *Dickens the Novelist*, 1970

Lester, V. Markham, *Victorian Insolvency: Bankruptcy, Imprisonment for Debt, and Company Winding-up in Nineteenth-Century England*, Oxford, 1995

McCalman, Iain, *Radical Underworld: Prophets, Revolutionaries and Pornographers in London, 1795–1840*, Oxford, 1988 (paperback edn, 2002)

McKillop, Alan Dugald, 'Thomson and the Jail Committee', *Studies in Philology*, Vol. 47, No. 1, January 1950

Marshalsea Press, *Where Dickens Dreamed of Little Dorrit*, 1926

Matthews, Betty, 'William Parke and the Royal Society of Musicians', *Musical Times*, Vol. 129, No. 1746, August 1988

Melville, Lewis, *The Life and Letters of Tobias Smollett (1721–1771)*, 1926

Mott, Graham, 'Was There a Stain upon Little Dorrit?', *Dickensian*, Vol. 76, No. 390, Spring 1980

Muldrew, Craig, *The Economy of Obligation: The Culture of Credit and Social Relations in Early Modern England*, Basingstoke, 1998

Ordish, T. Fairman, *Early London Theatres*, 1894

Owen, David, *English Philanthropy 1660–1960*, Cambridge, Mass., 1960

Parker, Alice, 'Tobias Smollett and the Law', *Studies in Philology*, Vol. 39, No. 3, Chapel Hill, North Carolina, July 1942

Peakman, Julie, *Lascivious Bodies: A Sexual History of the Eighteenth Century*, 2004

Pearce, Charles E., *'Polly Peachum': Being the Story of Lavinia Fenton (Duchess of Bolton) and 'The Beggar's Opera'*, 1913

Peebles, Gustav, 'Washing Away the Sins of Debt: The Nineteenth-Century Eradication of the Debtors' Prison', *Comparative Studies in Society and History*, Vol. 55, No. 3, Cambridge, 2013

Philpotts, Trey, *The Companion to Little Dorrit*, Mountfield, 2003

Philpotts, Trey, 'The Real Marshalsea', *Dickensian*, Vol. 87, No. 425, Autumn 1991

Prothero, I. J., *Artisans and Politics in Early Nineteenth-Century London: John Gast and His Times*, 1979 (paperback edn, 1981)

Rendle, William, *Old Southwark and Its People*, 1878

Rendle, William, and Norman, Philip, *The Inns of Old Southwark and their Associations*, 1888

Rizzo, Betty, 'Christopher Smart: A Letter and Lines from a Prisoner of the King's Bench', *Review of English Studies*, New Series, Vol. 35, No. 140, November 1984

Rosenfeld, Sybil, *The Theatre of the London Fairs in the Eighteenth Century*, Cambridge, 1960

Rotkin, Charlotte, 'The *Athenaeum* Reviews *Little Dorrit*', *Victorian Periodicals Review*, Baltimore, Vol. 23, No. 1, Spring 1990

Rubenhold, Hallie, *The Covent Garden Ladies: Pimp General Jack & the Extraordinary Story of Harris's List*, 2005

Sadie, Stanley (ed.), *The New Grove Dictionary of Music and Musicians*, 29 vols., 2nd edn, 2001

Schlicke, Paul (ed.), *The Oxford Companion to Charles Dickens*, Oxford, 2011

Sedgwick, Romney, *The House of Commons 1715–1754*, 2 vols., 1970

Slater, Michael, *Charles Dickens*, 2009

Staples, Leslie C., 'The Dickens Ancestry, Some New Discoveries', *Dickensian*, Vol. LXV, No. 290, Spring 1949

Stirk, Nigel, 'Arresting Ambiguity: The Shifting Geographies of a London Debtors' Sanctuary in the Eighteenth Century', *Social History*, Vol. 25, No. 3, October 2000

Survey of London, *Vol. XXV: St George's Fields (The Parishes of St George the Martyr, Southwark and St Mary Newington)*, 1955

Thornley, Isobel D., 'Sanctuary in Medieval London', *Journal of the British Archaeological Association*, New Series, Vol. 38, 1932

Tick, Stanley, 'Autobiographical Impulses in *The Haunted Man* (1848)', *Dickens Quarterly*, Vol. 18, No. 2, Baltimore, June 2001

Victoria County History, *The Victoria History of the County of Surrey. Vol. IV*, 1912

Whistler, Theresa, *Imagination of the Heart: The Life of Walter de la Mare*, 1993

White, Jerry, *London in the Eighteenth Century: A Great and Monstrous Thing*, 2012

White, Jerry, *London in the Nineteenth Century: 'A Human Awful Wonder of God'*, 2007

Wingent, R. M., *Historical Notes on the Borough and the Borough Hospitals*, 1913

Wroth, Warwick, *The London Pleasure Gardens of the Eighteenth Century*, 1896

Young, George F., 'The Marshalsea Re-visited', *Dickensian*, Vol. XXVIII, No. 223, Summer 1932

INDEX